THE CAMBRIDGE COMPANION TO COMICS

The Cambridge Companion to Comics presents comics as a multifaceted prism, generating productive and insightful dialogues with the most salient issues concerning the humanities. Its three sections provide readers with the histories and theories necessary for studying comics. Part I, Forms, maps the most significant comics forms, including material formats and techniques. Part II, Readings, brings together a selection of tools to equip readers with a critical understanding of comics. Part III, Uses, examines the roles accorded to comics in museums, galleries, and education. Individual chapters explore comics through several key aspects, including drawing, serialities, adaptation, transmedia storytelling, stereotyping and issues of representation, and the lives of comics in institutional and social settings. This volume emphasizes the relationship between comics and other media and modes of expression. The chapters offer close readings of vital works, covering a century of comics production.

MAAHEEN AHMED is Associate Professor of Comparative Literature at Ghent University, Belgium, where she leads a multi-researcher project on children and comics, which was awarded a prestigious European Research Council grant (no. 758502). She has published widely on comics, covering graphic novels and periodicals, both North American and European.

THE CAMBRIDGE COMPANION TO COMICS

EDITED BY
MAAHEEN AHMED
Ghent University

Shaftesbury Road, Cambridge CB2 8EA, United Kingdom

One Liberty Plaza, 20th Floor, New York, NY 10006, USA

477 Williamstown Road, Port Melbourne, VIC 3207, Australia

314–321, 3rd Floor, Plot 3, Splendor Forum, Jasola District Centre, New Delhi – 110025, India

103 Penang Road, #05–06/07, Visioncrest Commercial, Singapore 238467

Cambridge University Press is part of Cambridge University Press & Assessment, a department of the University of Cambridge.

We share the University's mission to contribute to society through the pursuit of education, learning and research at the highest international levels of excellence.

www.cambridge.org
Information on this title: www.cambridge.org/9781009255684

DOI: 10.1017/9781009255653

© Cambridge University Press & Assessment 2023

This publication is in copyright. Subject to statutory exception and to the provisions of relevant collective licensing agreements, no reproduction of any part may take place without the written permission of Cambridge University Press & Assessment.

First published 2023

Printed in the United Kingdom by TJ Books Limited, Padstow Cornwall

A catalogue record for this publication is available from the British Library.

Library of Congress Cataloging-in-Publication Data
NAMES: Ahmed, Maaheen, editor.
TITLE: The Cambridge companion to comics / edited by Maaheen Ahmed.
DESCRIPTION: Cambridge ; New York, NY : Cambridge University Press, 2023. | SERIES: Cambridge companions to literature | Includes index.
IDENTIFIERS: LCCN 2022059486 | ISBN 9781009255684 (hardback) | ISBN 9781009255691 (paperback) | ISBN 9781009255653 (epub)
SUBJECTS: LCSH: Comic books, strips, etc.–History and criticism. | Graphic novels–History and criticism. | LCGFT: Comics criticism.
CLASSIFICATION: LCC PN6710 .C33 2023 | DDC 741.5/9–dc23/eng/20221215
LC record available at https://lccn.loc.gov/2022059486

ISBN 978-1-009-25568-4 Hardback
ISBN 978-1-009-25569-1 Paperback

Cambridge University Press & Assessment has no responsibility for the persistence or accuracy of URLs for external or third-party internet websites referred to in this publication and does not guarantee that any content on such websites is, or will remain, accurate or appropriate.

Contents

List of Figures	*page* vii
List of Contributors	xi
Acknowledgments	xiii
Chronology	xiv
Introduction: Bridging Gaps *Maaheen Ahmed*	1

PART I FORMS

1	Comics Drawing: A (Poly)Graphic History *Simon Grennan*	25
2	Comics, Media Culture, and Seriality *Matthieu Letourneux*	46
3	Comics and Graphic Novels *Paul Williams*	63
4	Manga: An Affective Form of Comics *Jaqueline Berndt*	82
5	Digital Comics: An Old/New Form *Giorgio Busi Rizzi*	102

PART II READINGS

6	Comics and Multimodal Storytelling *Blair Davis*	125

vi   *Contents*

7 Comics Adaptations: Fidelity and Creativity   143
   Jan Baetens

8 Comics Genres: Cracking the Codes   166
   Nicolas Labarre

9 Life Writing in Comics   185
   Shiamin Kwa

10 Racialines: Interrogating Stereotypes in Comics   204
   Daniel Stein

11 Women and Comics: Politics and Materialities   225
   Maaheen Ahmed

12 Comics at the Limits of Narration   244
   Erwin Dejasse

PART III USES

13 Comics and Their Archives   267
   Benoît Crucifix

14 Readers and Fans: Lived Comics Cultures   287
   Mel Gibson

15 Comics in the Museum   308
   Kim Munson

16 Comics in Libraries   327
   Joe Sutliff Sanders

17 "Educationally Occupied": Learning with Comics   346
   Susan Kirtley

Further Reading   364
Index   369

Figures

0.1 Simon de Nantua (Rodolphe Töpffer), *L'Histoire d'Albert* (publisher unknown, 1845), p. 24. *page* 4

0.2 George Herriman, *Krazy Kat,* 24 September 1922. 7

0.3 "Lucy and Sophie Say Good Bye," *Chicago Tribune,* 7 May 1905. 9

0.4 Chris Ware, *Jimmy Corrigan: The Smartest Kid on Earth* (Pantheon, 2000), n. pag. 12

0.5 Emil Ferris, *My Favorite Thing Is Monsters* (Fantagraphics, 2017), n. pag. 15

1.1 Anonymous, "Norvic – the spring in a man's stride," *Men Only.* April 1960, p. 125. 29

1.2 Anonymous, "Heart Hunter," *Love Story Picture Library,* no. 1356. 1963, p. 47. 30

1.3 Katsushika Hokusai, *Hokusai painting, The Great Daruma at Honganji Nagoya Betsuin (Nishi-Honganji) in 1817.* 1817. 36

1.4 Marie Duval "Rinkophobia." *Judy, or the London Serio-comic Journal,* vol. 20, p. 62. 22 November 1876. 38

1.5 Winsor McCay, *Little Nemo,* Prelude, 1911. 42

2.1 Richard F. Outcault, "The Yellow Kid Inspects the Streets of New York," *The New York Journal,* 10 October 1898. 49

2.2 Final panels from three *Krazy Kat* strips from 4 September 1918, 7 September 1918 and 1 October 1918. 52

3.1 Miné Okubo, *Citizen 13660* [1946], University of Washington Press, 2014, p. 19. 68

3.2 A selection of graphic novels from the 1970s, showing the variety of physical formats. 70

3.3 Will Eisner, *A Contract with God and Other Tenement Stories* (Baronet, 1978), cover. 72

viii *List of Figures*

4.1 Osamu Tezuka. *Shintakarajima* (*Tezuka Osamu manga zenshū* 281) [1947] (Kodansha, 1984), pp. 12–13. — 88

4.2 Keiko Takemiya. *Tera e* vol. 1 [1977] (Square Enix, 2021), p. 111. — 93

4.3 Room-mates Serge and Gilbert. Keiko Takemiya. *Kaze to ki no uta* vol. 1 [1976] (Shogakukan, 1998), pp. 312–313. — 95

4.4 Jirō Taniguchi. *A Distant Neighborhood (Harukana machie)*. (Fanfare / Ponent Mon, 1998), p. 148. — 98

5.1 "Zach Weinersmith, "AI", *Saturday Morning Breakfast Cereal*, 2022". — 108

5.2 Marietta Ren, *Phallaina* (2016), promotional picture. — 112

5.3 Vidu, *L'immeuble* (2019), screenshot. — 113

6.1 Richard F. Outcault, "A Wild Political Fight in Hogan's Alley – Silver Against Gold" *New York World*, 2 August 1896. — 128

6.2 Winsor McCay, "Little Nemo in Slumberland" *Los Angeles Times*, 29 April 1906. — 130

6.3 *Flash Gordon's Trip to Mars* (1938) — 136

7.1 Olivier Deprez, *Le Château d'après Kafka* (*The Castle, after Kafka*) (FRMK, 2019), double spread, n. pag. — 150

7.2 Simon Grennan, *Dispossession* (Jonathan Cape, 2015), p. 18. — 154

7.3 First double spread of the drawn part of *fo(u)r watt* (Het Balanseer, 2019), n. pag. — 159

7.4 Last double spread of the drawn part of *fo(u)r watt* (Het Balanseer, 2019), n. pag. — 161

8.1 Mark Millar (w.) and Bryan Hitch (i.), The Ultimates 2 #9 January 2006. Marvel Comics — 170

8.2 Mark Waid (w.) and Andy Kubert (i.), *Ka-Zar* #4, August 1997. Marvel Comics. — 174

8.3 Stan Lee (w.) and Jack Kirby (i.), Fantastic Four #9, December 1962. Marvel Comics. — 177

9.1 John Porcellino, "Spotlight on: Opossums," *Map of My Heart*, Drawn & Quarterly, 2009, p. 96. — 188

9.2 John Porcellino, "They pulled around," *Map of My Heart*, Drawn & Quarterly, 2009, p. 28. — 194

9.3 John Porcellino, "I remember standing under this tree," *Map of My Heart*, Drawn & Quarterly, 2009, p. 30. — 196

List of Figures

9.4 John Porcellino, "It seems like nothing really matters," *Perfect Example*, Drawn & Quarterly, 2006, n. pag. — 200

9.5 John Porcellino, "King-Cat Top-forty. Winter '00-'01," *Map of My Heart*, Drawn & Quarterly, 2009, p. 227. — 201

10.1 Rudolph Dirks, "The Katzenjammer Kids Change Clothes with the Blackberry Brothers," *Chicago American Comic Supplement*, 2 September 1900, p. 2. — 211

10.2 Cover of Edward Windsor Kemble, *Comical Coons* (R. H. Russell, 1898). — 212

10.3 "Ebenezer." From Edward Windsor Kemble, *Kemble's Coons: A Collection of Southern Sketches* (R.H. Russell, 1897). — 214

10.4 Richard Felton Outcault, "Poor Lil' Mose on the 7 Ages," *New York Herald Comic Supplement*, 3 February 1901, p. 1. — 217

10.5 Richard Felton Outcault, "A True Ghost Story," *New York Herald*, 28 April 1901. — 218

10.6 Winsor McCay, "*Little Nemo in Slumberland*," *New York Herald*, 2 August 1908. — 220

11.1 Lynda Barry, "Dancing," *One! Hundred! Demons!* (Drawn & Quarterly, 2015), n. pag. — 232

11.2 Ebony Flowers, 'My Lil Sister Lena' in *Hot Comb* (Drawn & Quarterly, 2019), pp. 96–97. — 236

11.3 Weng Pixin, *Let's Not Talk Anymore* (Drawn & Quarterly, 2021). — 240

12.1 Rosaire Appel, *soundtrack/s* (Press Rappel, 2018), n. pag. — 247

12.2 Rosaire Appel, *Perturbation* (Adverse, 2019), n. pag. — 248

12.3 Andrei Molotiu, *The Panic*. From Andrei Molotiu. *Abstract Comics. The Anthology* (Fantagraphics, 2009), n. pag. — 250

12.4 Tim Gaze, untitled. From Andrei Molotiu. *Abstract Comics. The Anthology* (Fantagraphics, 2009), n. pag. — 253

12.5 Bianca Stone, *Poetry Comics from the Book of Hours* (Pleiades Press, 2016), n. pag. — 256

12.6 Renée French, *h day* (Picture Box, 2010), n. pag. — 259

13.1 Seth, *The Great Northern Brotherhood of Canadian Cartoonists* (Drawn & Quarterly, 2011), p. 103. — 268

13.2 Xeroxed reproduction of a 1926 comic strip by Milt Gross, sent out by Bill Blackbeard to Art Spiegelman in 1982 for possible inclusion in *RAW*. — 274

x *List of Figures*

13.3 First and last page of a .cbr file containing scans
of *True Love Problems and Advice Illustrated* no. 13, 1949,
Harvey Publications, hosted online at the Digital
Comics Museum.   279

14.1 A selection of British weekly comics and annuals.   289

14.2 Advertising poster for London shop, 'Dark They Were
and Golden Eyed' created by Bryan Talbot (1979).   292

14.3 Cover image of Fredric Wertham's *Seduction of the Innocent*
(Rinehart, 1954).   294

14.4 Cover of *Viz* no. 273, March 2018, Diamond Publishing.   298

14.5 The cover of the *Judge Dredd Annual*, 1983. Eagle Comics.   299

15.1 The first modern use of "cartoon." John Leech
(1817–1864). "CARTOON, No 1: Substance and
Shadow," *Punch*, July 1843.   309

15.2 Program cover for The Comic Strip:
It's Ancient and Honorable Lineage and Present
Significance (1942). Cover drawing by Fred Cooper.   313

15.3 Exhibition view of *The Cartoon Show: Collection of
Jerome K. Muller* at the Bowers Museum, Santa Ana,
CA. 1976.   317

15.4 Postcard design for *She Draws Comics: 100 Years of
America's Women Cartoonists,* Museum of Comic and
Cartoon Art, NY. 20 May to 6 November 2006.   321

15.5 *The Bible Illuminated: R. Crumb's Book of Genesis*,
installation view at the Hammer Museum, Los Angeles,
24 October 2009 to 7 February 2010.   323

16.1 *Superman's Girlfriend Lois Lane*, no 7, February 1959,
National Comics.   334

16.2 "Mr. Tawny's Fight for Fame." Originally published
in *Captain Marvel Adventures*, no. 126, November 1951,
Fawcett Comics.   336

16.3 *Pogo Possum*, no. 1, October-December, Dell.   338

16.4 *Pogo Possum*, no. 5, May–July 1951, Dell.   339

17.1 Sunni Brown, *The Doodle Revolution* (Penguin,
2015), p. 17.   356

17.2 Mike Rohde, *The Sketchnote Handbook*
(Peachpit Press, 2012), p. 27.   357

17.3 Emily Mills, *The Art of Visual Notetaking:
An Interactive Guide to Visual Communication
and Sketchnoting* (Quarto Publishing Group, 2019), p. 11.   359

Contributors

MAAHEEN AHMED is Associate Professor of Comparative Literature at Ghent University, Belgium

JAN BAETENS is Professor of Cultural Studies at KU Leuven, Belgium

JAQUELINE BERNDT is Professor of Japanese Language and Culture at Stockholm University, Sweden

GIORGIO BUSI RIZZI is Postdoctoral Researcher at Ghent University, Belgium

BENOÎT CRUCIFIX is Assistant Professor of Cultural Studies at KU Leuven and researcher at the Royal Library of Belgium

BLAIR DAVIS is Associate Professor of Media and Cinema Studies at DePaul University, USA

ERWIN DEJASSE is Scientific Collaborator at the Université libre de Bruxelles, Belgium

MEL GIBSON is Associate Professor of Childhood Studies at Northumbria University, UK

SIMON GRENNAN is Professor of Art and Design at the University of Chester, UK

SUSAN KIRTLEY is Professor of English at Portland University, USA

SHIAMIN KWA is Professor of East Asian Languages and Cultures and Comparative Literature at Bryn Mawr College, USA

NICOLAS LABARRE is Professor of American Culture at University Bordeaux Montaigne, France

MATTHIEU LETOURNEUX is Professor of Literature at the Paris Nanterre University, France

xii   *List of Contributors*

KIM MUNSON is an independent researcher based in San Francisco, USA

JOE SUTLIFF SANDERS is Associate Professor in the Faculty of Education
and Fellow at Lucy Cavendish College at the University of Cambridge

DANIEL STEIN is Professor of North American Literary and Cultural
Studies at the University of Siegen, Germany

PAUL WILLIAMS is Associate Professor of Twentieth-Century Literature
and Culture at the University of Exeter, UK

Acknowledgments

As with any academic endeavor, it is impossible to acknowledge everyone who contributed to the compiling of this *Companion*, offering help ranging from reading tips and fresh perspectives to moral support. This brief list is therefore inevitably inexhaustive. I have greatly benefited from the many kind comics scholars I have encountered since the earliest days of my entry into the field and the many inspiring colleagues from other fields.

Credit is due, first and foremost, to the excellent team of authors who agreed to contribute to this *Companion*. I could not have hoped for a better set of colleagues to work with. Special thanks to Christina Meyer, Rachel Miller, and Caitlin McGurk who participated in early discussions on chapters for this volume. I thank Ray Ryan for entrusting this project to me and for all his advice, Edgar Mendez for patiently and promptly responding to my many queries, Elizabeth Davey and Nagalakshmi Karunanithi for walking me through the later stages of the project, and Tim Ryder for his indexing work.

At Ghent University I was incredibly lucky to be surrounded by a team of enthusiastic, knowledgeable, and encouraging colleagues and friends: Eva Van de Wiele, Benoît Crucifix, Benoît Glaude, Giorgio Busi Rizzi, Margot Renard, Michel De Dobbeleer, and Dona Pursall. This list extends to the many collaborators and visiting scholars, including Jan Baetens, Shiamin Kwa, Hugo Frey, Kees Ribbens, Sylvain Lesage, Pedro Moura, Felipe Muhr, Sébastien Conard, Philippe Capart, Lara Saguisag, Ariane Holzbach, Wagner Dornelles, and María José Suárez.

Cheer was also provided by additional friends, family, some plants, and the occasional cat.

Chronology

Eighteenth Century

1732   William Hogarth, *A Harlot's Progress*

1796   Invention of lithography leading to the rise and boom of the illustrated press

Nineteenth Century

1814   Hokusai *Manga*

1819   Thomas Rowlandson, *The Tour of Dr. Syntax in Search of the Picturesque*

1827   Rodolphe Töpffer, *Amours de M. Vieux Bois*

1839–1840   *Jack Sheppard* by William Harrison Ainsworth, illustrated by George Cruikshank

1841   Cham (Charles Amédée de Noé), *Un génie incompris*

1854   Gustave Doré, *Histoire dramatique, pittoresque et caricaturale de la Sainte Russie*

1865   Wilhelm Busch, *Max und Moritz*

1867   Charles H. Ross, *Ally Sloper* (drawn by Marie Duval from 1869 onwards)

1879   Invention of Ben Day printing process

1896   R. F. Outcault, *The Yellow Kid*

1897   Rudolph Dirks, *Katzenjammer Kids*

1899   Frederick Burr Opper, *Happy Hooligan*

Twentieth Century

1903   Gustave Verbeek, *The Upside Downs*

1905   Winsor McCay, *Little Nemo in Slumberland*

1906   Lionel Feininger, *The Kin-der-Kids*

        Four-color (CMYK) printing used by the Eagle Printing Ink Company

1907   Bud Fisher, *Mutt & Jeff*

Chronology

1909	Rose O'Neill, *Kewpie*
1910	Grace Drayton, *Dottie Dimple*
1912	Cliff Sterrett, *Positive Polly* (later renamed *Polly and Her Pals*)
1913	George Herriman, *Krazy Kat*
	George McManus, *Bringing Up Father*
1918	Nell Brinkley, *The Brinkley Girls*
	Edwina Dumm, *Cap Stubbs and Tippie*
	Frank King, *Gasoline Alley*
1919	Frans Masereel, *Mon Livre d'heures*
1920	Oscar Jacobsson, *Adamson's Adventures*
1923	Otto Messmer, *Felix the Cat*
	Percy Crosby, *Skippy*
1924	Harold Gray, *Little Orphan Annie*
1925	Ethel Hays, *Flapper Fanny*
1928	Harold Foster, *Tarzan*
1929	Lynd Ward, *Gods' Man*
	Philip Nowlan (w.) and Dave Calkins (i.), *Buck Rogers*
	Elzie Crisler Segar, *Popeye the Sailor*
	The Funnies, Dell
	Hergé, *Les aventures de Tintin et Milou*
1930	Chic Young, *Blondie*
	Milt Gross, *He Done Her Wrong*
	Walt Disney (w.) and Ub Iwerks (i.), *Mickey Mouse*
1931	Chester Gould, *Dick Tracy*
	Henry Kiyama, *The Four Immigrants Manga*
1934	Alex Raymond, *Flash Gordon*
	Milton Caniff, *Terry and the Pirates*
	Lee Falk (w.) and Phil Davis (i.), *Mandrake the Magician*
	Al Capp, *Li'l Abner*
	E. O. Plauen, *Vater und Sohn*
1935	Marjorie Henderson Buell, *Little Lulu*
1937	Jackie Brown, *Torchy Brown in Dixie to Harlem*
	Dandy, DC Thomson
1938	Jerry Siegel (w.) and Joe Shuster (i.), *Superman* in *Action Comics #1*
	Beano, DC Thomson
	Ernie Bushmiller, *Nancy*
1939	Bill Finger (w.) and Bob Kane (i.), *Batman* in *Detective Comics* no. 27

	Bill Parker (w.) and C. C. Beck (i.), *Captain Marvel*
	Gladys Parker, *Mopsy*
1940	Will Eisner, *The Spirit*
1941	June Tarpé Mills, *Miss Fury*
	William Moulton Marsten (w.) and Harry Peter (i.), *Wonder Woman*
	Jack Cole, *Plastic Man*
	Joe Simon (w.) and Jack Kirby (i.), *Captain America*
	Vic Bloom (w.) and Bob Montana (i.), *Archie* in *Pep #22*
1942	Crockett Johnson, *Barnaby*
1944	Edmond-François Calvo (i.) and Victor Dancette (w.), *La bête est morte*
	Stuart Little (w.) and Ruth Atkinson (i.), *Patsy Walker* in *Miss America #2*
1945	Bill Woggon, *Katy Keene* in *Wilbur*
1946	Miné Okubo, *Citizen 13660*
1947	*All Negro Comics*, published by Orwin Cromwell Evans
	Joe Simon (w.) and Jack Kirby (i.), *Young Romance*
	Milton Caniff, *Steve Canyon*
1948	Walt Kelly, *Pogo* syndicated in *The New York Star*
1950	Arnold Drake et al., *It Rhymes with Lust*
1952	Osamu Tezuka, *Astro Boy*
	Harvey Kurtzman, *Mad Magazine*
1959	René Goscinny (w.) and Albert Uderzo (i.), *Astérix le Gaulois*
1961	Stan Lee (w.) and Jack Kirby (i.), *Fantastic Four*
1963	Stan Lee (w.) and Steve Ditko (i.), *Spiderman*
1967–1969	Hugo Pratt, *Una ballata del mare salato* (Corto Maltese)
1968	Robert Crumb, *Zap Comix #1*
1970	*It Ain't Me Babe*
1972–1991	*Wimmen's Comix*
	Justin Green, *Binky Brown Meets the Holy Virgin Mary*
	Keiji Nakazawa, *I Saw It: The Atomic Bombing of Hiroshima*
1976–2008	Harvey Pekar, *American Splendor*
1977	Pat Mills, *2000 AD*
1977–2004	Dave Sim, *Cerebus*
1978	Wendy Pini and Richard Pini, *Elfquest*
1980–1991	Françoise Mouly and Art Spiegelman, *RAW Magazine*
1980–1991	Art Spiegelman, *Maus*

Chronology xvii

1981	Gilbert, Jaime and Mario Hernandez, *Love and Rockets*
1982–1989	Alan Moore (w.) and Dave Lloyd (i.), *V for Vendetta*
1982–1990	Katsuhira Otomo, *Akira*
1984	Peter Laird and Kevin Eastman, *Teenage Mutant Ninja Turtles*
1985	Marv Wolfman (w.) and George Perez (i.), *Crisis on Infinite Earths*
1986	Frank Miller et al., *Batman: The Dark Knight Returns*
1986–1987	Alan Moore (w.) and Dave Gibbons (i.), *Watchmen*
1988	Grant Morrison (w.) and Charles Truog (i.), *Animal Man*
1989	Neil Gaiman et al., *Sandman*
1989	John Porcellino, *King-Cat comics*
1991–1998	Julie Doucet, *Dirty Plotte*
1991–2000	Frank Miller, *Sin City*
1992	Eric Drooker, *Flood!*
1993	Chris Ware, *ACME Novelty Library*
1993–1995	Joe Sacco, *Palestine*
1993–1997	Daniel Clowes, *Ghost World*
1994	Scott McCloud, *Understanding Comics*
	Paul Karasik (w.), David *Mazzucchelli* (i.), and Paul Auster (w.), *City of Glass: The Graphic Novel*
	Mike Mignola, *Hellboy*
1995–2000	Garth Ennis (w.) and Steve Dillon (i.), *Preacher*
1995–2005	Charles Burns, *Black Hole*
1996	Alan McGruder, *The Boondocks*
	Seth, *It's a Good Life If You Don't Weaken*
1997–2002	Warren Ellis (w.) and Darrick Robertson (i.), *Transmetropolitan*
1998	Jiro Taniguchi, *A Distant Neighborhood*
1999	Masashi Kishimoto, *Naruto*
1999	Posy Simmonds, *Gemma Bovery*

Twenty-First Century

2000–2003	Marjane Satrapi, *Persepolis*
2002	Bill Willingham, *Fables*
2003	Craig Thomson, *Blankets*
2003	Robert Kirkman (w.) and Tony Moore (i.), *The Walking Dead*
2004	Art Spiegelman, *In the Shadow of No Towers*

2005	Matt Madden, *99 Ways to Tell a Story: Exercises in Style*
2006	Alison Bechdel, *Fun Home*
	Gene Luen Yang, *American Born Chinese*
2009–2016	Andrew Hussie, *Homestuck*
2012	Richard McGuire, *Here*
2012	Brian K. Vaughan (w.) and Fiona Staples (i.), *Saga*
2014	Mariko Tamaki (w.) and Jillian Tamaki (i.), *This One Summer*
2014	G. Willow Wilson (w.) and Alphona (i.), *Ms. Marvel*
2015	Sonny Liew, *The Art of Charlie Chan Hock Chye*
	Nick Sousanis, *Unflattening*
2017	Emil Ferris, *My Favorite Thing Is Monsters*, vol. 1
2018	Nick Drnaso, *Sabrina*
2019	Lynda Barry, *Making Comics*
2020	Adrian Tomine, *Loneliness of the Long-Distance Cartoonist*
2021	Lee Lai, *Stone Fruit*

Introduction
Bridging Gaps

Maaheen Ahmed

Comics seem to have changed in recent years: superheroes are not a given, and when they are, they don't easily incarnate the good-evil binary; new superheroes, such as the latest Ms. Marvel, Kamala Khan, and the female Thor reverse established racial and gender stereotypes; powerful personal narratives (Art Spiegelman's *Maus*, Marjane Satrapi's *Persepolis*) have entered university classrooms, figuring very often but not exclusively in literature courses; art galleries and museums display and sell comics art; and perhaps, most importantly, comics are available in regular bookstores instead of specialist comic book shops or newsstands. This change encouraged the assumption that comics have grown up, offering content suitable for adults rather than child readers. Such narratives of comics growing up have been rightly criticized. Pointing out how the alleged maturing of comics in the 1990s was essentially a media hype, Roger Sabin traces a history of comics for adult readers which starts with the use of engraving in printing processes and the rise of satire in the eighteenth century, before leading to the publication of "the first modern comic," *Ally Sloper's Half-Holiday* in 1884 (17). Turning to the contemporary US American context, Christopher Pizzino problematizes the two sides of the comics *"Bildungsroman"* discourse: while it offers new opportunities for comics and attracts new readers, it also imposes the biases of legitimized literary and artistic media and increments anxieties against the supposed lack of value of mainstream comics. In our search for the artistic and literary elements in comics, we lose sight of the actual medium and flatten out aspects that are distinctive to it.

In many ways, the graphic novel incarnates the change implied by the alleged maturing of comics: its one-shot, book-length form (and sometimes size) and complex content calls for careful reading and rereading. Consider, for instance, the intertextual references in Alison Bechdel's *Fun Home*, ranging from James Joyce, Albert Camus, Colette and Henry James to pioneering homosexual and feminist authors such as Adrienne Rich,

Anaïs Nin, Barbara Love (*Sapho Was Right*) and Radclyffe Hall (*Well of Loneliness*). Often written and drawn by one author instead of several, the graphic novel edges closer to the kinds of works we are accustomed to classifying as highbrow, as opposed to the mass-produced items made by several, often anonymous hands. We frequently encounter this tension between high and low in academic and popular discourses around comics. While it may blur attempts for clear definitions – literary graphic novels versus popular comics? – such tension is productive. It tests the limits of literature and art and popular culture and can help trace how these limits mutate over time and in different contexts.

Charles Hatfield argues for understanding certain comics published from 1968 onwards as alternative literature, a literary form in its own right that does not need the graphic novel label. He traces the origins of personal, unabashedly confessional comics narratives that are imaginatively peppered with satire, science fiction and fantasy elements to the underground press, for which he takes the publication of Robert Crumb's *Zap Comix* as a starting point. Calling for a new kind of reading attuned to the specificities of the medium, the many "tensions," including imagetext and sequence and surface (32–67), require us to not only read (from left to right, for instance) but also to look (at the comics page in its entirety). The composite word, imagetext, as well the notion of constant tension between image and text were introduced by the art historian W.J.T. Mitchell to consider hybrid works such as William Blake's illuminated poems that rely on a complete synergy of words, images and lettering (89–107).

Like Hatfield and Pizzino, Bart Beaty offers a nuanced view of comics reception (and appropriation) in the art world, highlighting the limits of legitimization. Instead of getting tangled up in attempts to define comics – which can be problematic given the amount of comic-like artbooks and artbook-like comics, to give only one example – Beaty proposes understanding comics "as products of a particular social world" (43). Instead of formal properties, the contexts of production, framing, and reception contribute to our considering a work as comics. Comics can also be seen as "social objects" which, as Samuel L. Delany explains,

> resist formal definition, i.e., we cannot locate the necessary and sufficient conditions that can describe them with definitional rigor. Social objects are those that, instead of existing as a relatively limited number of material objects, exist rather as an unspecified number of recognition codes (functional descriptions, if you will) shared by an unlimited population, in which new and different examples are regularly produced. Genres, discourses, and genre collections are all social objects. And when a discourse

> (or genre collection, such as art) encourages, values, and privileges orig-
> inality, creativity, variation, and change in its new examples, it should be
> self-evident why "definition" is an impossible task (since the object itself,
> if it is healthy, is constantly developing and changing). (239; see also
> Hatfield 4)

The *Companion to Comics* considers comics as the host medium of forms such as the graphic novel, the comics magazine, the comic strip, the web comic, and other digital comics. This medium, a means of communication, of telling stories, constructing narratives and creating aesthetic experiences is essentially multimodal, very often, but not always, relying on words and images, different kinds of materialities (ranging from paper quality and binding to display locations) and even sound and animation (see Chapter 5 on digital comics). Different kinds of drawing styles – individualistic as opposed to streamlined "house" or series styles, a single artist as opposed to multiple, changing artists, digitized elements – play an important role in telling the story and creating aesthetic viewing and reading experiences. This bare definition of comics is naturally porous and should be understood as a compass providing an initial orientation. The chapters in this *Companion* continue to tease and explore possibilities of understanding comics, confirming that the medium is "infinitely plastic" (Hatfield xiv). In many ways, Jack Cole's *Plastic Man* embodies the modular potential of comics: like Mr Fantastic who appeared a few decades later, Plastic Man has an elastic body that can take any shape it wants (Spiegelman and Kidd). Such bodies incarnate the malleability and the visual potential of the comics form, both in the scope offered to the imagination and in the kinds of movement generated through the existence of multiple panels, different framing devices and page layouts.

Instead of boxing comics within fixed definitions, the more interesting way of approaching the medium is to trace its potentialities, to see how it works and how can we better understand it. For better understanding comics we need to turn to its diverse forms (Part I), the reading possibilities accounting for the diversity of comics production (Part II), and, last but not least, how the medium is framed in institutional and social contexts (Part III). The rest of this introduction turns to a few well-known (and one lesser known!) examples of comics to explain the basic elements of comics theory and history.

Even before the rise of the graphic novel, comics have showcased rich potential and variety and they have not always been for children alone. The association between children and comics is a product of the twentieth century with the appearance of "Children's Corner" sections in illustrated newspapers for adults around 1905 (Sabin 22), milking the attractiveness of pictures for children: too young to read, they could always look at and enjoy the pictures. That the earliest comics were intended for adults is evident from Rodolphe Töpffer's smart, ironic picture stories. His works, originally self-published, later avidly copied, famously drew praise from Goethe, who did not like caricature, nor did he seem to care much for Töpffer's prose and poetry (which outnumbered his comics). In the words of pioneering comics scholar David Kunzle:

> Goethe kept the two albums [*Mr. Cryptogame* and *Adventures of Dr. Festus*] a few days, "looking at only ten pages or so at a time, resting afterwards, because, he said, he risked getting an indigestion of ideas". In the written (dictated) judgement which Goethe was then pressed to render, he praised the artist warmly for being able to "draw multiple motifs out of a few figures", as "the most fertile inventor of combinations", and for his "innate, gay, and every-ready talent." (52)

Let's take a look at a page from Töpffer's *Histoire d'Albert* (Figure 0.1), published at the same time as *Histoire de M. Cryptogame* in 1845. It captures a moment when the antihero – all of Töpffer's protagonists are

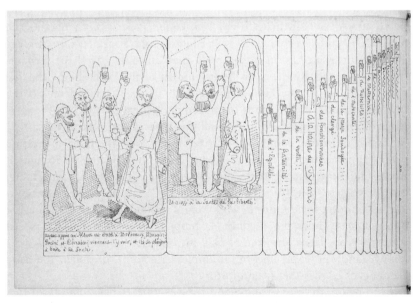

Figure 0.1. Simon de Nantua (Rodolphe Töpffer), *Histoire d'Albert* (publisher unknown, 1845), p. 24. https://gallica.bnf.fr/ark:/12148/btv1b85290242/f40.item

Introduction: Bridging Gaps 5

antiheroes – in one of his many moments of drinking, this time in a failing attempt to become a wine salesman, meets his Carbonari friends, with whom he had already participated in a botched revolution. The narrative voice is deeply ironic, pretending to sympathize with Albert while mocking his stupidity. Very rapidly, the revolutionary ideals of the three friends are confused and lost and they end up drinking to Metternich's health, the Austrian Chancellor who was one of the Carbonari's most fervent enemies. The drawings are amateurish and unfinished but one can see why they moved Goethe to offer a few words of praise: the lines are playful, the drawings are in constant movement, text and image work in symbiosis to convey the narrative's tone and flow without flattening it out. While we read the page from left to right, we also absorb it in its entirety (and perhaps even look at the end of each page before the beginning). Like comics and other serial fiction, such as the installments in which novels were published, the image also ends on a page turner; we are curious to see how this drunken encounter will end (not well, as suggested by the increasingly narrow panels, the incoherent words and indecipherable images). We might also be encouraged to revisit the entire album and discover new elements with each new reading since the simplicity of the images is misleading.

In his seminal *The Origins of Comics: From William Hogarth to Winsor McCay*, Thierry Smolderen examines William Hogarth's print cycles which produced "readable images [that] situated themselves between the *news* and the *novel*" (3). Already in the eighteenth century then, the medium of comics finds itself between modern print magazines and more literary publications, even though the novel did not have the canonical status it enjoys today. We can already see elements of both the press (satire, caricature) and the novel, especially in the long form, in Töpffer's comics. The picture stories are not simple imitations of the novel; they also mock its postures and preferences, recalling the satirical and caricatural affiliations of the comics medium. Many of the tenets of the novel and predilections of the nascent movement of romanticism – such as admirable, realistic protagonists and the emphasis on human emotions – are turned on their heads. The playful irreverence that we find in Töpffer's works, where a minor art pokes fun at itself and at the higher arts, persists in modern-day comics, many of which continue to cater to adult and mixed audiences, such as Georges Herriman's *Krazy Kat*, which ran from 1913 to 1944 and attracted an admiring readership that included the modernist poets, e. e. cummings and T.S. Eliot (see Heer and Worcester).

In *The Seven Lively Arts* (1924), writer and cultural critic Gilbert Seldes writes about *Krazy Kat*:

> It is rich with something we have too little of – fantasy. It is wise with pitying irony; it has delicacy, sensitiveness, and an unearthly beauty. The strange, unnerving, distorted trees, the language inhuman, un-animal, the events so logical, so wild, are all magic carpets and faery foam – all charged with unreality. Through them wanders Krazy, the most tender and the most foolish of creatures, a gentle monster of our new mythology. (244)

Notably Seldes situated comics among other "lively" elements of popular culture, including vaudeville, the circus, slapstick comedy, burlesque, musicals, the movies, especially those of Chaplin and Keaton, and jazz. The adjective "lively" is fascinating: these components of popular culture are alive, constantly in movement, in tune with their times. They are often joyous, even if that joy is bittersweet as readers of *Krazy Kat* will immediately acknowledge. Importantly Seldes places the higher and popular arts in dialogue, rather than in a hierarchical relationship.

Krazy Kat perfectly captures this dialogue between the "high" and "low," much like Töpffer's works. In Herriman's case, a modernist sensibility meets with the older tradition of nonsense. We are not yet in the realm of screwball comedy which became popular in American movies and comics in the 1930s. Nonsense, like comics, has a close affinity with children's literature. It defies adult logics and rationale, reverses established order. Consider, for instance, *Alice's Adventures in Wonderland* and Carl Sandburg's *Rootabooga Stories*. The latter offers a particularly apt comparison because of the important role accorded to the vastness of the American landscape where anything and everything is possible. In the comic in Figure 0.2, Krazy manages to create a fake shade. This "shady work" is a shelter from the sun for their love interest Ignatz.

Hannah Miodrag elaborates on *Krazy Kat*'s affiliation with nonsense: "The fractures Herriman creates between signifier and signified, the proliferation of words on one side and meaning on the other all refute [...] logocentrism" (30). In the comic in Figure 0.2, the fractures between signifier and signified unfold in part through word play, especially between the noun *shade*, Ignatz's obsession to find one, and the adjective *shady*, which is both a result of shade and something dishonest, even illegal. Krazy's painted "perminint" shade flirts with both significations of the adjective. Both characters adore repetitive forms, alliteration in Krazy's "cool, cam, comfitting" and hyperbole in both Ignatz's anger and Krazy's elaborate oral idiom ("Umbridge as us pillite pipples will say"). As Miodrag points out, the words are essentially ornamental and the story is carried by the pictures. The panel at the center with its exceptionally thick frame, in a comic which uses frames only sparingly, highlights the strip's

Introduction: Bridging Gaps 7

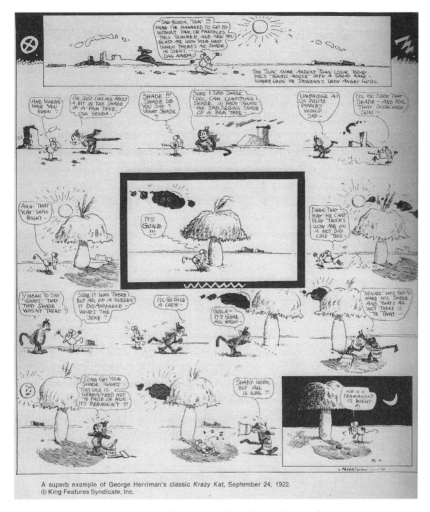

Figure 0.2. George Herriman, *Krazy Kat*, 24 September 1922

central problem: Ignatz's need for shade and the capricious clouds unpredictably killing the shade.

While in the *Krazy Kat* strip, we see Ignatz and Krazy in a relatively peaceful context (Ignatz contents himself with simply yelling at Krazy), the running joke punctuating many of the *Krazy Kat* strips is as follows: Ignatz waits with brick in hand for the most judicious moment to hit Krazy. He rarely misses his mark but Krazy takes these acts of brick-throwing as signs

8   MAAHEEN AHMED

of love which makes Ignatz angrier. This is the knot of nonsense propelling
the action in the comic but the repetition is never identical. The mouse
occasionally succumbs to the cat's love, for instance. But beyond Krazy's
love for Ignatz, nothing is certain in *Krazy Kat*: shades can be made
permanent, Krazy can be both male and female, and so on.

Like many strips relying on gag mechanisms, as masterfully broken
down and explained by Paul Karasik and Mark Newgarden in *How to
Read Nancy*, the anonymous, short-lived comic strip from 1905, *Lucy
and Sophie Say Good Bye* also relies on repetition of motifs with variations. These include modern, often urban, life and the subversion of
heterosexual expectations as the two women embrace. Like *Krazy Kat,
Lucy and Sophie Say Good Bye* is generally funny – when the two women
get away with their kiss in the face of mounting social pressure – but
occasionally also poignant and painful when the two women are forcibly
separated by human, mechanical, or natural forces.[1] Lucy and Sophie
hardly talk in the strip in Figure 0.3: their exchange is silent, unfolding
through their eyes and postures. The voices around them gradually get
louder and more urgent – children, schoolteacher, station master – who,
like most members of the public, the "crowd" we encounter in *Lucy and
Sophie* are quiet and patient at first and shocked, angry, and frustrated
when the women, ignoring all pressure, take their time to say their
goodbyes. Modern life, its speed, comforts, and anxieties were frequently
pictured and parodied in comics (Gardner, *Projections*; Bukatman). In
this strip, the women resist and even ignore the surrounding public's
haste; they create their own time and space. In the fourth panel, the
shock on the faces of the children and the ticket salesman is triggered
both by the kiss shared by the two women and the realization that the
train will be missed and the picnic cancelled. The strip ends in customary
chaos while Lucy and Sophie leave unscathed.

Lucy and Sophie Say Good Bye highlights the advantages of looking
beyond an established comics canon which can lead to new discoveries
and often subvert assumptions. This is why the chapters in this *Companion*
incorporate both well-known and lesser known works (see, in particular,
Chapter 5 on digital comics and Chapter 12 on comics at the limits of
narration).

Comics are lively, and modern and there's always more more than what
meets meets the eye. Even seemingly simple strips such as *Krazy Kat* and

---

[1] See Caitlin MGurk's insightful article on this unsigned short-lived comic.

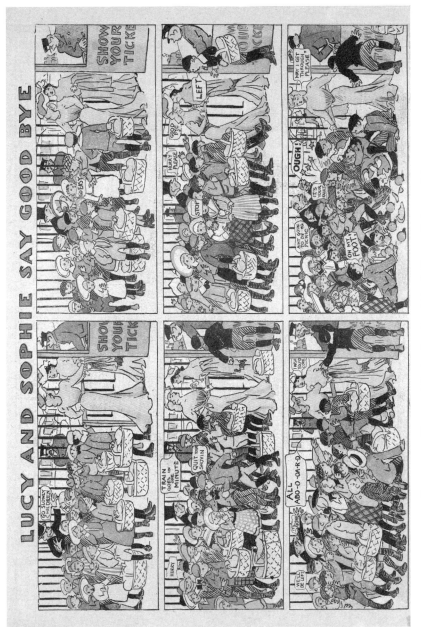

Figure 0.3. "Lucy and Sophie Say Good Bye," *Chicago Tribune*, 7 May 1905

Lucy and Sophie Say Good Bye, with their recurrent characters and motifs, reveal the mechanics of building suspense and resolving it with humor. Ernie Bushmiller, who prized the gag above drawing itself, used diverse techniques – incongruity, surprise, slapstick, verbal and visual puns, exaggeration, misunderstanding, irony, and absurdity – to entertain his readers on a daily basis (Karasik and Newgarden 69).

Reading comics, then, calls for honing new skills, paying attention to different kinds of details. Recently, Stephanie Burt has evoked enchantment and knowledge as a means of studying objects that still remain on the fringes of the academic radar, including comedy and comics (574). In Rita Felski's *Uses of Literature*, enchantment is the longest chapter, perhaps because of its intuitive and vast scope, encompassing a sense of wonder and fascination that is not limited to literature alone. Felski accords a few paragraphs to Hayao Miyazaki's anime, *Spirited Away*, among other works, including the B-movie *The Kiss of the Spider-Woman* and the Manuel Puig novel on which it is based. Found in all echelons of artistic, literary, and mass production, enchantment encourages engagement "with the affective and absorptive, the sensuous and somatic qualities of aesthetic experience" (Felski 76). Not limited to any one medium, such aesthetic experience offers a fresh way of studying works that do not fulfill familiar criteria of literary or artistic value.

Comics generate enchantment in different ways, many of which are channeled through images and action and the rest by the voices that concretize the story. Some enchantment is generated through the sheer size of the comics page. The *Krazy Kat* page, like any Sunday page, covering the entirety of a broadsheet and often in color, was a weekend treat, a pleasure for the eyes. Simulated movement can also be a source of enchantment. The overcrowded panels in *Lucy and Sophie Say Good Bye*, which are a recurrent feature of the strip, visualize the growing societal pressure that does not always leave the protagonists unscathed. All these panels are heady with movement and tension, much like Töpffer's playful pages.

As with any application of a literary concept to comics, the specificities of the medium need to be taken into account, including its tendency to destabilize and laugh at the assumptions and boundaries it relies upon, such as the frame or even the representativity of drawing.

Felski describes knowledge as follows:

> Through their rendering of the subtleties of social interaction, their mimicry of linguistic idioms and cultural grammars, their unblinking attention

> to the materiality of things, texts draw us into imagined yet referentially salient worlds. They do not just represent, but make newly present, significant shapes of social meaning; they crystallize, not just in what they show but in their address to the reader, what Merleau-Ponty calls the essential interwovenness of our being in the world. Their fictional and aesthetic dimensions, far from testifying to a failure of knowing, should be hailed as the source of their cognitive strength. (104)

Here knowledge is not really about facts or even intertextual knowledge. Felski is particularly interested in social knowledge, learning about others and about contexts. Such sharing of knowledge and experience has also encouraged innovation and experimentation in the comics form. It can explain, at least in part, the immense success of graphic novel memoirs and autobiographies (or autographics, to use Gillian Whitlock's term) which have attracted considerable popular and academic interest. Comics capture life experiences in different, often very personal and intimate ways (Chute; Køhlert). The medium does not simply convey and construct knowledge; it encourages us to reflect on the very construction and communication of knowledge and on the processes of signification. The process of breaking a narrative into panels also gives the illusion of unveiling the mechanisms of stringing together a story (or a joke) and some comics contain self-reflexive spins or commentary on the medium. We can already see that in the *Krazy Kat* strip where the joke is anchored in the drawn essence of the comic; it only works because *Krazy Kat* is a comic and allows for the fixing of shades.

Knowledge in comics takes a multimodal form, beginning with the act of drawing itself, which can function as a way of thinking. One of the first pages of Chris Ware's award-winning graphic novel *Jimmy Corrigan: The Smartest Kid on Earth* offers us insights on both the personal level of the young, fatherless protagonist and the social context he finds himself in (Figure 0.4). The page is laden with individual and collective aspirations and anxieties, many of which are channeled through tropes associated with the superhero genre. In the first tier, the boy is running late but he can't help playing with a mask, part of a superman costume. Once in the car, he sticks an arm out and pretends to fly. While his impatient mother's words are outside of the frame, dominating the entire page, we never see her entire face. Like the superhero universe, this is a man's world, confirmed by the long panel in the third tier introducing the car show where the superman actor is scheduled to make an appearance.

Ware instils deep irony into his comic by displacing the codes of superhero comics to ordinary, small-town existence. Jan Baetens and Hugo Frey have discussed in detail how *Jimmy Corrigan* "is a goldmine

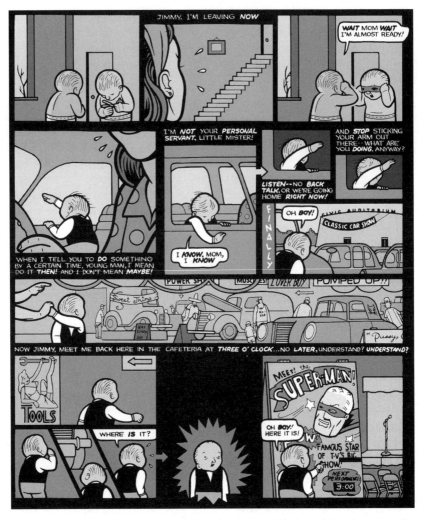

Figure 0.4. Chris Ware, *Jimmy Corrigan: The Smartest Kid on Earth* (Pantheon, 2000), n. pag. Reproduced with kind permission of the artist.

of grammatextual imagination and clever questioning of the borders between text and paratext, but is also a work that rethinks the graphic novel system in this regard (and many others as well)" (159). Originally coined by Jean-Gérard Lapacherie, grammatextuality draws attention to the graphic elements of written text (152–153): the font or style and size of writing, its placement on the page, and the relationships it establishes with other elements on the page. Gérard Genette introduced the term paratext to include all the elements surrounding a narrative, from the title page and cover to the discourse propelled by the text, ranging from interviews to promotional material (*Palimpsests* 3–4). Such paratext is displaced and rewoven in *Jimmy Corrigan* where ads of the fictive comic, *Jimmy Corrigan, the Smartest Kid on Earth* are interspersed throughout the graphic novel. This also alludes to the story's beginnings as a comic book which was inevitably more fragmented, combining more than one story line, letter columns, and imagined advertisements.

Comics such as *Jimmy Corrigan* confirm the need for an interdisciplinary toolbox to study comics. Cultural history (Gabilliet), Bourdieusian field theory which focuses on cultural capital and the hierarchy of the arts (see Beaty), transmedia connections with film (Gardner; Davis; Bukatman), narratological approaches (Mikkonen), comics as communication and language (Miodrag), print culture (Smolderen), drawing theory (Grennan), genres (Labarre), especially the superhero (Hatfield and Heer), race (Wanzo), life writing (Chute; Chaney) are all part of the wide gambit of comics studies. We encounter all of these dimensions in this *Companion*.

Many of the early insights into the specificity of comics come from the artist-theoretician Scott McCloud. McCloud bases his understanding of comics as a sequential art form on the prolific cartoonist Will Eisner. For McCloud much of the magic of comics lies in the "gutter", the space in between panels which encourages readers to fill in the gaps in the comics narrative. McCloud also discusses the different kinds of representation and suggests that simplified representations with minimal individualistic detail allow for greater reader identification. Much has been made of the gutter as a privileged space of reader involvement, so much so that we sometimes forget that such spaces of interpretation are present not only between panels but within and across panels. Reader involvement is activated on multiple levels: drawing, panels, page layout, references to other literary, artistic, and popular works.

Comics theorists such as Pierre Fresnault-Deruelle and Thierry Groensteen identify a tension on the comics page between linear and tabular systems. The former is present in strips, such as newspaper comics, and the latter is present in comic books, albums, and the graphic novel. In emphasizing the networked aspect of comics Groensteen introduces the notion of braiding (*tressage*) as a central feature of the system of comics which establishes connections beyond the obvious, sequential ones: these connections unfold on visual and semantic levels across fragments of panels within and beyond the comic (147). This infuses a comic with multiple reading possibilities. Similar to McCloud's and Eisner's emphasis on sequentiality, the reader's role is crucial in unpacking the many winding, braided paths in a comic.

Layout is another medium-specific aspect of comics that needs to be accounted for alongside sequential and network elements. Groensteen suggests two variables for understanding page layout: regular or irregular; discrete or ostentatious (97). These factors elaborate on the work performed by the page layout along aesthetic and narrative dimensions while accounting for reader participation. With the exception of *Lucy and Sophie Say Good Bye*, the examples discussed earlier have irregular layouts that occupy different positions on the scale of discrete to ostentatious, with the *Krazy Kat* and *Histoire d'Albert* excerpts being less ostentatious than the *Jimmy Corrigan* page: the layout of the *Histoire d'Albert* page captures the increasing drunkenness and reduced lucidity of Albert whereas the layout in *Krazy Kat* highlights the longwinded process of procuring a shade for Ignatz alongside the moments of tension and resolution. The layout of the *Jimmy Corrigan* page captures the complexity of mental and physical movement across a brief span of time.

The potential of comics is also evident when they exploit their close connections with other media or arts. Emil Ferris' masterful *My Favorite Thing Is Monsters* offers rich insight into the medium's engagement with its own history, other media, and its ability to stretch its own limits.

My Favorite Thing Is Monsters is the diary of Karen, a mixed-race, queer girl growing up in a poor neighborhood in Chicago during the 1960s. It braids diverse genres ranging from detective comics to graphic memoir. The death of Karen's upstairs neighbor Anka is the central crime that Karen tries to resolve, but the story is full of other mysteries and connections. That Anka is a Holocaust survivor alludes to the strong Holocaust memoirs told in comics form, starting with Spiegelman's *Maus*. The graphic novel's pages imitate spiral-bound notebook pages: the metal of the spiral binding remains only indexically present through photographic reproduction and contrasts with the drawn images, which vary from slightly cartoonish to intensely realistic. While panels and word balloons are recurrent, each page or double page functions as an organic entity.

Knowledge and enchantment are closely intertwined in these pages. Knowledge is transmitted through the artworks Karen visits regularly at the Art Institute of Chicago. Figure 0.5 shows Karen's friend Franklin's enchantment with the paintings, which mirrors Karen's fascination and affective connections to the artworks. With their imaginations, the

Introduction: Bridging Gaps 15

Figure 0.5. Emil Ferris, *My Favorite Thing Is Monsters* (Fantagraphics, 2017), n. pag. © Emil Ferris. Courtesy of Fantagraphics Books (www.fantagraphics.com).

children inhabit the paintings and breathe life into them. They also reflect ways in which we as comics readers can revisit and reconsider images, engaging with them on interactive and affective dimensions and imbuing them with new social meanings. Franklin draws connections between

Lucas Cranach's portrait of Magdalena of Saxony and a superwoman. Even without such explicit parallels, the act of redrawing the oil painting on a comics page opens a dialogue between the different kinds of arts and status accorded to them.

In addition to portraying social meaning and weaving intertextual and intermedial knowledge, *My Favorite Thing Is Monsters* also demonstrates how comics personalize stories. This unfolds through the imitation of a young girl's diary, her drawings and texts. Knowledge and enchantment are personified by the ghostlike Sandy because she appears at a moment in school when Karen, who is regularly bullied, is particularly alone. Sandy, Karen's imaginary friend, steps in to offer a human connection. She personifies possibilities of (imagining) socializing, offering the companionship that Karen longs for. Their hug, which dominates a page, is rich in affect, emphasizing the warmth of the gesture against the actual emptiness of the imaginary hug.

Ferris draws her graphic novel with ballpoint pens, which entails meticulous drawing skills. Her distinctive drawing style mediates the artworks in the Art Institute of Chicago, while also visualizing Karen's voice. Ferris' drawing bridges the graphic novel's storytelling and (fictional) diary functions. Philippe Marion introduced the term graphiation to explain how artists establish personal styles through negotiating collective tendencies, the demands of the particular story being told, and personal inclination (see Baetens and Frey 137). Graphiation emphasizes how what we see on the comics page is not simply the trace of an artist's hands and how that trace is molded by multiple factors. This trace has the power to fascinate us viewer-readers because it stems from the artist's hand (rarely in the fully literal sense owing to the many digital tools used for touching up images), testifies to their skill, and channels our perception and reactions. Comics drawing and, more specifically, graphiation channel knowledge and enchantment.

These examples show how comics mediate between the story or narrative moment, the potential reader, and their experience. These mediations rely on comics-specific tools and are influenced by a complex set of historical and cultural factors which are elaborated upon by the chapters in this *Companion*.

As we have seen, the medium of comics encompasses not merely the funnies or the graphic novel, but a range of publications, all of which are connected through a deep history of drawing and implicated in the mechanisms of consumer culture. Part One on *Forms* maps histories and affordances of the most significant comics forms, with "forms" being understood in a broad sense, including material formats and techniques, such as drawing. Simon Grennan contextualizes comics drawing in the broader histories of image making, and shows how it unfolds in a dialogic relationship with the context, with drawers or drafters and with readers and viewers. He then introduces Smolderen's concept of polygraphy or the combination of different graphic registers to generate humor.

One of the defining elements of comics, especially comic strips and comic books, is their seriality. Matthieu Letourneux draws connections between comics aesthetics and the logics of serial media that were established by the burgeoning print industry of the eighteenth century. He argues that the comic books or floppies introduced a new kind of seriality that was dependent on stories that would extend across issues, often ending on cliffhangers.

While seriality has long been considered a dominant feature of comics, the graphic novel counters that assumption. However, the graphic novel is not as new as we might think. Considering the graphic novel "as a concept, a label and a way of publishing comics," Paul Williams traces a recent history of the graphic novel from the woodcut novels of the 1920s and 1930s to the rise of the direct market in the 1970s and the turning point of 1986 which saw the publication of *Maus*, Alan Moore and Dave Gibbons' *The Watchmen*, and Frank Miller's *The Dark Knight Returns*.

Focusing on key manga that have attracted critical attention in the West, Jaqueline Berndt adopts a formal approach, elaborating an aesthetics of eyes in manga. Unpacking the representation of eyes in works by internationally renowned mangaka such as Osamu Tezuka, Keiji Nakazawa, and Jirō Taniguchi, Berndt argues for considering manga as an affective comics form.

The final chapter in *Forms* turns to the latest addition to the comics corpus, digital comics. Giorgio Busi Rizzi introduces three kinds of digital comics formats and possible parameters, including immersion and agency, for comparing them with print comics and for appreciating their distinctiveness. Moving from comics drawing to key formats and the digital mode of comics making and publishing, *Forms* introduces readers to the material diversity and complexity of the comics form, paying special attention to the visual dimensions of the medium and its connections to popular culture and publishing dynamics.

Readings brings together a selection of tools to equip readers with a critical understanding of comics encompassing diverse, topical perspectives. These critical readings interweave two trajectories: one focuses on the connections between comics and other media (film, animation, literature, poetry) on both material and generic grounds whereas the other questions normative stances and broaches issues of representation. Although at first blush, such an interweaving may seem counterintuitive, it reflects the multifaceted and intertwined possibilities of comics readings and takes advantages of the medium's moments of self-reflection and changing trends in comics scholarship.

Blair Davis' chapter on comics as multimodal storytelling expands on the media connections established by comics, tracing their concurrent emergence and divergent histories as well as the moments of transmedial convergence. Complementing Letourneux's discussion of seriality in trans-media comics franchises, Davis traces the changing forms of transmedial comics stories, from early B-movies and animated shorts to television shows from the late 1940s and 1950s, Netflix series, and superhero blockbusters. Jan Baetens turns to another key media interacting with comics, literature. Focusing on four different kinds of literary adaptations in comics, Baetens discusses possible techniques for transposing novels to visual narratives. He shows how experimental comics can break away from the unwritten rule of fidelity to host medium and use creative approaches that end up being truer to the original work than more literal adaptations. Nicolas Labarre considers genre as a label that is more useful than specific, as a blueprint and as a contract (comparable to the pact established by serial media discussed by Letourneux). Labarre elaborates on the functions of genres, their transmedia lives and implications, genre (self-)parody and performance, social functions, and, ultimately, the limitations of genres, especially when genres become architexts and are connected across media and discourses (see Genette, *Architext*).

Shiamin Kwa then draws our attention to one of the most-discussed genres in comics studies, life writing and graphic memoir. She elaborates on the effects of immediacy generated by John Porcellino's zines and how the zine format foregrounds the aporetic nature of Porcellino's mode of life writing in comics. Expanding on issues of representation and representativity, Daniel Stein discusses print media from the turn of the nineteenth century through the lens of racialines: "the broadly entertaining and increasingly popular confluence of the drawn line and the blackened spaces it encapsulates in the graphic rendition of stereotypical 'blackness.'" He examines both the perpetuation of Black stereotypes as well as moments when they unsettled racist imagery and narratives. My chapter on women and comics begins with a brief history of women and comics including women comics artists and comics for women. Turning to three contemporary graphic novels by female artists, I focus on how the materialities of drawing styles and writing, especially collage, work to interweave personal and the collective stories. Closing *Readings*, Erwin Dejasse explores possibilities for reading comics that test the limits of narrative coherence and disregard clear story lines. These include drawing parallels between abstract comics and music, and considering poetry comics through the lens of "plastic signs" where both image and word are graphic and polysemous.

Part Three on *Uses* covers the roles accorded to comics in different sociocultural and institutional settings and practices, from readerships and shops to museums, libraries, and archives. Benoît Crucifix explores the archival workings of comics, juxtaposing reflections on how comics create and interact with their own archives to the concerns raised by the actual archiving of comics. Mel Gibson discusses how comics reader and fan communities have evolved in the UK and the US, changing according to the places selling comics, from newsstands to specialist comics shops that appeared in the late 1960s. She elaborates on the objecthood of comics in collector and fan circles, the establishment of taste cultures (Woo), and the gender and age discrepancies in fan interactions. Tracing a brief history of comics in museums and galleries through landmark exhibitions starting from the 1930s, Kim Munson discusses the changing status of comics in museums alongside the practices for displaying comics as artworks and as objects to be read. Turning to libraries, Joe Sutliff Sanders elaborates on the complex relationship between comics and librarians, especially librarians' animosity towards comics and the attempts made by comics to court them through encouraging reading, especially before the infamous Comics Code. Susan Kirtley closes the *Companion* with one of the most prominent "uses" of comics: education. She examines the educational roles of comics, on possibilities of teaching with comics, teaching about comics, and encouraging multimodal literacy. Comics, Kirtley argues, offer ideal tools – through doodling or sketchnoting, for instance – for thinking in an increasingly multimodal world.

The time has come, as Jared Gardner recently suggested, to fine-tune our goggles towards a better understanding of the many forms of comics: moving away from the nice neighborhood of the graphic novel to the far wider world of comics ("Nice Neighborhood" 597). Moving from the forms and material dimensions of comics to key perspectives for looking at and reading comics and the roles accorded to comics in social and institutional contexts, this *Companion* tries to capture the broad, multifaceted possibilities for approaching the medium of comics.

WORKS CITED

Comics

Anonymous. "Lucy and Sophie Say Good Bye", *Chicago Tribune*, 7 May 1905.
de Nantua, Simon (Rodolphe Töpffer). *Histoire d'Albert*, 1845.
Ferris, Emil. *My Favorite Thing Is Monsters*, vol. 1. Fantagraphics, 2017.
Herriman, George. *Krazy Kat*, 24 September 1922.
Ware, Chris. *Jimmy Corrigan: The Smartest Kid on Earth*. Pantheon, 2000.

Secondary Sources

Baetens, Jan and Hugo Frey. *The Graphic Novel: An Introduction*. Cambridge University Press, 2014.
Beaty, Bart. *Comics Versus Art*. University of Toronto Press, 2012.
Burt, Stephanie. "Why Not More Comics?" *PMLA*, vol. 134, no. 3, 2019, pp. 572–578.
Chute, Hillary L. *Disaster Drawn: Visual Witness, Comics and Documentary Form*. Harvard University Press, 2016.
Davis, Blair. *Movie Comics: Page to Screen/Screen to Page*. Rutgers University Press, 2017.
Delany, Samuel L. "Politics of Paraliterary Criticism." *Shorter Views: Queer Thoughts and the Politics of the Paraliterary*. Wesleyan University Press, 1999, pp. 218–270.
Felski, Rita. *The Uses of Literature*. Wiley-Blackwell, 2008.
Fresnault-Deruelle, Pierre. "From Linear to Tabular (1976)." *French Comics Theory Reader*. Translated by Ann Miller and Bart Beaty. Leuven University Press, 2014, pp. 121–138.
Gabilliet, Jean-Paul. *Of Comics and Men: A Cultural History of American Comic Books*. Translated by Bart Beaty and Nick Nguyen. University Press of Mississippi, 2010.
Gardner, Jared. *Projections: Comics and the History of Twenty-first-century Storytelling*. Stanford University Press, 2012.
"A Nice Neighborhood." *PMLA*, vol. 134, no. 3, 2019, pp. 595–600.
Genette, Gérard. *The Architext: An Introduction*. Translated by Jane E. Lewin. University of California Press, 1992.
Palimpsests: Literature in the Second Degree. Translated by Channa Newman and Claude Doubinsky. University of Nebraska Press, 1997.
Grennan, Simon. *A Theory of Narrative Drawing*. Palgrave Macmillan, 2017.
Groensteen, Thierry. *The System of Comics*. Translated by Bart Beaty and Nick Nguyen. University Press of Mississippi, 2009.
Hatfield, Charles. *Alternative Comics: An Emerging Literature*. University Press of Mississippi, 2005.
Heer, Jeet and Kent Worcester. *Arguing Comics: Literary Masters on a Popular Medium*. University Press of Mississippi, 2004.

Karasik, Paul and Mark Newgarden. *How to Read Nancy: The Elements of Comics in Three Easy Panels*. Fantagraphics Books, 2017.

Køhlert, Frederik Byrn. *Serial Selves: Identity and Representation in Autobiographical Comics*. Rutgers University Press, 2019.

Kunzle, David. *Father of the Comic Strip: Rodolphe Töpffer*. University Press of Mississippi, 2007.

McCloud, Scott. *Understanding Comics: The Invisible Art*. Kitchen Sink Press, 1993.

McGurk, Caitlin. "Lovers, Enemies, Friends: The Complex and Coded Early History of Lesbian Comics Characters." *Journal of Lesbian Studies*, vol. 22, no. 4, 2018, pp. 336–353

Mikkonen, Kai. *The Narratology of Comic Art*. Routledge, 2017.

Miodrag, Hannah. *Comics and Language: Reimagining Critical Discourse on the Form*. University Press of Mississippi, 2013.

Mitchell, W. J. T. *Picture Theory: Essays on Verbal and Visual Representation*. University of Chicago Press, 1994.

Pizzino, Christopher. *Arresting Development: Comics at the Boundaries of Literature*. University of Texas Press, 2016.

Sabin, Roger. *Adult Comics: An Introduction*. Routledge, 1993.

Seldes, Gilbert. *The Seven Lively Arts*. 1924. http://xroads.virginia.edu/~Hyper/SELDES/seldes.html Accessed 3 August 2022.

Smolderen, Thierry. *The Origins of Comics: From William Hogarth to Winsor McCay*. 2000. Translated by Bart Beaty and Nick Nguyen. University Press of Mississippi, 2014.

Spiegelman, Art and Chipp Kidd. *Jack Cole and Plastic Man: Forms Stretched to their Limits*. Chronicle Books, 2001.

Wanzo, Rebecca. *The Content of Our Caricature: African American Comic Art and Political Belonging*. NYU Press, 2020.

Whitlock, Gillian. "Autographics. The Seeing 'I' of Comics." *Modern Fiction Studies*, vol. 52, no. 4, 2006, pp. 965–979.

Woo, Benjamin. "The Android's Dungeon: Comic-Bookstores, Cultural Spaces, and the Social Practices of Audiences." *Journal of Graphic Novels & Comics*, vol. 2, no. 2, 2011, pp. 125–136. doi.org/10.1080/21504857.2011.602699

PART I
Forms

CHAPTER I

Comics Drawing
A (Poly)Graphic History

Simon Grennan

Drawing Encompassing Comics

It is easy to bring to mind the drawn forms that derive specifically from the comics medium, because they are so few, so frequently repeated, and so familiar. These drawn forms encompass both *mise-en-page* (or the way drawn marks are arranged relative to each other and to a viewer or reader) and *mise-en-scène* (or the depiction of a story or storyworld). Drawing is not only mark-making, mapping and indexing, writing and planning, layout and interface, but also scene-making and story-showing.

We are able to determine which forms of drawing derive specifically from comics by answering a single question in the case of each possible type of drawing: "Do we know the form of drawing elsewhere, before the emergence of drawing traditions that now identify the comics medium?" If not, we might assume that the form of drawing in view derives specifically from comics.

Answering this question does not imply that all forms of drawing have had similar uses or have prompted similar responses from different people in different times and places. They have not. In fact, exactly the same forms of drawing have signified in widely different ways at different times. However, heterogeneity does not contradict the fact that some forms of drawing appear to derive from the comics medium, its current iterations and uses, and the circumstances in which the medium emerged.

The forms of drawing that derive specifically from the comics medium include (i) speech balloons, thought bubbles, and narration boxes; (ii) gutters; (iii) panel borders; (iv) time-changing arrows and number sequences; and (v) a clutch of visual symbols for invisible forces.

Speech balloons, thought bubbles, and narration boxes are categorically distinct from the appearance of written comments and naming scrolls or scrolls of speech in earlier drawings. Before the advent of the comics medium, the functions that these types of drawing perform had not been recognized (Cohn; Groensteen; Forceville, Veale, and Feyaerts). Gutters are not simply the spaces between images, found in drawings elsewhere (Berlatsky). Panel borders use *mise-en-page* to place the reader or viewer relative to a *mise-en-scène* or to arrange a number of *mise-en-scènes*. They do not entirely replicate the drawn thresholds between times and spaces that appear in many decorative architectural schemes before the twentieth century, although there are striking functional, though not contextual or semiotic, similarities (Verstappen; Whistler). Drawn symbolic visualizations of changes in time in comics, such as arrows and number sequences, are used to direct reading. They are distinct from indexical, propositional, and purely directional arrows or number sequences, found elsewhere, which do not unfold a visual story (Witek). The clutch of drawn symbols for invisible forces – such as odor, heat, or exasperation and for the visual blurs, compressions, and elisions that visually represent motion in static media – are known as "pictorial runes" (Kennedy 589–605) or "indicia" (Walker; Shinohara and Matsunaka). The use of clusters of dots to represent immanent energy or a numinous environment within a depicted storyworld is a rare example of a form of drawing that devolves to named drafters (Jack Kirby and Steve Ditko), sometimes known as "Kirby Krackle" (Foley). The "pictorial runes" and "Kirby Krackle" of the comics medium are unlike drawings of invisible energy seen elsewhere.

These drawing innovations are relatively recent additions to the ever-expanding, global, and heterogeneous field of ways and forms of drawing, where each process and type of drawing realizes the different circumstances in which it is made. Drawings have been made for a very long time indeed, since 71,000 BC.

Drawing encompasses comics, in the sense that the ways and forms of drawing employed to make and to understand comics are largely not comics specific, with the exceptions detailed earlier. More precisely, the comics medium offered and continues to offer a set of circumstances that intervene in the history of drawing, as other forms have also intervened in the past.

All innovations in the history of drawing have appeared in this way: a specific set of circumstances allows the creation and use of a particular type of drawing. Often, a new way of drawing or type of drawing adapts an older type to new circumstances. When the comics medium first evolved, it largely transformed and made new use of older drawing processes and forms. The comics medium emerged according to the possibilities that a set of eighteenth- and nineteenth-century European circumstances and a set of nineteenth-century circumstances in China and Japan had to offer. Subsequent formal additions to the range of opportunities for drawing have built upon and adapted these older ways and forms, only occasionally changing them beyond recognition (St. Fleur; Smolderen; McCarthy).

The Circumstances of Comics

There is no single genealogy of the drawn forms in which comics have been produced and used, because the medium arose out of a range of different circumstances and exploits different traditions of drawing. It is also not possible to define the comics medium according to the small number of formal innovations that the medium has contributed to the wide field of drawing, because many drawings that are recognized and used as comics do not feature them.

Rather, each age revises the history of forms of drawing retrospectively, building upon previous revisions and rejecting, ignoring, or transforming how past forms are considered. Different forms of drawing have been devised and produced at different historical moments, through the creation or development of new relationships between drafters, writers, publishers, viewers, and readers, as well as the repetition of old ones.

Traditions have emerged out of these relationships, between groups of producers and consumers of comics, some long-standing. These relationships have often included the repetition of ways of drawing, writing, publishing, and reading. These repetitions of ways of making and using comics make it possible to identify different groups and to compare ways of working and reading.

In art history, groups of producers have been known as "schools." The techniques and business of being an artist involved learning to repeat ways of working through apprenticeship to an established artist. With the production of comics, producers are grouped together, who make comics that are formally similar, are made in similar ways, and/or have similar users. It is possible to identify styles of drawing that derive from different comics drafters and groups of drafters making comics in different drawing traditions or genres. According to Meyer, style is "a replication of patterning, whether in human behavior or in the artefacts produced by human behavior, that results from a series of choices made within some set of constraints" (3).

It is difficult to isolate these styles of comics drawings from larger practices of visualization in graphic design, design and illustration, fine art and advertising, both older and concurrent with their use in comics.

This is not to say that a range of different visual styles and generic practices of comics drawing are not immediately identifiable. Rather, it is not usually possible to isolate a style of drawing to a type of comics alone. Comics drawing styles are often described by the sub-genres of comics that they produce: *shōjo*, Big Foot, Marcinelle, Marvel, and many, many others. Readers recognize and expect to find types of content relative to specific drawing styles. We do not expect to find drug-inflected stories of American counterculture drawn in the style of *shōjo* (girls) manga, for example. The impact of changes in drawing style upon plots and storyworlds has been amply demonstrated in drawing experiments that map shifts in meaning against shifts in drawing style, by Madden, Sykoryak, and Grennan (*Narrative Drawing*, 161–250).

In addition, drawing styles are almost always produced in the context of larger relationships between different media, different media producers, and, crucially, types of readers who buy and use commercial print and other products. The drawing style of a 1960s English print advertisement for men's shoes (Figure 1.1) is a blithe stylistic clone of the drawing style of a romance comic of the same period (Figure 1.2).

There are exceptions, such as the comics-specific invention of "Kirby Krackle" mentioned earlier, plus the clear identification of the drawing styles of recognizable, named drafters. But these unique and autographic styles of drawing are only comics-specific forms in the sense that the drafter-auteurs draw most frequently for comics. In fact, if the contemporary American cartoonist R. Kikuo Johnson makes an editorial drawing for the cover of *The New Yorker* magazine, it is drawn in the style of Kikuo Johnson, not in the style of "a comic by Kikuo Johnson."

Sometimes, drafters, writers, and publishers directly influence each other's ways of working. Readers also see how their contemporaries are making use of comics and follow suit. Learning how to become a drafter, writer, or reader is often a case of direct experience. However, sometimes these schools (of art) or groups (of comics) have been identified retrospectively by scholars or other drafters. For example, in 1977 the term *ligne claire* (clear line) was applied retrospectively to the work of a number of French and Belgian drafters by Dutch comics artist Joost Swarte. He recognized and named formal similarities in the work of a range of drafters working over a period of forty years, although the term would not have meant anything to the previous drafters themselves. The term has been widely adopted since.

The different forms that comics have taken and the names given to them always provide evidence for the relationships between the producers

Comics Drawing: A (Poly)Graphic History

Figure 1.1. Anonymous, "Norvic – The Spring in A Man's Stride," *Men Only*, April 1960, p. 125.

30 SIMON GRENNAN

Figure 1.2. Anonymous, "Heart Hunter," *Love Story Picture Library*, no. 1356, 1963, p. 47.

and users who made and used them. This includes the different terms for the medium as a whole – comics, *bandes dessinées, manga, fumetti, sensacionales, historietas, lubki,* and others. Different forms map out these relationships and evidence the past and current uses to which the medium is put. For example, the Italian term *fumetti* specifically names the medium after the form of speech balloon drawings (puffs of smoke), whereas the French *bandes dessinées* (drawn strips) foregrounds the newspaper publishing origin of the medium in the French language, and the English language "comics" locates the medium even more specifically on the "entertainment" pages of a newspaper.

Therefore, specific comics forms, including types of drawing, are frequently associated with specific historical situations, including specific types and styles of drawing, publishing business methods, types of social structures, and types of people. It is even possible to associate specific emotional sensations and different ideas and beliefs with the comics forms that these ideas and beliefs produce.

Alternatively, some comics scholars have attempted to map an encompassing genealogy of the drawn forms that the comics medium has taken. The idea parallels the creation of frequently revised definitions (seeking to answer the question "what is a comic?"). This type of analysis is based on the identification of shared formal properties in comics produced in widely different times and places, and for different uses (Eisner; Peeters; McCloud; Groensteen; Postema; Earle; and others).

Most recently, this approach to defining comics has reached a watershed, with the recognition of these properties in widely different media, other than comics. Chris Gavaler proposes the existence of a "comics form" that ranges far beyond the circumstances, history, craft, and users of comics. According to this idea, drawing (or, rather, being drawn) cannot be one of the small set of cross-media properties that constitute the "comics form," because this "form" can be found in media that are not drawn.

Recognition and Reading

More circumstantially, Ian Hague asks, "how do we recognise comics?" (10). The question aims to articulate the ways in which the circumstances in which comics are made and used produce and revise the forms in which comics appear. Recognition underpins an equally profound question about the causes and consequences of drawing and reading comics: "how do we use comics?" Although the answer is an easy one ("we read them"), reading itself throws up some complex issues for drawing.

The history of reading, like the history of drawing, encompasses the ways in which comics have been recognized and used. It steers us resolutely towards a comprehension of the comics medium that always mutualizes the circumstances of comics and their drawn forms. Following Hague, we can approach drawing in the medium of comics as responses to historical changes of the circumstances in which comics are read.

In this sense, it is key to understand comics drawing as a popular literature that multiplies and alters ways of reading. There are three overarching traditions of recognizing and reading comics: *manga*, comics/comix/graphic novels, and *bandes dessinées*. These traditions are not exclusive (there are ways of recognizing and reading comics that do not fall within their generic horizons) but, in each tradition, groups of readers are habituated to find a range of ways to access products, types of publication, and types of mark-making (including color, layout, and writing), genres, and plots (Jauss and Benzinger). To describe these different expectations of different types of comics drawing, we must compile brief encompassing descriptions of the three different circumstances of drawing, distributing, and reading in the three traditions.

A small list of key aspects allows us to describe the different circumstances in each tradition. The list includes: the motivations for drawing, buying, and reading a comic; where and when it is drawn and read; who is drawing, distributing, and reading; the reader's generic expectations of the ways in which the comic styles the stories and worlds that it shows; and, finally, the drawn forms that emerge from the congruence of the other aspects. To some extent, this list is mindful of Peterson and Anand's article, "The Production of Culture Perspective," which aims to describe how "symbolic elements of culture are shaped by the systems within which they are created, distributed, evaluated, taught and preserved." These include "technology, law and regulation, industry structure, organization structure, occupational careers and market" (311). Of course, Peterson and Anand approach production only, whereas this list summarily incorporates formal characteristics, including types of drawing and reading, relative to drawing.

Until relatively recently, it might have been plausible to describe these reading traditions according to the languages or even nationalities of their readers. The comics strip was Anglophone, *bandes dessinées* were Francophone, and manga was Japanese, Chinese, and Korean: the manga tradition is a postwar Japanese phenomenon, with direct parallels in both China/Chinese (*manhua*), Korea/Korean (*manhwa*), and, more recently, English (Brienza). In the last twenty years, these language demarcations have become more complex, as global markets have embraced translations and forms have been imported, exported, and transformed, modifying these traditions (Grennan, "Influence").

The word "reading" also reveals a definitive characteristic of the medium and has foundational implications for the recognition of types of drawing in comics. Comics are visual literature. Other drawn media are viewed. Alternatively, we read writing. Viewing might be said to encompass reading (we can't read without viewing, but we can view without reading), but the two activities are different and distinct. However, the comics medium somewhat confounds these distinctions, because it requires both viewing and reading (Forceville, Veale, and Feyaerts). There are wordless comics (they devolve to viewing), but readers' recognition of them as comics incorporates the idea of writing, even if writing is absent.

More crucially, comics drawings are largely encountered in diverse print media or, more recently, in digital media that adapt and transform the reading conventions of print media. In the main, print media has produced traditions of reading, such as left-to-right or down and up sequences, page turning and scrolling, rather than traditions of viewing, such as locating the body relative to an imagined scene. There are exceptions to print's historical imperative to read, such as book illustrations and visual instructions.

However, these exceptions only reveal their historical relationship to the forms and circumstances in which writing, rather than drawing, has emerged as print media (Hall; Brake, "Writing"). Drawing in the comics medium is one of these exceptions, in that readers' expectations of print literature are met with drawings rather than writing. As a result, the physical push and pull between the rhythm of reading and the rhythm of viewing is a general characteristic of the comics medium in every tradition.

Print and Comics: Accumulating Diverse Indices

In the long history of drawing, the craft of making visual representations has frequently been organized and described by media, bundling together the purpose of the drawing, the drafter (or drafters), their materials, and their circumstances. A printmaker was distinct from a painter and a painter was distinct from a technical drafter. These media and the skills required to manipulate them were technically precise and clearly defined. Each medium was produced by its own traditions and, as a result, these traditions defined the medium (Petherbridge).

We are often in the habit of describing drawing media – or the means by which drafters make marks and the surfaces that they mark – according to the skills that the drafter has to acquire to use them. When we push together these descriptions, of media and skills, we are also describing the possibilities for making one type of mark or another, which are open to the drafter.

If we accept this way of describing media, skills, and possibilities, it follows that the types and styles of media – and the uses that the drafter makes of them – also describe the drafter's body, when they are making a mark. For example, the term "hand-drawn" implies a range of possible body gestures and body postures. These are quite distinct from the body gestures and postures implied by the term "typeset," for example. These gestures and postures have histories that parallel and produce the uses of different drawing media themselves. The gestures and postures are learned and recognized.

In the twentieth century, ideas about drawing started to focus more intently upon the drafter's body and away from the capacities, practices, and traditions of different media. Drawing became a topic of debate about the body itself (Meskimmon and Sawdon).

However, the body was always present in drawings as defined by media. The body is found in the earliest discussions of artistic style, or the representation of the individual traits of a particular drafter or artist in the way in which they fulfill their craft. A unique style of production has always been thought of as a personal signature and, as such, has been considered as an unmediated means of experiencing the individual traits of the drafter (Szép; Kukkonen; Gardner).

Whatever other function the mark might have, drawn marks always record the ways in which they are made. This record does not find its origin in the characteristics of any medium, but rather in the characteristics of the drafter's body. The mark that records the way in which it is made finds significance in its physical origin. The drawn mark is always a sign of the activity of its production. Its significance lies in pointing to the origin of its own making, in the actions of the drafter's body (Peirce).

The description also applies to every drawing, regardless of the medium in which it is made. This might sound counterintuitive. What of those mark-making media that interpose multiple boundaries between the drafter and the mark, such as digital drawing media? In fact, these media still index the activities of the drafter's body, but in ways that are widely different from each other. In fact, these media index diverse bodies.

Drawings trace the drafter's body and readers find significance in them as originating from the drafter's body. In print media, however, these origins are visibly and tangibly embedded alongside the traces of many other bodies – the origins of the production and distribution processes of print media in the bodies of printers, paper manufacturers, machinists, and distributors (Brake, "Writing"; Grennan, "Marie Duval").

The diversity of people, activities, and traces, significantly brought together in printed drawings, is deftly represented in a woodcut print by the Japanese artist Hokusai, depicting himself at a spectacular event that he had organized, to show off his drafting skills, by making a monumental ink drawing of the monk Daruma (Figure 1.3).

Hokusai made a printed drawing of himself making a drawing at a performance event, with the crucial change from direct index (trace) to printed index coming between the artist, the viewer, and the event itself. There is really only one event here (and it is not the depicted event, it is the print), although the indices of the people that produced it are diverse, numerous, and uncountable – the reading of the indices that produce the print, the activities of the paper makers and ink makers, knife makers and block manufacturers, the scale of the print production, the knife cuts in the small wood block, the tiny amounts of colored ink that made the impression on paper, the transport of the print to the shop, its display, and sale to different people.

The print inculcates a sense of vertigo, caused by the extreme, abrupt differences in size between the depicted scene (the size of the drawing of Daruma at the event) and the size of the print in the reader's hands. It is reinforced and enlarged by material differences between the huge sheet of canvas in the scene and the sheet of paper on which the print was made, to be held in the hand. The reader is huge in comparison to the depicted drawing of Daruma's head, which in turn is huge in comparison with the depicted Hokusai and members of the crowd. And yet Daruma's drawn head is bigger than the reader. Hokusai is simultaneously big and small.

The depicted event in 1817 was singular, time-specific (past), and, as a participant, you had to be there. However, the print is multiple and constantly revised at different times in different places. Hokusai is in the picture, at a single event in 1817, of which he was the star. But the printed drawing exists in hundreds of locations, alongside the many indices of his collaborators. It is these contrasting effects, simply brought about by accumulating the indices of diverse bodies in the process of printing a drawing, that make an experience of this print so vital and compelling a revelation of the characteristic diversity of body indices in print media.

Smolderen argues that the indexical diversity of print media was made visible in the self-conscious use of contrasting drawing styles, topics, and craft

Figure 1.3. Katsushika Hokusai, *Hokusai painting, The Great Daruma at Honganji Nagoya Betsuin (Nishi-Honganji) in 1817*. 1817.

methods by drafters in the early history of European and American comics. Exemplified in the printed drawings of William Hogarth, he describes the European and American visual cultures of the mid-eighteenth century as "already saturated with a seemingly infinite variety of graphic systems" (9).

Many of these graphic systems are so deeply disconnected from the experiences of current viewers – and even scholars – that it can be difficult to navigate the ways in which Hogarth articulated competing systems in the same drawings or sets of drawings. The task is not made easier by the acclaim with which he was heralded in his lifetime and his subsequent enduring reputation, which can make his innovations and visual riskiness appear inevitable, in retrospect. Smolderen describes Hogarth's serial prints as analogous, for readers, to the experience of wandering at a fair, where accumulated diverse drawn sensations and ideas are punctuated by the rhythm of passing by, that is, by the readers themselves (4).

However, as Maidment (1992, 2014) and Brake (2001) have shown, it was not until the early nineteenth century that the business of print pervaded visual culture to the extent that multiple, competing genres, products, styles of production, and visual regimes battled for readers and sought to create new readerships, new ways of reading, and new types of drawing. Unlike Hogarth's readers (print collectors who were relatively well-off literate men, purchasing as connoisseurs), nineteenth-century periodical readers were massively heterogeneous, increasingly verbally and visually literate across all classes. They were strikingly involved in creating, mixing, and dissolving established ways of reading, viewing, and thinking.

The boom in the entertainment industries produced, in daily lives, exactly the conditions that Smolderen describes as visible in Hogarth's serial prints, or "polygraphic humor," a "multi-layered visual text saturated with allusions to conflicting systems of representation (ranging from the highly rhetorical language of history painting to the rebellious insolence of graffiti drawings," packed with "stylistic collisions, ironic contrasts and hybridisation" (9).

However, it was the nineteenth-century business of periodical print that made this "polygraphic" drawing comprehensible, attractive, and saleable to readers; created the conditions in which the indexing of the bodies, activities, and ideas of multiple producers – from drafters to news vendors – was foregrounded; and produced the medium of comics. By the last quarter of the nineteenth century, the use of contradictory styles in the same drawing in print was utterly recognizable to readers. In the most visually accomplished of cases, different drawing styles were associated with particular ways of living, styles of dress, political opinions, and types of persons, so that the use of different styles of drawing indicated the relationships, struggles, and antagonisms between different people. Polygraphic drawing was used and recognized as the acutest (and funniest) social commentary.

A good example of this is provided in a drawing by the London cartoonist and actor Marie Duval (Figure 1.4). Duval made use of two

Figure 1.4. Marie Duval "Rinkophobia." *Judy, or the London Serio-comic Journal*, vol. 20, p. 62, 22 November 1876. © The Marie Duval Archive 2021.

recognizable styles in the same drawing. The woman skating is young, fashionable, and attractive to men. She is drawn in the style of contemporaneous women's fashion illustrations. Indeed, the figure was probably traced directly from one of these. In contrast, the people skating around her are drawn in a completely different style displaying a lack of formal visual arts training and appearing more like spontaneous doodles than anything else. The young woman's style is serene. She has means and status. She will overcome. Those around her are poor and are making a bad show. They are styled for struggle, failure, and ignominy.

Duval, as readers understood her, also had to transform (or restyle) her own body, in order to draw in different styles. Visual arts training always involved the learning of specified body postures and movements as well as craft techniques (Duffield Harding), whereas the casual, untrained drafter could simply "dash down" a drawing (Ross and Wilson 110). On one hand, the trained style in which the young woman is drawn constrained Duval's technical activities and demonstrated skill (if only at recognizing the style elsewhere and tracing). On the other hand, the untrained style of the falling skaters indexes Duval unleashed. These two body attitudes also represented Duval's opinions about her characters. Did Duval laud the fashionable young woman with her choice of drawing style and show disapprobation by drawing the others differently? Or is the polygraphic contrast showing that the young woman will inevitably fall (literally) to the level of the untrained, the unconstrained, and the failed?

This way of pushing drawing styles together offers the best visual match to another of the ideas that root polygraphy. Smolderen's term adapts the term "polyphony" from literary theory, replacing "speech" with "drawing," so that multiple voices are replaced by multiple visualizations. Bakhtin explains that "what unfolds. . .is not a multitude of characters and fates in a single objective world, illuminated by a single authorial consciousness; rather a *plurality of consciousnesses, with equal rights and each with its own world*, combine but are not merged in the unity of the event." (176, italics in original). This is what I mean when I write that Duval transformed her body, in using different styles in a single drawing. Bakhtin adds that "almost no word is without its intense sideward glance at someone else's word" (203). This is also made explicit in the visual relationships between styles, types of people, and ideas in "Rinkophobia." Duval's styles and methods were not produced in isolation, but in dialogue, indexing a set of social and bodily relationships, plus opinions, in the real world.

A similar dialogue underpins the bound-breaking early nineteenth-century work of Rodolphe Töpffer. He also self-consciously adopted of an untrained style (prefiguring Duval) in counterpoint to stifling or illiberal contemporaneous reading conventions. Smolderen proposes that the types and styles of Töpffer's drawings visualized a "satirical debate with the idioms of progressive action" such as mechanization, standardization, centralized global time, new shared units of measurement, and rules-based logistics, all of which became pervasive in the second industrial revolution, at the time when Töpffer was drawing (51). He did this by combining contemporaneous graphic types from different origins, which were recognized as radical by readers, such as the codified visible gestures of melodrama stage acting and "the Romantic ideal of the arabesque" (49).

Töpffer started to make his drawings for circulation among friends. Original drawings were passed around. It is significant that these domestic drawing and reading activities appeared in the realm of contemporaneous home entertainments and pastimes, such as playing music, singing and acting, collaging, decoupage, embroidery, watercolor painting, and sketching. Töpffer's drawings were unofficial, unprofessional, and private. For Töpffer's friends, humor was sparked by the ways in which his drawing style visualized and commented upon some of the familiar contradictions of their daily lives.

This combinatory visualization of the familiar became truly polygraphic when Töpffer's drawings began to be reproduced in print. When that occurred, drawings in the domestic style of amateur dramatics, parlor antics, and social visits were repurposed as a radical new entertainment for sale. Private drawings became public, multiple copies joined the mainstream of periodical literature and the visible indices of the people making this happen joined Töpffer's once-private marks, to make a syncretic and diversely indexed medium – comics.

Stage acting and visual production practices have fed the medium ever since, including the ways in which it employs drawing styles and types. Hogarth pops up retrospectively in this context. In some ways, the relationship between the stage acting and production of the 1750s and Hogarth's serial prints prefigured the relationship between Töpffer and the on-page visualization of melodramatic acting style. Hogarth's portrait of actor David Garrick in the role of Richard III (1745) literally visualizes the actor gesturing "horror." Similar codified body postures produce the characters throughout Hogarth's *mise-en-scène* in the stories in his serial prints.

In fact, we find this relationship, between performance practices and drawing, across the three drawing and reading traditions of the comics medium. This is recognized by readers in all three traditions. The reciprocal influence of types of visual style, alongside types of story, between Osamu

Comics Drawing: A (Poly)Graphic History

Tezuka's 1953 manga "Princess Knight" and the all-female musical theatre the Takaratsuka Review, based in his hometown, is well known.

Both Tezuka's drawing style and the performing style of the Review relied upon audiences' and readers' recognition of types of visualization in the much older Japanese Kabuki theatre tradition, which was accumulated, recreated and recontextualized. These included the visualization of men as women and vice versa and a range of visual codes, including *mei* (or holding a pose and pausing the action at a significant moment), *aragoto* (equating exaggerated body movement with heroism and the "significant exit" or *roppo*) and the *kumadori* make-up style, which visually codifies drawn marks on the actors faces with specific character traits. "Both Tezuka's construction of space and the stylized posing and expression of emotions of his characters in his early works (hand gestures, posing on tiptoe with hands pressed on chest, and so on)" derive from the particular, recognizable practices of cross-dressed drama exemplified by the Review and the older Kabuki tradition (Hikori 301).

The early twentieth-century drawings of American drafters George Herriman and Winsor McCay demonstrate similar impulses, to simultaneously exploit multiple drawing styles and visual regimes (often performance regimes), accumulating and physically indexing diverse collaborators. Their drawings tangled with, drew upon, and influenced the development of moving image and audio recording and the emerging comprehension of their audiences (Sattler).

Smolderen's analogy of wandering at a fair in the serial drawings of Hogarth is even more apposite with Herriman and McCay, given that their drawings immediately adopted and then transformed the sensations, styles, practices, and devices of spectacle and variety in movies, sometimes becoming movies themselves. The reading environment into which they poured their serial newspaper drawings was bursting with a teeming, familiar variety (Morton).

In the first decile of the twentieth century, movies were shown anywhere, as public events and fairground attractions, in a general commercial attempt to become as pervasive and all-encompassing as newsprint. The drawings of Herriman and McCay joined movie and adapted the panoply of sensations on offer at entertainment events. These recklessly (and sensationally) mixed illustrated songs, colored glass slides (stereopticon projection), beverage, food, sheet music, newspaper and merchandise sales, live narrators, dance and acrobatic interludes, musical accompaniment, diegetic sound, slapstick and claptraps, multiple stage acting traditions, call and response, plus the practices of magic and illusionist shows.

Figure 1.5. Winsor McCay, *Little Nemo*, Prelude, 1911.

Both McCay and Herriman also animated their drawings as movies, helping to create the movie medium. In an illuminating parallel with Hokusai, with different means for an entirely different audience, McCay appeared as the drafter in the prelude to one of his own drawn animated films, doubling and re-doubling the polygraphic indices, as Hokusai had done 100 years earlier (Figure 1.5)

Conclusion

It is not possible to isolate the comic medium by describing the specific types of drawing that comics has contributed to the wide field of such a heterogeneous and ancient set of practices, habits, relationships, and images as drawing. Drawing encompasses comics or, rather, the medium of comics intervened, and continues to intervene, in the history of drawing.

Drawings index, and sometimes directly trace, the sequence, rhythm, and character of the past gestures that the drafter used to draw the marks. Distinctly, printed drawings are also indices of the people, activities, and situations in which they were produced and distributed. They technically mediate between the bodily activities that accumulate to create and work machines to such a degree that they cannot be thought of as individual body traces. They might be thought of as the indices of groups of activities. The relationship between writing and speech provides a useful analogy for the relationship between drawings and print. Drawings reproduced through print are not the equivalent of recorded speech. Rather, print must be described as the equivalent of machine-generated speech.

In the nineteenth century, the business of periodical print produced the opportunities and the imperative for the comics medium to accumulate multiple diverse indices of the labour and ideas of production collaborators, visualized in accumulated, contrasting drawing styles and different ways of reading. Participating in a boom in varieties of visual, moving, and audio entertainment, distribution, reading, and viewing comics have emerged as polygraphic, characterized by a wide, energetic, and often self-contradictory or pivoting range of drawing styles and visual regimes and their consumers.

WORKS CITED

Comics

Duval, Marie. "Rinkophobia." *Judy, or the London Serio-Comic Journal*, vol. 20, 22 November 1876, p. 62.
Madden, Matt. *Ninety-nine Ways to Tell a Story: Exercises in Style*. Jonathan Cape, 2007.
Sikoryak, Robert. *Masterpiece Comics*. Drawn & Quarterly, 2009.
Tezuka, Ozamu. *Princess Knight*. Kodansha, 1953–1956.

Secondary Sources

Allen, Robert. *Vaudeville and Film 1895:1915: A Study in Media Interaction*. University of Iowa Press, 1977.
Bakhtin, Mikhail. *Problems in Dostoevski's Poetics*. University of Minnesota Press, 1977.
Berlatsky, Eric. "Lost in the Gutter: Within and between Frames in Narrative and Narrative Theory." *Narrative*, vol. 17, no. 2, 2009, pp. 162–187.
Brake, Laurel. "Writing, Cultural Production, and the Periodical Press in the Nineteenth Century." *Writing and Victorianism*, edited by J. B. Bullen. Addison Wesley Longman, 1997, pp. 54–72.
  Print in Transition, 1850–1910. Palgrave, 2001.
  Journalism and the Periodical Press in Nineteenth-Century Britain. Cambridge University Press, 2017.
Brienza, Casey. *Manga in America: Transnational Book Publishing and the Domestication of Japanese Comics*. Bloomsbury, 2016.

Cohn, Neil. "Beyond Word Balloons and Thought Bubbles: The Integration of Text and Image." *Semiotica*, no. 197, 2013, pp. 35–63.

Duffield Harding, James. *Lessons on Art*. David Bogue, 1849.

Earle, Harriet. *Comics: An Introduction*. Routledge, 2021.

Eisner, Will. *Comics and Sequential Art: Principles and Practices from the Legendary Cartoonist*. W. W. Norton, 2008.

Foley, Shane. "Kracklin' Kirby: Tracing the Advent of Kirby Krackle." *Jack Kirby Collector*, no. 33, 2001. www.twomorrows.com/kirby/articles/33krackle .html Accessed 15 September 2021.

Forceville, Charles, Tony Veale, and Kurt Feyaerts. "Balloonics: The Visuals of Balloons in Comics." *The Rise and Reason of Comics and Graphic Literature: Critical Essays on the Form*, edited by Joyce Goggin and Dan Hassler-Forest. McFarland, 2010, pp. 56–73.

Gardner, Jared. "Storylines." *Substance*, vol. 124, 2010, pp. 53–69.

Gavaler, Chris. *The Comics Form: The Art of Sequenced Images*. Bloomsbury, 2022.

Grennan, Simon. *A Theory of Narrative Drawing*. Palgrave Macmillan, 2017.

"The Influence of Manga on the Graphic Novel." *The Cambridge History of the Graphic Novel*, edited by Jan Baetens, Hugo Frey, and Stephen Tabachnik. Cambridge University Press, 2018, pp. 320–336.

"Marie Duval and the Technologies of Periodical Print." *Marie Duval: Maverick Victorian Cartoonist*, edited by Simon Grennan, Roger Sabin, and Julian Waite. Manchester University Press, 2020, pp. 118–133.

Groensteen, Thierry. *The System of Comics*. Translated by Bart Beaty and Nick Nguyen. University Press of Mississippi, 2007.

Hague, Ian. *Comics and the Senses: A Multisensory Approach to Comics and Graphic Novels*. Routledge, 2014.

Hall, David, ed. *Cultures of Print: Essays in the History of the Book*. University of Massachusetts Press, 1996.

Hikori, Hori. "Tezuka, Shōjo Manga and Hagio Moto." *Mechademia*, vol. 8, 2013, pp. 299–311.

Jauss, Hans Robert and Elizabeth Benzinger. "Literary History as a Challenge to Literary Theory." *New Literary History*, vol. 2, no. 1, 1970, pp. 7–37.

Kennedy, J. M. "Metaphor in Pictures." *Perception*, vol. 11, no. 5, 1982, pp. 589–605.

Kukkonen, Karin. *Studying Comics and Graphic Novels*. Wiley, 2013.

Maidment, Brian. *Into the 1830's: Some Origins of Victorian Illustrated Journalism: Cheap Octavo Magazines of the 1820s and Their Influence*. Manchester Polytechnic Library, 1992.

Comedy, Caricature and the Social Order, 1820–1850. Manchester University Press, 2014.

McCarthy, Helen. *A Brief History of Manga*. Octopus, 2014.

McCloud, Scott. *Understanding Comics: The Invisible Art*. William Morrow, 2001.

Meskimmon, Marsha and Phil Sawdon. *Drawing Difference*. Bloomsbury, 2016.

Meyer, Leonard. *Style and Music: Theory, History and Ideology*. University of Chicago Press, 1989.

Morton, Drew. "Sketching under the Influence? Winsor McCay and the Question of Aesthetic Convergence between Comic Strips and Film." *Animation*, vol. 5, no. 3, 2010, pp. 295–312.

Peeters, Benoît. *Case, planche, recit*. Casterman, 1991.

Peirce, Charles. *Semiotics and Significs*. Indiana University Press, 1977.

Peterson, Richard and Narasimhan Anand. "The Production of Culture Perspective." *Annual Review of Sociology*, vol. 30, 2004, pp. 311–334.

Petherbridge, Deanna. *The Primacy of Drawing: Histories and Theories of Practice*. Yale University Press, 2004.

Postema, Barbara. *Narrative Structure in Comics: Making Sense of Fragments*. RIT Press, 2013.

Ross, Charles Henry and Dower Wilson. *Flirting Made Easy: A Guide for Girls*. Dalziel Brothers, 1882.

Sattler, Peter R. "Ballet Méchanique: The Art of George Herriman." *Word & Image: Journal of Visual Enquiry*, vol. 8, no. 2, 1992, pp. 133–153.

Shinohara, K. and Matsunaka, Y. "Pictorial Metaphors of Emotion in Japanese Comics." *Multimodal Metaphor*, edited by Charles Forceville and Eduardo Urios-Aparisi. De Gruyter, 2009, pp. 265–293.

Smolderen, Thierry. *The Origins of Comics: From William Hogarth to Windsor McCay*. University Press of Mississippi, 2014.

St. Fleur, Nicholas. "Oldest Known Drawing by Human Hands Discovered in South African Cave." *The New York Times*, 2018. www.nytimes.com/2018/09/12/science/oldest-drawing-ever-found.html. Accessed 15 September 2021.

Szép, Eszter. *Comics and the Body: Drawing, Reading and Vulnerability*. Ohio State University Press, 2021.

Verstappen, Nicolas. "Crossing Panel Borders: Transnational Constrained Comics Composition and Mindful Development Communication." *Mindful Communications for Sustainable Development: Perspectives from Asia*, edited by Kalinga Seneviratne. Sage, 2018, pp. 236–261.

Walker, Mort. *The Lexicon of Comicana* [1980]. iUniverse, 2000.

Whistler, C. T. "Fantasy and Reality: Tiepolo's Poetic Language at Wutzburg, Verona and Madrid." *Verona Illustrata*, vol. 2018, 2017, pp. 101–118.

Witek, Joseph. "The Arrow and the Grid." *A Comics Studies Reader*, edited by Jeet Heer and Kent Worcester. University Press of Mississippi, 2009, pp. 149–156.

CHAPTER 2

Comics, Media Culture, and Seriality

Matthieu Letourneux

The aesthetics of comics are deeply linked to serial logics. Since the end of the nineteenth century, with the success of Richard Outcault's *Yellow Kid* and *Buster Brown* comics or Winsor McCay's *Little Nemo in Slumberland*, the reader's pleasure has been attached to recurring characters and familiar comics structures that can be found from one issue to the next. The adventures of *Buck Rogers* or *Terry and the Pirates*, continuing week after week, offered another experience of seriality: not the variation of successive stories (series), but the continuity of a comic strip with constantly renewed action (serial). Subsequently, comic books, with their plethora of titles based on superhero teams, such as the Justice League or the Avengers, have sought to build reader loyalty through similar principles of serialization.

The serialities of comics can therefore only be understood through situating them in the broader framework of media history and its transformations. The two historically dominant formats, the comic strip and the comic book, are each linked to their own medium or publication format – the newspaper and the magazine, respectively – and to their rhythms of production and consumption. It is these rhythms and media constraints that comics exploit in their serial forms. The serialized stories and the principle of comic repetition of gags and their structure in the case of the comic strip, as well as the use of recurring characters, are different ways of aesthetically exploiting the communicational logics of the formats: their periodicity, the standardization which they induce, the principles of editorialization, or the structuring of brand identity and the generic, easily reproducible, nature of media. The authors conceive seriality as a principle of variation around implicit or explicit conventions that arouse the reader's interest. The aesthetic pleasure of the reader resides paradoxically on the attention that she pays to originality (changes and innovations introduced within the serial framework), where a reader little familiar with the series

This chapter benefited from initial exchange and comments from Christina Meyer.

46

would see only repetition. Over time, serialization practices have taken various forms in comics. Examples include parallel series, spin-offs developed around secondary characters, or efforts to connect series through creating (new) narrative and diegetic unity. It is nevertheless still possible to understand such serialization practices through the principles of repetition and variation that derive from media logics.

Serial Comics and Press Culture

In its broadest definition, seriality engages a relation to an object (an artistic work or a commodity) mediated by a series of other objects that share common characteristics with it, and through which it is apprehended. From this perspective, seriality does not pose an aesthetic or narrative question. It is above all a material question. In our daily experience, series comprise of objects manufactured in a certain quantity. In this, seriality is deeply linked to the logics of production of market capitalism (Kelleter). If, in creative fields, serial aesthetics have held an increasingly important place during the nineteenth and twentieth centuries, it is simply because the development of a production system that is increasingly standardized and manufactures goods in increasingly large quantities has imposed a serial relation to the objects. Such standardization favored the emergence of an aesthetic sensibility based on homogenized systems and their variations. The development of the press, one of the first mass-produced commodities, was an early expression of this serial culture. At the same time, the newspaper thematized the serial principle in its form, through a system of regular columns and features creating and punctuating reader expectations, day after day or week after week (Beetham; Thérenty).

Newspapers with similar formats and subjects, issues of the same newspaper, headings fixing recurrent themes and building reader loyalty are all examples of serial products. During the same period, the easy reproduction and marketing of engravings and the proliferation of advertisement posters and leaflets in the public space, standardized illustrations in newspapers and other serial publications, favored an aesthetic sensibility attuned to images. This pictorial seriality was exploited by illustrators and caricaturists transposing on the page, through series of images, the experiments with moving pictures taking place at the same time through a multitude of visual devices (see Smolderen; Gunning). The success of *Hogan's Alley* and the Yellow Kid, the character imagined by Outcault, is deeply linked to the *New York World*, the newspaper for which Outcault created the Kid in 1895, and then to the *New York Journal*, in which

Outcault continued to draw (Meyer). The recurrence of the Yellow Kid exploits the periodicity of the medium to produce expectations in the reader and increase her pleasure through the familiarity established with the character and his eccentricities (Figure 2.1).

If the massive *Yellow Kid* panels seem to explode in a multitude of fragmented images, it is because the development of comics cannot be conceived independently from that of the press and of the increasing space accorded to the image in the public sphere. They are emblematic of the increasingly visual media and serial culture established during the nineteenth century. All these elements of popular culture share certain key features, such as standardized formats and serial temporalities and, in the case of comic books, an editorial reading pact that attaches the reader to a serial publication despite the heterogeneity of its content and its contributors.

Since they offer stories in pictures, comics are deeply linked to the media on which they are printed because, unlike text, the image imposes a specific kind of relationship to the space of the page, or has this relationship imposed by the publisher or the printer. Historically the supports for comics are first those of the press, which followed a double rhythm: that of the daily newspaper and of the Sunday papers. Then came the comic books in the 1930s, for a long time essentially linked to the distribution systems of kiosks and small shops. Comic books and comic strips can thus be described as tied to the logics of periodicals, inseparable from the newspaper or magazine that publishes them. Such supports are linked to a specific format and design, which guarantee stability and define an editorial reading pact. The reader of *Mutt and Jeff* or *Terry and the Pirates* is above all a regular consumer of the newspaper in which she discovers the strips. She appreciates the thematic and stylistic unity of the newspaper, its political opinions, the informational hierarchies it proposes, or certain columns and editorials. Comics are only one of the features to which the reader is attached. In other words, the periodicity of comics is part of a global serial economy, especially the seriality of the medium (newspaper genres and formats, issues from the same title, article genres. . .).

This serially induced pleasure is evident in the case of comic books. Originally, most comic book titles offered a lead series (like "Superman" for *Action Comics*) and several secondary series (in *Action Comics*, for example, "Three Aces" or "Zatara"). For the fan, these other series also contribute to the attractiveness of the title. And in some cases, such as anthology comic books (e.g., EC horror comics), the reader's loyalty is based on the genre and tone of the different stories, which in itself formed a coherent series (that of horror stories). Even if the reader of these anthology comic books

Figure 2.1. Richard F. Outcault, "The Yellow Kid Inspects the Streets of New York," *The New York Journal*, 10 October 1898.

does not find the same characters from one issue to the next, the reading pact is serial in that the consumer buys a periodical with expectations related to the previous issues they have read, and which are predetermined by the publication. From this perspective of editorial seriality, publishing houses usually offered comic books specializing in one genre: romance, westerns, crime, superheroes, and more, echoing the tactics of pulp fiction and periodicals from the interwar period from which the first comic book publishers borrowed heavily (see Jones). The relationship to genre is another way to drive serial expectations that may have been defined at the editorial level.

Thus, the earliest comic books already articulate material seriality (that of the periodical), editorial seriality (that of the magazine's identity), and generic seriality (which means that most comic books adhere to certain generic codes permitting easy identification by the reader; see Chapter 8 on comics genres). In addition to these features, there is often a logic of diegetic seriality, since the titles generally have one or more recurring characters, and these characters these characters very quickly acquire their own comic books: this is the case with *Superman* in 1939, *Batman* in 1940, but also with much more obscure characters, such as *Amazing Man* (1939), *Mystery Men* (1939), *Blue Bolt* (1940), etc. But if this definition (of a series with a recurring character) is the most common one of seriality, it is important to understand that these four levels – material, editorial, generic, and diegetic seriality – are deeply connected to each other (see Letourneux, *Fictions*). Each time, they establish a relationship to what Gérard Genette calls an architext, which corresponds to "the entire set of general or transcendent categories – types of discourse, modes of enunciation, literary genres – from which emerges each singular text" (17). The architext thus designates the conceptual category and the encyclopedia of its associated characteristics: it is produced by the unifying function of the press title (an issue of *Zap Comix* or *Tales of Suspense* is considered in relation to the unity of the title), of the genre (a horror comic from EC or a romance story from *Teen-Age Romance* are related to generic expectations), the thematic series (a machine by Rube Goldberg makes sense in relation to his other poetic and absurd machines), the recurring character series (a *Batman* or *Li'l Abner* story is linked to the encyclopedia produced by the other adventures), or the (trans)media universe (a *Star Wars* comic makes sense in a universe made up of films, books, video games, etc.). This relationship to the work mediated by the series to which it belongs and to the architext that defines its perception determines both the choices made by the creators and the reader's mode of aesthetic attention.

Series Aesthetics and Periodicity: Comic Strips in the Newspaper Economy

As we have seen, comic strips and comic books are themselves caught up in the serial logics described earlier because they are part of a publishing context that engages a serial relationship with the medium. As a result, the periodic, temporal constraints of media have repercussions on the aesthetics of the artworks. The first serial model to emerge was the comic strip, published in newspapers and Sunday supplements. Deeply linked to the logic of these periodicals, the comic strip offers regular encounters with the characters according to two principles. In order to distinguish between these two models, we can refer to the classical opposition between "series" and "serial" (see Gardner, "History"). The term "series" designates a set of stories with recurring characters that are independent of each other, and which can be read in any order. This is the case, for instance, in the *Peanuts* comic books, in which each comic strip offers a complete gag. The notion of "serial" refers to a set of episodes or stories linked together by narrative and chronological features that imply an order of reading. The plots of comic strips such as *Nick Carter* and *Brick Bradford* continue from one issue to the next and cannot be understood outside this continuity.

The first dominant serial model is that of the complete story, very brief and generally humorous, which revolves around a character or a handful of recurring characters (but not always: Rube Goldberg, for example, specialized in creating a thematic series based on nonsensical machines since the 1910s). Such stories diegetize the principle of seriality by incorporating the seriality of the format in which they appear (such as the newspaper) in the story lines: *Buster Brown, Mutt and Jeff* or later *Peanuts* are based on a limited number of character types. This limited system of characters, usually associated with a world that is also reduced to a few settings, determines a series of rules that constitute, much like Umberto Eco's repertoire of *topoi*, a game of constraints, with the reader. The series offers an extremely readable thematic and narrative encyclopedia. Within fixed storytelling formulae, authors can make different combinations, and offer a multitude of variations often crystallizing around recurrent crises. This deliberate choice to use the same processes to intensify the serial aesthetic is further enhanced by the choice made by many artists to propose a range of recurring expressions and poses for their characters (from *Krazy Kat* to *Peanuts* or *Bringing up Father*), thus intensifying, in the drawing itself, the effects of iterations and variations likely to provoke laughter (Figure 2.2).

52 MATTHIEU LETOURNEUX

Figure 2.2. Final panels from three *Krazy Kat* strips from 4 September 1918, 7 September 1918 and 1 October 1918.

Comics, Media Culture, and Seriality

In Charles M. Schultz's *Peanuts*, for example, Snoopy's imaginary identities, Charlie Brown's psychoanalysis sessions with Lucy, Lucy's love for Schroeder are all recurring sequences that generate laughter precisely because readers know the author's routines and tastes in advance as well as the ways in which they will be renewed (see Vaillant; Wiltse). The pleasure of reading these comic strips is based on the principle of repetition with variation around limited rules that form the architext of the series (similar to what Eco has described as the dialectic of repetition and improvisation, or innovation). Such strips need the rhythm of the periodical that serves as its background to be fully exploited, since it is the familiarity with the conventions and the recurring characters that produces the reader's pleasure. Pleasure is accentuated by the pauses between the issues of the periodical, which exploit the rhythm leading from the expectation to the pleasure of finding the conventions again while escaping the saturation that a continuous reading of successive strips would have produced.

The second dominant serial model in the newspaper is the serial comic strip. It was established in 1929, when *Tarzan* and *Buck Rogers* were published in strips. The success of comic strip serials was to last for a long time, producing long-running series, such as *The Heart of Juliet Jones*, which lasted from 1953 to 2000. Borrowing from models tried and tested since the nineteenth century in the field of novels, these serials published in the press obey the same principles of loyalty as their ancestors. They aim at inciting the reader to subscribe in order to not miss any episode of their favorite series. While humorous comic strip series exploit the return of the same character and the variation around certain gags, adventure or romance comic strips such as *Tarzan* or *Juliet Jones* are based on a principle of incompleteness, dramatized by the effects of narrative tension. Such tension is ensured by a crisis concentrated in the final panels (in the form of cliffhangers, for instance) inviting to read the next installments (see Gardner, "History"). The serial comic strip seems to escape the linearity of a series since the same story continues from issue to issue. But, in addition to the fact that the serial generally takes the form of a series of successive adventures defining shorter narrative units (confrontation with an enemy, sentimental encounter, or new expedition), the rhythm of publication actually imposes a serial logic itself. The discontinuous and hyper-sequential character of the strips informs the narrative; it leads the narration to adopt a form favoring a reading that invests the rhythm of the installments and their temporality, concentrating on the episode and on the short narrative sequences, and reducing the superstructure to an indefinite and open unit. In a series such as Alex Raymond's *Flash Gordon* (1934), the character lives through a series of micro-adventures at a frantic pace: a plane crash, a fight against monsters, a duel in an arena, a battle in a spaceship, all follow one another in a few dozen strips. The episodes form a series that holds the reader's attention much more than the general plot, which is very vague (defeating Ming, coming back to earth, etc.). Finally, the very rhythm of each delivery, with its first panel summarizing the relevant preceding events and its final panels opening up a (new) crisis, imposes a repetitive structure which works as a series based on the reader's aesthetic sensibility to narrative rhythms: from installment to installment, the reader finds the same rhythms, the same dynamics of reviving interest and relaunching the narrative. It is this double movement of repetition and progression (and thus of transformation) which produces the pleasure of the narrative, and which installs the serial in series logics.

Serial Aesthetics and Periodicity: Comic Books

Dependent on a media ecosystem that is different from that of newspapers, comic books introduce important variations in the serial economy in comparison to the comic strip model. If comic books at first served to republish comics previously issued in newspapers and periodicals, certain titles from 1934 onwards devoted themselves to previously unpublished stories (see Gabilliet 13–19). The comic book also imposed a different relationship between readers and stories by offering a longer story (of several dozen pages), based on plot unity or an episodic logic strong enough for each episode, with its fixed number of pages, to be read as a semi-independent story (a mixed model, between the series and the serial, encouraging readers to buy the next episode).

The media economy of the comic book differs from that of the comic strip in that the medium is entirely devoted to the publication of comics. It therefore combines the serial logics of periodicals, genres, and characters. Thus, at the end of the 1930s, the *Action Comics* fan loved the periodical, the superhero story genre, and the character of Superman at the same time. In the first decades, a character was generally first tested in an anthology comic book; if successful, the character would become the title character of their own periodical, making the reader loyal to the character and to the comic book title as a whole.

Comics, Media Culture, and Seriality

This concordance between the character, the genre, and the editorial title has favored plot standardization. The reader's pleasure stems from finding their favorite character every month, but they also enjoy a certain kind of adventure, a certain story format, comparable narrative structures, a set of recurrent protagonists, and thematic motifs that constitute the identity of the series. It is a total experience of seriality that is offered to the reader, further enhanced by the coherence produced, in the kiosk, by the range of similar titles (e.g., different stories featuring western actors as heroes in the 1950s), romance comic book series, superhero comics (see Letourneux, "The Editors"): all these genres are marked by similar covers and a strong repetition of plots because the formats and the competition between publishers impose a logic of standardization which lead the reader to have specific expectations.

But it would be wrong to see in this reading pact a simple principle of repetition. Indeed, for the consumer, the choice to buy one periodical rather than another within a standardized offer is based above all on a logic of distinction. Where a cursory reader would see only repetition, the fan identifies essentially variety (see Letourneux, *Fictions*). It is the same pleasure of variety that determines the fan's relationship to the adventures of their favorite character: new enemies, new perils, new sentimental twists (e.g., in the life of Spider-Man or in the interactions between the X-Men). Familiarity with the conventions of the series translates into a hypersensitivity to the effects of renewal, transformation, or appropriation. This contributes to promoting the development of fan communities, circulating, within the series, from one work to another, and soon, as we will see, from one set of works to another (see Jenkins). Fan interest in these logics of variation has undoubtedly affected the structures of the works by progressively favoring serialization effects, with love or dramatic plots evolving in the background. Although this process is old in comic books[1], it remained superficial for a long time because the variations did not really alter the repetitive serial structure of the series (see Friedenthal). The process only became a recurrent means of enriching the fictional universe in the 1970s. Chris Claremont exploited this principle in the new *X-Men* series he wrote from 1975 onwards, multiplying the departures, conflicts, or deaths of team members like so many twists from a soap opera,

---

[1] Well-known examples include "If This Be My Destiny...!" (1966, in three parts) by Stan Lee and Steve Ditko, known to have contributed to the humanization of Peter Parker, or Amazing Spider-Man # 121, with the death of Gwen Stacy, which will haunt the character lastingly.

exemplifying the semi-serialized turn in series with recurring characters. It is not only a question of keeping the reader loyal by inviting them to buy the next issue to read the continuation, but to exploit the possibilities of continuing and enriching characters and their world within the constraints and possibilities of serialization. This open-ended nature of the work explains why comic books have given rise to intense hermeneutic activity on the part of fans, who project themselves into the rest of the story or engage in interpretations of its overall meaning. Letters columns in comic books or fan conventions provide platforms for these exchanges. In return, publishers are receptive towards readers' comments and preferences and do not hesitate to reorient their series according to fan reactions (Kelleter). It is in this sense that one can say that a serial narrative remains always open and susceptible to see its global meaning altered.

Fragmentation, Consolidation, and Transmedia Iteration

With the domination of comics publishing by DC and Marvel from the 1960s onwards, and the importance of superheroes in their offer, serialization processes became more complex. Publishers were keen to develop and deepen their offer of characters, especially as rightsholders of the titles, in lieu of the authors. Characters were consequently promoted like brands, following several strategies. The first one is to decline them in parallel series. Such a practice began very early: already in 1939, the adventures of Superman were proposed in *Superman* alongside *Action Comics*, before the character was gradually declined in dozens of comic book series, alone or with other superheroes, but also in films, in Big Little Books, other publications, and offshoots (see Freeman, "Up"; for more on transmedia narratives, see Chapter 6).

The second way to make the series bear fruit is to expand it to series with derived characters, often to attract new audiences. This is the case of Superboy, a teenage version of Superman, aiming to attract a young readership (1944, then 1949 for the title itself), or of Lois Lane (1958, as titular character) seeking to seduce female readers. The practice is striking in the case of the publisher of Archie comics (originally MLJ Magazines) which transitioned from being a publisher with a broad catalog, to one focusing on the Archie universe, multiplying series around its main character, Archie and his friends. Betty, Veronica, Jughead, and Reggie have all had their own dedicated series, producing a perennial diegetic universe that in turn consolidates the identity to the whole publishing house.

The third strategy follows logically from the previous one. It concerns the cross-fertilization of the brands that the characters become, by multiplying crossover series (like teaming up Superman and Batman in *World's Finest Comics* in July 1954). Comic books presenting teams of vigilantes from different series (such as the *Justice League*, launched by DC in 1960, or *The Avengers* for Marvel in 1963) multiplied, contributing to the feeling of a diegetic continuity beyond the specificity of the characters. It is Marvel that has developed this principle of diegetization of editorial production in the most rationalized manner by seeking to unify all the series into a coherent universe. The process started in the 1940s, but accelerated in the 1960s – under the impetus of Stan Lee, Jack Kirby, and Steve Ditko – to progressively reach an important degree of sophistication by multiplying references from one series to another (Méon; Friedenthal). They thus invited readers to circulate among the different productions of the publisher (Flanagan). This effort of diegetization became progressively central in the rapport established between publishers and fans (Friedenthal). It also led a publisher like DC to produce stories that aimed to resolve the contradictions accumulated through the development of characters in parallel series, like *Crisis on Infinite Earths* (1985), which narrativized the creation of an official history of the DC universe by destroying universes that no longer conformed to the overarching narrative (Klock). The world of DC, like that of Marvel, thus corresponds to consolidating the unity of the universe of each of the series-brands (Spider-Man, Iron Man, X-Men) towards a diegetized industrial brand (Marvel or the Marvel universe), a universe constituting of a series of series. This multiplication of intertwined narrative arcs has resulted in a shift in the reader's interest from the story or series to series of series that organize themselves into a more or less coherent world.

Such an evolution of characters and their universe into a constellation of series can thus be explained by editorial decisions linked to commercial choices. To take just one example, when, in the 1980s, Marvel and DC massively invested the market of specialized bookstores, they adapted their production to these new distribution channels, and multiplied their series in order to seduce a public of collectors, thus producing numerous parallel series in a small number of issues, or complete stories around serial characters published in the form of graphic novels (Gabilliet 85–97; for more on graphic novels see Chapter 3). These tighter narratives, strongly structured around a plot and offering a singular vision, are also an opportunity for successful authors to develop personal interpretations of the fictional universe associated with a character, negotiating between serial logics and authorial singularization strategies.

Frank Miller's Batman (*The Dark Knight Returns*, 1986) or Mark Millar's communist Superman (*Red Son*, 2003) are two famous examples; but the reconfigurations offered by series such as Marvel's *Civil War* (2006), inviting the reader to witness a generalized confrontation of superheroes, or *Annihilation* (engaging the Marvel universe in cosmic stakes, 2006) are other examples of singularization, less anchored in a style than in a relationship to the fictional world. From then on, the possibility for authors to reinvent characters and their worlds has transformed characters into architexts destined to be reinvented, relaunched, reconfigured. As soon as the character is declined in different media and parallel series, the consumer becomes attentive to the variations that exist between the versions offered: one-shots, miniseries, spin-offs, crossovers are perceived as so many different versions, sometimes evaluated through an author's distinctive style or their ability to reinvent the codes of the series. For a few decades now, authors have been encouraged to assert their styles and are free to choose the degree of character continuity they want to retain. This authorial turn (which had already been partly initiated in the 1970s) was to have major consequences for the way in which the relationship between the works and the serialized ensembles was conceived. Over time, Spider-Man, Batman, or Superman ceased to be perceived as series and became more and more like brands that could be declined into parallel series which occupied different niches, investing in varied aesthetics or tonalities, following a logic of specialized standardization characteristic of pop culture in the post-Fordist era.

From the 1970s onwards, post-Fordist production methods favored the emergence of specialized product lines within major brands (as opposed to the standardized products of the Fordist era), aimed at differentiated audiences and enriching the brand image by declining it across different products. This resulted in a strong shift towards brand value, with products figuring as components of a strong identity (or elements of brand storytelling). This practice, characteristic of the choices made by brands as different as Nike or Apple, is even more striking in the cultural industries. When Marvel or DC choose to develop one or several short series around existing characters, to enhance secondary characters, or to revisit an event narrated in an old comic book, they do it more and more according to a global strategy that actually engages the identity of the brand and the whole transmedia ecosystem (Letourneux, "Penser").

However, from the 1990s onwards (with the success of Tim Burton's *Batman*), another major turning point occurred in the serial logic surrounding comics characters as publishers began explicitly integrating a transmedia identity into their conception of a popular character. In reality, this turn builds on a phenomenon that has existed since the origin of comics; the great comic book characters were declined across different media from the very beginning, producing parallel media series (Meyer); in the interwar period, comic strip characters were declined in parallel series in Big Little Books, film serials, radio series, toys, cartoons. Following this logic of development across different media supports, each of these media series enriches the character's universe with their own logic, which encourages publishers to develop certain aspects explored in other media in their comics. In the 1960s, the development of the group The Archies, comprising musicians figuring as characters of the Archie comics universe, confirmed the transmedia destiny of comics, simultaneously affecting the choices the choices made in the comics by the publishing house.

But the way in which, since the 1960s, Marvel has conceived the development of its flagship series according to their potential for television franchises and derivative products is another manifestation of this need to think of the series beyond the unity of their diegetic developments, in the light of their industrial and transmedia developments (Johnson). Such a movement has in fact occurred in both directions. Just as many children in the late 1960s first knew Spider-Man as a cartoon character before discovering the comic books – as is the case with Hopalong Cassidy, in the 1950s, and Tarzan, during his long career, who appeared as characters from cinema, novels, or comic books (Kackman) – the close links woven from the beginning between comics and other media (Gardner, *Projections*) call for a transmedia perspective and the need to think about the diegetic (in)consistencies alongside industrial and material constraints (see Davis). This is even more prominent today with the displacement of the transmedia polarization from comics to films (in other words, from the opposition between Marvel and DC to the confrontation between Disney and Warner). With the rise of film series, the increasingly peripheral position of comics in the franchise system requires us to think of the development of comic book series in terms of a constant dialogue with a center represented by the cinema and all the merchandising it generates.

The famous "Marvel Cinematic Universe" thus represents a turning point towards a multimedia serial universe which now has a cinematographic center. The choices made in the comics are certainly not simply a record of the decisions made by the new cinematic center of attraction, but they regularly manifest their importance. That Mark Millar decided to give Samuel L. Jackson's features to Nick Fury in 2002, making the new version of the character a transmedia figure, manifests such a turn (Yockey).

Conclusion

As we can see, reflection on seriality should not be limited to an analysis of the series of a character's adventures and the world in which they evolve. It brings into play the logics of the media and the ways in which stories and brand identities are structured and communicated; it also engages principles of generic serialization, which explains why we always attach serial expectations to genres. As for diegetic seriality (that of the character and fictional universe), while it is largely explained by these other serial logics, it also depends on the strategic choices of media industry actors and, increasingly, on the power relations between the different media that participate in the reiteration and valorization of characters.

WORKS CITED

Comics

Action Comics. Detective Comics, 1938–2011.
Herriman, Georges. *Krazy Kat*, 4 September, 7 September and 10 October, 1918.
Outcault, Richard F. "The Yellow Kid Inspects the Streets of New York," *The New York* Journal, 10 October 1898.

Secondary Sources

Beetham, Margaret. "Open and Closed: The Periodical as a Publishing Genre." *Victorian Periodicals Review*, vol. 22, no. 3, Fall, 1989, pp. 96–100.
Davis, Blair. *Movie Comics: Page to Screen, Screen to Page*. Rutgers University Press, 2017.
Eco, Umberto. "The Myth of Superman." Translated by Natalie Chilton. *Diacritics*, vol. 2, no. 1, 1972, pp. 14–22.

"Innovation and Repetition: Between Modern and Post-Modern Aesthetics." *Daedalus*, vol. 114, no. 4. *The Moving Image*, 1985, pp. 161–184.

Freeman, Matthew. "Up, Up and Across: Superman, the Second World War and the Historical Development of Transmedia Storytelling." *Historical Journal of Film, Radio and Television*, vol. 35, no. 2, 2015, pp. 215–239.

Friedenthal, Andrew J. *Retcon Game: Retroactive Continuity and the Hyperlinking of America*. University Press of Mississippi, 2017.

Gabilliet, Jean-Paul. *Of Comics and Men: A Cultural History of American Comic Books*. University Press of Mississippi, 2009.

Gabriele, Sandra and Paul S. Moore. "The *Globe* on Saturday, the *World* on Sunday: Toronto Weekend Editions and the Influence of the American Sunday Paper, 1886–1895." *Canadian Journal of Communication*, vol. 34, no. 3, 2009, pp. 337–358.

Gardner, Jared. *Projections: Comics and the History of Twenty-first-Century Storytelling*. Stanford University Press, 2012.

"A History of the Narrative Comic Strip." *From Comic Strips to Graphic Novels*, edited by Daniel Stein and Jan-Noël Thon. De Gruyter, 2013, pp. 301–322.

Genette, Gérard. *Palimpsests*. Translated by Channa Newman and Claude Doubinsky. University of Nebraska Press, 1997.

Glaude, Benoît and Olivier Odaert. "The Transnational Circulation of Comic Strips Before 1945." *Journal of European Popular Culture*, vol. 5, no. 1, 2014, pp. 43–58.

Gunning, Tom. "The Art of Succession: Reading, Writing, and Watching Comics." *Comics & Media, Critical Inquiry*, vol. 40, no. 3, 2014, pp. 36–51.

Jenkins, Henry. *Comics and Stuff*. New York University Press, 2020.

Jones, Gerard. *Men of Tomorrow: Geeks, Gangsters and the Birth of Comic Book*. Basic Books, 2004.

Kelleter, Frank, "'Five Ways' of Looking at Popular Seriality." *Media of Serial Narrative*, edited by Frank Kelleter. Ohio State University Press, 2017, pp. 7–34.

Latour, Bruno. *Reassembling the Social: An Introduction to Actor-Network-Theory*. Oxford University Press, 2005.

Letourneux, Matthieu. *Fictions à la chaîne*. Seuil, "Poétique," 2017.

"'The editors have cast me in comic stories', Comic books, western stars e transmedialità." *Bande à part 2, fumetto e transmedialita*, edited by Giuliana Benvenuti, Sara Colaone, and Lucia Quaquarelli. Morellini Editore, 2019, pp. 47–65.

"Penser les fictions sérielles en régime postfordiste." *Cahiers de Narratologie*, no. 37, 2020. https://doi.org/10.4000/narratologie.10488

Meyer, Christina. *Producing Mass Entertainment: The Serial Life of the Yellow Kid*. Ohio State University Press, 2019.

Sabin, Roger. *Comics, Comix & Graphic Novels*. Phaidon, 1996.

Smolderen, Thierry. *The Origins of Comics: From William Hogarth to Winsor McCay*. Translated by Bart Beaty and Nick Nguyen. University Press of Mississippi, 2014.

Thérenty, Marie-Ève. *La Littérature au quotidien*. Seuil, "Poétique", 2007.

Turner, Mark W. "Periodical Time in the Nineteenth Century." *Media History*, vol. 8, no. 2, 2002, pp. 183–196.

"The Unruliness of Serials in the Nineteenth Century (and in the Digital Age)." *Serialization in Popular Culture*, edited by Rob Allen and Thijs van der Berg. Routledge, 2014, pp. 11–32.

Vaillant, Alain. "Portrait de l'humoriste moderne en serial rieur. À propos d'Alphonse Allais." *Belphégor*, no. 14, 2016, *Sérialités*, n. pag. https://journals.openedition.org/belphegor/740

CHAPTER 3

Comics and Graphic Novels

Paul Williams

Introduction

Artist Charlie Adlard: "If there's one phrase I loathe, it's the graphic novel" (quoted in Flood). Writer Alan Moore: a "marketing term [...] that I never had any sympathy with." Creator Marjane Satrapi: "I don't very much like this term of graphic novel. I think they made up this term for the bourgeoisie not to be scared of comics." Hardly ringing endorsements from creative talents whose international reputations were forged in the graphic novel form!

The international spread of this term has not been celebrated unreservedly, with good reason: readers will have their own examples of when "graphic novel" has been used loosely or cynically. In 2008 the scholar Hillary Chute called it the "official catchphrase" for a broad variety of projects "in the medium of comics" (462 n2). Walk into a library or bookshop and the signage will reflect the term's wide use, but comics creators, fans, reviewers, and academics are not so sanguine about its ubiquity. Given that scholars also refer to "graphic narratives," "graphic literature," and "graphic memoir," does comics studies need to talk about graphic novels?

The academics Jan Baetens and Hugo Frey think so. In *The Graphic Novel: An Introduction* (2015) they make the case that graphic novels deserve attention as "exceptional" adult-oriented comics characterized by formal experimentation and sophisticated content: "contemporary graphic novels display genuinely significant, although rarely absolute, variation from the preexisting comics and comix traditions" (Baetens and Frey 1–4). Baetens and Frey believe the graphic novel is a "medium [that] is part of other, more-encompassing cultural fields and practices (graphic literature, visual storytelling)" but distinguishable from newspaper

---

With thanks to Seiko Buckingham and Denis Kitchen for their assistance with permission requests.

63

cartoons and periodical comics on the basis of "complex and variegated" form, "serious" and/or non-fictional subject matter, "strong preference for the book format," and the graphic novel's association with particular publishers and types of retailer. Baetens and Frey stress this is "not a closed list of essential features" and that definitions of the graphic novel might change over time or only operate at specific times and in certain places (7–21).

Is there a danger in ring-fencing a certain group of comics as more complex and innovative than others? Christopher Pizzino in *Arresting Development: Comics at the Boundaries of Literature* (2016) proffers that canonizing a small body of texts as "a respectable kind of reading" excludes the vast majority of comics and renders them "naturally inferior and immature." For Pizzino, the "legitimacy the graphic novel possesses" delegitimizes the medium of comics as a whole and should be considered "conflicted and unstable" (22–45). This chapter does not set out to defend "graphic novel" – "those two, sometimes unloved, words" (Baetens and Frey 4) – but I do want to equip readers to wade into these debates. To go about studying graphic novels raises all sorts of questions and issues: is there an implicit valuation of some comics (those most resembling literary texts) over others? Do critics risk focusing on novelistic aspects of a text (such as dialogue or character development) at the expense of other features? Does a focus on the graphic novel occlude certain subject positions?

I plan to explore the graphic novel as an object of aspiration (a desired future for comics) and as a material product generated out of particular historical contexts. The latter is important because, while supremely talented creators have helmed ambitious, questing experiments, their long-form comics did not appear by sheer force of will; specific conditions needed to exist for graphic novels to be completed, published, distributed, and sold. In what follows I offer a chronology of the graphic novel since the nineteenth century, with an emphasis on US graphic novels since the mid-1960s (when the term was coined in relation to comics). Three key definitions of the graphic novel are in play: (i) a long, complete narrative; (ii) book publication, either hardback or softcover; and (iii) a particularly sophisticated text deserving esteem for its literary and artistic merit. When someone hails a graphic novel, it is often the case that all three meanings are invoked, but not always; these definitions aren't automatically in alignment, and as Pizzino noted, the graphic novel is a highly unstable category. I have not restricted myself to texts labelled as "graphic novels" and include instances such as "picture novels," "visual novels," and "comics novels," opening up a long history going back to the 1820s.

Comics and Graphic Novels

Drawing Novels in the Nineteenth Century

The idea of calling a long-form comic a "novel" or publishing it in book form begins in the first half of the nineteenth century, when eight such texts were produced by the Genevan writer and educator Rodolphe Töpffer. The earliest manuscript for Töpffer's French-language comics narratives has been dated to 1827, with *Histoire de Monsieur Jabot* the first to be published in 1833. Töpffer described the form he pioneered as the "*histoire en estampes*" (story in prints, picture story) but a reviewer in the 1840s had no hesitation asserting that Töpffer "draws novels" (Kunzle xi, 1, 187). Töpffer's oblong albums of long-form comics proved popular and circulated widely; at first his original books were passed between admirers, but from the mid-1830s onwards they were translated into multiple languages (and sometimes bootlegged without Töpffer's permission). He inspired artists around Europe to make similar books, prominent examples of which include George Cruikshank's *The Loving Ballad of Lord Bateman* (1839), Cham's *Impressions de voyage de Monsieur Boniface* (1844), Alfred Crowquill's *Pantomime: To Be Played As It Was, Is, and Will Be, at Home* (1849), and Gustave Doré's *L'histoire de la Sainte Russie* (1854). Töpffer's albums travelled further still and pirated editions were published in the United States in 1842 (Smolderen 53–73; some titles have been shortened).

After the 1850s, long comics narratives gradually disappeared but comic strips became increasingly visible in newspapers in the latter part of the nineteenth century. Their popularity was exploited with reprint books, an early example of which in the United States was the 1897 edition of Richard F. Outcault's *Hogan's Alley* (Meyer 42). In the UK this practice had already led to Marie Duval's long comics narrative *Ally Sloper: A Moral Lesson*, published as a book edition in 1873 (Sabin, "Ally Sloper"). Reprinting newspaper strips in books still takes place, and while daily strips rehearse a different narrative logic to most graphic novels,[1] on occasion books of strips alter the original order of publication and provide new material to create self-contained stories for the book edition.

Woodcut Novels

Woodcut novels were a vibrant form of comics-making in the 1920s and 1930s, influenced by the broader artistic revival of woodcut techniques at the end of the nineteenth century. Woodcut novels took their aesthetic

---

[1] Some graphic novels deliberately mimic one-page strips, such as Daniel Clowes's *Wilson* (2010).

style from political cartoons, Christian iconography, and German Expressionism, and typically displayed one panel per page. Narratives tended towards the didactic and allegorical and offered a critique of urbanization, industrialization, capitalism, and militarism (Beronä 10–13). They emerged in Geneva in 1918, when political cartoonist Frans Masereel produced *25 Images de la passion d'un homme*, a protest against class inequality. In 1919 his most popular woodcut novel was published, *Passionate Journey*, the narrative of a male protagonist navigating a bewildering and corrupt city (Beronä 15–16, 21–24).

Masereel's books caught the imagination of artists across Europe and North America and a series of long-form comics for adult readers were published from the 1920s to the 1950s. Notable titles include Otto Nückel's *Destiny: A Novel in Pictures* (1926), Helena Bochořáková-Dittrichová's *Childhood* (1931), and Giacomo Patri's *White Collar: A Novel in Linocuts* (1940). Most of the books called "woodcut novels" were not made with woodcuts at all, but by using engraving tools to create prints out of lead, wood, or linoleum. One constant was the absence of speech balloons (though readers might be oriented by billboards or newspaper headlines placed within panels), hence their description as "picture novels" by the art historian Hellmut Lehmann-Haupt in 1930 (612).

The leading proponent of the form in the United States was Lynd Ward. An artist studying in Germany in the late 1920s, Ward saw Masereel's woodcut novels and produced similar work using wood engraving upon his return to America. New York book editor Harrison Smith and British publishing house Jonathan Cape released Ward's first book *Gods' Man* in October 1929, the narrative of which focuses on the apparent contradiction between commercial success and artistic integrity. Even now Cape is a major graphic novel publisher, and it is significant that woodcut novels were released by established trade presses: these were not obscure experiments but reached a large audience of readers. Despite being published the same month as the New York Stock Exchange crash, *Gods' Man* went into six printings and sold 20,000 copies over the following four years (Ward 20–24). Perhaps because they came from literary publishing houses, woodcut novels commonly featured "novel" in their subtitles.

During the 1930s, Ward's woodcut novels became longer and more complex, leading to his most extended and multilayered work *Vertigo* (1937). The themes recurring across his books include America's slide towards fascism, urban poverty, organized struggles for better pay and working conditions, racist violence and the legacy of slavery, and the place of art and utopianism in a country without hope for the future. These political commitments were present in most of the woodcut novels published up to the middle of the twentieth century, the last notable example being Laurence Hyde's *Southern Cross: A Novel of the South Seas Told in Wood Engravings* (1951), an indictment of the social and ecological fallout of atomic-bomb testing in the Pacific.

Graphic Novels in Mid-Century America

Many mid-century US graphic novels shared similar themes with the woodcut novels: James Thurber's *The Last Flower: A Parable in Pictures* (1939), Don Freeman's *It Shouldn't Happen* (1945), and Si Lewen's *The Parade* (1957) are all antimilitarist allegories that reject speech balloons (some have captions or dialogue running opposite or under the panels). Like those creators, Miné Okubo was an artist and commercial illustrator, but her *Citizen 13660* (1946) came out of a very different context. Okubo was one of more than 100,000 Japanese Americans detained during the Second World War: between 1942 and 1944 Okubo was interned in camps in California and Utah, during which time she produced the hundreds of ink sketches that became the book *Citizen 13660* (Creef 4–7).

Early in the narrative, Okubo is forced to register at a Civil Control Station, after which her surname is replaced by the serial number 13660 and her household property is confiscated (Figure 3.1). While she waits, Okubo draws herself reading "the 'funnies' until my number was called," and she pictures the soldiers on guard in such a way that the barrel of a gun hovers near her head (19). For cultural historian Kimberley L. Phillips, Okubo's "seemingly calm perusal of the comic pages floats as her silent rebellion against" government aggression, an act of resistance against the dehumanization of Japanese Americans by the US state (110). Elsewhere in *Citizen 13660*, Okubo individualizes Japanese Americans and shows their spirit and humor in defiance of the racist stereotypes found in 1940s comic books and political cartoons (Hong xvi).

In 1950, two crime comics publishers experimented with paperback publishing. Fawcett Publications brought out *Mansion of Evil* credited to Joseph Millard ("A complete novel in words and pictures") and St. John Publications released the "Picture Novel" *It Rhymes with Lust*, written by Arnold Drake and Leslie Waller and drawn by Matt Baker, and *The Case of the Winking Buddha* by Manning Lee Stokes and Charles Raab. In this period, crime and horror comics were under the spotlight for glamorizing law-breaking and encouraging moral depravity. In 1947 an anti-comics movement began in the United States that saw public comics burnings, local bans on specific genres, and jeremiads by public intellectuals (Wright 86–107). This activity climaxed in 1954, when members of the comics

Figure 3.1. Miné Okubo, *Citizen 13660*, 1946, University of Washington Press, 2014, p. 19. © 1946, 1973, 1983 by Miné Okubo

industry testified in front of the Senate Subcommittee on Juvenile Delinquency (Nyberg 53–84). When these graphic novels were published, crime comics were being attacked for undermining the nation's integrity; if the label "novel" was a bid for legitimacy, it didn't bring lasting advantage to either company. Neither Fawcett nor St. John produced any more paperback comics and both ceased publishing comics altogether by the end of the 1950s (Gabilliet 45–46).

Enter: the "Graphic Novel"

The term "graphic novel" emerged in November 1964, courtesy of fan-critic Richard Kyle's "Wonderworld" newsletter,[2] and it was elaborated in

---

[2] "Wonderworld" was part of *CAPA-alpha*, the first amateur press association dedicated to comics. Ideally once a month, members of *CAPA-alpha* exchanged newsletters as a means of circulating their thoughts, sketches, and reviews with fellow fans.

fanzines by Kyle and his peers. His initial proposal was that the future of comics lay in periodicals ("comic books") because, unlike newspaper strips, artists had more space on the page. Furthermore, periodicals offered the opportunity to tell longer stories ("Wonderworld" 1–4). Length was key because, no matter how brilliant a comic might be, at present "no mood is sustained long enough to reach into the heart and mind of any but the uncommon reader" (Kyle, "Graphic" 41–42). Repeatedly praising Harvey Kurtzman's short stories, Kyle hoped that the creator might attempt a "novel-length" version of the war comics he produced at publisher EC. How long should a graphic novel be? In 1966 Kyle mooted 75–100 pages or longer ("Graphic" 42); in 1967 he thought it should take around 60–90 minutes to read (Kyle, Letter 35–36). Calling these longer comics "graphic novels" was part of their prestige brand; Kyle thought his new term would attract a highly literate readership of "intelligent adults" and usher comics towards their rightful "place in the literary spectrum" (Kyle, "Wonderworld" 4).

As these conversations unfolded in fandom, creators and readers of mainstream comics identified the lengthening narratives at Marvel Comics as novels. Writer Stan Lee and artists including Jack Kirby and Steve Ditko were innovating with the superhero genre, ratcheting up the personal angst and civilian difficulties that their protagonists faced, extending narrative arcs across multiple issues, and presenting interwoven storylines in each issue. Letters from readers hailed these longer narratives as novels (Jackson; McGregor) and the Marvel personnel followed their lead. Jack Kirby moved to Marvel's rival DC in 1970 and told the *New York Times* he was inventing several new series that as a whole constituted a "continuing novel" (Braun 55).

Further sources of graphic novels were Grove Press and Olympia Press, New York publishers specializing in erotica, avant-garde literature, and literature in translation. Grove serialized three long-form comics in house magazine *Evergreen Review* before reprinting them as books: *Barbarella* (1966) by Jean-Claude Forest and *The Adventures of Jodelle* (1967) by Pierre Bartier and Guy Peellaert, both translated from the French, and Michael O'Donoghue and Frank Springer's *The Adventures of Phoebe Zeit-Geist* (1968) (Baetens and Frey 44). Olympia released *Filipino Food* in 1972, a wordless, psychedelic sequence of images by Ed Badajos, a political cartoonist in the underground press.

Another major development in the 1960s was the emergence of underground comix. For most of the decade, comix creators published their work in national satire magazines and in the underground newspapers that could be found in major cities and around college campuses. A boom in periodical comix began in 1968: these were chiefly sold via mail order or in record shops, alternative bookstores, and the head shops catering to countercultural consumers. The comix boom peaked in 1972, followed by a crash in the number of new titles sold (Gabilliet 81–82). Underground creators could pursue intensely personal, noncommercial projects compared to the mainstream industry, which still adhered to the Comics Code drawn up in response to the moral panic of the 1950s; the Code restricted comics to child-suitable fare, severely limiting the representation of sex, violence, drug-taking, and moral ambiguity. Underground creators did produce long narratives, but one-off book publication – Dan O'Neill's *Hear the Sound of My Feet Walking.. Drown the Sound of My Voice Talking..* (1969) and Richard Corben's *Bloodstar* (1976), for example – was rare. More common were long-form comix released as periodicals, such as Lee Marrs's *The Further Fattening Adventures of Pudge, Girl Blimp* (1973–1978) and Justin Green's seminal autobiography *Binky Brown Meets the Holy Virgin Mary* (1972).

Figure 3.2. The variety of physical formats adopted by 1970s graphic novels can be seen here: from left-to-right, Jack Katz, *The First Kingdom*, Wallaby, 1978 © 1978 by Jack and Carolyn Katz; Sanho Kim, cowritten by Michael Juliar, *Sword's Edge, Part I: The Sword and the Maiden*, Iron Horse, 1973 © 1973 by Iron Horse Publishing Co., Inc.; Gil Kane, cowritten by Archie Goodwin [uncredited], *Blackmark*, Bantam, 1971 © 1971 by Bantam Books, Inc.; Burne Hogarth, adapted by Robert M. Hodes from an original text by Edgar Rice Burroughs, *Tarzan of the Apes*, Watson-Guptill, 1972 © 1972 by Edgar Rice Burroughs, Inc.

Also in the 1970s, veterans of the mainstream comics industry, some of whom communicated with fans and referred to "graphic novels" themselves, devised long comics narratives published in book form (Figure 3.2). These included Gil Kane's postapocalyptic sword-and-sorcery adventure *Blackmark* (1971; cowritten by Archie Goodwin), Burne Hogarth's *Tarzan of the Apes* (1972), and Sanho Kim's *Sword's Edge* (1973). One of the longest projects (over 750 pages in total) was written and drawn by Jack Katz, a former mainstream comics artist whose *The First Kingdom* was serialized in periodicals between 1974 and 1986. Prefiguring later modes of graphic novel production, Wallaby Books reprinted the first six issues as a book edition in 1978. In the same year, Baronet published Will Eisner's *A Contract with God*, the paperback edition of which was emblazoned with "graphic novel" on its front cover (Figure 3.3).

One of the most important changes for the development of the graphic novel was the start of the direct market in 1973. Rather than distribute comics in mixed bundles on a sale-or-return basis through national magazine distributors to drugstores and newsstands, the direct market saw specialist comic shops place advance orders for specific titles with distributors dedicated to comics. This shift had implications for the whole ecosystem of US comics. Before 1973, fewer than a dozen specialist shops selling new comics operated in the United States; retailers found getting hold of new titles every month a difficult and unreliable process. The direct market allowed the number of comic shops to grow markedly, and their primary clientele was ardent fans who tended to be older than the casual consumers buying their comics from newsstands. Fans had more money to spend and publishers recentered their output on this consumer base, trialing new products such as book editions and glossy magazines. The shift towards fans as near-exclusive consumers of US comics was gradual, however, and direct market sales only overtook the sale-or-return method in the mid-1980s (Beerbohm 82).

Another repercussion of the direct market was the appearance of new publishers. The sale-or-return system required an issue of a comic to be printed in the hundreds of thousands to have a chance of making a profit (Beerbohm 82). The direct market, on the other hand, allowed companies to publish comics in small print runs and still be commercially viable. Low initial capitalization meant new presses could enter the market, such as independent publishers appealing to fans of mainstream comics with parodies or more adult variations of established series (as in the underground, comics distributed via the direct market did not have to abide by the Comics Code). Eclipse was one of the first independents and it started

Figure 3.3. Will Eisner, *A Contract with God and Other Tenement Stories* (Baronet, 1978) © Will Eisner Studios, Inc.

releasing graphic novels in 1978 with writer Don McGregor and artist Paul Gulacy's postapocalyptic action-adventure *Sabre*. McGregor and Gulacy had both worked at Marvel but Eclipse offered what the mainstream industry did not permit in the 1970s: royalty payments, ownership of the intellectual property that creators generated, and almost-unrestricted artistic autonomy.[3] This was the attraction of the independents, giving creators the freedom to experiment with genres and length and to imagine texts that did not have to be suitable for very young readers.

Alternative comics were also invited into existence by the direct market. Alternative comics consisted of small presses and self-publishing creators exploring genres such as autobiography, history, reportage, comedy, and soap opera. Influenced by the underground, alternative comics were typically published in black and white (with color covers), made by unchanging creative teams (often a single person), and rarely followed a monthly publication schedule. Many alternative creators pursued long-form comics in serialization, but unlike the commercial logic dominating the mainstream industry in the late twentieth century, these narratives were devised to come to a halt once the story was told rather than be perpetuated indefinitely. Having a definite sense of an ending made such narratives amenable for republication in book form; the renewed popularity of the graphic novel at the start of the twenty-first century was underpinned by alternative comics serialized in the 1990s and then reprinted as single books, such as Daniel Clowes's *Ghost World* (1997), Chris Ware's *Jimmy Corrigan: The Smartest Kid on Earth* (2000), Joe Sacco's *Palestine* (2001), and Lynda Barry's *One! Hundred! Demons!* (2002). As the scholar of comics Charles Hatfield puts it, "the direct market [. . .] gave birth to a new sense of aesthetic possibility, spurred by the example of the undergrounds. [. . .] [The] much-discussed 'graphic novel' owed its very life to this new market" (Hatfield 25).

1986 and All That

Historians of the graphic novel are fascinated by the year 1986, calling it an "*annus mirabilis*" (Clarke 206) and wondering whether it was the "greatest year" (Duncan, Smith, and Levitz 65) in the medium of comics. Why? Because of three softcover books and a twelve-issue DC series that

---

[3] There were isolated occasions in the 1970s when creators' rights were contractually acknowledged in the mainstream, such as the royalties Steve Gerber received for the *Kiss* magazine-format comic published by Marvel (Howe 183–196).

began serialization in 1986, the latter republished as a book edition the following year. With these four titles, the concept of the graphic novel entered further into the world of bookstores, libraries, broadcast news, and newspaper supplements. Under titles such as "Are Comic Books Growing Up?" (Johnson D1) journalists noted with surprise the number of adults spending money on graphic novels.

Two of the books were revisionist superhero titles based on properties owned by DC. *Batman: The Dark Knight Returns*, written and penciled by Frank Miller, was serialized February–August 1986 as a prestige format miniseries and released as a collected edition later that year; writer Alan Moore and artist Dave Gibbons's *Watchmen* was serialized October 1986–September 1987 and reprinted in book form almost immediately after its serialization. Miller and Moore produced pioneering work in the revisionist superhero genre earlier in the 1980s with their respective runs on *Daredevil* and *Saga of the Swamp Thing*, and they exercised even greater creative control over *The Dark Knight Returns* and *Watchmen*; Marvel and DC were granting certain creators more autonomy to stop talent migrating to the independents. Revisionist superhero comics were increasingly visible in the second half of the 1980s as part of the targeting of older fans as consumers: these comics expected readers to know the generic conventions of the superhero genre and assumed that fans would enjoy seeing those conventions subverted with stories probing the ethics of vigilantism and the political and psychosexual implications of superheroic violence.

The first volume of Art Spiegelman's *Maus* was released by Pantheon Books in August 1986. If revisionist superhero graphic novels surprised journalists because of the incongruity of superheroes having sex and launching their own toy lines, *Maus* challenged preconceptions about comics in a very different way, following two intertwined narrative tracks: Art Spiegelman's fraught relationship with his aging father Vladek in the 1970s and 1980s and Vladek's experience of the Holocaust in the 1930s and 1940s. Spiegelman's unexpected move was an extended metaphor in which different nationalities and ethnic groups are visualized as animals: Jews as mice, Germans as cats, Poles as pigs, Americans as dogs, and so on. In doing so, Spiegelman gave visual form to how the Jews were constructed as vermin by a genocidal ideology of antisemitism (Spiegelman 113–118).

Furthermore, *Maus* unpicks and transgresses the visual metaphor even as it extends it through the narrative, mocking Nazism's desire to compartmentalize and hierarchize ethnicities. This is done by (for instance) depicting the children of German and Jewish parents with a combination of feline and mouse characteristics, underlining how human groups cannot be imagined as discrete units in the same way families in animal taxonomy operate. In *Maus* the animal identities are not necessarily there at birth: for much of the book the characters appear as anthropomorphic animals, but on occasion they are drawn as humans wearing animal masks, such as in Volume Two, when Art depicts himself at the drawing board in 1987 contemplating the death of his parents, the enormity of the Holocaust, and the success of *Maus*'s first volume. Also in Volume Two, Art reveals his sketchbook to the reader, sharing his uncertainty over how to draw his wife Françoise Mouly, a French convert to Judaism. These strategies let the reader know that, while visually structured to convey the dehumanizing language used to persecute Jews, Spiegelman's text does not endorse it – *Maus* insists on the fallibility of this way of thinking and its terrible consequences.

Not as prominent as those three graphic novels, the 1986 Doubleday edition of Harvey Pekar's *American Splendor* also deserves mention. This was a collection of short autobiographical pieces about working-class life in Cleveland, Ohio, that originally appeared in Pekar's *American Spendor*, the series he had self-published since 1976.

It is hard to establish reliable like-for-like sales, but by July 1988 *Batman: The Dark Knight Returns* had sold 85,000 copies and the first volume of *Maus* 100,000 copies (McDowell E7). Publishing houses – including Pantheon, Warner Books, and Doubleday – commissioned graphic novels themselves, a mix of original projects, editions of previously published comics reprinted under license, and adaptations of prose fiction by well-known authors (Sabin, *Adult Comics* 104, 177). Of the graphic novels of 1986, *Maus* has had the greatest impact, the subject of over a hundred scholarly articles. Its global footprint is staggering: the *Maus* books (volume two was released in 1991) have each sold more than a million copies in the United States and *Maus* has been translated into approximately thirty languages (Spiegelman 152).

Maus was serialized in *RAW*, an avant-garde comics anthology situated at the crossroads of multiple comics traditions. *RAW* was edited by Mouly and Spiegelman and appeared as a magazine (1980–1986) and then in paperback form (1989–1991). It provided a platform for surviving members of the underground, as well as featuring alternative comics creators, European comics visionaries, and artists known for their gallery installations. *RAW* straddled the worlds of comics and art: in 1978 Mouly and Spiegelman established RAW Books and Graphics in the SoHo area of Manhattan, a district of factories and warehouses undergoing gentrification as artists relocated to the area. The first publication that RAW Books and Graphics released was *The Streets of Soho Map and Guide*, a handbook detailing SoHo's galleries, restaurants, and stores (Heer 49–52). As an expensive anthology ($7.95 in 1986) sold in art bookshops and galleries, *RAW* closely resembled the Downtown arts scene's mixed-media magazines (Kelly 328–329).

Showcasing creators associated with the *RAW* anthology, RAW Books and Graphics released a series of books in the 1980s, including *Jimbo* (1982) and *Invasion of the Elvis Zombies* (1984) by Gary Panter, *How to Commit Suicide in South Africa* (1983) by Holly Metz and Sue Coe, *Jack Survives* (1984) by Jerry Moriarty, *Big Baby: Curse of the Molemen* (1986) by Charles Burns, and Coe's *X* (1986). Preceding the late 1980s flurry of interest in the graphic novel by publishing houses, *How to Commit Suicide in South Africa* was reprinted by Random House in 1984. They may have been books, but these RAW One-Shots retained the anthology's experimental sensibility: *Invasion of the Elvis Zombies* was sold with a free flexidisc, and with its oversized corrugated cardboard covers and taped spine, the *Jimbo* book is profanely positioned between punk self-destruction (designed to deteriorate with multiple readings?) and a precious coffeetable art object.

Written shortly after the late 1980s boom, Roger Sabin's *Adult Comics: An Introduction* (1993) cast a suspicious eye over the media coverage that graphic novels received: "'Comics Grow Up' became a regular headline in the arts pages" but "the coverage tended to concentrate on the novelty aspect [. . .] (at times, it was almost a case of 'wow! comics about holocaust victims and psychopathic superheroes!')." Colluding with the journalists who stressed the supposedly unprecedented adult audience, publishers' advertisements sought to convince consumers that, with the graphic novel format, comics had been deodorized of the association of juvenility and arrested development. Adults were reassured they could read a graphic novel in public without stigma, but this marketing strategy ignored the long history of adult comics and book editions (Sabin, *Adult Comics* 91–93, 176).

Based on brittle foundations, the 1980s graphic novel boom was not sustained; in the early 1990s, trade presses cut back their graphic novel lines and bookshops reduced their shelf-space. There were many reasons for declining bookstore sales: economic recession, the evaporation of graphic novels' "novelty value," and the absence of graphic novels as good as the books that initially garnered attention. Furthermore, the fundamental status of comics with the reading public had not changed a great deal (Sabin, *Adult Comics* 110–115, 178).

Twenty-First-Century Graphic Novels

If 1986 was the start of a short-lived boom, more sustained growth has been underway since the turn of the century. Up to 2007, annual sales of graphic novels grew at a staggering rate: figures for 2003 were up nearly fifty percent on the year before, and the following year saw an increase of around thirty-five percent (Reid, "US Graphic Novel" 15). This trajectory has wobbled a little, but the overall direction is one of growing sales and literary esteem. At the start of the twenty-first century, the popularity of translated Japanese comics (manga) in softcover editions spurred book-stores and libraries to increase the shelving devoted to other book-format comics. In other words, strong manga sales enabled graphic novels originally published in English to gain visibility too (Brienza 60–61, 162–163; Reid, "US Graphic Novel"). Retailers and librarians were empowered to take these steps because educational psychologists revised earlier dismissals of comics as detrimental to literacy; in the 2000s it was widely accepted that comics encouraged reading skills and attracted hard-to-reach demographics into libraries (Lopes 166).

In accordance with this seal of approval from educators and librarians, new graphic novel publishers have emerged with a focus on children and young adults. These include publishers such as Papercutz and TOON Books (the latter established by Françoise Mouly) and imprints such as First Second (an imprint of the publisher Macmillan) and Graphix (Scholastic). Graphic novels for children or teenagers are not completely new, but the scale of the market is remarkable: Scholastic printed a million copies to launch Raina Telgemeier's children's graphic novel *Guts* in 2019. DC has tilted towards younger readers by recruiting personnel from the children's or YA field, such as executive editor Michele Wells (formerly of Penguin Random House and Disney Worldwide Publishing), prose writer Lauren Myracle, and comics creators Mariko Tamaki and Gene Luen Yang (Reid, "BookExpo 2019"; Reid, "In Her First"). Yang won the Young Adult Library Services Association's Michael L. Printz Award for literary excellence in YA literature for *American Born Chinese*, published by First Second in 2006; he recently wrote DC's *Superman Smashes the Klan* (2020, with art provided by Gurihiru, the Japanese artistic team Chifuyu Sasaki and Naoko Kawano).

There is now a substantial back catalogue of diverse graphic novels with which librarians and retailers can keep their shelves stocked. As in the 1980s, the popularity of graphic novels has prompted book publishers such as Penguin and Faber to (re)enter the market. Many graphic novels released by trade presses have joined *Maus*, *American Born Chinese*, and *Watchmen* on school and university syllabi, books such as Marjane Satrapi's *Persepolis* (2000–2003), Alison Bechdel's *Fun Home* (2006), and Adrian Tomine's *Killing and Dying* (2015). *Maus* received a Pulitzer Prize in 1992, and graphic novelists keep gaining more literary accolades this century: MacArthur Fellowships (so-called Genius Grants) have been awarded to Ben Katchor (2000), Alison Bechdel (2014), Gene Luen Yang (2016), and Lynda Barry (2019). Ware's *Jimmy Corrigan* won the UK *Guardian* newspaper's First Book Award and an American Book Award in 2001, *Time* magazine selected Bechdel's *Fun Home* as best book of 2006, and in the UK *Dotter of Her Father's Eyes* (2012) by Mary M. Talbot and Bryan Talbot won the Costa Biography Award. Graphic novels have ceased to be novelties on literary award shortlists, though such occasions continue to garner comment from the media as unprecedented events. This was demonstrated by the press reports on the longlisting of Nick Drnaso's *Sabrina* (2018) for the Man Booker Prize: *The New York Times* called *Sabrina*'s nomination "a major breakthrough" for the graphic novel format (Marshall).

If length and literary respectability continue to be signal components of the graphic novel, another part of its meaning – book publication – is less fixed than ever as graphic novelists play with the materiality of texts. Lynda Barry's *Syllabus: Notes from an Accidental Professor* (2014) is designed to look like a composition notebook for students (Kashtan 69–75), Chris Ware's *Building Stories* (2012) is a box of comics, and Art Spiegelman's *In the Shadow of No Towers* (2004), an archive of newspaper strips and a memoir of 9/11, is an oversized edition with heavy pages. The heft of *In the Shadow of No Towers* evokes a strongbox as well as the durable books for young children printed on thick card. Writing in 2011, Jan Baetens comments that *In the Shadow of No Towers* goes against a "sanitized version of the graphic novel" obsessed with seriousness of content, lone authorship, and "bookishness" (1151–1152).

Due to the rise of reading comics via digital devices, a wave of contemporary creators publish their graphic novels serially in online increments. Where they sense a viable audience, creators re-release their narratives in book form (or licence their graphic novels to a print publisher). Significant twenty-first-century graphic novels such as Josh Neufeld's *A. D.: New Orleans After the Deluge* (2009), Jeremy Love's *Bayou* (2009 and 2011), and writer Paul Tobin and artist Colleen Coover's *Bandette* (2013–present) were all available in digital form before print. While turning an online graphic novel into a book is sought by many creators as a totem of prestige and a means of monetizing free-to-access online content, print is not necessarily the ultimate goal of digital graphic novelists. Creators express their respect for online serialization because it offers a way of honing one's craft and slowly building a readership via word of mouth (Kashtan 103–107).

Responding to Richard Kyle's hopes for the future of comics, in 1966 the comics fan Henry Steele intimated that longer narratives necessitated book publication, "hard-cover 'graphic novels' of several hundred pages, [printed] not on a periodical basis, but as individual publishing ventures like conventional novels" (37). It's telling that Steele's imagination jumped to a hardback graphic novel, conflating the "conventional novel" with a weighty iteration of book publication. But digital texts remind us that long-form comics don't need to live inside books to thrive. In the mid-1960s, a small cohort of US comics fans spoke of the graphic novel in hushed tones as a distant possibility, but almost sixty years on, the question is no longer whether graphic novels are part of comics' future, but what lies in the future of the graphic novel: which material formats might be utilized? What stories might be told? Who will find a voice through this unstable cultural form? That instability is an engine of artistic potential that continues to attract comics creators, even if the term itself divides opinion.

WORKS CITED

Comics

Okubo, Miné. *Citizen 13660* [1946]. University of Washington Press, 2014.
Sedlmeier, Cory, ed. *The Fantastic Four Omnibus*. Vol. 2, Marvel Worldwide, 2013.
Ward, Lynd. *Storyteller without Words: The Wood Engravings of Lynd Ward with Text by the Artist*. Abrams, 1974.

Secondary Sources

Baetens, Jan. "Graphic Novels." *The Cambridge History of the American Novel*, edited by Leonard Cassuto, Cambridge University Press, 2011, pp. 1137–1153.
Baetens, Jan and Hugo Frey. *The Graphic Novel: An Introduction*. Cambridge University Press, 2014.
Beerbohm, Robert L. "Secret Origins of the Direct Market, Part One: 'Affidavit Returns' – The Scourge of Distribution." *Comic Book Artist*, no. 6, Fall 1999, pp. 80–91.
Beronä, David A. *Wordless Books: The Original Graphic Novels*. Abrams, 2008.

Braun, Saul. "Shazam! Here Comes Captain Relevant." *New York Times*, 2 May 1971, pp. SM32+.

Brienza, Casey. *Manga in America: Transnational Book Publishing and the Domestication of Japanese Comics*. Bloomsbury Academic, 2016.

Chute, Hillary. "Comics as Literature? Reading Graphic Narrative." *PMLA*, vol. 123, no. 2, 2008, pp. 452–465.

Clarke, M. J. "The Production of the *Marvel Graphic Novel* Series: The Business and Culture of the Early Direct Market." *Journal of Graphic Novels and Comics*, vol. 5, no. 2, 2014, pp. 192–210.

Creef, Elena Tajima. "Following Her Own Road: The Achievement of Miné Okubo." Robinson and Creef, pp. 3–10.

Duncan, Randy, Matthew J. Smith, and Paul Levitz. *The Power of Comics: History, Form, and Culture*. 2nd ed., Bloomsbury Academic, 2015.

Flood, Alison. "New Comics Laureate Charlie Adlard Declares War on 'The Graphic Novel.'" *Guardian*, 17 Oct. 2006, www.theguardian.com/books/2016/oct/17/new-comics-laureate-charlie-adlard-declares-war-on-the-graphic-novel. Accessed 10 May 2021.

Gabilliet, Jean-Paul. *Of Comics and Men: A Cultural History of American Comic Books*. Translated by Bart Beaty and Nick Nguyen, University Press of Mississippi, 2010.

Hatfield, Charles. *Alternative Comics: An Emerging Literature*. University Press of Mississippi, 2005.

Heer, Jeet. *In Love with Art: Françoise Mouly's Adventures in Comics with Art Spiegelman*. Coach House, 2013.

Hong, Christine. Introduction. *Citizen 13660*, by Miné Okubo [1946]. University of Washington Press, 2014, pp. vii–xxiv.

Howe, Sean. *Marvel Comics: The Untold Story*. HarperCollins, 2012.

Hutler, Charles. Letter. *Fantastic Four*, no. 53, August 1966. Sedlmeier, p. 617.

Jackson, Donald. Letter. *Fantastic Four*, no. 56, November 1966. Sedlmeier, p. 687.

Johnson, Steve. "Are Comic Books Growing Up?" *Chicago Tribune*, 28 August 1986, pp. D1+.

Kashtan, Aaron. *Between Pen and Pixel: Comics, Materiality, and the Book of the Future*. Ohio State University Press, 2018.

Kelly, Mike. "Art Spiegelman and His Circle: New York City Comix and the Downtown Scene." *International Journal of Comic Art*, vol. 10, no. 1, 2008, pp. 313–339.

Kunzle, David. *Father of the Comic Strip: Rodolphe Töpffer*. University Press of Mississippi, 2007.

Kyle, Richard. "Wonderworld." *CAPA-alpha*, no. 2, November 1964, pp. 1–4.

"Graphic Story Review." *Fantasy Illustrated*, no. 5, Spring 1966, pp. 3–4, 41–42.

Letter. *Fantasy Illustrated*, no. 7, Spring 1967, pp. 35–36.

Lehmann-Haupt, Hellmut. "The Picture Novel Arrives in America." *Publishers Weekly*, 1 February 1930, pp. 609–612.

Lopes, Paul. *Demanding Respect: The Evolution of the American Comic Book*. Temple University Press, 2009.

Marshall, Alex. "Graphic Novel in Running for Man Booker Prize for First Time." *New York Times*, 23 July 2018, www.nytimes.com/2018/07/23/books/booker-prize-graphic-novel-ondaatje.html. Accessed 2 February 2019.

McDowell, Edwin. "America is Taking Comic Books Seriously." *New York Times*, 31 July 1988, p. E7.

McGregor, Don. Letter. *Fantastic Four*, no. 48, Mar. 1966. Sedlmeier, pp. 500–501.

Meyer, Christina. *Producing Mass Entertainment: The Serial Life of the Yellow Kid*. The Ohio State University Press, 2019.

Moore, Alan. Interview. *Blather.net*, 17 October 2000, www.blather.net/projects/alan-moore-interview/northhampton-graphic-novel/. Accessed 10 May 2021.

Nyberg, Amy Kiste. *Seal of Approval: The History of the Comics Code*. University Press of Mississippi, 1998.

Phillips, Kimberley L. "To Keep a Record of Life: Miné Okubo's Autographic *Manga* and Wartime History." Robinson and Creef, pp. 99–110.

Pizzino, Christopher. *Arresting Development: Comics at the Boundaries of Literature*. University of Texas Press, 2016.

Reid, Calvin. "US Graphic Novel Market Hits $200M." *Publishers Weekly*, 18 April 2005, p. 15.

"BookExpo 2019: Graphic Novels for Everyone." *Publishers Weekly*, 5 June 2019, www.publishersweekly.com/pw/by-topic/industry-news/bea/article/80364-bookexpo-2019-graphic-novels-for-everyone.html. Accessed 27 June 2020.

"In Her First YA Graphic Novel, Lauren Myracle Takes on Catwoman." *Publishers Weekly*, 20 March 2019, www.publishersweekly.com/pw/by-topic/industry-news/comics/article/79584-in-her-first-ya-graphic-novel-lauren-myracle-takes-on-catwoman.html. Accessed 27 June 2020.

Robinson, Greg and Elena Tajima Creef, eds. *Miné Okubo: Following Her Own Road*. University of Washington Press, 2008.

Sabin, Roger. *Adult Comics: An Introduction*. Routledge, 1993.

"Ally Sloper: The First Comics Superstar?" *Image [&] Narrative*, vol. 4, no. 1, 2003, www.imageandnarrative.be/inarchive/graphicnovel/rogersabin.htm. Accessed 31 May 2021.

Satrapi, Marjane. Interview. *New York Times Magazine*, 21 Oct. 2007, www.nytimes.com/2007/10/21/magazine/21wwwln-Q4-t.html#:~:text=I%20don't%20very%20much,to%20be%20scared%20of%20comics. Accessed 10 May 2021.

Smolderen, Thierry. *The Origins of Comics: From William Hogarth to Winsor McCay*. 2000. Translated by Bart Beaty and Nick Nguyen, University Press of Mississippi, 2014.

Spiegelman, Art. *MetaMAUS*. Edited by Hillary Chute, Viking-Penguin, 2011.

Steele, Henry. Letter. *Fantasy Illustrated*, no. 5, Spring 1966, p. 5.

Ward, Lynd. *Storyteller without Words: The Wood Engravings of Lynd Ward with Text by the Artist*. Abrams, 1974.

Wright, Bradford W. *Comic Book Nation: The Transformation of Youth Culture in America*. Rev. ed., Johns Hopkins University Press, 2003.

CHAPTER 4

Manga
An Affective Form of Comics

Jaqueline Berndt

In the late twentieth century, the word *manga* entered usage in Western languages, and nowadays it designates primarily graphic narratives made in or associated with Japan, in distinction from North American comics and Franco-Belgian *bandes dessinées*. But not all comics made in Japan pass as manga abroad, just as the word *anime* does not necessarily reflect the broad scope of animated film created there. In addition to country of production, both popular and academic discourse also categorizes manga according to style, format, and sociocultural disposition. Manga narratives are regarded as "a cheap form of fiction generating demand for new products on a daily and weekly basis" (Grennan 321), and as appearing in "digest-sized tomes printed backwards and populated by large-eyed, pointy-chinned, pinch-faced adolescents who all look so much alike" (Harvey 167). Outside of Japan, these narratives circulate typically in the format of trade paperbacks (*tankōbon*) that maintain the Japanese reading direction from right to left.[1] Hard-cover editions with flipped pages such as *Buddha* by Osamu Tezuka (1928–1989)[2] are apparently not manga enough to be shelved in the same bookstore corner.

This narrow notion of manga leaves us with two options: either to concentrate on Japan's domestic scene and verify traits exhibited by Japanese comics across production modes, publication venues, genres, readerships, and historic periods, or to conceptualize manga along lines other than national ones, as a form of comics that has certain traits in common with similar non-Japanese graphic narratives. Thierry Groensteen's insistence on the applicability of a universal rather than culturally specific comics studies framework makes a case for the latter (Groensteen 51). Keeping in mind the specific conditions that gave rise to

---

[1] See Kacsuk, also for the "Made in Japan" notion as conditioned by media and institutional factors.
[2] Japanese names are indicated in the Western order. The romanization of Japanese words follows the modified Hepburn system.

82

Manga: An Affective Form of Comics

manga in its local setting, this chapter promotes a transcultural approach through a form-conscious discussion and conceptualizes manga as an affective type of graphic narrative.

Manga has already attracted ample interest pertaining to its ways of expressing emotions (see Groensteen; Abbott and Forceville; Tsai). But the focus on emotions tends to foreground how a given state of mind is captured or visually encoded, presuming psychologized and consciously acting subjects who are human, or humanlike, individuals. While the psychologization of fictional characters has been highly conducive to the sociocultural recognition of comics, in recent years, the critical focus has shifted from characters as individual entities to imaginary, as well as pragmatic, connections between multiple actors (intradiegetically, between characters; transdiegetically, between characters and readers; and extradiegetically, between readers via characters). Closely related, the potential of material surfaces to channel readers' attention has gained prominence in scholarship. These shifts have been articulated, among other things, in the name of affect as an intensive, overwhelming force that involves the reader effortlessly in embodied and material ways.[3] Giving critical preference to affect over emotion is a matter of prioritization rather than opposition: it implies placing the emphasis on the reader, their being affected by comics-specific devices in favor of close interrelations that eventually blur the line between self and other, inside and outside, subject and object of gazing. Characters' faces, and in particular eyes, recommend themselves as a prime example here.

The pictorial device of huge eyes has famously been regarded as a hallmark of manga, although onomatopoeia and script, pictorial runes,[4] linework, and panel layout are all equally important for the operation of affect in this type of comics. Focusing on eyes allows for a discussion of media-cultural particularities, and also for questioning the applicability of cinematic concepts, which are often taken for granted in comics criticism, such as the power dynamics of gazing. In its focus on manga eyes as both an attention-drawing and interconnecting device, this chapter goes beyond their exclusive attribution to *shōjo* (girls) *manga* and widens the view to approach something closer to an ocular history that includes boys (*shōnen*) comics, as well as graphic narratives for an older audience, occasionally categorized as alternative manga abroad. The examples illustrating crucial

---

[3] Schneider (10-11) provides a compact overview of affect theories in the context of comics studies.

[4] Speed lines, flourishes, popped veins, and other non-iconic graphic elements (Abbott and Forceville 106).

84   JAQUELINE BERNDT

historical instances here have been selected in view of the exceptional amount of Anglophone comics criticism they have generated. They include Keiji Nakazawa's historical manga for children *Barefoot Gen*; Keiko Takemiya's *shōjo*-esque style in the science fiction narrative *To Terra* and her pioneering boys love manga *The Poem of Wind and Trees*, as well as Jirō Taniguchi's graphic novel, *A Distant Neighborhood*. Before zooming in on how they employ eyes, however, a brief survey of manga's reception outside Japan is necessary.

Obscured Diversity

The earliest translated editions of comics from Japan were dominated by *gekiga*. This term was coined by comics artist Yoshihiro Tatsumi (1935–2015) in 1957 in order to distinguish the then new graphic narratives created by him and his peers from previous serials aimed at children, especially those by Tezuka. In the beginning, *gekiga* was exclusively published for book-rental shops (*kashihon'ya*), but over the course of the 1960s *gekiga* artists, stories, and styles were, for the most part, absorbed by magazines of the major publishing houses to become part of *seinen* (youth) *manga*. Decades later, North American comics criticism came to promote *gekiga* as an alternative to the global manga boom that flourished in the form of licensed printed translations from the late 1990s to the late 2000s (see Suter).

Yet, best-selling serials targeted to adolescent readers and not *gekiga* have shaped what is recognized as manga today. This began with *Dragon Ball* by Akira Toriyama (b. 1955), and *Sailor Moon* by Naoko Takeuchi (b. 1967). The production, distribution, and consumption of their localized versions were neither indebted to *gekiga* nor to *Barefoot Gen* by Nakazawa (1939–2012), the actual progenitor of translated manga editions. The first two of *Barefoot Gen*'s ten volumes had already been released in English in 1976, attracting little interest from the comics community.[5] Comics from Japan only gained attention in 1987 with the publication of a translated edition of Tatsumi's short stories and the first issues of *Lone Wolf and Cub* by writer Kazuo Koike (1936–2019) and artist Gōseki Kojima (1928–2000). The latter serial was highly influential in terms of visual storytelling, as can be seen in page layouts deviating from the conventional grid and including unframed images drawn directly into the uninked space in, for example, *Ronin* (1983–1984) by Frank Miller (b. 1957). In the

---

[5] See Sabin on the reception of *Barefoot Gen* from peace book to graphic novel and manga.

same vein, *Akira* by Katsuhiro Ōtomo (b. 1954) acquired considerable fame from 1988 onwards, in tandem with its animated movie adaptation. This *gekiga*-like narrative that often places the reader in the driver's seat, as McCloud has so aptly put it (*Understanding* 114), resonated with science fiction fans. Addressing a mature audience open to realist storytelling, *Akira* did not directly connect to the notion of manga that began to gain ground around a decade later. The fact that it was first published in a lavishly flipped and colored Americanized version is indicative of the audience intended initially.

The type of manga most prominent today has been identified as "a popular visual literature of escapism" (Grennan 321). Representative of Japan's comics mainstream, it is characterized by fictional entertainment featuring cute characters, highly formulaic visuals, and game-like narrative structures deliberately left incomplete with regard to narrative coherence and the overall ending: "all of [the narrative and pictorial] techniques amplif[y] the sense of reader participation in manga, a feeling of being part of the story, rather than simply observing the story from afar" (McCloud *Making*, 217). Narrative twists fueled by intense emotions rather than rational reasoning may easily appear as escapism in the face of sociopolitical, or autobiographical representation. But this type of manga (usually published by big media corporations) also facilitates active engagement, from empathizing with characters and filling in narrative gaps to the formation of taste communities in which fans create, critique, and cosplay. Its "visual language" – highly shareable due to codification – has the potential to be put to both exclusive and inclusive, industry-compliant and subcultural, use, as practices inside and outside of Japan show.

Regardless of whether the emphasis is on Japanese particularity or, more specifically, on a corporate style that invites participation, the diversity of graphic narratives in Japan stays out of the picture. This includes the constricted notion of *gekiga* as essentially noncorporate, which ignores not only its industrial cooption but also the studio system run by Tatsumi's historic peers such as Takao Saitō (1936–2021). Another recurrent blind spot is the segmentation of corporate comics along the lines of age and gender, or more precisely, the inclination to take the masculine genres – *shōnen manga* (for boys) and by extension *seinen manga* (for youths) – as the standard. In addition to subject matter or artists' gender, this standard makes itself felt in the treatment of panel and page.

In his meta-comic *Understanding Comics, the Invisible Art* Scott McCloud highlighted some particularities of Japanese comics. He included *shōjo manga*, but only with regard to facial and background expressions,

86   JAQUELINE BERNDT

not the genre-specific interplay between panel and page. While McCloud's aspect-to-aspect type of panel transitions has been related to *shōjo manga* traditions of communicating internal rather than external motion (e.g., by Tsai 476–477), these traditions are more prominently represented by devices that trigger an alternation of the visual frame between panel and page rather than tracing individual panels in sequence (Groensteen 63). Elaborate multiframes were initially introduced by female artists in the 1970s together with narratives that privileged interiority and interpersonal relations over physical action and fierce competition. McCloud referenced *The Rose of Versailles* by Riyoko Ikeda (b. 1947) (*Understanding*, 133).[6] Yet, the *shōjo*-esque features of Ikeda's manga – emotive page compositions and hyper-feminine character imagery – were actually due to the artist's compromise between the girl readership of the magazine and her own aspirations to create *gekiga* (which is evident in the serial's dynamic fight scenes and the occasional inclusion of historical realism).

A manga such as Takeuchi's *Sailor Moon*, which entwined affectionate poses with girls fighting, was available in English only after 1997. Since then, narrative tropes, multiframe designs, and pictorial runes derived from girls manga have become part of fusion styles that stretch across Japan's traditional genres and beyond its national borders. Examples that undermine the assumption of influence – that is, the often one-directional and as such hierarchical relation between supposedly discrete entities – are Jen Wang's modernized Cinderella tale, *The Prince and the Dressmaker*, and Alice Oseman's queer romance series *Heartstopper*. Young adult graphic fiction like this may be regarded as inspired by manga, although not necessarily called by that name.

Manga Eyes

In the 1980s, European comics critics perceived manga as culturally too specific and therefore too exclusive for non-Japanese readers to enjoy effortlessly. Nowadays, manga is "one of the most recognizable styles of representation" (Cohn 153). This recognizability often draws upon character design, most notably the eyes. Regardless of size, eyes have been the main device for evoking (or quelling) affection in Japan's modern visual

---

[6] Ikeda's manga is properly credited as distinct from two other pictorial citations of *shōjo manga* heroines. At the time, a translated excerpt of *The Rose of Versailles* was available, together with excerpts from *Barefoot Gen*, Tezuka's *Phoenix*, and Leiji Matsumoto's *Ghost Warrior* (in Schodt 1998/1983).

media: "[i]n contrast to 'Western' emoticons where most attention is paid to representing the mouth, the most important part of *kaomoji* [facial characters] are the eyes" (Giannoulis and Wilde 3). Comics have undoubtedly contributed to that importance, and not only *shōjo manga*. In general, characters depicted with huge eyes suggest a sympathetic nature and a very young age (which recalls Konrad Lorenz's *Kindchenschema*). As such, big eyes easily stand in for comics, a medium traditionally targeting children and disparaged as childish. Large, round eyes embellished with long lashes and articulate pupils may affect the reader in several ways, with close-up shots potentially enhancing the intensity of the interaction.

Close-ups of faces or eyes are usually traced back to Tezuka, who is probably best known as the creator of *Astro Boy*. Tezuka has entered manga history as a cartoonist who, in the immediate postwar period, provided children with dynamic, cinematically informed adventure stories. His professional debut, the almost 200-page-long *New Treasure Island* (*Shintakarajima*, script by Shichima Sakai, 1947), is a good example in this regard. The manga begins with the protagonist Pete riding a car (Figure 4.1). To generate the sensation of racing, the perspective shifts from side to frontal view and, as if to zoom in on Pete's face, the shot size changes across the four vertical panels into which the page is broken down, including an extreme close-up of his eyes. On the top of the next page, the subject and object of gazing are intertwined, as a little dog appears in Pete's right eye. The dog was crossing the street when it suddenly froze in shock, facing Pete (and the reader). Finally, in the fourth panel, it sits down bathed in sweat, but no longer framed by the black ring that turned out to be Pete's iris. This iris carries a little notch on the lower right, foreshadowing the psychologization of manga characters that became a staple of extended graphic narratives.

Due to his eyes, Pete was perceived by Japanese readers of the immediate postwar period as highly approachable and radically modern. Aided by sweat drops in previous panels and reinforced by the onomatopoeia superimposed onto the page, the close-up of eyes with pupils endowed the protagonist with something like interiority. In the 1950s, Tezuka also elaborated on the proportion of black and white within the pupil, and added eyelashes, eyebrows, and eyelids (Natsume 81–89). This design went hand in hand with increasingly mature stories of life and death: cinematically informed nonverbal storytelling facilitated irreversible narrative events, and characters began to assume psychological depth; it suffices to recall Astro Boy's childhood trauma, his rejection by Dr. Tenma, and the resulting emotions that motivate his later actions. Consequently, big eyes came to suggest preexisting interiority.

Figure 4.1. Suggesting emotions through an iris with a notch.
Osamu Tezuka, *Shintakarajima* (*Tezuka Osamu manga zenshū* 281) [1947] (Kodansha, 1984), pp. 12–13. Read from right to left. ©Tezuka Productions, 1947.

Mitigating Violence

Like Tezuka's early comics – in particular *Kimba, the White Lion* – Nakazawa's *Barefoot Gen*, arguably the first manga to cross language borders, combined fatal events and mortal characters with the consideration of children. Its protagonist Gen is an elementary schoolboy in Hiroshima when the atomic bomb is dropped on August 6, 1945 (at the end of the first of ten volumes). The ensuing conflagration kills half of his family. Over the course of eight years, Gen meets many atomic-bomb victims like himself, and he experiences numerous sad partings. Eventually, his mother succumbs to radiation sickness. But Gen himself survives due to his ability to bounce back, or his "plasticity" (see Lamarre). This is implied graphically on the manga's first page by the use of jumping-jack postures and it is exemplified later in the narrative, for example, through an astonishing rise from the dead after having fainted and being dumped on a pile of corpses. Animating still images and operating in part as comic relief, Gen's plasticity mitigates, in all its improbability, historically realist violence.

In his introduction to the first volume of an early translated edition, Art Spiegelman noted two things about *Barefoot Gen* that connect to the discussion here. First, he found the manga "cloyingly cute, with special emphasis on Disney-like oversized Caucasian eyes and generally neotenic faces" (n.p.). And second, he discerned a specific way of visually communicating intense emotions: "Gen's pacifist father freely wallops his kids with a frequency and force that we might easily perceive as criminal child abuse rather than the sign of affection that is intended" (n.p.). The translation of affects into physical acts has been a common trope in graphic narratives for boys: manga-literate readers approach these acts not as mirroring a historical reality but rather as invoking media-specific conventions that convey a reality effect of their own, namely, an emotional probability, a shareable feeling. A similar example of emotional expression via non-facial information is the loss of hands in the serial *Yotsuba!*: "neither to be taken literally, nor as exemplifying a feature of the 'super-deformed' technique [. . .] cueing a character's loss of control, predominantly through being overcome by emotion" (Abbott and Forceville 103–104).

Informed by such conventions, the behavior of Gen's father can be taken lightly, but other instances of graphic violence cannot. Especially noteworthy are the atomic-bomb victims who, with their melting skin, reappear nightmarishly over the course of the narrative. In contradistinction to Gen, their eyes are small, completely black, and without pupils, as if signaling that they are already lost, incapable of bouncing back to the realm of the living (Yoshimura 267–275). Gen's mother, for example, is accorded an intermediary position: her eyes have pupils but when she witnesses her family dying, they are covered by hatching in a way that is reminiscent of horror manga.

Japanese manga critics maintain that the clear divide in *Barefoot Gen* between those who are meant to survive and those doomed to die – and the clear dissociation from the latter – can be traced back to the fact that its serialization began in *Weekly Shōnen Jump*, the magazine for boys that became the flagship of the manga industry in the late 1980s. Previously, Nakazawa had published a few short stories on the same subject matter in non-mainstream magazines for young adults, such as

JAQUELINE BERNDT

Manga Punch.[7] Inclining towards a *gekiga* style, these stories neither anonymized the dying nor deprived them of dialogue. This gave them the appearance of hovering between life and death, and resulted in an uncanniness that was considered inappropriate for a young readership. *Barefoot Gen* answered to the ambiguity by adjusting *gekiga* to the requirements of *shōnen manga*, drawing a clear line between Gen as subject and the black-eyed victims as object. This is evident in the existence of pupils or lack thereof, and further in the contrast between big and small eyes.

Small eyes were characteristic of *gekiga*'s departure from child-oriented manga. Child-oriented manga, however, used them to distinguish between protagonist and secondary characters, friend and foe, self and other. Gen's big eyes set him apart as the central character with whom the reader is supposed to identify, or more precisely, share intense emotions. As part of "performative images," they indicate an inner consciousness that is "less a reflection than a site of emotions not acted upon" (Kajiya 240). In other words, they operate in an affective way, bringing forth potential emotions that have not been actualized yet. But they might also come across as Caucasian, not just due to their own size and shape but more specifically, in juxtaposition to the smaller and slanted eyes of other characters like Gen's Korean neighbor, Mr. Pak. In manga, narrow eyes are easily perceived as a means of "othering." Rather than identification, they invite instantaneous dissociation, which may range from impulsive refusal to admiration from afar.

More than "Mirrors of the Soul"

Manga eyes are largely read as representations, especially of ethnicity. To which type of reader such readings apply, and at which point in the medium's history, is too controversial a matter to be treated cursorily within the constraints of this chapter (see Berndt 269–272). Instead of focusing on what manga eyes may reference, this section highlights how they interconnect what is normally divided, using *shōjo*-like examples.

Eyes interconnect characters with each other, and characters with readers. Whenever *shōjo manga* is critically addressed, extreme close-ups of eyes filled with highlights of diverse shapes tend to take center stage. But manga eyes do not have to be big to involve readers affectively. *Sailor Moon*, for instance, features characters that are cross-eyed or X-eyed, have clenched or arched eyes, and also "eye-umlauts" in the form of hearts or

---

[7] Published monthly from 1967 to 1985.

Manga: An Affective Form of Comics

spirals (see Cohn). Such pupil-less eyes do not serve the "omnipotence of the narrative" (Groensteen 56) by revealing what lies beneath; they operate as surface devices that involve readers by virtue of cuteness, "a locus for intimacy, care and affection" (Gn 55), that "affects because of its difference to the subject" (50).

Yet, even big eyes are not always or inadvertently representations of interiority. As pointed out above, through the example of *Barefoot Gen*, eyes become cues for characters' positions and feelings by means of juxtaposition. The resulting difference, however, is not necessarily fixed. It often varies contextually, according to the partner with whom a certain character is pictorially paired. In *shōjo manga*, differences in size and shape have served to distinguish pure-hearted, affect-driven young girls from calculating adult women, but also masculine and feminine character traits. The latter is particularly evident in manga narratives that evolve around the trope of the (not necessarily cross-dressing) "girl in male attire" (*dansō no shōjo*). A representative historical example is *The Rose of Versailles*. One of its protagonists, the female Oscar, who was raised as a man and trained as a military officer, comes to guard Queen Marie-Antoinette as a woman in male attire. This Oscar exhibits narrower eyes and shorter eyelashes, as well as a longer face with a sharper jawline, in comparison to female characters, but whenever she is depicted next to a man whom she adores, she acquires rounder "feminine" forms (Oshiyama 165–170). In intimate moments with her beloved André, who is of lower social rank than her, faces and eyes become uniform in shape, suggesting an equal standing beyond gender and class. Two decades after *The Rose of Versailles*, *Sailor Moon* followed in its steps, at least with regard to gender performance, with the introduction of Haruka, or Sailor Uranus. Engaged in a relationship with a female peer, Haruka exhibits more masculine traits (and uses a masculine first-person pronoun) in everyday school settings, while assuming more feminine ones when fighting as a magical girl.

Instead of character pairs, dreamy-looking single characters in close-up have been one of the most prominent features of *shōjo manga* since the 1950s. When placed in collage-like, multilayered compositions where they are orbited by multiple pictorial and linguistic fragments (especially popular since the 1970s), these facial close-ups seem to reflect what is going on inside. But on closer inspection, the huge eyes often appear lost in space, staring dead ahead, and lacking a specific focus. Obviously, they are neither directed inwards nor to the reader, and they do not address any specific intradiegetic pictorial element. Such eyes suggest indifference towards the divide between inner and outer reality, depth and surface, subject and object, or conversely, they make the opposites meet. Keiko Takemiya (b. 1950) used this device frequently in her 1000-page-long science fiction serial *Towards the Terra*. Published in a *seinen*, not *shōjo*, manga magazine, it anticipated the conjoining of feminine and masculine genre traits that is quite common today.

Towards the Terra unfolds in an authoritarian future where allegedly immaculate humans are fabricated by erasing childhood memories in a so-called adult exam. At the core of the narrative is the opposition between the new breed of humans and the Mu, a deviant species equipped with psychic powers. The manga's protagonist, Jomy Marcus Shin, becomes an intermediary between the two. At the beginning, he is contacted by the Mu's chief, Soldier Blue, with the request to assume leadership. This encounter takes the form of telepathy (Figure 4.2). The page that conveys the significant moment features three Jomys. In the middle ground, on the right, he appears to be floating in free space, with drooping head and shoulders. In the lower and smaller panel insert, he is asleep, eyes closed; the upper panel insert, an extreme close-up, shows him wide-eyed and with his right hand raised as if in defense. Although turned towards Soldier Blue, who is depicted in full-body length on the left gesturing towards the "first" Jomy on the right, the "third" Jomy's gaze does not point at the telepathic intruder. Rather, the open eyes play a pragmatic role: they provide a nodal point for the reader to stitch together the fragments of the page, including the monologue lines that convey Soldier Blue's voice as perceived by Jomy in his state of trance.

Horror manga, especially the unpredictable body-horror type, also employs close-ups of eyes. In the case of Junji Itō (b. 1963), this relates to *shōjo manga*, as he has largely published in female-oriented magazines such as *Monthly Halloween* and *Nemuki* since his professional debut in 1987. But in his graphic narratives, characters' eyes do not ensure the unity of the page. On the contrary, staying within bordered panels that are to be read one by one, they reinforce fragmentation. Still, Itō's uncannily veined eyes and Takemiya's affectively sparkling ones have something in common: neither provide psychologized substantiation for the narrative events.

Figure 4.2, for example, is composed in a way that involves the reader in Jomy's experience of telepathic communication: we see what he sees with his inner eye, and we hear what he hears. But the image of suggested subjectivity, Jomy's internal view, includes a view on Jomy from the outside, and the interiority is not about hidden emotional truths. After all, it is telepathy that conjoins inner and outer reality, as well as the different characters and places. Thus, the display of interiority can be

Figure 4.2. Telepathic intrusion of Soldier Blue (on the left) into Jomy's interiority. Keiko Takemiya, *Tera e* [1977], vol. 1. (Square Enix, 2007), p. 111. ©1977–2007 Keiko Takemiya.

contagious, or affective, insofar as it involves the reader, but it is not necessarily representing a subject vis-à-vis an object through a gaze. Unfocused eyes invite us to cross the line that separates characters from each other as well as the reader: they invoke the impression that certain feelings do not belong to any specific character, but to all involved parties, up to and including the reader. Other prominent identifiers of *shōjo manga* fulfil a similar purpose, for example, unframed soliloquy-like lexia, speech balloons without tails, and the regularly objected visual "sameness" of characters. The latter is often employed to suggest interchangeable, or equal, character positions, as demonstrated through the example above. But it may also extend beyond individual texts and occur across genres. Jomy, for example, resembles one of the protagonists from Takemiya's most famous manga series, *The Poem of Wind and Trees*.

This long-running serial, first published in a manga magazine for girls, has become famous as a pioneer of the boys love genre (initially called *shōnen'ai* in Japanese and usually known as *yaoi* abroad). Set in France in the 1880s, *The Poem of Wind and Trees* features two adolescent boys – Serge and Gilbert – who become lovers, try to live independently as a couple, and are ultimately separated by death, after two years of narrated time. Gilbert is the wind mentioned in the manga's title. His beauty, as well as his mysteriously promiscuous and imprudent behavior, affect the characters around him, beginning with Serge. Gilbert's centrality to the narrative materializes in numerous pages that single him out. Medium shot panels, or close-ups with only his right eye sparkling and his left eye staying hidden under a strand of hair, constitute him as the ultimate object of attention (Figure 4.3). Lecherous gazes (by characters as well as readers) objectivize him, but strangely enough, he plays along, up to and including sexual assaults, even rape. This does not necessarily freeze him in the position of a helpless victim. Often, "[h]e executes agency through acknowledgement, manipulation and re-turning of the gaze" (Antononoka 235). This agency is further expressed through sudden changes in his portrayal, from still postures to energetic jumping and running. Consequently, Gilbert's one-eyed appearance – with the visible eye unfocused – comes across as both self-protective and belligerent, inward- and outward-oriented. While confirming power-based divides, he also subverts them, visually as well as narratively.

In the context of this chapter, it is noteworthy that the manga's narrative presents Gilbert's behavior not as prudent or calculated, but affect-driven. A multi-volume flashback provides some background information, introducing the complicated relationship with his father Auguste

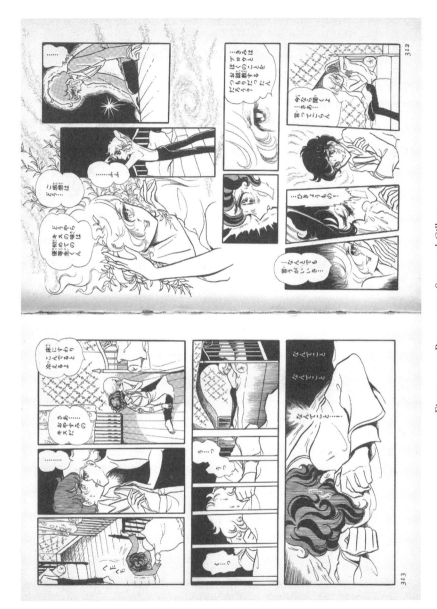

Figure 4.3. Room-mates Serge and Gilbert.
Keiko Takemiya, *Kaze to ki no uta* [1976], vol. 1 (Shogakukan, 1998), pp. 312–313.
Read from right to left. ©1998 Keiko Takemiya.

who pretends to be his uncle, and his frequent exposure to child abuse. But rather than unresolved trauma the narrative foregrounds the way he was brought up – as a feral child, unspoiled by civilization – to explain what makes him act rashly and impetuously. Furthermore, the narrative focuses less on rationalizing Gilbert's behavior than on foregrounding Serge's strong attachment to him. Serge serves as the main focalizer, who mediates between the initially targeted girl readers, and the boy characters who not only replace the traditional boy-meets-girl configuration, but also twist it into a story of fluid positions. Similar to the other examples discussed above, in Takemiya's graphic narratives, large eyes facilitate the removal of feelings from individual subjects whose identity rests on separation from others; their affectivity operates as an invitation to share, rather than to observe, feelings.

Interconnecting Different Spheres

As a crucial affective device for involving readers, manga eyes often go hand in hand with cartoonish exaggeration and narrative improbability. Their employment is unusual in graphic narratives of a more subdued and personal tone, such as Jirō Taniguchi's (1947–2017) *A Distant Neighborhood*. Initially serialized in a *seinen manga* magazine alongside Saitō's studio-produced *gekiga*, *A Distant Neighborhood* sends its 48-year-old protagonist back to his 14-year-old self, a junior-high school student living in a small town, who sees his father leave the family and his mother die a few years later. Time travel eventually helps him resolve the related trauma and revisit his own attitude towards being a husband and a father. This is narrated in a highly subjective manner,[8] beginning with the protagonist's frequent monologues. Rendered in the past tense, his adult inner voice is always present, even while he relives the events of his youth (and engages in monologue as well as dialogue in the present of the past). There is also the famous graveyard sequence in the first chapter, where he slides into the past for the first time. While the transition itself is conveyed through wordless panels that feature nature devoid of people in "non-character-bound focalisation" (Mikkonen 146), its result is presented from a visual first-person perspective with sneakers, legs, and hands spotted by the protagonist before he himself enters the picture again.

A Distant Neighborhood has been found to be "emotionally charged" (Beaty 152) in an introspective way. But the narrative does not compensate

---

[8] For a narratological analysis, see Mikkonen 129–49.

for an action-packed plot by representing characters' affects, as would be expected from girls manga. It does not exert affective pressure on the reader either, as it forgoes pictorial runes that evoke cuteness, uses onomatopoeia sparingly, does not privilege visual storytelling at the expense of verbal text, gives preference to regular panel layouts, and embeds the characters in detailed three-dimensional spaces. In general, this manga distinguishes between foreground and background, human actor and environment, speaker and listener, inner and outer voice. Consequently, it stands to reason that Taniguchi is perceived as "more classically 'European' than stereotypically Japanese" (Beaty 147). But while publishers such as Casterman have attempted at "divorcing him from his manga roots" (148), in reality, Taniguchi employs techniques that make both his "literary" and his "genre comics," which appear in different imprints and formats abroad (154), comparable to the examples mentioned above. This explains why it takes much less time to read the 400-page *A Distant Neighborhood* than graphic novels that have emerged from the Euro-American small-press realm.

Not all panels in *A Distant Neighborhood* show detailed spaces. Mimetic depictions are occasionally replaced by abstract momentum lines, for example, when the high school boys do sports or brawl, and conversations between the protagonist and members of his family often take place against a blank background, as if to concentrate all attention onto the speakers, who are mainly presented in shot/reverse shot sequences and from the chest upwards. The most intriguing device, however, is the frontal close-up of the eyes. Four extreme close-ups appear in *A Distant Neighborhood*, and all of them stretch over a whole tier in the middle of the page. Except for the half-closed eyes in the second graveyard scene (Taniguchi 85), all of them convey a sensation of shock, a surprise, or a flash of insight, induced by an overlapping of past and present (59, 148, 353, Figure. 4.4). While the narrative as a whole grounds characters' actions from a psychological perspective through references to childhood trauma, for instance, the extreme close-ups of eyes conjoin the spheres that are otherwise so neatly divided: past and present, the protagonist's inner and outer reality, self-conscious emotion and affective response. As such, these eyes signal what becomes increasingly apparent: that the entire narrative is one continuous monologue, less objective than the meticulously drawn, photorealist imagery might suggest.

As a manga-typical element in a seemingly atypical graphic narrative from Japan, close-ups of eyes appear not often, but memorably in Taniguchi's introspective narratives, reflecting the continuity between

Figure 4.4. The protagonist's 14-year-old self of the past conjoined with the inner voice of the present 48-year-old overcome by the realization that he behaves like his father. Jirō Taniguchi, *A Distant Neighborhood (Harukana machie)*, translated by Kumar Sivasubramanian, graphic adaptation by Frédéric Boilet. (Fanfare/Ponent Mon, 1998), p. 353. ©PAPIER/Jiro TANIGUCHI via BCF Tokyo.

corporate mainstream and alternative comics. Even Taniguchi's narratives are informed by a standardized publication format that harks back to serialization in commercial magazines (in his case, of *seinen manga*): its formal characteristics, monochromy, abstract backgrounds, and a certain preference for fragmentation, lengthy panel sequences without words, and a prevalence of faces stand out. In the Japanese context, it was the manga magazine that spurred readers' affective investment and encouraged the development of such devices. But a highly affective type of comics is by no means limited to Japan, and enormous eyes are not limited to manga either, as Taniguchi's style helps to confirm.

Coda

This chapter juxtaposed two options at the beginning: the conceptualization of manga as affective comics, and the search for commonalities across different genres of comics made in Japan prior to the age of webcomics. The fact that they are closely interrelated was demonstrated through graphic narratives by Takemiya and Taniguchi. Being anything but exhaustive, the discussion foregrounded the critical potential of an affect-centered approach by focusing on the (in)famous eyes in manga. It showed how they capture the reader's attention by virtue of the materiality of imagetext prior to any representational considerations. It further analyzed how eyes invite the reader to stitch the visible fragments of a page together, and conduce indifference towards the divisions between inside and outside, seeing and being seen, deep meaning and surface attraction, individualized emotions and shared feelings. This is not to say that representation and its interpretation do not matter in highly affective forms of comics. Rather, it is to acknowledge traits of comics that have been traditionally suspected to be childish, escapist, or acritical as is the case with manga. Laying open their specific potential, however, calls for a shift in focus from pursuing *what* manga is, to *how* manga is, how it engages characters and readers in specific contexts.

WORKS CITED

Comics[9]

Ikeda, Riyoko. *The Rose of Versailles (Berusaiyu no bara)*, in *Margaret*, 1972–73.
Koike, Kazuo (w.), and Kojima, Gōseki (i). *Lone Wolf and Cub (Kozure Ōkami)*. Kodansha, 1970–76.

---

[9] The titles listed here refer to the original place of publication.

Miller, Frank. *Ronin*. DC, 1983–84.

Nakazawa, Keiji. *Barefoot Gen* (*Hadashi no Gen*), in *Weekly Shōnen Jump* and others, 1973–87.

Oseman, Alice. *Heartstopper*. Hachette, 2018–.

Ōtomo, Katsuhiro. *Akira*, in *Young Magazine*, 1982–90.

Takemiya, Keiko. Toward the Terra (*Tera e*), in *Monthly Manga Shōnen*, 1977–80.

  Poem of Wind and Trees (*Kaze to ki no uta*), in *Weekly Shōjo Comic* 1976–82, and in *Petit Flower*, 1982–84.

Takeuchi, Naoko. *Sailor Moon* (*Bishōjo senshi*), in *Nakayoshi*, 1992–97.

Taniguchi, Jirō. *A Distant Neighborhood* (*Harukana machi e*), in *Big Comic*, 1998–99.

Tatsumi, Yoshihiro, *Good-Bye and other stories*. Catalan Communications, 1987.

Tezuka, Osamu. *New Treasure Island (Shintakarajima)*, text by Shichima Sakai. Ikuei, 1947.

  Astro Boy (Tetsuwan Atomu), in *Shōnen*, 1952–68.

  Kimba, the White Lion (*Jungle Taitei*), in *Manga Shōnen*, 1950–54.

  Buddha, in the magazines *Kibō no tomo*, *Shōnen World* and *Comic Tom*, 1972–83.

Toriyama, Akira. *Dragon Ball*, in *Weekly Shōnen Jump*, 1984–95.

Wang, Jen. *The Prince and the Dressmaker*. First Second, 2018.

Secondary Sources

Abbott, Michael and Charles Forceville. "Visual Representation of Emotion in Manga: 'Loss of Control' Is 'Loss of Hands' in *Azumanga Daioh* Volume 4." *Language and Literature*, vol. 20, no. 2, 2011, pp. 91–112.

Antononoka, Olga. "Communicating Emotions: How Commercial Manga for Women Approaches 3.11." *Kritika Kultura*, no. 26, 2016, pp. 222–242. DOI: 10.13185//KK2016.02612

Berndt, Jaqueline. "*SKIM* as *GIRL*: Reading a Japanese North American Graphic Novel through Manga Lenses." *Drawing New Color Lines: Transnational Asian American Graphic Narratives*, edited by Monica Chiu. Hong Kong University Press, 2014, pp. 257–278.

  "Takemiya Keiko: Mangaka with an Educational Mission." Ibid. *Manga: Media, Art, and Material*. Leipzig University Press, 2015, pp. 107–137.

Beaty, Bart. "Jirō Taniguchi: France's Mangaka." *Comics Studies Here and Now*, edited by Frederick L. Aldama. Routledge, 2018, pp. 144–160.

Cohn, Neil. *The Visual Language of Comics: Introduction to the Structure and Cognition of Sequential Images*. Bloomsbury, 2013.

Giannoulis, Elena and Lukas R. A. Wilde. "Introduction." *Emoticons, Emoji and Kaomoji: The Transformation of Communication in the Digital Age*, edited by Elena Giannoulis and Lukas R. A. Wilde. Routledge, 2019, pp. 1–22.

Gn, Joel. "A Lovable Metaphor: On the Affect, Language and Design of 'Cute'." *East Asian Journal of Popular Culture*, vol. 2, no. 1, 2016, pp. 49–61.

Grennan, Simon. "The Influence of Manga on the Graphic Novel." *The Cambridge History of the Graphic Novel*, edited by Jan Baetens, Hugo Frey, and Stephen E. Tabachnick. Cambridge University Press, 2018, pp. 320–336.

Groensteen, Thierry. *Comics and Narration*. Translated by Anne Miller. University Press of Mississippi, 2013.

Harvey, Robert C. "Manga Now and Manga then: Tatsumi's Gekiga and the Hokusai Origin of the Species." *The Comics Journal*, no. 284, July 2007, pp. 167–174.

Kacsuk, Zoltan. "Re-Examining the 'What is Manga' Problematic: The Tension and Interrelationship between the 'Style' Versus 'Made in Japan' Positions." *Arts*, vol. 7, no. 26, 2018, n.p. https://doi.org/10.3390/arts7030026

Kajiya, Kenji. "How Emotions Work: The Politics of Vision in Nakazawa Kenji's *Barefoot Gen*." *Comics Worlds and the World of Comics*, edited by Jaqueline Berndt. International Manga Research Center, 2010, pp. 227–243. http://imrc.jp/images/upload/lecture/data/245-261chap17Kajiya20101224.pdf

Lamarre, Thomas. "Manga Bomb: Between the Lines of *Barefoot Gen*." *Comics Worlds and the World of Comics*, edited by Jaqueline Berndt. International Manga Research Center, 2010, pp. 263–307. http://imrc.jp/images/upload/lecture/data/262-307chap18LaMarre20101224.pdf

McCloud, Scott. *Understanding Comics, the Invisible Art* [1993]. Harper Perennial, 1994.

Making Comics: Storytelling Secrets of Comics, Manga and Graphic Novels. William Morrow, 2006.

Mikkonen, Kai. *The Narratology of Comic Art*. Routledge, 2017.

Sabin, Roger. "*Barefoot Gen* in the US and UK: Activist Comic, Graphic Novel, Manga." *Reading Manga: Local and Global Perceptions of Japanese Comics*, edited by Jaqueline Berndt and Steffi Richter. Leipzig University Press, 2006, pp. 39–58.

Schneider, Greice. "Affect." *Key Terms in Comics Studies*, edited by Erin La Cour, Simon Grennan, and Rik Spanjers. Palgrave Macmillan, 2021, pp. 10–11.

Schodt, Frederik L. *Manga! Manga! The World of Japanese Comics*. 1983. Kodansha International, 1998.

Spiegelman, Art. "Barefoot Gen: Comics after the Bomb." Nakazawa, Keiji, *Barefoot Gen: A Cartoon Story of Hiroshima*, vol. 1, translated by Project Gen, Last Gasp, 2004, n.p.

Suter, Rebecca. "Japan/America, Man/Woman: Gender and Identity Politics in Adrian Tomine and Yoshihiro Tatsumi." *Paradoxa*, no. 22, 2010, pp. 101–122.

Suzuki, Shige (CJ). "Teaching Manga: A Medium-Specific Approach Beyond Area Studies." *Manga!: Visual Pop-Culture in Art Education*, edited by Masami Toku and Hiromi Tsuchiya Dollase. InSEA Publications, 2020, pp. 208–217.

Tsai, Yi-Shan. "Close-ups: An Emotive Language in Manga." *Journal of Graphic Novels and Comics*, vol. 9, no. 5, 2018, pp. 473–489.

CHAPTER 5

Digital Comics
An Old/New Form

Giorgio Busi Rizzi

Although digital comics have gained popularity since the 2000s, they remain a multifaceted (if not contradictory) object, often difficult to frame theoretically. This is because, rather than identifying a specific object, digital comics is an umbrella term that embraces profoundly different forms developed over more than thirty years, that only have some kind of digital mediation in common.

Artists exploring digital comics have often professed their intention of pushing them to the limits, expanding their form by relying on the affordances of the digital support (hyperlinks, audio, animation, playability), and navigating the potentially boundless space that Scott McCloud called "infinite canvas" (222). Nevertheless, the more unconventional works have so far managed to attract only a marginal audience, and are sometimes not even considered as *comics*. In contrast, most digital comics formally differ very little from those printed on paper, retaining their layout and static nature, and leveraging their digital environment to reshape editorial processes and participatory practices.

This chapter navigates this complexity, mapping digital comics from a formal and sociocultural point of view, retracing their historical evolution, and situating them in the contemporary media landscape. It will then reflect on their specificities regarding immersion and agency, and address issues of participation and preservation.

So, What Are Comics, Again?

Let's begin by addressing the comics elephant in the room.

In their overview of the subject, Darren Wershler, Kalervo Sinervo, and Shannon Tien observe that "it's far from clear what 'digital comics' actually

This work was made possible by a Special Research Fund (BOF) fellowship (01P03819) awarded by Ghent University.

Digital Comics: An Old/New Form

references, because comics are at once a medium, a set of genres, and a series of different 'formations' that combine a system of production and circulation, a cultural and ideological component, and physical format" (256). Part of this difficulty probably depends on the fact that the medium's birth owed to the recombination of a series of practices rather than a technological novelty, as pointed out by Lorenzo Di Paola (18–20). This inherently hybrid nature, and the different evolutions of its most significant artistic traditions (Anglo-American, Franco-Belgian, Japanese, and Korean) have contributed to the difficulty of formulating a definition univocally accepted by most scholars and authors. "Medium," in turn, is a difficult concept to define, because it connotes as much technological and material devices as it does semiotic (cognitive and modal) regimes and cultural (social, institutional, economic) aspects. For this reason, I propose a more fluid conception of comics, based on both formal and sociocultural elements, which can encompass digital comics as peripheral, hybrid types of comics.

On a formal level, most definitions of comics point to a combination of text and images on one side, and sequentiality on the other, as pivotal characteristics. Nonetheless, purely formal definitions often hypostatize the affordances of a medium, leveraging medium specificity to emphasize what a media product should (not) do. In this way, they inevitably imply a canon of what could be considered comics, generally based on (and more fitting for) the tradition taken as a point of departure; and they will either risk excluding this or that eccentric form (abstract, non-narrative comics, silent comics, single-panel comics, and so on) or try stretching their formulation to encompass a specific outlier. However, this is not to say that formal definitions have no reason to exist, and that all media should behave in the same way. On the one hand, one can appeal to a weak idea of medium specificity, delineating what media *typically* do, rather than what they must do – that is, for a descriptive tool based on the practices, rather than the affordances, of a medium[1]; on the other, one can get around the problem of the finiteness of categorizations by understanding comics according to parameters. We can thus identify a series of characteristics, and define as "comics" any artifact that shows a sufficient combination of these characteristics – so that, in the face of a low (non-prototypical) or missing parameter, the others compensate by being present and/or proto-typical. The parameters I suggest are words/images interplay

---

[1] For a summary of ongoing debates about medium specificity, see Carroll.

(multimodality); paper support (hence, a static nature); hand-drawing; iconicity[2]; narrativity; the panel/grid framing; a cognitive network between panels/images (generating closure, tabularity, and arthrology); the expression of temporality through spatiality; and the reader's freedom in terms of pace and direction of their reading that I propose to call "browsability."

This formal definition, however, works better in combination with an overarching socio-pragmatic one, reminding us that, in the final instance, "the 'social fact' of [comics'] conventional distinctiveness cannot be treated in a transhistorical or transcultural manner" (Thon and Wilde 234); namely, that in the end "a comic is what is produced or consumed as a comic" (Hague 27) by a community. Indeed, as Ian Gordon suggests, what matters is the "political economy" of comics "as a cultural institution tied to concrete historical circumstances, not a form in the abstract" (23). This ultimately allows us to discard the Bayeux tapestry or Trajan's column as examples of comics, and consider Grant Morrison's Batman #663 not just as narrative prose supplemented by illustrations (hence, formally, an illustrated book), but as a comic issue embedding something that cannot be read as such on a mere formal level.

What We Talk about When We Talk about Digital Comics[3]

Having clarified what I mean by "comics," I believe it is also necessary to explain what I mean by "digital," since the digital dimension of comics can involve several levels of mediation. A caveat: it is misleading to imagine digital comics in binary opposition to paper ones. On the contrary, the digital shift encouraged further mutations of the comics medium, which has been hybridized with video games, e-literature, animation, and so on, borrowing their imaginary and formal vocabulary ("camera" movements, branching paths, music soundtracks, and so on). The dichotomy that will often resurface in this chapter nonetheless helps explaining the peculiarities of digital comics in relation to common understandings of comics.

The first mediation concerns the creation process: drawing, inking, coloring, lettering, paginating, etc.[4] Even in the case of most paper comics,

---

[2] According to McCloud, iconicity is the property of simplification thanks to which comics can evoke, for example, a face by simply drawing a circle with two points and a line: 24–59.

[3] The structure of this chapter is highly indebted to an essay I wrote for a volume entitled *Pixel. Letteratura e media digitali* (edited by Beniamino Della Gala and Lavinia Torti). I thank the editors for allowing me to rework some passages.

[4] To these, one may add the recently opened possibility, still difficult to assess, of creating comics relying on generative AIs such as DALL-E2, Midjourney, Stable Diffusion, and the like.

these phases are nowadays mainly, if not entirely, carried out by digital means, because they offer immediate control of choices and reversibility of mistakes that would be impossible to achieve by working only with ink on analog supports. Similarly, for some time now the industrial (re)production and distribution (printing, shipping, etc.) of printed comics has been increasingly automated. Such use of digital tools should be seen as means of production instead of distinctive qualities of their outcomes. Hence, these interventions are not a criterion for determining whether a comic is "digital."

A contrasting reflection can be made when considering digitized paper comics, that some see as a completely different category from born-digital ones. Although I am arguing that what ultimately counts is the digital status of the final product, it is always important to consider when this digitization process happens: it can be part of the production phase (the artist works with ink on paper, the comic is then scanned and digitally reworked); it can be part of the reproduction and distribution phase (the final object often existing in parallel with its twin paper specimen); and it can be part of the afterlife of a comic, being digitized, legally or illegally, to redistribute or preserve it. In this sense, digitized comics surely pertain to digital culture; hence, they partake in the mediations that ultimately define our object of interest, displaying structural and formal character-istics that derive from the specific affordances of digital texts. These are related on the one hand to the materiality of the supports that host the comics (CD-ROMs, hard disks, cloud storages, or the Internet), which determines their potential ephemerality and whether they can be accessed online and/or offline; and on the other, to the technological and cogni-tive adaptations affecting the act of reading: the supports (smartphones, tablets, PCs, VR viewers) and technologies (e.g., the guided view fea-tured by some platforms) through which digital comics are read, the gestures that they entail and allow for, and how they consequently modify the reading process. To this, one may add the digital trajectories of (both paper and digital-born) comics: the participatory practices that take place through the Web, including piracy; the physical nature of digital comics and its implications for property and consumption; and the risk of coding obsolescence. However, they have a constitutive difference from born-digital comics.

One of the reasons why defining comics has always been difficult pertains to their hybrid nature, which originally stemmed from the lack of technological changes in respect to already existing media. It is then paradoxical, to some extent, that after those changes did appear – after, as Julien Baudry mentions, graphic software and instruments, the Web, and the many screens through which we consume those comics ("Paradoxes" 4) – one advocates for some untouched unity of the medium. Yet, in light of what was said, I argue that digital comics, whether born-digital or significantly remediated, can be seen as a different form compared to paper comics, while belonging to the medium of comics. This perspective reflects the sociocultural practices that encourage authors, users, and scholars to identify specific products as digital *comics*. At the same time, defining such works as *digital* comics and foregrounding their different media qualities, it accounts for the technological shift that results in different affordances and different semiotic strategies in respect to paper.

We therefore need new parameters to better identify digital comics and take this change in modality into account. Digital comics will be less prototypical comics, whose core characteristics only partially overlap with those of traditional ones: their reliance on words/images interplay (multimodality) is possibly complexified by the presence of sounds and animations (multimediality); the support is digital (potentially allowing for a dynamic nature); the panel/grid framing is sometimes replaced and embodied by the screen surface; the cognitive network connecting panels/images may be stressed/replaced by means of hyperlinks; the possibility of a heterochronous or a homochronous mode may result in a (sometimes partially) predetermined reading pace and in a twofold temporality (spatial and/or chronological); and the reading directions can be freer, allowing for a certain degree of playability and what I propose to call "explorability," in contrast to the "browsability" of paper comics.

Always Historicize: The Birth (and Growth) of Digital Culture

A fuller understanding of the heterogeneity of digital comics comes from retracing their historical trajectory. We can identify four phases of digital culture, determined by different paradigms: personal computing; network computing; digital renaissance; platform economy[5]. These phases have shaped the dominant forms in the history of digital comics:

1. Personal computing (circa 1985–2000), when PCs become widespread, and the interest of tech companies in proving the usefulness of their products meets the curiosity of practitioners. For

---

[5] This reconstruction is partially based on Mondoux; for different ones, see Baudry; Wershler et al. For the sake of brevity, I will only make reference here to the main Western comics traditions, that is, Franco-Belgian and Anglo-American. This should be complemented with an overview of the different evolution of digital culture in Asia and its repercussions on manga/manhwa.

Digital Comics: An Old/New Form 107

the first time, comics – notably, Mike Saenz and Peter Gillis' *Shatter* (1985–1986) and Pepe Moreno's *Batman: Digital Justice* (1990) – are created using a computer; several videogame companies (Infocomics, Ubisoft, etc.) experiment with the comics form; and these two directions eventually converge, giving birth to the first digital comics that venture into the multimedia potential of the form: on CD-ROMs, Edouard Lussan's *Opération Teddy Bear* (1996) and Simon Guibert and Julien Malland's *John Lecrocheur* (1998), which rehashed the adventure game format, and Voyager Company's *The Complete Maus* (1994), which supplemented Spiegelman's original comic book with interviews, sketches, and archival material.

2. Network computing (circa 1995–2010), when the Internet appears and expands, geographically and in terms of the amount of time the average user spends on it every day. During this phase, online comic strips gain popularity. They are comics that leverage digital practices to provide their readers with a serialized product. As a result, their static nature echoing paper strips can be explained both as a consequence of the limits in computation (a heavier webpage would take more time to load) and as a way to anchor the form in something the audience is already familiar with, subtly remediating it in a new environment (e.g., by featuring a hover text). Many of these comics still exist and are read by a large and loyal audience. Notable examples include Mike Krahulik's *Penny Arcade* (1998–), Nicholas Gurewitch's *The Perry Bible Fellowship* (2001–), Zach Weinersmith's *Saturday Morning Breakfast Cereal* (2002–, see Figure 5.1), Ryan North's *Qwantz* (2003–), Joey Comeau and Emily Horne's *A Softer World* (2003–2015), Randall Munroe's *Xkcd* (2006–), Kate Beaton's *Hark! A Vagrant* (2007–2018), Reza Farazmand's *Poorly Drawn Lines* (2008–). Some comics, nonetheless, experimented more with "unnatural" formats and flash animation: notably, one can mention Charley Parker's *Argon Zark* (1995–2009).

3. Digital renaissance[6] (circa 2005–2015). This phase is symbolically introduced by three watershed events: the spread of self-publishing platforms and blogs; the ubiquity of game culture, propelled by ever-increasing computational and connection capacities, and its subsequent visual and narrative impact; and the growing interest of

---

[6] I borrow the concept from Joel Waldfogel (despite using it with some liberty).

Figure 5.1. Zach Weinersmith, "AI", Saturday Morning Breakfast Cereal (2022)

authors in digital comics due to the increasing legitimacy of the form, as demonstrated by Scott McCloud's influential *Reinventing Comics*. Harnessing these tensions, several authors seek to create online and offline digital comics that aim to take full advantage of the affordances of the comics medium: noteworthy examples include Sutu's *NAWLZ* (2008), Julian Hanshaw's *The Art of Pho* (2011), and Ezra Claytan Daniels' *Upgrade Soul* (2012). From a formal perspective, this is a flourishing period, with many authors experimenting with unusual formats and diverse platforms. Nevertheless, these comics rarely manage to reach a wide audience, struggling to consolidate and overcome the phase in which they can be seen as media of attraction – a term that Rebecca Rouse, when discussing mixed reality, borrows from "cinema of attraction," to describe media products that are "unassimilated, interdisciplinary, seamed, and participatory" (105).[7]

4. Platform economy (2010–present). While the phenomenon is broad and complex[8], we can sketch at least three aspects concerning the correlation between platforms and comics. The first case is platforms that host (and generally sell) comics, usually focusing on one specific format, hence directly mediating layout choices and reading processes. For instance, ComiXology (2013–) and Izneo (2010–), hosting mostly skeuomorphic comics (i.e., those that remediate the layout and static nature of paper comics); Thrillbent (2012–2016), Electricomics (2015–2016), and Turbointeractive (2017–), based on panel delivery; Verticalismi (2015–2018), Delitoon (2011–), Webtoon (2004–), and Tapas (2012–), featuring vertical scrolls. The second case is that of crowdfunding and support platforms, such as Kickstarter (2009–), Indiegogo (2007–), Patreon (2013–), or Kofi (2012–), used by self-published authors to directly reach their readers and acquire funds. The third case is social media, which have not only established themselves as an intermediate stage of publication (authors often begin there, consolidate their fanbase, and then move on to paper), but have also markedly determined the evolution of the form.

From the beginning, digital comics have explored most of the affordances of digital storytelling, incorporating multimedia, hypertextual and interactive elements, albeit within the limits of existing computational technology[9]; and when that technology advanced, allowing for new and different affordances, digital comics experimented with it. At the same time, they remediated and borrowed from traditional comics forms to better anchor themselves in the tastes and habits of the readers, while undergoing a process of convergence that further blurred media bound-

---

[7] "I owe this insight to Lorenzo Di Paola".

[8] For an overview of the relation between platform economy and webcomics, see Nicolle Lamerichs.

[9] In this regard, one must remember that the opportunities of digital culture are accompanied by corresponding inequalities (in terms of hardware, infrastructures, and access) that have heavily shaped the socio-geographical distribution of digital technology so far.

aries in terms of language, forms, and imaginary. After a long mutation, digital comics' primary concern seems nowadays consolidating their formal independence, reaching economic stability and cultural legitimacy (see Baudry).

Partly in reaction to this, paper comics are experiencing what Aaron Kashtan calls a "crisitunity" – that is, both a crisis and an opportunity (17) – fueled by "biblionecrophilia," or the fetishizing nostalgia for the book object counterposed to the digital turn (54). This led a growing number of authors to "kindle-proof" paper comics (76), that is, develop forms that are impossible to effectively transpose to a digital environment – think of Chris Ware's *Building Stories* (2012), whose fragmentation and abundance of formats make it virtually undigitizable[10].

The (Changing) Shape of Comics

The umbrella term of "digital comics" as all kinds of comics that are read and consumed on digital supports still calls for clarification. I argue that there are three possible categories[11] of digital comics: skeuomorphic ones; comics modulating their inter-panel succession; comics featuring intra-panel expansions.

1. The first category regroups skeuomorphic comics: static and framed by a grid-like layout, they remediate and closely resemble their print counterparts.

This is the most common type of digital comics, encompassing both digitized paper comics and the majority of born-digital comics. Why do so many digital comics rely on replicating the panel/strip/page structure? According to Ernesto Priego and Peter Wilkins, this is not "because of an inherent conservatism or unwillingness to experiment but rather because the grid's enframing is such a powerful generative technology" (17). An additional reason is that many comics aim at a parallel publication, synchronous or asynchronous, on different supports. This usually happens in two circumstances: either the same comics are sold simultaneously on paper and digitally (usually through one of the previously

---

[10] This point calls for nuance: see Kashtan for a deconstruction of this purported "undigitizability" (54–90).
[11] For a different typology, see Magali Boudissa.

mentioned platforms), or authors use digital venues as a promotional vehicle for a subsequent publication on paper. In both cases, formats allowing for minimal (if any) changes when moving to another medium are the most economical strategy. This is the case with many comics hosted on social media: often autobiographical or commenting current events, sometimes absurdist, they try to maximize their viral potential by getting as many reposts as possible and allow to monetize their popularity

2. The second category includes comics modulating their layout with inter-panel successions that use digital affordances to do things that paper comics cannot do as effectively or evidently. They either rely on scrolling (a), conceiving the screen as a window on a potentially infinite surface, free from the constraints of the page and able to take all possible directions; or on panel delivery (b), presenting the readers one panel at a time and only revealing the following one once they click/tap on it.

Despite their purportedly limitless possibilities, the infinite canvas theorized by McCloud is not a frequent option in digital comics, which prefer avoiding an excessive polycentrism of the readers' gaze and preserve its unidirectionality (Tirino 84–85). Indeed, the scroll format (a) has imposed itself in its simpler version, by framing a single panel at a time and directing navigation in one direction, usually through a vertical movement (long naturalized as the unmarked reading path on the Internet). This is the mechanism adopted by webtoons, highly successful in Korea and now popular worldwide. There are also hybrids between this and skeuomorphic comics, exemplified by what the French call "blog-BD," where the grid-like layout is navigated through scrolling vertically.

The scroll principle nonetheless allows for captivating experiments: letting the represented space escape in every direction far beyond the initial visible area (the special episode "Click and Drag" of Randall Munroe's *Xkcd*, 2012); punctuating a vertical scroll with a soundtrack and a Java code that makes the panels fade once being read, thus embodying the dementia of the protagonist (*These Memories Won't Last* by Sutu, 2015); or combining a horizontal scroll with a parallax effect (Stevan Živadinović's *Hobo Lobo of Hamelin*, 2011–2014) and a geolocated soundtrack, as in Marietta Ren's *Phallaina* (2016, see Figure 5.2), which merges its panels into a flowing continuum, each region connected to the next by porous boundaries.

Figure 5.2. Marietta Ren, *Phallaina* (2016), promotional picture

Digital comics relying on panel delivery (b) encompass three very different objects: Balak's "turbomedia" (see his influential graphic essay *About Digital Comics*), which relies on the presentation mechanism described earlier, and is usually hosted on dedicated websites; the guided view reading mode (I will discuss it in the following section); and comics hosted on social media, the semantic unity of which is formed by the posts, each regrouping a discrete number of panels that the reader unveils by clicking/tapping. This format is extremely popular on Instagram, where it has evolved to feature most often four single square panels (Instagram's default layout) followed by the whole composition, itself shaped as a gridded square encompassing all the preceding panels. Although it may not look like a technical breakthrough, this simple remediation of the strip form has become very successful, and confirms the elasticity and adaptability of the comics medium.

Here too, there is space for experimentation: Lorenzo Ghetti and Carlo Trimarchi's *To Be Continued* (2014–2017) is a serialized superheroes webcomic that displays fascinating examples of both scrolling and panel delivery combined with many more features relying on digital affordances.

3. The third category encompasses comics featuring intra-panel expansions that allow for a different perception of the storyworld in comparison to traditional comics. One can further distinguish between comics featuring enhanced panels (motion comics and AR comics) and those featuring explorable panels (hypercomics and VR comics).

Motion comics incorporate audio and animations (flash, gifs, and so on) on a static background, usually keeping emanata and balloons. The system has attracted considerable criticism because it alters the reading rhythm, which aligns with the duration of sounds and movements, and because the simultaneous presence of text and audio may be seen as semiotically ambiguous or redundant. Despite this, recent examples of motion comics have gained critical acclaim, such as Matt Huynh's *The Boat* (2014), a vertical scroll featuring short animations and hyperlinks leading to paratextual glosses; or André Bergs' *Protanopia* (2017), a very short comic that uses sensor-induced motion to animate otherwise static panels.

Augmented Reality comics are often hybrid media objects, primarily paper works that can be enhanced with a smartphone (by pointing the camera at specific points of certain pages), but they can also be born-digital comics that use AR to add information to the story. Rob Shields' *Neon Wasteland* (2019), François Schuiten's *La Douce* (2012), and Sutu's *Modern Polaxis* (2014) are good examples of the former, Mike De Seve's *Operation Ajax* (2010) of the latter.

Hypercomics are comics with a multilinear, game-like narrative structure which requires users to choose between several possible paths. Excellent examples are Margarita Molina Fernandez's *2* (2021) or those that Daniel Merlin Goodbrey, an accomplished theorist-practitioner, hosts on his site alongside his academic contributions (2000–2014). Vidu's *L'Immeuble* (2019, see Figure 5.3) hybridizes this category with turbo-media to create a hypertextual, navigable story of a building that calls to mind Perec's book, *Life: A User's Manual*.

Finally, Virtual Reality comics are set in a computer-simulated, three-dimensional environment perceived through a VR device. The format does not seem to be (for now) at ease with comics, despite some interesting experiments: Walkie Entertainment's *Archipelago* (2018) and the VR adaption of Marc Antoine Mathieu's *Sens* (2016) or Richard McGuire's

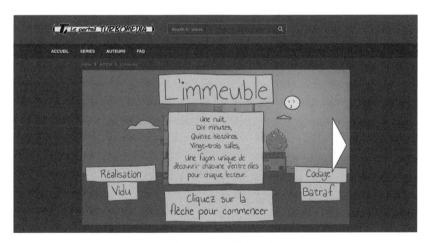

Figure 5.3.   Vidu, *L'Immeuble* (2019), screenshot

Here (2020). Given the characteristics of VR environments, it is nevertheless contested whether they can still be considered comics.

How to Do Things with (Digital) Comics: Agency, Immersion, and Panel Delivery

In the collective imaginary, digital comics – at least those belonging to our second and third categories – always maximize interactivity, reaching quasi-videogame playability, and immersivity, leveraging their support to provide ample and navigable storyworlds. But is it the case? Can interactivity be reduced to playability? And isn't directly relating immersion to how visually detailed or interactive a narrative a trivialization of how immersion works?

To better understand how (digital) comics shape their reading processes, both cognitively and materially, I thus propose considering four types of agency: narrative (a), interpretive (b), material (c), and social (d). (I will discuss the latter in the following section.) All have a relationship of some kind, often ambivalent, with the immersion that a text seeks to solicit, be it phenomenological, emotional, material, or social. Throughout these categories, I want to reconsider the relation digital comics entertain with paper ones.

I prefer to call "narrative agency" (a) what is usually referred to as "interactivity" – the kind provided by videogames or e-literature. While digital media are particularly apt to accommodate for interactive mechanisms and allow for high narrative agency, nothing prevents paper comics from doing the same (adopting multilinear structures such as branching paths). Moreover, paper comics traditionally enable a very high level of interpretive agency. Interpretive agency (b) which takes place on textual and visual levels, is made of the cognitive processes involved in the reception of a story, the set of inferences and correlations that readers project onto what they are reading. These processes serve to fill two kinds of gaps: textual gaps, namely, events that are not explicitly present in the narrative, but that we understand must have happened (see Iser); and visual gaps. The latter are related both to the level of detail (McCloud's aforementioned "iconicity") and to the relationships between panels, either successive, requiring the kind of mental editing that McCloud calls "closure"[12] (60–93), or non-successive, enlivening a network of visual and semantic references (see Groensteen's "general arthrology," 171–186). All these processes imply the readers' activation of a network of semiotic,

---

[12] For a more efficient reworking of the concept, see Mikkonen (38–45).

intertextual, and real-life references that they possess (what Iser calls "repertoire").

Narrative and interpretive agency directly affect immersion: they are intertwined to both phenomenological immersion (encompassing spatio-temporal and narrative-hermeneutic processes) and emotional immersion (affective and narrative-ludic processes[13]). In principle, when this kind of agency is limited, immersion is limited as well (although immersion is often seen as an abandonment to being transported by a story; see Gerrig).

Material agency (c) has a close link to material immersion (which includes kinesthetic and technological processes). Both depends on the gestures that users are able (and choose) to make, which in turn stem from the materiality and design of the interface with which they interact. Three issues are at stake: the (de)naturalized nature of those gestures; whether readers keep control of the reading pace; and whether they can see the whole page and zoom in/out.

As Benoît Crucifix and Björn-Olav Dozo observe, the reader of e-comics can be given "the role of the 'animator' through clicking, scrolling, swiping, and other movements" (584), creating a set of gestures analogous to those of paper reading. Of course, naturalized gestures (such as turning a paper page, clicking on an arrow, or scrolling) and denaturalized ones (such as clicking on a half-hidden link or recomposing a narrative scattered on loose sheets) imply a very different cognitive load. As a consequence, the relation between material agency and immersion is complex and multifaceted, since a more challenging, denaturalized gesture has the potential to maximize as well as disrupt both. A different possibility is that sound and/or animation are present. This option problematizes the equation between temporality and spatiality typical of paper comics, abandoning the heterochrony (i.e., the users' control of their reading rhythm) that characterizes them – an outcome that some see as determining whether such objects should be considered comics. In this case the relation between material agency and immersion seems to be inversely proportional: when the duration of animations cannot be interrupted, the text dictates and delimits its time of consumption, minimizing the users' material agency while (in theory) maximizing their immersion.

A peculiar case in this regard is that of the aforementioned panel delivery. When abandoning the grid in favor of a succession of single panels, digital comics renounce the element that has historically held

---

[13] Phenomenological immersion mirrors both narrative and interpretative agency, while emotional immersion does not have an agentic counterpart.

together the structure, marked the rhythm, and guided the reading process of paper comics (Priego and Wilkins). This has an impact on both narrative and interpretive agency: leaving out the grid means that readers are hindered in their freedom to wander, mentally and physically, through comics, and generates a breakdown of the network of relationships and references between panels. Usually, comics find another way to supply what is missing by remediating different sense-making strategies, and amongst panel delivery-based comics, turbomedia try to keep the grid structuring. However, while Balak's original conception was meant to be a productive, integral feature of the way he envisioned turbomedia, it also substantiates the superimposing mechanism of the guided view – the optional reading mode adopted by ComiXology, Marvel, and Izneo. Guided view acts as a permanent zoom in, reorganizing skeuomorphic comics based on grid-like layouts by fragmenting them and progressively revealing one new panel (or part of it) at a time when users click or tap on the image. Conceived to let users control their reading pace, this system improves readability, noticeably on small devices like smartphones, where the mediation of the support has a higher toll on material immersion. Nevertheless, it does so by imposing a preordained reading progression and hindering the perception of the entire page (as it was originally conceived). Further, the system is not at ease with non-rectangular, unconventional panels. Consequently, material agency is limited, and interpretive agency is disrupted, since rhythm, layout, and arthrology are drastically altered. The repercussions on immersion are nonetheless more ambiguous: is it maximized by the opportunity of appreciating the details inside a panel or limited by the impossibility of cognitively processing the panels in sequence? The different answers to this question are probably the reason behind the ambivalent reception of the system.

Returning to the comparison (and the alleged competition) between paper and digital comics in light of their different possibilities in terms of immersion and agency, we must evidently reject the notion of a media hierarchy: digital comics offer their readers formats and features based on digital affordances, which prompts a series of cognitive processes beyond the capabilities of paper; at the same time, they give up another set of cognitive processes typical of paper comics. Of course, a similar reasoning can be made when comparing digital comics with any other medium – which proves once again that no medium is inherently "more powerful" than another. Instead, medium specificity and the narrative peculiarities of each text establish relationships of consonance (the text explicitly leverages the affordances of its medium), dissonance (the text chooses to go against the characteristics most often associated with that medium), or, perhaps more often, convergence (texts and medium align, eventually creating a new object that does not foreground all the affordances of the medium, but only those most productive on a sociocultural level).

Digital (After)Lives: Participation, Piracy, and Preservation

As mentioned, one type of agency had yet to be discussed here. Social agency (d) has profoundly changed in the transition from paper to digital: on the one hand, it now encompasses the new actions – what Rick Shivener calls the "extensive agency" of digital comics readers, their capacity for "downloading, reprogramming, editing, rescaling, redistributing, and circulating" (57) comics. To this one may add liking, reposting, and all the other practices that take place through social media and modulate social immersion. On the other hand, most participatory modes that predated the Internet and that have always been an integral part of comics culture – exchanging ideas with the authors, remixing, speculating, commenting, and so on – have experienced an acceleration, a geographical expansion, and a growing disintermediation. This has allowed many authors to live off the support of their fan communities alone, through crowdfunding or merchandising sales. *Homestuck* (2009–2016), a mammoth comic series created by Andrew Hussie, is one of the best examples of this interactive process of growth: it evolved from a webcomic to becoming the hub of a series of transtextual and transmedial branches, particularly thanks to a highly active community that turned it into a participatory narrative ecosystem (Busi Rizzi).

At the same time, comics are no strangers to the centralization and concentration that has invested other fields of digital culture in the last years: with the advent of platform economy, smaller businesses had to shut down, while others (usually owned by multinationals) have resisted in the face of a market where users are often unwilling to pay for the consumption of intangible, un-collectable objects. Comics conglomerates have tried to counteract this through flat subscriptions that give access to impressively large catalogs, but nonetheless limit the number of issues one can hold simultaneously[14] and prohibit sharing files by means of DRMs and encryptions.

---

[14] For example, at the time this article was written, ComiXology or Marvel Unlimited offered access, respectively, to over 25,000 and almost 30,000 titles, but only enabled the simultaneous downloading of a relatively minimal number of them (12 for Marvel, 50 for ComiXology).

As a result, the platformization of comics curbs most of the exchange practices that have long characterized comics culture, channeling them towards a more orderly consumption that does not allow for any behavior leaning towards piracy[15]. Indeed, when copies are not encrypted, piracy is a significant part of the digital culture surrounding comics: borrowing and lending comics can be easily done on the Internet through hosting platforms (Dropbox, WeTransfer, etc.), websites, and peer-to-peer software. The difference, quite ironic given that stakeholders prevent the material ownership of the digital comics that are legally available, is that borrowed paper comics ultimately had to be restituted to their owner (and bought anew if one wanted to keep them), while unprotected digital comics, once downloaded, are forever available to the users. Furthermore, while lending or donating physical objects are one-at-a-time gestures, uploading is both repeatable and multidirectional, allowing for the formation and management of what Abigail De Kosnik calls "rogue archives." An example of the latter are websites hosting scanlations, translations of manga realized and uploaded online by fan communities which are illegal but precious cultural mediators of products often neglected by foreign markets, hence otherwise unreachable, untranslated, or translated only long after the original publication (see also Chapter 13 on comics and their archives).

Rogue archives are not, of course, the only way of preserving comics in the digital realm. A growing number of projects aim at the digitization and preservation of otherwise perishable comic material (early comics, magazines, fanzines, and so on), working to perpetuate a fundamental, still understudied part of our cultural heritage. This nonetheless shines a light on the paradoxical relationship digital culture holds with memory and ephemerality. While the digital seems to be the ideal environment for the preservation of paper comics, in fact, its current configuration also constantly endangers digital comics. Indeed, as De Kosnik observes, although the Internet "began as a fantasy of the perfect archive, a technology that would preserve the vast record of human knowledge in its entirety" (44), due to the inevitable obsolescence of hardware and software, "the networked computing system fails completely as a memory machine" (46). Digital media are "degenerative, forgetful, erasable" (Chun 160): supports break and become unreadable, programming languages change, plugins are not developed anymore, the rent of web domains is no longer paid, and so on. And although preservation tools such as the Internet Wayback Machine can only save "a skeleton of a page, full of fragmented links

---

[15] For a more detailed discussion of this issue, see Sinervo; Stevens and Bell.

and images" (169), not much has been done so far to use them to preserve digital comics (and similar objects), which are consequently far more ephemeral than their print counterparts. Accounting for this perishability and developing strategies to counteract it is one of the challenges of contemporary digital (comics) culture.

Conclusion

This chapter traced a genealogy and offered a typology of digital comics that acknowledges their evolution, complexity, and heterogeneity. It delineated an object that, despite a long history, is still hybrid, unfinished, evolving, not so much in its formal experimentations as in its plastic ability to adapt, reinvent itself, incorporate new practices and remediate the different paradigms of print and digital culture. One cannot help being curious about what (most) digital comics will look like in a few more years.

WORKS CITED

Comics

Ren, Marietta. *Phallaina*. Small Bang, 2016.

Vidu (Victor Dulon). "L'immeuble." *T, le portail TURBOMEDIA*, 2019. https://turbointeractive.fr/limmeuble/ [Accessed 31 July 2022].

Weinersmith, Zach. "AI". *Saturday Morning Breakfast Cereal*, 11 June 2022 [Accessed 31 July 2022].

Secondary Sources

Aggleton, Jennifer. "The Proper Serious Work of Preserving Digital Comics." *UK Web Archive Blog. The British Library*, 9 August, 2017, https://blogs.bl.uk/webarchive/2017/08/digital-comics.html [Accessed 31 July 2022].

Balak (Yves Bigerel). *About Digital Comics*, 2009. http://balako1.deviantart.com/art/about-DIGITAL-COMICS-111966969 [Accessed 31 July 2022].

Baudry, Julien. "Paradoxes of Innovation in French Digital Comics." *The Comics Grid: Journal of Comics Scholarship*, vol. 8, no. 1, 2018, pp. 1–24.

Cases-pixels. PUFR, 2018.

Boudissa, Magali. "Typologie des bandes dessinées numériques." *Bande dessinée et numérique*, edited by Pascal Robert. CNRS Éditions, 2016, pp. 79–99.

Busi Rizzi, Giorgio. "Il fumetto digitale tra sperimentazione e partecipazione: Il caso Homestuck." *H-ermes. Journal of Communication*, no. 18, 2020, pp. 45–72.

Carroll, Noël. "Medium Specificity." *The Palgrave Handbook of the Philosophy of Film and Motion Pictures*, edited by Noël Carroll et al. Palgrave Macmillan, 2019, pp. 29–47.

Chun, Wendy H. K. "The Enduring Ephemeral, or The Future Is a Memory." *Critical Inquiry*, vol. 35, no. 1, Autumn 2008, pp. 148–171.

Crucifix, Benoît and Björn-Olav Dozo. "E-Graphic Novels." *The Cambridge History of the Graphic Novel*, edited by Jan Baetens et al. Cambridge University Press, 2018, pp. 574–590.

De Kosnik, Abigail. *Rogue Archives: Digital Cultural Memory and Media Fandom.* MIT Press, 2016.

Di Paola, Lorenzo. *L'inafferrabile medium. Una cartografia delle teorie del fumetto dagli anni Venti a oggi.* Alessandro Polidoro Editore, 2019.

Gerrig, Richard. *Experiencing Narrative Worlds: On the Psychological Activities of Reading.* Yale University Press, 1993.

Gordon, Ian. "Comic Strips." *Comics Studies: A Guidebook*, edited by Charles Hatfield and Bart Beaty. Rutgers University Press, 2020, pp. 13–24.

Groensteen, Thierry. *Système de la bande dessinée.* Presses Universitaires de France, 1999.

Hague, Ian. *Comics and the Senses: A Multisensory Approach to Comics and Graphic Novels.* Routledge, 2014.

Iser, Wolfgang. *The Act of Reading: A Theory of Aesthetic Response.* John Hopkins University Press, 1978.

Kashtan, Aaron. *Between Pen and Pixel: Comics, Materiality, and the Book of the Future.* Ohio State University Press, 2018.

Lamerichs, Nicolle. "Scrolling, Swiping, Selling: Understanding Webtoons and the Data-driven Participatory Culture around Comics." *Participations*, vol. 17, no. 2, November 2020, pp. 211–229.

McCloud, Scott. *Understanding Comics: The Invisible Art.* Kitchen Sink Press, 1993.

Reinventing Comics: How Imagination and Technology Are Revolutionizing an Art Form. Paradox, 2000.

Mikkonen, Kai. *The Narratology of Comic Art.* Routledge, 2017.

Mondoux, André. *Histoire sociale des technologies numériques.* Éditions Nota Bene, 2011.

Priego, Ernesto and Peter Wilkins. "The Question Concerning Comics as Technology: *Gestell* and Grid." *The Comics Grid: Journal of Comics Scholarship*, no. 8, 2018, pp. 16–41.

Rouse, Rebecca. "Media of Attraction: A Media Archeology Approach to Panoramas, Kinematography, Mixed Reality and Beyond." *International Conference on Interactive Digital Storytelling*, edited by Frank Nack and Andrew S. Gordon. Springer, 2016, pp. 97–107.

Shivener, Rick. "*Re-theorizing* the *Infinite Canvas:* A Space for Comics and Rhetorical Theories." *Perspectives on Digital Comics: Theoretical, Critical, and Pedagogical Essays*, edited by Jeffrey S. J. Kirchoff and Mike P. Cook. McFarland, 2019, pp. 46–62.

Sinervo, Kalervo A. "Pirates and Publishers." *The Comics World: Comic Books, Graphic Novels, and Their Publics*, edited by Benjamin Woo and Jeremy Stoll. University Press of Mississippi, 2021, pp. 208–233.

Stevens, J. Richard and Christopher Edward Bell. "Do Fans Own Digital Comic Books? Examining the Copyright and Intellectual Property Attitudes of Comic Book Fans." *International Journal of Communication*, no. 6, 2012, pp. 751–772.

Thon, Jan-Noël and Lukas Wilde. "Mediality and Materiality of Contemporary Comics." *Journal of Graphic Novels and Comics*, vol. 7, no. 3, 2016, pp. 233–241.

Tirino, Mario. "Nuvole e pixel. Per una lettura sociologica del fumetto sperimentale contemporaneo." *Sguardi dalle scienze sociali*, edited by Alessandra Santoro and Luca Bifulco. Funes, 2018, pp. 69–94.

Waldfogel, Joel. *Digital Renaissance*. Princeton University Press, 2018.

Wershler, Darren, et al. "Digital Comics." *Comics Studies: A Guidebook*, edited by Charles Hatfield and Bart Beaty. Rutgers University Press, 2020, pp. 253–266.

PART II
Readings

CHAPTER 6

Comics and Multimodal Storytelling

Blair Davis

The medium of comics spans numerous centuries, platforms, and modalities. Where they were once found only in printed formats, they now exist on paper and in a variety of digital forms. Where they were once found primarily in newspapers and magazines, now they are also published in the form of comic books, graphic novels, webcomics, digital comics, and variety of other formats. At their core, comics are made up of both words and images, whatever the publishing venue. This very combination of images and words makes comics multimodal; both the printed word and the visual image existed in other media long before comics arose, but the unique combination of words and imagery contained in comics make the medium a unique multimodal experience whether they are read on paper or a screen.

As the publishing industry evolved throughout the nineteenth and twentieth centuries, comics could be found in a growing number of venues. From newspaper strips to pulp magazines to hardcover collections and comic books, readers engaged with the medium of comics in numerous ways, often buying them in numerous formats (such as reprinted collections of popular daily newspaper strips like *Foxy Grandpa*, *The Brownies*, and *Bringing Up Father* in the early decades of the twentieth century, or comic books like *Famous Funnies* and *Popular Comics* that collected numerous such strips beginning in the 1930s). Regardless of the format, the combination of words and images unique to comics saw readers experience a unification of two separate modes of content – navigating the meanings of not only the written words and the drawn images but also what the collective message of both in tandem meant. Simply put, with comics we process the information from the words we read and the images we see, but we construct and reconstruct further meaning from the combination of words and images because of their distinct relationship with one another across panels and pages.

While comics are a static medium, given the fact that the images don't actually move, many creators have either sought to replicate the experience of the moving image through various formal conventions while others have allowed their work to be adapted (or, in more cases than not, their editors or publishers have allowed it) by the film and television industries, allowing for these stories and characters to be represented through new methods of multimedia and multimodal storytelling. As new digital platforms flourished in the late twentieth and early twenty-first centuries, new formats such as webcomics and motion comics added movement to the hybrid of words and images that was once limited to print formats, often with mixed results (especially in the case of the latter, such as the 2008 *Watchmen* motion comic).

Print-based comics, their adaptations, and their new digital counterparts have allowed the comics medium to expand how it uses words and images in tandem with one another to convey information and tell stories. The biggest Hollywood studios, including Disney and Warner Bros., have built franchises around teams of characters like the Avengers and the Justice League, in turn altering the images that comics readers experience when they pick up those characters' print-based adventures. Digital comics have also altered how we can experience the modalities of reading comics, with technologies such as "guided view" and text-to-speech offering new ways of enjoying comic books in ways that printed editions do not offer. The medium of comics has evolved as the technologies used to produce and consume them have changed, but the multimodal nature of reading comics and their unique combination of words and images has endured regardless of how they are made by creators and accessed by fans.

From Print to Celluloid

As a popular artform, comics have thrived for centuries. Political cartooning that satirized various social and governing forces can be traced back to the late eighteenth and early nineteenth century in the work of such artists as James Gillray and George Cruikshank. Newspapers and magazines were their main forums, and while most such instances were single-panel cartoons and not multi-panel strips, these early comics frequently contained complexities in their arrangement of words and images. In many cases, the text appeared within the panels themselves while at other times it was placed along the exterior bottom edge of the panel. Often the figures spoke dialogue housed within word balloons, while sometimes the dialogue emanated from mouths without the structure of a balloon to encase it. In each example, the reader had to navigate between information conveyed through both textual and visual means while negotiating any contradictions (often deliberate and satirical in nature) therein while also navigating the physical confines of the panel's terrain in terms of how words and images are arranged.

When artists like Rodolphe Töpffer began specializing in multi-panel comics by the 1830s, readers further navigated the relationships between multiple panels and the boundaries between them. Töpffer anchored textual captions in separate rectangular boxes beneath each of his panels, while Richard Doyle's multi-panel comics for *Punch* magazine in the mid-1800s also regularly placed captions beneath each image. The latter did not use formal panel borders to separate each image, using instead the negative space of the page to create de facto panel borders. In so doing, the textual captions appear in the blank spaces between the bottom of one panel and the top of another – spaces which we now refer to as part of the gutters of the page.[1] The nineteenth century was a period of regular experimentation for comics creators in terms of how and why stories were told, and the ways in which artists used different conventions to arrange how readers engaged with both text and images was part of that process of exploring new possibilities.

In the final decade of the 1800s, the medium pivoted in response to the trends of industrial modernism and the syndicated distribution of newspaper content across multiple cities and markets. In 1895 (the same year that films began to be screened in public for mass audiences thanks to the Lumière brothers and their Cinematograph in France), the arrival of a character nicknamed "The Yellow Kid" cemented the popularity of color comic strips in the Sunday editions of American newspapers with the debut of Richard F. Outcault's *Hogan's Alley* (1895–1898) in the May 5 edition of *New York World*. Depicting life in a working-class area much like that found within New York's tenement neighborhoods of the period, *Hogan's Alley* starred a young boy named Mickey Dugan (best known as the "The Yellow Kid" for the long yellow shirt he always wore, see Figure 6.1).

Outcault's strip was immensely popular, as were Rudolph Dirks' *The Katzenjammer Kids* in 1897 and Frederick Burr Opper's *Happy Hooligan* in 1900. Their success spawned a wide range of other comic strips in the first few years of the twentieth century, both on Sundays in color and weekdays in black and white (see Harvey; Gordon). Daily strips tended to be more modest in size and scale, typically featuring between four and six panels in

---

[1] For further theoretical explanations and applications of how the gutter function within comics, along with the roles played by other formal conventions of the medium like word balloons, captions, panels, and frames, see McCloud, *Understanding Comics*, Groensteen, *System of Comics* and Postema, *Narrative Structure in Comics*.

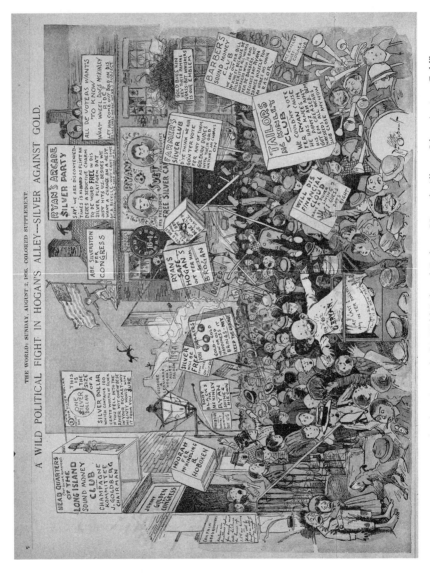

Figure 6.1. Richard F. Outcault, "A Wild Political Fight in Hogan's Alley – Silver Against Gold," *New York World*, 2 August 1896.

an overall rectangular arrangement across part of the page. Sunday strips were usually much more elaborate and ambitious in how they used words and images, thanks not only to color printing but also in how they could encompass the entire dimensions of a whole newspaper page: the 29.5-inch by 23.5-inch dimensions of a Sunday strip on broadsheet newspaper page was inordinately larger than a daily strip (which was often as wide as the page, but only a few inches in height, allowing for multiple strips per page).

In turn, *Hogan's Alley* offered readers a plethora of text embedded both among and within the imagery that made up one giant panel – along with spoken dialogue, we find slogans and messages appearing across billboards, signs and on clothing within the strip's urban environment, and were often to be read in no apparent order, unlike comic strips with several sequential panels or even a progression of text meant to be read from left to right within a single panel. Comics collector and historian Bill Blackbeard noted that "Outcault captioned his cartoons extensively with pronouncements or dialogue by the principals. His drawings are so arresting that we might be inclined to gloss over the captions with their tight, small print and seemingly endless loquaciousness, but they are often amusing in their own right, revealing [a sharp] ear for slang" (Blackbeard 29). Outcault's work compelled the reader to take an even more active role in negotiating how words and images connected on the page than that of most previous comics creators. This shows how comics is an ever-evolving medium. Unlike other media which often replace one format with another (such as the replacement of silent cinema and black and white movies with talkies and Technicolor), comics regularly adds new formats while keeping the old ones active. Comic books did not replace comic strips, just as webcomics did not replace other formats either.

In the first few years of the twentieth century, as newspaper strips boomed in popularity, new creators like Winsor McCay pushed the boundaries of comics' potential for formal and narrative innovation even further. In strips like *Little Sammy Sneeze* (1904–1906), McCay played with how motion and temporality could be represented both within and across panels as he chronicled the destructive capabilities of a young boy's powerful sneezes. In *Dream of the Rarebit Fiend* (1904–1911) and *Little Nemo* (1905–1927), he experimented with how comics could represent the surreal and fantastic worlds of our dreams (see Figure 6.2): from his innovative use of perspective to his creative distortions of figures and objects to the ways in which he turned panel frames into malleable constructs that defied both publishing traditions and the laws of physics within his dream-induced narrative worlds (Bukatman).

Figure 6.2. Winsor McCay, "Little Nemo in Slumberland" *Los Angeles Times*, 29 April 1906.

Comics and Multimodal Storytelling

While McCay's work inspired other creators to attempt similarly playful approaches, only a few comics artists attained lasting success with their deliberately experimental approaches to the medium. Gustave Verbeek had a nine-year run with *The Terrors of the Tiny Tads* from 1905 to 1914, while George Herriman's *Krazy Kat* ran for over three decades between 1913 and Herriman's death in 1944. Increasingly, as newspaper syndicates solidified their comic strip lineups by the 1920s and 1930s, like King Features (*Blondie, Flash Gordon, Popeye*), United Features (*Ella Cinders; L'il Abner, Tarzan*), and McNaught (*Boob McNutt, Dixie Dugan, Joe Palooka*), the needs of narrative seriality and endearing characterization saw more conventional approaches to how creators ordered their words and images within panels, as well as how panels were arranged on the page.

Whereas earlier creators often played with the size and shape of their panels and the imagery within them, panel sizes became more standardized by the 1930s as storytelling often emphasized dramatic realism in keeping with the parallel influence of pulp literature in this era. The emphasis on experimentation in the work of McCay, Verbeek, and Herriman gave way to the fast-paced, ongoing adventures of Harold Gray's *Little Orphan Annie* (1928–2010), Chester Gould's *Dick Tracy* (1931–present) and Milton Caniff's *Terry and the Pirates* (1934–1973), among others. The earliest comic strips of the twentieth century were often in search of their dominant conventions, which in turn saw the techniques of Verbeek and McCay give way to those of Gray, Gould, and Caniff in later decades.

When the comic book publishing format emerged in the mid-1930s with series like *Famous Funnies* (1934–1955) and *Popular Comics* (1936–1948), it began by reprinting newspaper strips. In turn, series which subsequently created new content for their comic books rarely departed from the formal conventions of comic *strips* as far as how text and image were handled within particular panels. Panel borders were typically rigid (lacking the pliability of McCay's work), while captions and word balloons were ordered in a way that prioritized expedience and readability over playfulness and novelty. Some creators, like Will Eisner and Jack Kirby experimented with new approaches in the pages of *The Spirit* (1940–1952) and *The Fantastic Four* (Vol. 1, 1961–1998) – Kirby played with size and scale in his drawings of god-like celestial beings like Galactus (see Hatfield), while Eisner often folded the series' title lettering into the cityscape of the narrative world itself. Other artists like Lily Renée and Alvin Hollingsworth often pushed the limits of how their characters' bodies might be abstracted and distorted, especially within the horror genre in features like "The Werewolf Hunter" and series like *Eerie*.

Towards the end of the twentieth century, creators like Moebius, Chris Ware, and J.H. Williams further tested the multimodal limits of combining text and image in their work, pushing the boundaries of the medium even further with their creative panel arrangements, figure designs, and unconventional storytelling approaches. Whereas comics creators often turned away from the experimentation found in the work of McCay and Herriman as newspaper syndicates and comic book publishers sought to tell new types of stories, there is a noticeable return to trying new visual approaches among many creators in the late twentieth century.

In recent years, comic book adaptations like those of the Marvel Cinematic Universe, have led a whole new generation of media consumers to become fans of comics, often turning to the adventures of their favorite heroes on the page after having seen them on the screen. But the popularity of comic book movies has precursors that date as far back as the dawn of the 1900s when silent films brought the most popular comics characters of the day to theater screens (Davis, *Movie Comics*). Newspaper strips like *The Katzenjammer Kids* (1897–2006), *Happy Hooligan* (1900–1932), *Foxy Grandpa* (1900–1918), and *Buster Brown* (1902–1923) were turned into black and white silent short films – only around one minute in length at first, but often faithfully adapting the premise and basic narrative from particular installments of a certain day's strip that had been published fairly recently.

The first *Happy Hooligan* film from 1900, for instance, adapts an installment of the strip from a few months prior in which Happy attempts to warn an organ grinder who is about to be arrested by a police officer. Both the strip and the film show the organ grinder playing music in the street while a woman in a window grows increasingly upset at the noise. Happy warns the musician and pushes him out of the way as the officer approaches, but when the woman grabs a bucket of water to deter the organ grinder it is the policeman who ends up getting wet instead. Rushing inside to confront the woman, Happy can't believe his luck after he is accused by the officer of being the one creating a disturbance. Both the film and the strip contain the same basic narrative details, but the film lacks the strip's color format, dialogue, and even the diagonal composition which allows readers to see the officer approaching over several panels – creating a sense of expectancy that the film lacks by having the officer enter abruptly from stage-right.

While cinema lacked sound (and, as a result, dialogue and voice-over narration) at first, directors eventually found ways to overcome the inability to record actors speaking, relying on intertitles – passages of text

Comics and Multimodal Storytelling

inserted on title cards between two live-action shots – to allow audiences a variation on the types of textual content found in the captions, word balloons, and onomatopoetic sound effects of comics. Intertitles anchored the surrounding shots with textual information much as a caption within or beneath a comics panel does, providing film viewers with more context to better understand what they are seeing and/or telling us what the characters are saying in similar ways to how comics readers process the information in captions and word balloons. In both cases, the text is separate from the image, but the audience gains a greater understanding of the story's events as a result of both modalities being used in tandem.

Just as comics developed sound effects like "Ka-pow!," "Thwip!," and "Snikt!" to compensate for the medium's lack of sound, so too did cinema develop its own devices to overcome the same limitation in its early years. In adapting McCay's *Dream of the Rarebit Fiend* in 1906, director Edwin S. Porter – now recognized as one of the most talented creators of cinema's earliest era – had to rely on the emergent technologies of the film medium to attempt a faithful recreation of the kinetic, dream-induced fervor regularly found in McCay's work. Whereas McCay could ground his phantasmagorical images with the dialogue of his oft-bewildered characters as they reacted to the unfolding events, Porter's adaptation lacks the ability to add this layer of characterization since cinema lacked sound (and the film also foregoes the emerging practice of intertitles). While many modern film fans might prefer to watch live-action superheroes rather than read their textual source material, the challenges inherent in Porter's adaptation given the technical limitations of filmmaking in this era shows us how in many ways we can see comic strips as the more sophisticated visual medium in the early years of the twentieth century, even though movies and newspaper comic strips share contemporaneous origins circa 1895.

McCay soon became a filmmaker himself, turning both *Little Nemo* and *Dream of the Rarebit Fiend* into animated films between 1911 and 1921 while also creating the influential *Gertie the Dinosaur* (1914). He directed himself in *Winsor McCay: The Famous Cartoonist of the N.Y. Herald and His Moving Comics* (1911), his first film, which combined live-action sequences of McCay at his drawing board with animated segments including characters from *Little Nemo*. In the film's opening, McCay's talents are put to the test: "Winsor McCay agrees to make four thousand pen drawings that will move, one month from date" reads an early intertitle as he makes a bet with a group of men (including fellow cartoonist George McManus) that he can add motion to his drawings. Another intertitle soon reads, "Winsor McCay, at desk, showing four thousand drawings ready for

Vitagraph Company's moving picture camera," as two workers carry in bundles of paper and barrels of ink (labelled "Drawing Paper" and "Ink" in big, black letters for the audience's benefit, reminding them of the material components needed to make comics).

As the group of men gather in McCay's studio to assess his progress, the cartoonist starts up a film projector and his drawings spring into motion: we watch as lines begin to form on a blank page, soon taking the shape of a character named Flip from *Little Nemo*. This animation is then followed by a shot of McCay's hand as he draws the same image in real time, after which we watch as Flip moves before the camera and is joined by two other characters from the strip, Impie and Nemo. Flip and Impie leap, tumble, and then stretch and shrink their bodies to distorted lengths akin to how we might see them in a fun-house mirror, showing off the potential of animated films to allow their characters to move in unnatural ways and assume misshapen forms.

In so doing, McCay's characters bend the laws of physics with their movements on screen in the same way that they regularly do on the page; in both cases, however, they do so in ways that other visual media like photography and live-action cinema cannot achieve naturally. The pen lines which constitute the very basis of the imagery in both comics and animation are inherently prone to approximation instead of verisimilitude. But the visual imagery of both comics and animation are generated by human hands and not the mechanical apparatus of a camera, which begs the question of exactly how many words a hand-drawn picture is worth and what the relationship is between those words and that image when placed together on the page or on screen.

Even though many film fans prefer adaptations of comics to their printed counterparts, Hollywood hasn't always been able to come to terms with the ways in which the comics medium handles abstraction along with its unique combination of words and images. In 1933, Paramount attempted to make a live-action film musical called *Funny Page* in partnership with King Features Syndicate starring several newspaper strip characters (Davis Movie Comics, 26–30). But the project fell apart when they realized the difficulty in bringing characters like Popeye, Blondie, and Dagwood and the Katzenjammer Kids to the screen in live-action form. Popeye's jaw and forearms are unnaturally large, as are the black ovals which constitute Dagwood's eyes, meaning that no actor could embody such roles without some kind of alteration. Make-up effects were deemed insufficient to properly recreate the physical distortions of these popular characters' faces, and rubber masks were tested out but also abandoned.

With both options, the actors would be rendered unrecognizable (a hard sell for audiences and vain movie stars alike). The masks might have allowed actors to more closely resemble the drawn features of the characters in a way that make-up could not, but without the ability to move their mouth it would have been difficult for audiences to know who was speaking. Word balloons – with their textual recreation of speech and their clear demarcation of who is talking thanks to how the tail of the balloon is pointed in the direction of the speaker – solve that problem, while animation can easily make the characters' mouths move.

So, while comics, animation, and live-action cinema each combine the modalities of words and images, each medium has its own limitations when it comes to how it handles those elements. As Christopher Pizzino reminds us, "the reading experience as a whole [with comics] typically has bodily and sensory aspects that are quite distinct, and that are both enabled and demanded by the material and spatial qualities of the medium." He notes, for instance, how "the reading experience could scarcely be more different than that of a printed text" such as a prose novel, "whose spatial arrangements, under the hand and eye of the reader, feel mostly or entirely incidental to the flow of discourse" (19).

From Celluloid to Television to Transmedia Storytelling

The silent film era saw numerous comic strips adapted into movies, from animated shorts based on *Krazy Kat* and *Mutt and Jeff* to feature films like *Tillie the Toiler* (1927), *Harold Teen* (1928), and *Bringing Up Father* (1928). Whereas *Funny Page* never came to be as a star-studded musical in the 1930s, Hollywood did find success in that decade – in which sound filmmaking was now commonplace – by adapting several newspaper strips into lower-budget B-films and chapterplay serials. The aviation-centered strip *Tailspin Tommy* was turned into a pair of serials in 1934 and 1935, with audiences returning to the theater each week for the next installment of the multi-part film. *Dick Tracy* was given his own serial in 1937 followed by three sequels between 1938 and 1941, while other popular strips were the basis for *Ace Drummond* (1936), *Jungle Jim* (1937), *Radio Patrol* (1937), *Secret Agent X-9* (1937), *Tim Tyler's Luck* (1937), *Red Barry* (1938), *Buck Rogers* (1939), and *Mandrake the Magician* (1939). In each case, elaborate make-up effects and rubber masks are nowhere to be seen, with actors like Ralph Byrd and Buster Crabbe embodying characters like Dick Tracy and Buck Rogers with just their costumes and charisma to identify them as their comic strip counterparts. Such films embraced the

Figure 6.3. *Flash Gordon's Trip to Mars* (1938)

limitations of live-action cinema in adapting comics, in other words, forgoing any attempt to give Dick Tracy a literally square jaw, for example, and instead embracing the fact that visual images work inherently differently within the two media.

Crabbe also starred in three *Flash Gordon* serials between 1936 and 1940 in which the title hero battles arch nemesis Ming the Merciless, which were both immensely popular among audiences and highly influential to the development of the science-fiction genre in cinema. The second serial, *Flash Gordon's Trip to Mars* (1938), took a unique approach to replicating its source material as each chapter recaps what came before in the previous installment. While most serials summarize the major plot points with text-based title cards for viewers returning each week for the next chapter, *Flash Gordon's Trip to Mars* does so by having one of Ming's guards view a series of comics panels on a view screen (Figure 6.3). As the guard turns a dial, the panels advance on the guard's screen as the audience is treated to numerous drawn images with textual captions beneath. Here, an active parallel is made between the acts of film spectatorship and the process of reading comics thanks to the literal recreation of comics panels for cinemagoers – an approach that was later taken on occasion in twenty-first-century comic book cinema as well, as we will see.

Similar approaches to using comics panels as chapter serial recaps were used in *Ace Drummond* (1936), although without having a character look at the panels on a screen. Instead, the panels appear to be in a newspaper, with other strips surrounding it (we can see the bottom of a *Jungle Jim* strip above the *Ace Drummond* panels, for example). As the final panel gives us the last of the requisite information about the previous installment of the serial, the image dissolves into a live-action version of the drawn image. Hollywood regularly used advertising rhetoric surrounding how movies allowed readers favorite comics characters to "come to life," with the formal strategy of transitioning from a static comic panel to the live-action equivalent serving as a visceral embodiment of that marketing strategy. One ad for the 1931 film *Skippy* based on Percy Crosby's popular comic strip promised viewers that they would at last meet the character "in person," while another ad for the film shows Skippy bursting through a torn newspaper page, as if he is literally bursting through from the comics page (Davis *Movie Comics*, 17–18).

In the 1940s and 1950s, B-movie adaptations of comic strips continued. Films based on *Blondie* continued a successful run of over two dozen entries between 1938 and 1950, while four feature films based on *Dick Tracy* appeared between 1945 and 1947. There were also numerous B-films based on the western strip *Red Ryder* released between 1944 and 1950 as well as those adapted from the strips, *Joe Palooka* between 1946 and 1951 and *Jungle Jim* between 1948 and 1956. A few superheroes got their own adaptations in live-action serials, including *Adventures of Captain Marvel* (1941), *Batman* (1943), *Captain America* (1944), and *Superman* (1948). The latter resorted to replacing actor Kirk Alyn with an animated doppelganger to make the Man of Steel fly, while in *Captain Marvel* the titular hero took flight thanks to a wooden dummy on a wire. While the artifice of both approaches is readily apparent, numerous fully animated *Superman* short films were made between 1941 and 1943. Initially created by Dave Fleischer (whose Fleischer studios created the popular *Betty Boop* and *Popeye* series of cartoons), the Superman shorts remain beloved by comics fans, once again showing how animation achieved what photorealism could not.

When television made its mainstream debut in the 1940s, it wasn't long before there were programs based on comic strips – many of which had previously been adapted as films. There were television series based on *Blondie* (1957), *Buck Rogers* (1950), *Dennis the Menace* (1959), *Dick Tracy* (1950–1951), *Flash Gordon* (1954), *Joe Palooka* (1954), *Jungle Jim* (1955–1956), *Red Ryder* (1951), *Terry and the Pirates* (1952–1953), and *Steve Canyon* (1958–1959), all of which were half-hour, serialized live-action shows. But before television producers began casting actors in the roles of popular comics characters, some were first transported to the screen in a more literal form. In 1948, a format known as telecomics brought comics to television by using voice actors to read dialogue while the images were shown panel by panel. Eisner's *The Spirit* was featured in this format in 1948 while a series called *Telecomics* used King Features Syndicate strips like *King of the Royal Mounted* in 1949. The latter program was sold to NBC in 1950 and its named changed to NBC Comics, while another station used the comic book *Classics Illustrated* to produce similar telecomics using that series' popular adaptations of famous literary works (Davis *Movie Comics,* 180–181).

Telecomics proved short-lived in the early days of television, but the idea would resurface decades later in the form of "motion comics." But as television programming entered the 1960s, new approaches to adapting comics to the screen emerged. Marvel partnered with Grantray-Lawrence Animation to produce *Marvel Super-Heroes* in 1966, using artwork from actual comics pages to bring viewers the adventures of Captain America, Iron Man, the Hulk, Sub-Mariner, and Thor. Drawings by Jack Kirby, Don Heck, and others that had already been published in various issues of *Avengers, The Incredible Hulk,* and other Marvel series. Movement was added to the artwork to make the characters speak, jump, and fight, while actors added their voices. Like *Telecomics, Marvel Super-Heroes* is an example of what Jay Bolter and Richard Grusin call remediation, whereby the content of one medium is repurposed for use in another medium. Unlike adaptation, which takes a story told in one medium and tells it in another, remediation preserves aspects of the content's modalities as presented in the original medium: much like how cinemagoers engage with the medium of radio when the film's characters listen to an actual radio broadcast, how television programs can be broadcast within movie theaters (i.e., how episodes of the *Adventures of Superman* television show were combined to make various feature films in the 1950s; see Davis, *Battle*) or how the internet can allow us to experience radio and television content in new forms like YouTube, television viewers engage with literal comic book images when watching *Marvel Super-Heroes* and *Telecomics.*

A similar attempt was made to create series around several DC Comics characters like Metamorpho using the artwork of Ramona Fradon, but when DC saw the result they disliked the animation and the project never surfaced (Brunet and Davis 253). Instead, DC allowed Filmation Associates to create *The New Adventures of Superman* and *The Adventures of Superboy* in 1966 using a more traditional approach to animation that did not involve repurposing original artwork from the comics. Marvel did the same with Grantray-Lawrence's animated *Spider-Man* series and Hanna Barbara's *Fantastic Four* in 1967, while DC offered up

The Superman/Aquaman Hour of Adventure in 1967, *The Adventures of Batman* in 1968, and *Super Friends* in 1973. The 1960s and 1970s also saw several live-action television series and specials starring many of the most popular Marvel and DC heroes, including *Batman* (1966–1968), *Shazam!* (1974–1976), *Wonder Woman* (1975–1979), *Spider-Man* (1977–1979), *Captain America* (1979), *Doctor Strange* (1978), and *The Incredible Hulk* (1977–1982).

The serialization involved in how comic books tell stories similarly worked well for television scripts. By the 2000s, the shared narrative universe of Marvel Comics would also be mirrored in the storytelling approach taken in such Netflix series as *Daredevil* (2015–2018), *Jessica Jones* (2015–2019), *Luke Cage* (2016–2018), *Iron Fist* (2017–2018), and *The Defenders* (2017), while DC did the same with such series as *Arrow* (2012–2020), *The Flash* (2014–), *Supergirl* (2015–2021), *Black Lightning* (2017–2021), and *DC's Legends of Tomorrow* (2016–). Such shows use the model of "complex" storytelling practices described by Jason Mittell in *Complex TV: The Poetics of Contemporary Television Storytelling*, whereby there is often a blurring of the "lines between episodic and serialized narratives" (2).

In producing numerous animated and live-action versions of their characters, publishers tacitly alter how viewers engage with their printed counterparts. Whether new readers or returning ones, the experience of seeing a hero's adventures on screen changes – consciously or not – how we understand the drawn, static form of that character's image. The animated or live-action image of that character informs how we interpret the drawn version, much as our memories of being with a loved one in person informs how we process their image in a photograph or how standing before a famous work of art in a museum fundamentally alters how we later engage with mediated representations of that same artwork.

Accordingly, comic book cinema reached a turning point in 1978 with the release of Richard Donner's *Superman*. As the first big-budget superhero film ever produced, *Superman*'s special effects delivered on the promise of its advertising pitch that audiences would believe that a man could fly – a tacit acknowledgment from Hollywood that its previous incarnations of flying superheroes were less than convincing given how they were made on limited budgets. While few comic book movies from the 1980s and 1990s are as influential as Donner's *Superman* with the exception of Tim Burton's *Batman* (1989), neither of those films attempted any kind of remediative approaches in how they brought their source material to the screen. Some directors, however, evoked the medium in very direct ways. George Romero used animation in *Creepshow* (1982) to suggest that the film's sequences were taken from the actual panels of a comic book in the EC tradition, zooming out from the page to show the issue lying discarded in the street. Ang Lee went a step further in *Hulk* (2003), layering multiple frames across the screen at once to suggest the presence of comics panels – evoking the medium much like *Flash Gordon's Trip to Mars* did decades earlier. Given how Romero and Lee are both considered to be preeminent, auteur directors, such creative approaches to comic book cinema should be celebrated and perhaps emulated more often.

While Marvel does not use remediative visual strategies in their MCU oeuvre, the opening credits of their movies do feature the Marvel logo in the form of panels being flipped, briefly paying tribute to the page-based origins of such films. Instead of using strategies of remediation in their films, Marvel embraced transmedia storytelling instead – extending their narratives across multiple media platforms such as Disney+ shows like *WandaVision* and *Loki* as well as tie-in comic books. Since 2008, Marvel has published various single-issue and limited series comics that serve as preludes to the stories in recent or upcoming films, such as *Captain America: First Vengeance* (2011), *Marvel's Guardians of the Galaxy Prelude* (2014), and *Marvel's Infinity War Prelude* (2018). Such comics explore the narrative world of the films further, foreshadow certain plot points, and expand further on various subplots as way of allowing fans of the films to extend their engagement with the cinematic narratives further across multiple media platforms.

Conclusion: Motion Comics and Beyond

Marvel and DC also dabbled in the briefly popular phenomenon of motion comics in the early 2000s, which offers a hybrid experience of reading and viewing a comic book much like *Telecomics* did in earlier decades. Motion comics use the pages and panels of actual comic books to create a hybrid of animated and static imagery, while voice actors once again replace word balloons and captions. The result is what comics scholar Drew Morton calls "the suggestion of movement (through zooms, pans and tilts, and montage) rather than smooth and fully rendered character metamorphosis" (132). While motion comics based on such series as *Astonishing X-Men*, *Black Panther*, and *Watchmen* proved popular in the first decade of the twenty-first century, with the latter even airing on television when the 2009 film adaptation was released, the format proved to be more of a fad than a lasting addition to the variety of formats in which comics fans engage with the medium's various hybrids of words and images.

Despite the demise of motion comics, comics continue to flourish in a variety of new formats. As Andrew Aydin notes in his graphic novel *Run: Book One* about the life of John Lewis, comics storytelling involves "both the narrative *and* the visual, blending the two in a hopefully successful marriage that builds understanding that neither element could create alone" (129) – a process that occurs for comics readers regardless of where, how, and in what format one accesses them.

Whether paper or pixel-based, the medium's unique combinations of text and pictures produces an end result for the reader that creates a greater meaning because of how each mode is used in tandem. Digital versions of comics continue to grow in popularity on such services as ComiXology and Marvel Unlimited, while webcomics have allowed a new generation of creators like Kate Beaton (*Hark! A Vagrant*) and Mike Krahulik and Jerry Holkins (*Penny Arcade*) to gain widespread readership. Webcomics began as a format that was housed on individual websites, but soon gained wider distribution via social media platforms such as Twitter and Instagram. These new forms of circulation are a reminder that comics are not bound to the printed page from which they emerged centuries ago. But at the same time, the modalities of words and visual images have remained at the core of the medium regardless of the platform through which readers engage with comics.

WORKS CITED

Comics

Lewis, John, Aydin, Andrew, Fury, L., and Nate Powell. *Run: Book One*. Abrams Comicarts, 2021.
McCay, Winsor. "Little Nemo in Slumberland" *Los Angeles Times*, 29 April 1906.
Richard F. Outcault, "A Wild Political Fight in Hogan's Alley – Silver Against Gold" *New York World*, 2 August 1896.

Secondary Sources

Blackbeard, Bill. "The Yellow Kid, the Yellow Decade." *R.F. Outcault's The Yellow Kid: A Centennial Celebration of the Kid Who Started the Comics*. Kitchen Sink Press, 1995, pp. 16–136.
Bolter, Jay David and Richard A. Grusin. *Remediation: Understanding New Media*. MIT Press, 2000.

Brunet, Peyton and Blair Davis. *Comic Book Women: Characters, Creators and Culture in the Golden Age*. University of Texas Press, 2022.

Bukatman, Scott. *The Poetics of Slumberland: Animated Spirits and the Animating Spirit*. University of California Press, 2012.

Davis, Blair. *The Battle for the Bs: 1950s Hollywood and the Rebirth of Low-Budget Cinema*. Rutgers University Press, 2012.

Movie Comics: Page to Screen/Screen to Page. Rutgers University Press, 2017.

Hatfield, Charles. *Hand of Fire: The Comics Art of Jack Kirby*. University Press of Mississippi, 2011.

Harvey, Robert C. *Children of the Yellow Kid: The Evolution of the American Comic Strip*. Frye Art Museum, 1998.

Gordon, Ian. *Comic Strips and Consumer Culture, 1890–1945*. Smithsonian Institution Press, 1998.

Groensteen, Thierry. *The System of Comics*. Translated by Bart Beaty and Nick Nguyen. University Press of Mississippi, 2007.

McCloud, Scott. *Understanding Comics: The Invisible Art*. HarperCollins, 1993.

Mittell, Jason. *Complex TV: The Poetics of Contemporary Television Storytelling*. New York University Press, 2015.

Morton, Drew. "'Watched Any Good Books Lately?': The Formal Failure of the Watchmen Motion Comic." *Cinema Journal*, vol. 56, no. 2, 2017, pp. 132–137.

Pizzino, Christopher, "On Violation: Comic Books, Delinquency, Phenomenology." *Critical Directions in Comics Studies*, edited by Thomas Giddens. University of Mississippi Press, 2020, pp. 13–34.

Postema, Barbara. *Narrative Structure in Comics: Making Sense of Fragments*. RIT Press, 2013.

CHAPTER 7

Comics Adaptations
Fidelity and Creativity

Jan Baetens

Comics and Literature: A Difficult Match

It may come as a surprise that, in comparison to cinema, for instance, so few comics and graphic novels are based on literary source texts.[1] Even if their number is now rapidly growing, the absolute numbers of literary comics adaptations remain relatively low. In addition, this type of adaptation is more often seen as a problem than as an opportunity, in spite of some major achievements as well as the growing acceptance of the graphic novel as a new literary genre (Baetens and Frey). This chapter aims at giving an overview of this difficult encounter between comics and literature, while trying to bypass the traditional barrier of the fidelity issue, generally used as a scarecrow to discourage authors to risk a literary adaptation in comics form. Instead of taking fidelity in the traditional sense of the word and thus repeatedly asking whether the adapting comic succeeds in faithfully reproducing the characteristics and qualities of the adapted literary text, the following pages will address fidelity from a different point of view, not as an obstacle or a sword of Damocles but as a possible springboard for new and creative reinterpretations that do not solve the fidelity problem by simply throwing it out of the window but by trying to find new solutions (Baetens "Comics and Literature"; *Adaptation*).

---

[1] To avoid any confusion: this chapter will not address two types of comics, however deeply rooted in literary culture, that are not really adaptations in the real sense of the word. First, the nonfictional genre of the *biopic* (comics on authors, see, for instance, on Joyce as seen through his daughter's eyes, the graphic novel by Mary M. Talbot and Brian Talbot, *Dotter of Her Father's Eyes*, London: Cape, 2012), and second, the fictional genre of what would be the comics equivalent of the *Hollywood novel*, namely, fictional stories situated in the professional environment of writing and the publishing industry (see, for instance, on the "lost generation" in Paris, work by Jason, *The Left Bank Gang*, Seattle: Fantagraphics, 2001). Similarly, we will also not include discussions on the adaptation of poetry, which raises different questions.

143

For many decades, comics have been considered the absolute opposite of "real" literature. The antagonism between words and images, high and low, culture and commerce, adult and child or adolescent, willing suspension of disbelief and unresisting surrender to manipulation, was nearly complete and creative interaction between both extremes of the cultural spectrum close to inexistent.[2] The only way to mix comics with literature – but not the other way round! – was to take benefit of the former's appeal to young audiences in order to prepare for the reading of the latter. As we all know, this was the explicit didactic program behind the infamous "Classics Illustrated" series (first run 1941–1969, with nearly 170 issues), the comics version of the bowdlerization of literature. "Classics Illustrated" may be the series we love to hate, but its long-standing success and the creative impulse it has given to many would-be authors[3] should not obnubilate the existence of other, properly literary but more experimental adaptations in more respected venues than comic books, catering to other reader groups with the help of other formulas, such as the astonishing one-page comics book reviews in general magazines, rediscovered by Chris Ware in his guest-edited issue of McSweeneys (Ware 2014).

Experiments of this kind, however, remained marginal and one will have to wait for the graphic novel movement, starting in the late 1980s and setting itself through as a real new strand in comics in less than one decade, to notice a more open attitude toward literary adaptations. Yet even then, adaptation is far from being center stage. Rather than trying to build cultural capital by borrowing from literature with a capital L, the graphic novel, in the US and elsewhere the heir of the countercultural comix, explores the untapped possibilities of the comics medium by investing genres that had hardly been present in mainstream production. No super-heroes, SF, crime fiction, horror, romance, adventure strips, and the like, but autobiography, semi-autobiography (autofiction), biography, history, and journalism – typically literary genres, but not genres that at the start of comix and graphic novel movement were judged essential to literature, a concept still strongly associated with or reduced to fiction, more

---

[2] One can only notice here the more relaxed approach of scholars and researchers in book history (including library history and bookshop history), a discipline that often devotes much time and space to this special type of word and image publication (Nixon).

[3] An astounding example is described in Jerome Charyn's *The Man Who Grew Younger* (1963), where the narrator's brother, a wild and undisciplined boy, almost a juvenile delinquent, spending more time in the streets than in school, seriously tries to invent his own comics superhero strip by finding his inspiration in the first "Classic Comics presents" series, the original name of "Classics Illustrated." Among the titles mentioned by Charyn are *Ivanhoe* and *The Three Musketeers*.

specifically "literary" fiction, that is "nongenre" fiction (on the importance of the "brows" in comics studies, see Pizzino).

Literature, in other words, is definitely a feature of the graphic novel, as demonstrated by the emphasis on first- or third-person voices in storytelling, the suspicion of any seamless combination of words and images, the preferences of unconventional plotting, the play with conflicting perspectives, the progressive shift from magazine to book publication and the adoption of typically bookish and literary techniques and mechanisms such as the chapter structure of long narratives, which contrasts starkly with the daily or weekly installment structure of long-running comics series (Dürrenmatt). Yet all this is not literary adaptation. Besides, literary authors working as graphic novelists preferred the writing of *original* stories, although with a strong literary intertext. In the anglophone context, Neil Gaiman's *The Sandman* is a good example, in the French production one might think of the work by novelist and scriptwriter Benoît Peeters in his collaboration with comics artist François Schuiten in the *Obscure Cities* [*Cités Obscures*] series (Baetens *Rebuilding*). It will take more time and perhaps a sharper awareness, thanks to a better circulation of works originally made in lesser-known languages in the now strongly globalized comics market,[4] to make room for literary adaptations.

Some Roadblocks and a Turning Point?

There are many reasons, next to the more anecdotal explanation of the poor quality of some of the most commercial and definitely low-brow productions, to explain this reluctance toward the use of existing literary texts as source material for comics adaptations. The most general one is of course the *misology* that has accompanied the visual turn as one of its unspoken shadows. The shift from a text-oriented to an image-oriented culture, which does not necessarily involve the disappearance or downsizing of the presence of words (it suffices to think of the spectacular return of orality in digital poetry, if not in digital culture in general), has gone hand in hand with an increasing suspicion of all things verbal or linguistic. For many creators in the field of visual narrative, to rely upon a work of literature seems to jeopardize the autonomy and thus creativity of the

---

[4] Translation, however, remains a very unequally organized business, which probably explains the absence of a pioneering author such as the Uruguayan-Argentinean author Alberto Breccia (1919–1993) on the English market. Well translated in French, Breccia is often considered the ultimate reference as far as literary adaptations are concerned, with seminal work on Poe and Lovecraft, among others.

image, eventually imprisoning all forms of visual thinking to a kind of visual rhetoric (Baetens "Visual Rhetoric"), that is, to an ancillary use of the image which remains at the service of the word. Moreover, and this is an important difference with cinema (Murray; Gelder), there does not seem to be an added commercial value in the use of highly prestigious literary sources: today, ambitious literary adaptations are more a niche product, uninteresting for the larger market that has turned to other types of adaptations.

A second reason for the unwillingness to tap into the literary heritage or even the more contemporary production has to do with the social and cultural desire of distinction. Graphic novels – the situation of mass-market is not comparable in this regard – are extremely cautious to avoid confusion with two well-established genres that in spite of their visually rich and intellectually challenging successes continue to fall prey to the already mentioned danger of visual rhetoric: *illustration* on the one hand, the *picture book* on the other hand (Nikolajeva and Scott). In their best cases, both practices establish fascinating protocols to strike the right balance between showing and telling, but even when their showing is much more or even completely something else than the mere visualization or transposition of their telling, there still is the fear that the underlying textual model might disrupt the desired equality between text and image and thus jeopardize the relative independence of the combined media. Frequent examples of this are Robert Crumb's *Genesis* (2009), a rather literal book-length adaptation of the biblical source text, and the three-volume anthology edited by Russ Kick, *The Graphic Canon*, two projects that are clearly closer to the model of illustration than to that of truly creative visual narrative. Their problem is not fidelity – as we will see, faithful adaptations can prove highly creative – but their turning away from the proper narrative possibilities of comics in favor of the more traditional regime of illustration. The attempt to shift from image to narrative is not always there, and to a certain extent similar remarks might apply to the equally renowned Proust adaptation by Stéphane Heuet, whose drawings are now also exhibited and reprinted in special portfolios as individual drawings, explicitly labeled as "illustrations" in a French art gallery ("Proust Art"[5]).

A third but certainly not final reason is the changes in the social and creative profile and status of the comics artist, who tries to escape the restrictions of the traditional production line of the Taylorized studio work, characterized by a strong labor division and the difficulty for visual

---

[5] https://proust.art/fr/

artists to participate in the creative labor of script writing.[6] The desire to break free from the limitations of the studio context has pushed many visual artists either to become their own scriptwriter or to shy away, in the cases when they continue to collaborate with a writer, from the model of the literary adaptation, which would further strengthen the no-longer-accepted tutelage of the word. The long-standing institution of wordless comics and graphic novels (Beronå) testifies to the strategic and symbolic relevance of elaborating new work outside the boundaries of the verbal and literary markers.

Today things have changed a lot, however, and the recent (small) hype of literary adaptations in a comics country such as France is an important symptom in this regard. Ever since the fast-growing acceptation of comics and graphic storytelling in the cultural field, one notices that the comics artists themselves have adopted a more easy-going attitude toward literature. To adapt is now no longer seen as a genuflection to a more prestigious ancestor, but as proof of a newly established comradeship. This situation is not without irony, though, for at the moment when the world of comics is now establishing a less complex relationship with the traditional center of high culture, namely, literature, it is literature itself that is no longer capable of keeping up appearances and maintaining its centrality in the larger cultural field.[7]

The most important factor of change is, however, the new vision of adaptation that is now replacing the old-fashioned antagonism between fidelity and creativity, the former threatening the use of literary models given the danger of reducing adaptation to illustration, the latter even more aversive to literary source texts which are seen as an obstacle to the development of personal storytelling. (It is well known that autobiography and semi-autobiography or autofiction are among the genres that have most spectacularly benefited from the shift from comics to graphic novels.) Today, these views on adaptation no longer hold, not only for commercial reasons (as powerfully shown by Murray and Gelder, fidelity as well as literature are indispensable players in the modern adaptation game), but also for purely artistic and creative reasons.

---

[6] For an interesting exception to this rule, see the work of Jack Kirby as analyzed in Hatfield (2011), who convincingly shows the limits of all binary thinking that opposes the idea of mass production and originality.

[7] Bob Dylan's Nobel Prize, certainly a well-deserved tribute, reflects the shifting power relations between the arts, and what is important to notice is perhaps less the choice of the artist than the relative lack of importance of the Nobel Prize for literature in this case: Dylan didn't need it and it will not change the way his work will be remembered.

On the one hand, adaptation is now seen as an inherently interpretive gesture, which means that even adaptations aiming at complete fidelity inevitably offer a new vision of the adapted work (Hutcheon and O'Flynn; Cléder and Jullier; Boillat and Philippe). On the other hand, the very notion of fidelity is no longer a synonym for slavish interpretation and thus an inevitable lack of creativity, but as a challenge that makes room for new types of creativity (as can be seen for instance in the special subgenre of comics adaptations that maintain the integral version of the original version, taking the risk to be misjudged as comics "illustrations" rather than as comics "creations"[8]). To be faithful is far from being simple. It is instead the freedom one takes toward the original that is in many cases too easy and too lazy a solution, while the process of trying to faithfully adapt may be a good example of so-called constrained or conceptual, that is, rule-based creativity; this is a key issue and procedure in all forms of contemporary cultural production which has radically dismantled the age-old conflict between "creative" and "uncreative" ways of writing (Perloff; Goldsmith).

Literary Texts: The Words and the Rest

If one agrees that fidelity concerns are perfectly companionable with the creative impulse of constraint-based production[9], the first thing to do is to examine what exactly is the object of the adaptive process. Literary works are no monoliths but mosaics of elements of very different nature and status and according to the type of item or aspect that is adapted, the work will inevitably raise very different questions. Yet before entering into some detail and giving some examples, it is equally necessary to make three preliminary observations.

First of all, it should be noted that a literary text, even when exclusively made of words, that is without illustrations, is in quite some cases already an intermedial object, not only because words themselves are intermedial objects (Mitchell; Baetens and Sánchez-Mesa), but also because they have already been adapted or are part of a larger network where words and

---

[8] A good example would be the work by Dutch comics artist Dick Matena, who has followed this policy in his adaptation of several classics of Dutch and Flemish literature.

[9] In modern literature, constraint-based writing, which replaces the idea of "inspiration" by the use of preconstructed formal rules, is best illustrated by the Oulipo group (originally French, but nowadays with important worldwide connections). Within Oulipo, there exists a branch of constrained comics production called "Oubapo" ("ouvroir de bande dessinée potentielle" or *workshop for potential comics*), best illustrated in the US by the work of Matt Madden.

images intermingle. In other words: at the moment of deciding to make a comics adaptation, the visual artist will have to establish a dialogue with the existing visual intertext of the text under scrutiny.

Here are some typical examples, from various types of adaptation ranging from the traditional to the decidedly experimental. A huge crowd-pleaser, the mainstream Proust adaptation by Stéphane Heuet (2001–2007) has been violently attacked by the scholarly audience for proposing a bowdlerized version of *Remembrance of Things Past* (originally published 1913–1927).

Critical voices mainly highlighted the mismatch with the selected drawing style. Instead of borrowing his inspiration from the late Claude Monet, whose *Water Lilies* series were the implicit model of Proust's fictional ideal painter, Elstir, Heuet chose to work in an elementary clear line style, close to Tintin but light-years away from Monet's post-impressionism (as Heuet's series evolves, he will, however, adopt a more historically "faithful" style).

Dispossession (2015), Simon Grennan's adaptation of one of the later novels by Anthony Trollope, *John Caldigate* (1879), is a good mix of old and new in the domain of comics adaptation. The aim of the work is to present Trollope's work, scorned today as a little old-fashioned, to a modern audience via an adaptation that rejuvenates the novel while sticking as closely as possible to the original. The chosen drawing style reflects this strategy, since it combines increased expressionism with a critical but immediately recognizable dialogue with Trollope's illustrators, some of them very prestigious such as John Everett Millais. An even more complex case is represented by the adaptation of Kafka's unfinished novel *The Castle* (1926) by Belgian woodcut artist Olivier Deprez (2019), who also succeeded in seamlessly bringing together tradition and invention (Figure 7.1): his own experimental style, permanently oscillating between figuration and abstraction, proves capable of integrating two different visual models – on the one hand the expressionist drawings of Kafka himself, who used to make symbolically charged sketches in the margins of his manuscripts, drawings that eventually became famous thanks to their frequent use as cover illustrations; on the other hand the tradition of the wordless Masereel-like woodcut graphic novels, which emerged during the last decade of Kafka's life and whose "primitivist" style has become the standard for most narrative woodcuts ever since.

A second general observation has to do with another inherent duplicity of the literary text. Even if the work has no direct intermedial counterpart, it always contains at least two different types of elements: those that can

Figure 7.1. Olivier Deprez, *Le Château d'après Kafka* (*The Castle, after Kafka*) (FRMK, 2019), double spread, n. pag. Courtesy of Olivier Deprez, © Olivier Deprez & FRMK, 2003

materially be observed in the text (things such as the number of words, the chapter division, the use of metaphors, or the description of the characters) and those that have to be inferred from the reading. Genre is a good point in case: all texts have genre markers, weak or strong, but even when the

Figure 7.1. (*cont.*)

author or the publisher gives explicit genre indications (this is a spy novel, this is a romance, etc.), readers still have the possibility to make different readings (in a spy novel one can prioritize the romance elements, or vice versa). Literary works do not always include a user's manual. This fundamental openness applies to many aspects of a novel, such as its mood (some readers will judge "sad" a work that others will experience as "ironic;" its irony can be seen as either "mild" or "biting," etc.) or its rhythm (the readerly experience of rhythm is one of the most subjective dimensions of reading, but it plays a key role in the adaptive process; although the readerly experience of narrative rhythm remains partially subjective, the shift from a "fast-paced" original to a "slow-paced" adaptation or vice versa is generally experienced as disturbing and most adaptations try to be faithful in this regard, even if in other regards they abandon any kind of fidelity policy).

A good example of the "dark side" of a literary text and the threats and opportunities it can generate for a comics adaptation can be found in Martin Vaughn-James's 1975 *The Cage*, a fascinating and unfortunately less-known forerunner of the graphic novel movement. This two hundred-page black and white album with no human characters does not refer to specific literary texts. Yet, it is a very faithful adaptation of the "spirit" of the French New Novel and its attempt to establish new forms of storytelling that can do without the "outdated" concepts of character, plot, psychology, and message (Robbe-Grillet). The "narrative" of these works is that of the permanent change of forms and figures morphing into other forms and figures in ways that are simultaneously surprising and perfectly understandable.

Third, it cannot be denied that most discussions on comics adaptations of literary works are heavily biased by the corpus they choose to study. Granted, most of these adaptations revisit the same canonical masterpieces, over and over again (Austen, Dickens, Melville, Carroll, Wilde, to name some of the usual suspects), and this restriction has of course a strong impact on how adaptation is understood, namely, as a two-stage rocket with first the narrative transformation of the literary story into a new plot and second the visual transformation of the script into the language of comics. Interesting as these adaptations may be, they do not cover the whole field. We will therefore turn to a few other examples and conclude this chapter with a very unconventional case.

Some Aspects of Fidelity in Adaption

Roughly speaking, and readers may recognize in what follows a variation on Brian McFarlane's fundamental opposition between "transfer" and "adaptation proper," one could start from the following grid: 1) elements or aspects of the original text that can respectfully be transposed (and this faithful transfer can of course involve a great deal of creativity), 2) elements or aspects that have to be modified (but this modification does never mean that it cannot be done in a faithful manner), and 3) elements that are not present in the source text, but that are added in the adaptive process (a historical reading of adaptation informs us that in certain cases this artistic license is even seen as the *conditio sine qua non* of fidelity[10]). But let's put some meat on these bones and give some examples, which will immediately show the tight interaction between the various types.

Type 1: *elements that can be adapted.* It is commonly accepted that plots as well as actual words can more or less easily be transferred from novels to comics. Yet in most cases, comics artists still have to face the thorny issue of word count. Many novels have a number of words that is simply too large to be directly transposed (unless of course the publisher allows for the complete reuse of the original text, which is perfectly thinkable but in practice quite rare and by the way not always very satisfactory, since it increases the danger of reducing the images to mere illustrations of the words). Hence the necessity of cutting down the source material. This reduction is not always a treachery, as shown by the already mentioned Trollope adaptation by Simon Grennan (Figure 7.2). Provocatively subtitled "A novel of few words," this comics version of the extremely lengthy *John Caldigate*, a typical Victorian three-decker, does not only succeed in offering the "essence" of the novel's multiple plot lines, leaving aside a great number of elements and adopting a rather elliptical style of visual storytelling, thus bringing to the fore the "showing" rather than the "telling," it also manages to install a new rhythm that smartly transfers the fundamental quality of Trollope's art as a novelist, namely, "equality," that is the identical treatment of all elements of the fictional world and the pursuit of a narrative rhythm without slowing down or speeding up. This equality is achieved through the combination of a twofold technique: on the one hand, the perfect coincidence of each page with a story unit (without relying on the traditional installment technique of nineteenth-century serialization, the plot is neatly divided in independent segments, each of them occupying exactly one page), on the other hand the systematic use of a special rhythm at page layout level (the 3 × 2 grid of the book evolves according to the rhythmic pulse of a waltz, page after page). By doing so, Grennan transposes a verbal feature (continuous plot rhythm, equality

---

[10] The key document in this regard is the polemical debate launched by New Wave critic and later director François Truffaut against traditional methods of literary movie adaptation, which strongly emphasized the necessity of "inventing" new scenes in order to faithfully reproduce something that would otherwise remain nonadapted.

Figure 7.2. Simon Grennan, *Dispossession* (Jonathan Cape, 2015), p. 18.
Courtesy of Simon Grennan, © Simon Grennan & J. Cape

Comics Adaptations: Fidelity and Creativity

of word count on the page) in a way that is both extremely creative and perfectly faithful to Trollope's storytelling techniques.

Type 2: *elements that have to be changed.* As already seen in the Grennan example, it would not be wise to separate the various types of elements that are part of the adaptive process. *Dispossession* offers a singular treatment of length, rhythm, and word count – all elements that can (theoretically speaking) be transferred from novel to comics – but it does so by linking this work with a special treatment of its page layout, an aspect that inevitably changes in the transposition of a novel to comics (the page grid of a comic can never be the mechanical transposition of the printed surface of a page). Analogous mechanisms are at play in comics that strongly focus on the issue of page layout: their work is at its best when they succeed in drawing connections with other dimensions of the novel.

An interesting example of this policy is given by the comics adaptation of Paul Auster's *City of Glass* (1991), the first book of his New York Trilogy. Coauthored by Paul Karasik (script) and David Mazzuchelli (drawings), this adaptation powerfully relies on the use of medium-specific comics features, such as the systematic use of a regular 3 × 3 grid. Karasik and Mazzucchelli manage to showcase a large number of formal variations on this basic component, while progressively disclosing its manifold thematic and symbolic layers. As explained by David Coughan, this grid does not only refer to the novel's setting (New York; symbolically the Tower of Babel), it also gains a metafictional dimension. Quinn, the protagonist of Auster's novel, is in search of the prelapsarian language and since the book as well as the comics adaptation is always looking for the best way to translate words into images, the methodical use of the grid can be seen as a quest for the prelapsarian form of comics language. Quoting from the introduction by Art Spiegelman, the coeditor of the "Neon-Lit" series where the book first appeared, Coughan argues:

> If Karasik and Mazzucchelli are presenting their *City of Glass* as words turned into images, but images objectified, mattering, then perhaps it is possible that Quinn finds the prelapsarian tongue, a language of signs, not in *City of Glass,* but more truly in *City of Glass: The Graphic Novel.* Perhaps this is what Spiegelman means when he says, "By insisting on a strict, regular grid of panels, Karasik located the Ur-language of Comics: the grid as window, as prison door, as city block, as tic-tac-toe board" (iii). (845)

An analogous case can be made for the treatment of time in Grennan's *Dispossession,* also open to this kind of metafictional interpretation. In this book, the focus on the page, as material unit dividing the plot into semi-autonomous units, and the subsequent focus on the Waltz-like arrangement of the grid, which invites the reader to exceed the merely linear succession of the panels in order to grasp the global organization of the page, display the medium-specific interweaving of time and space at the level of the reading of comics; the sequential structure of the images (which we read panel after panel, row after row) is always mixed with the so-called tabular association of the same images in a larger visual composition (we normally start reading at the bottom right of the page, then scan the page as a whole and eventually resume linear reading top left).

Type 3: *elements that are added*. Readers will immediately think here of color, and they are right, provided they realize that black and white is no less a color, very different from the black and white balance of the printed text of a page, and that this addition of color as a medium-specific layer should always be addressed in relationship with other layers and aspects of the work. Thus color in *Dispossession* is more than just a chromatic enhancement of the internal organization of the page: it is a key factor in the acknowledgment of the mutual relationships between the six panels of the average page, which may go unnoticed without the help of this anything but "decorative" feature.

Given the many differences between words and images, most comics elements belong to this third type, rather than to the first two. However, the traditional impact of plot and story, the logical consequence of the almost exclusive interest in comics adaptations of nineteenth-century novels, often leads to an underestimation of the importance of these medium-specific elements. The strengths and weaknesses of an adaptation do not depend on the more or less clever adaptation of story and plot; they are instead deeply dependent on the ability of the artist to answer questions such as: How do I draw a character that is not described in the novel? How do I translate the difference between the various ways in which the novel frames a dialogue, for instance, by distinguishing between "X, she says" and "X, she whispers"? Some comics authors decide, for instance, to "displace" this verbal information from the face to the hands (Baetens *Adaptation*, 71–85, for the case of Jacques Tardi).

The most salient intervention as addition is of course the introduction of an implicit or explicit author's comment on the source material, which is generally explained by the temporal as well as ideological gap between the original literary work and the adapted comics. What matters here, is that these interventions are often justified in the name of... fidelity: what the authors of the new version try to bring to the fore is not necessarily a "counter"-reading, but a more complete and authentic reading.

In the case of Cham's 1863 comics serialized reinterpretation of Victor Hugo's 1862 blockbuster *Les Misérables*, entitled "*Les Misérables* by Victor Hugo. Read, meditated, commented and illustrated by Cham" (for a modern reprint, see Kunzle 481–523), the satirical intention is crystal-clear with, for instance, author's messages hinting at plagiarism and frequently poking fun at the oversentimental treatment of the social drama. In *Dispossession*, however, the creative intervention is much more subtle and multilayered. By inserting a totally new and well-developed postcolonial subplot, including the use of aboriginal language, in a book of "few words," the author does not file an ideological lawsuit against Trollope's "white supremacy," but shows instead how a novel such as *John Caldigate* proves capable of producing multiple and noncanonical readings.

World Literary Heritage and Post-Comics: Watt

Experimental comics are anything but new, but the rise of the graphic novel has allowed the growth of a now well-published phenomenon: *abstract comics* (Molotiu). Abstraction, which refers here to the non-figurative aspects of its drawings, is not incompatible with a strong rhythmic and thus narrative dimension (Baetens, "Abstraction"). Literature is undoubtedly an essential partner in the broader context of what others are now calling *post-comics*, a field that comprises abstract comics but aims more generally at dismantling all traditional dichotomies between word and image in sequential narrative (Conard, *Post-Comics*). To illustrate some of the possibilities of such a post-comics treatment of literature with a type of work hardly taken into account in the debates on literary adaptations in comics, we will end this chapter with a short presentation of *fo(u)r watt*, Sébastien Conard's version of Samuel Beckett's 1953 novel *Watt*.

Let us start with how the artist confronts the source material. Like all those having to work with literary material of some length, Conard addresses the issue of textual contraction and he does so in a radical way. Rather than trying to summarize Beckett's plot, he shrinks the 250 pages of the novel to four brief quotes, all capable of being read as statements on the role of time and space in art. After this sweeping distillation, Conard also abolishes the difference between text and paratext (Genette). Two of the four quotes appear in the middle of the book (i.e., as "text"), whereas two others function as opening and closing epigraphs (i.e., as "paratext"). This maneuver draws attention to the spatiality of the text, more precisely to the fact that the text's emplacement is part of its meaning and that this place is not only a matter of sequential arrangement (what comes first, what comes next, etc.), but also of its spatial relationship to the book as an object. In *fo(u)r watt*, the work is not what one finds "between two covers," it is an object that merges text and paratext in one single material composition, with no distinction between pages and covers. The title already announces this fusion, since it is at the same time a fragment of one of the quotes ("for watt's sense of chronology was strong, in a way, and his dislike of battology was very strong"), a possible dedication (this book is "for Watt"), and a verbally modified title that becomes both a question ("what for?") and an indication of how to read ("please pay attention to the rule of four"). Moreover, the title on the front cover is repeated in mirror writing on the back cover, which adds a strong temporal dimension to the key feature of space: by asking the reader to read from right to left, Conard emphasizes the notion of orientation, which strongly combines space and time, not only in general but always in relationship with the host medium of the work.

The initial treatment of Beckett's novel goes thus in two directions: on the one hand a drastic reduction, on the other hand the introduction of new features that aim at giving keys on how to start reading the work. In this regard, the foregrounding of "four" highlights the interaction between four possible aspects of the page: left page and right page (the spatial double spread) are combined with the two sides of the double-sided page (the temporal dimension of turning the pages). At the same time, this framework allows to see the birth of the image in a post-comics adaptation. Instead of only illustrating Beckett's novel (for it remains possible, in spite of the work's minimalism, to "recognize" some of the successive settings of Watt's adventures), Conard proposes a visual interpretation of the general aspects and categories of his initial contraction and introduces a set of basic components (dots, lines, chromatic fields, each of which allows for abstract and figurative readings) and then builds a sequence that can also be read in either figurative or abstract ways. Such an approach is an extremely creative variation on what is often considered a default option of experimental narrative, namely, *database narrative*, that is, the sequential combination of a preexisting non-sequentially ordered archive or collection of elements (Manovich). *fo(u)r watt* is doing exactly the opposite: the book does not derive a narrative from an archive, it builds an archive through its narrative; it invents new forms that embody the visual possibilities of a general program and plays with new combinations that explore their transformations in what is both an abstract and a figurative plot, actively using the material properties of page and book and eventually bringing the sequence to its close in a way that mirrors the circularity of the whole work (which in last instance is determined by the closure as well as the double orientation of the book: a set of twenty-two pages to be read from left to right and right to left).

When we compare the first and last double spread of Conard's post-comics adaptation (well knowing that these pages are not the "beginning" and the "end" of the work itself, which starts and ends with the paratext and the covers), the creative logic of the adaptation comes immediately to the fore (Figures 7.3 and 7.4).

Figure 7.3. First double spread of the drawn part of *fo(u)r watt* (Het Balanseer, 2019), n. pag. Courtesy of Sébastien Conard, © Sébastien Conard & Het Balanseer

Figure 7.3. (cont.)

Comics Adaptations: Fidelity and Creativity

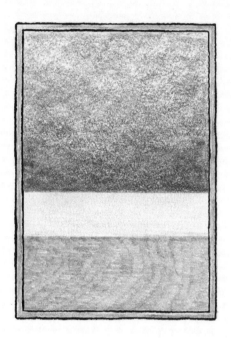

Figure 7.4. Last double spread of the drawn part of *fo(u)r watt* (Het Balanseer, 2019), n. pag. Courtesy of Sébastien Conard, © Sébastien Conard & Het Balanseer

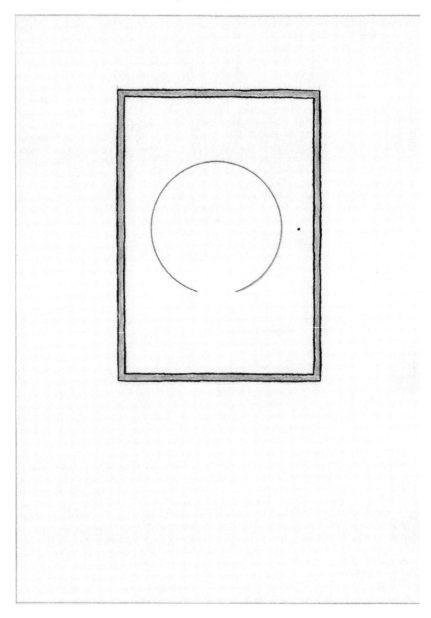

Figure 7.4. (*cont.*)

Comics Adaptations: Fidelity and Creativity

The double spreads showcase all the visual elements that will be used throughout the work (dots, lines, white, grey and black color fields, simultaneously abstract and figurative) as well as the fundamental operations of any material treatment of its underlying rules. One finds, for instance, examples of addition, subtraction, substitution, and permutation, that is, the four basic mechanisms of verbal or visual rhetoric.

As a literary comics adaptation, *fo(u)r watt* is not only highly experimental but also, and perhaps very paradoxically, much more readable than its conventional counterparts. Conard's book is indeed totally WYSIWYG. We can see how Beckett's words become a program, how this program is materialized in visual signs, and how these signs are arranged according to the features of their host medium. All this can be discovered, discussed, judged by any reader without the help of external commentaries. In that sense, the creativity of Conard's work is double: first, because it is an original contribution to a field that is often trapped by the pitfalls of illustration; second, because it allows the reader to become creative herself, through the fact that the author shares with his readers the rules of his game.

WORKS CITED

Comics

Auster, Paul, Paul Karasik, and David Mazzucchelli. *City of Glass: The Graphic Novel*. Faber, 2005. Rev. ed. of *Neon Lit: Paul Auster's City of Glass*. Avon, 1994.

Conard, Sébastien. *fo(u)r watt*. Het Balanseer, 2019.

Crumb, Robert. *The Book of Genesis Illustrated*. Norton, 2009.

Deprez, Olivier. *Le Château, d'après Kafka*. FRMK, 2019.

Grennan, Simon. *Dispossession*. Jonathan Cape, 2015.

Heuet, Stéphane. *In Search of Lost Time: Swann's Way*. Translated by Arthur Goldhammer. Liveright Pub, 2015.

Kick, Russ. *The Graphic Canon*, 3 vol. Seven Stories Press, 2012–2013.

Molotiu, Andrei. *Abstract Comics. The Anthology: 1967–2009*. Fantagraphics, 2009.

Vaughn-James, Martin. *The Cage*, 2nd revised edition. The Coach House Press, 2013 [1975].

Ware, Chris. *McSweeney's Quarterly Concern, No. 13: An Assorted Sampler of North American Comic Drawings, Strips, and Illustrated Stories*. McSweeneys, 2004.

Secondary Sources

Baetens, Jan. "Visual Rhetoric and Visual Thinking." *Eloquent Images*, edited by Mary E. Hocks and Michelle Kendrick. MIT Press, 2003, pp. 179–199.

"Abstraction in Comics." *SubStance*, vol. 40, no. 1, 2011, pp. 94–113.

"Comics and Literature." *The Oxford Handbook for Comics Studies*, edited by Frederick Aldama. Oxford UP, 2019. Online. DOI : 10.1093/oxfordhb/9780190917944.013.35

Rebuilding Story Worlds: The Obscure Cities by Schuiten and Peeters. Rutgers University Press, 2020.

Adaptation et bande dessinée: Éloge de la fidélité. Les Impressions Nouvelles, 2020.

Baetens, Jan and Hugo Frey. *The Graphic Novel: An Introduction*. Cambridge University Press, 2014.

Baetens, Jan and Domingo Sánchez-Mesa. "Literature in the Expanded Field: Intermediality at the Crossroads of Literary Theory and Comparative Literature." *Interfaces*, vol. 36, 2015, pp. 289–304.

Beckett, Samuel. *Watt*. Olympia Press, 1953.

Beronä, David. *Wordless Books: The Original Graphic Novels*. Abrams, 2008.

Boillat, Alain and Gilles Philippe. *L'Adaptation. Des livres aux scénarios*. Les Impressions Nouvelles, 2018.

Charyn, Jerome. *The Man Who Grew Younger*. Harper and Row, 1963.

Cléder, Jean and Laurent Jullier. *Analyser une adaptation*. Flammarion, 2017.

Conard, Sébastien, ed. *Post-Comics: Beyond Comics, Illustration and the Graphic Novel*. Het Balanseer, 2020.

Coughan, David. "Paul Auster's *City of Glass*: The Graphic Novel." *Modern Fiction Studies*, vol. 52, no. 4, 2006, pp. 832–854.

Dürrenmatt, Jacques. *Littérature et bande dessinée*. Garnier, 2013.

Gelder, Ken. *Adapting Bestsellers: Fantasy, Franchise and the Afterlife of Storyworlds*. Cambridge University Press, 2019.

Genette, Gérard. *Paratexts: The Thresholds of Interpretation* [1987]. Translated by Jane E. Lewin. Cambridge University Press, 1997 (1987).

Goldsmith, Kenneth. *Uncreative Writing*. Columbia University Press, 2011.

Hatfield, Charles. *Hand of Fire: The Comics Art of Jack Kirby*. University Press of Mississippi, 2011.

Hutcheon, Linda and Siobhan O'Flynn. *A Theory of Adaptation*. Routledge, 2013.

Kunzle, David. *Cham: The Best Comic Strips and Graphic Novelettes*. University Press of Mississippi, 2019.

Manovich, Lev. *The Language of New Media*. MIT Press, 2001.

McFarlane, Brian. *Novel to Film: An Introduction to the Theory of Adaptation*. Clarendon Press, 1996.

Mitchell, W. J. T. "There Are No Visual Media." *Journal of Visual Culture*, vol. 4, no. 2, 2005, pp. 257–266.

Murray, Simone. *The Adaptation Industry*. Routledge, 2012.

Nikolajeva, Maria and Carole Scott. *How Picture Books Work*. Routledge, 2001.

Nixon, Mark. "Comics and Graphic Novels." *The Book in Britain. Volume VII. The Twentieth Century and Beyond*, edited by Andrew Ash, Claire Squires and I.R. Willison. Cambridge University Press, 2019, pp. 555–564.

Perloff, Marjorie. *Unoriginal Genius*. University of Chicago Press, 2010.

Proust.Art. https://proust.art/fr/

Pizzino, Christopher. *Arresting Development: Comics at the Boundaries of Literature*. Texas University Press, 2016.

Robbe-Grillet, Alain. *For a New Novel* [1963]. Translated by Richard Howard. Northwestern University Press, 1992.

Truffaut, François. "Une certaine tendance du cinéma français". 1954. Online English version at *New Wave Film.com*: www.newwavefilm.com/about/a-certain-tendency-of-french-cinema-truffaut.shtml

CHAPTER 8

Comics Genres
Cracking the Codes

Nicolas Labarre

Genres serve as common and efficient shortcuts through the sprawl of popular fiction. For instance, when Austin Price reviewed the work of mangaka Junji Ito in 2018 for *The Comics Journal*, he described the artist as "the premier *horror comics* talent of our era" [my emphasis] in the very first sentence of the text, below the reproduction of four black-and-white panels showing a huge bandaged creature waking up (Frankenstein's monster, from Ito's adaptation of Mary Shelley's novel) (Price). The title and the opening characterization of the author imitate a content warning, discouraging certain readers from delving into an article discussing and presenting gruesome imagery. Price then refines his initial claim, by noting that Ito's work is "singular" and cleverly suggests that his horror comics often include "comic horror." The text thus states that Junji Ito works within the genre of horror, as identified by a major critical institution, but also that he exceeds the boundaries and expectations of that label. Meanwhile, "horror comics" serves a pragmatic objective in keeping away certain readers, who may not care about the specificities of Ito's output but are keen on avoiding a broad range of content, based on a shared assumption of what contemporary horror may look like.

A generic label performs several discursive and social functions, with varying degrees of specificity and with the understanding that it cannot fully account for the work it is applied to. This multifaceted and somewhat slippery use of genre is not singular to the article or the *Comics Journal*: it points to the fact that genres are constantly negotiated discursive formations, for which usefulness trumps specificity.

Functions of Genres

In his influential *Film/Genre*, film scholar Rick Altman identifies three main functions of genres: as *blueprints*, as *labels*, and as *contracts* for viewers (Altman 14). Furthermore, genres possess a *structure*, which corresponds perhaps more strongly to shared assumptions about them, and refers to defining features or to narrative formulas: the setting for a western, the representation of sex in erotic works, the endangerment of the body in horror, etc. However, Altman sees this structure less as an absolute than as the consensual by-product of the various social functions accomplished by the genres. Genres are mutable categories, flickering groupings, the boundaries of which are frequently challenged and evolve over time. They are discursive, social constructions, not platonic ideals. As such, they are only relevant insofar as they are useful. Broadly defined, the functions described by Altman are not specific to any medium; however, the social groups and institutions producing these discourses, or to put it differently, the identity of the users of genres, are contingent. They depend not only on the medium but also on the specific historical and cultural context.

Altman's *blueprint* function refers to the act of creating works within a genre, or taking account of classical generic structures so as to purposefully deviate from them. The genre is then understood as a set of features, a roadmap, which can be followed or open new paths.

The *label* function is useful to advertisers, distributors and cultural intermediaries such as libraries or bookstores. Genre then serves as a mode of classification, a box to tick in online databases or the choice of a shelf or section to display a given book.

Finally, the *contract* refers to expectations. Viewers, or readers in the case of comics, use genres to manage their expectations, both prior to consumption of a given cultural object and afterward. The Junji Ito article in *The Comics Journal* offers a typical example of the process, since it starts by positioning the mangaka within a genre – the better to ward off certain readers – then compares the expectations of the genre to the actual comics.

Of course, these functions interact constantly: the blueprint is useful inasmuch as it facilitates efficient labeling, which helps manage expectations, while a well-received work can quickly feed back into the blueprint. This does not imply that labeling engenders conformity: a creator may willfully deviate from generic blueprints yet rely on (or be forced to conform to) classical labeling, thus creating surprise among readers and possibly shifting the entire system to accommodate this deviation. For instance, *House of Secrets* #85 (1970) contains a two-page story, "Reggie Rabbit" (Len Wein and Ralph Reese), in which anthropomorphic animals are revealed to be disgruntled alien invaders who eventually leave Earth on a glittering 1950s comics rocket. This has little to do with horror, but it was published in a long-running horror/fantastic anthology, often tinged with humor. In this case, labeling and expectations aligned closely, but the blueprint did not: the story is arguably made much more memorable by this generic framing than if it had been published as satire in the *National Lampoon*, which Reese frequently worked for. Later stories published in *House of Secrets* do not offer evidence of a change in the blueprint but "Reggie Rabbit" does shift readerly expectations by suggesting the comic book may have been open to more radical deviations from its erstwhile formula; it opens up the range of plausible narratives which readers might expect from the series.

As indicated earlier, the functions of genres in comics, films, and literature are broadly similar. Furthermore, genres help bridge the gap between media by offering a shared taxonomy. Labels such as "horror" or "romance" are useful in part because they can serve to market cultural products or to shape expectations across popular media. They foreground the incessant intermedial exchanges at work in popular culture and reflect what Benoît Berthou calls the "cumulative logic" of cultural consumption: a broad survey of French readers of comics published in 2015 indicated, for instance, that comics readers played videogames nearly twice as much as the general population (64% against 36%) and were also more frequent cinemagoers (82% against 57%) (Berthou 120). Given these figures, which would likely be replicated in other countries, genres serve as convenient intermedial navigation tools, alongside other meaningful organizing principles, such as brands (Disney, Marvel, etc.), characters (Sherlock Holmes, Batman, My Little Pony, etc.) and authors (though author names across media are often akin to brand; e.g., "a Stephen King movie").

Genres across Media

Intermedial circulations are central to comics publishing and reading. As Shawna Kidman has shown in her institutional history of US comics: "At no point in history did comics develop in isolation; they were both deeply informed and deeply impactful on the culture industries writ large" (Kidman 4). This presence in a complex media ecosystem involves direct transpositions and adaptations but also a variety of mutual influences, which confirms the usefulness of discursive categories spanning several media. For instance, the superhero genre does not have the same history in comics and in movies, but the similarities between movies like *The Incredibles* (Bird, 2004) and *The Fantastic Four*, regardless of their respective medium of origin, can be explained by examining the way the whole superhero genre has spread from one medium to another.

These transmedia genres tend to have an even weaker structure than medium-specific versions, since they have to accommodate a broader range of users and discursive situations, and typically apply to extensive bodies of texts. Defining most genres is often an exercise in futility (even apparently clear-cut cases, such as the western or pornography, which could be defined, respectively, by a setting and a legal framework, are open to ambiguities and borderline cases, not to mention cultural specificities); definitions become more fluid when attempting to consider genres across media.

Beyond the variety of usages that they have to accommodate, the amorphousness of transmedia genres can be explained in two ways. The first is the specific history of genres in each medium: they evolve over time, and successful innovations are then taken into account by their users. To take one example, superhero comics in the early 2000s moved closer to a cinematic model of representation, typified by the early issues of *The Authority* (Ellis and Hitch, DC/Wildstorm, 1999–2000) and refined in *The Ultimates* (Millar and Hitch, Marvel, 2002–2007) (see Figure 8.1). These influential comic books integrated a "widescreen" aesthetic, with black margins and long horizontal panels typically occupying the whole width of the page, combined with radical decomposition of movement in action scenes and abundant use of photographic references. Later superhero comics could then choose to adopt or to ignore this "cinematic" style, making it a significant creative bifurcation in the genre's blueprint. That distinction between cinematic and non-cinematic superhero stories is of course not applicable to superhero films of the same period: an important historical juncture in the comics version of the genre is thus not replicated in the film version or in the transmedia version. Conversely, the Batman TV show in 1966–1967, introduced a version of the superhero genre on television inspired by the 1940s serial and ignoring the transformations of the genre in comic books in the ensuing decades. In addition to adopting a campy tone, the TV show foregrounded the diverging histories of the genre in the two media, and was for years regarded as an aberration by superhero fans (Reynolds 43).

A second phenomenon can help explain the lack of specificity of transmedia genres: media affordances, or mediageny. Media affordances refer to the specific possibilities of a given medium – such as the possibility for film to reproduce sound. The concept of "mediageny," devised by Philippe Marion ("Narratologie médiatique"), offers a slightly different version of the same idea by suggesting that certain media may be especially

Figure 8.1. Mark Millar (w.) and Bryan Hitch (i.), The *Ultimates* 2, no. 9, January 2006. Marvel Comics.

appropriate for a specific type of content.[1] Both ideas point to the fact that media have specific properties, respectively, considered as ontological or conventional, which shape the type of content they offer. It is hard to imagine how certain videogame genres, such as the First-Person Shooter, could even exist in comics, for instance, since they rely on properties which the medium does not have (spatial continuity, movement control, etc.). Beyond these cases of radical incompatibility, genres within a medium often resort to specific formal strategies. Much has been written, for instance, about the rhetoric of the archive in graphic memoirs – which led, for instance, Alison Bechdel to redraw the pages of the novels she discusses in *Fun Home*, so as to make sure everything in the book bore the trace of her own hand (Cvetkovich; Chute 185–186). The adaptation of *Fun Home* as a musical in 2013 also sought to convey authenticity, but did so through very different means, notably through the embodied performance of the singers (Anderst).

The two interacting factors, history and mediageny, can result in a drift, whereby medium-specific versions of genres come to differ so much that transmedia labeling no longer functions. The "graphic memoir" may be a marginal example of such a drift: it is a comics version of the broader "memoir" genre, but also, arguably an autonomous and medium-specific body of work. However, as I have argued elsewhere, while medium-specific versions of popular genres constantly deviate from the broader intermedial umbrella term, these multiple versions are regularly realigned: successful works exert their influence across media either through officially sanctioned transpositions – *The Ultimates* had been designed as a blueprint for the *Avengers* movies and served that role – or by exerting an influence on creators in other media (Labarre, *Understanding Genres* 23–24). Even comics genres that function in constant dialogues with other media – such as horror, or the western (Wandtke; Martinez; Goodrum and Smith) – undergo such drifts apart from their meaning in other media before aligning again: the domestic horror of many 1950s comics starkly differed from the shape of the genre in other media at the time, but their influence later helped reshape horror films and novels. These moments of intermedial realignments help ensure the continuing relevance of broad genre labels. When they fail to occur, the process simply generates new genres

---

[1] This helps circumvent the problem raised by marginal examples that imbue a medium with atypical properties. *Most* comics do not involve diegetic smells, but some have included "scratch-and-sniff" systems, for instance (Hague 136–138). Mediageny avoids this issue by describing what is plausible, rather than possible, in a given medium.

which may then expand to other media: such was the case when the superhero genre emerged as distinct from adventure narratives in other media in the late 1930s.

The Superhero Genre

Superheroes have formed the most influential genre in the history of comic books. After the creation of Superman in *Action Comics* #1, these characters dominated the market until the end of the Second World War. Contrary to popular histories, they did not disappear afterward but they did fade away, to become prominent again in the 1960s and then, arguably, from the 1980s to the present day.

The existence of the superhero genre cannot be contested. If you were to create your own superhero story, you would probably have a blueprint or mental scheme at your disposal, possibly involving a traumatic origin story and certainly having the hero use extraordinary abilities to stop crime. If you had to market a superhero story, you could direct the online platform ComiXology to file it under the appropriate generic label, "superhero," where it would coexist with the output of dedicated publishing institutions, such as DC or Marvel. If you were so inclined, you could also seek out academic texts, such as *The Superhero Reader*, in which scholars confirm the currency of the label. Finally, as a reader, the mention of the superhero may bring to mind specific characters and is likely to provide a useful starting point to help you decide whether you want to read a specific comic book or not. In addition to fulfilling these various functions, the label appears remarkably stable: it can be applied to texts spanning decades, and it is difficult to think of an alternative denomination ("capes and tights"?).

Several authors have attempted to provide a definition of the genre, or, as I have described it earlier, a definition of its structure. The most influential of these attempts was by Peter Coogan in his book *Superhero: The Secret Origin of a Genre* (2006) and has been reprinted or commented upon in numerous readers and textbooks (Heer and Worcester; Hatfield et al.; Duncan and Smith; Hatfield and Beaty). According to Coogan, who draws notably from the conclusion of a 1939 trial on the alleged plagiarism of Superman, superheroes have three main characteristics: a pro-social mission, superpowers, and a distinctive identity, including a codename and a costume (Coogan 30–60). Coogan also notes that all of these three elements may be downplayed or even completely absent, even in canonical examples such as the Batman (created in 1939) or the Hulk (1961).

This is of course a very broad definition but making it more specific would require moving away from an overview of the genre to a more openly historicized approach. For instance, superhero narratives of the early 1940s frequently include horror elements, with various monsters, haunted castles, and mad scientists. By the late 1950s, these elements had been excised from comic book publishing through the Comics Code, and superhero stories gave a more central role to themes, designs, and plots associated with science fiction and engineering. Shortly afterward, Marvel Comics took to integrating elements of romance and self-parody, before opening up to horror again as restrictions on the genre waned in the 1970s. In short, the ahistorical approach to the genre, much like the intermedial one, erases features which would have been seen as key to the genre at specific points in time, in order to account for the broadest possible range of text.

Furthermore, Coogan's model does not explain how the fairly stable consensus since the late 1930s was constructed. Nor can it offer an absolute way to distinguish what belongs to the genre and what does not. Asterix the Gaul fills certain criteria but is not usually labeled a superhero by virtue of being a French comic hero, for instance. Conversely, Marvel's Ka-Zar, essentially a copy of Tarzan, has nevertheless been a key component of several superhero tales. Originally a pulp character in a jungle setting in the 1930s, Ka-Zar was reintroduced in an episode of *The Uncanny X-Men* in 1965. Ka-Zar has been published by Marvel in a format and with creators associated with superhero fiction and has frequently been shown interacting with superheroes. Unlike Tarzan himself, Ka-Zar functions *at least for a sizable group of readers* as a super-hero: he is described as such on his (user-maintained) *Wikipedia* page, in several entries of the (user-maintained) *Grand Comic Book Database* as well as on the (retailer-curated) ComiXology app. Ka-Zar may be a marginal case, yet the character functions as part of the superhero genre, and has even been the main attraction in titles marketed and presumably con-sumed as superhero fiction (Figure 8.2).

To understand the plasticity of the superhero genre, it may be useful to turn to one of its canonical examples: *Fantastic Four*. An often-told story suggests that the series was created in 1961 as a reaction to DC's team of superheroes, The Justice League. Yet, *Fantastic Four* only partially resem-bles that model. The first issue recounts their transformation as a horrify-ing experience, describes them as reluctant, squabbling protagonists, before pitting them against an army of giant subterranean monsters. The issue does not use the phrase "superhero" or any variation thereof and repeatedly

Figure 8.2. Mark Waid (w.) and Andy Kubert (i.), *Ka-Zar* no. 4, August 1997. Marvel Comics.

emphasizes the monstrosity of its protagonists rather than their superhuman nature. In fact, only one of the four characters, the Human Torch, corresponds to a preestablished component of the genre: a character with the same name had been popular in the 1940s, and the figure of the flying man is likened to Superman when bystanders are shown declaring "Look! A blazing burning comet!//No!! It's not a comet!! It's – It's –," echoing the recurring line, "It's a bird, it's a plane, no, it's Superman!", introduced in the 1940 radio show and used in various media afterward. In the second issue, the team, still in civilian clothes, repels an alien invasion by showing their leader pictures taken from giant monster comics, themselves clearly inspired by the giant monster science-fiction films of the 1950s.

In subsequent issues, the connection with the superhero genre is clarified in three ways. First, some of the narrative choices follow the genre's blueprint, bringing in colored uniforms, a secret base with elaborate gadgets and super-powered villains (most memorably Dr. Doom). Secondly, the stories include explicit intertextual references to established superhero texts. In #4, the Human Torch is shown reading a comic book featuring Namor, a character created by Bill Everett in 1939, before Namor himself shows up in the story. The series still includes non-superhero references, especially to *Frankenstein*, but the explicit allusions to 1950s sci-fi quickly become rarer; the comic book is not positioned as *only* a superhero series, but as a plausible update and extension of the genre. The gradual emergence of a shared superhero universe is part of that strategy.

The third strategy, chaperoning genre identification, consists in selecting and presenting testimonies from the readers who describe their own perception of the comic book. Letter columns are a place of co-construction in which publishers acknowledge the reception of the comic book while curating and in some cases inventing these messages (Stein; Labarre, *Heavy Metal* 100; Licari-Guillaume), and they offer a fitting forum for the co-construction of genres. The first mention of superheroes in *Fantastic Four* is to be found in the letter column to the third issue (March 1962) – the first issue to have one – in which a reader notes: "It's nice to see a group of super-heroes who aren't naturally buddy-buddy." Strikingly, this message appears in the same issue when the costumes and other conventional superhero features are introduced.

Early issues suggest that this affiliation is not that clear-cut for all readers, with multiple references to other possible genres. The letters frequently debate the identity of a possible fifth member, or of a replacement for one of the existing characters. In #7, a reader from New Jersey suggests that this new member could be "a scientific genius and assists Mr. Fantastic, or a wizard who uses magic to fight crime – or perhaps an alien from space." The list seems to imply that the generic affiliation of the title was still up for debate: none of these characters is characteristic of the superhero genre, though all of them could possibly work in that context. In fact, the letter as printed, ended with a: "What do you think?" addressed to the editors (and not the creators). The generic negotiation was also happening outside the comic book itself: *Alter Ego*, a fanzine very much focused on superheroes discussed *Fantastic Four* in the context of the best comics of 1961 and included an original drawing of The Thing by Jack Kirby, inviting readers to buy the publication.

These glimpses into the various discourses suggest that the title quickly migrated towards the superhero genre, as the result of a dual movement of consolidation and expansion: it foregrounded recognizable elements of established superhero prototypes, and it simultaneously shifted the boundaries of the genre by virtue of its success. This process culminated in-text in #9, an issue in which the Fantastic Four realize they cannot afford the rent for their expansive headquarters in NYC. The story is tongue-in-cheek, verging on self-parody (a vein Marvel fully embraced with the *MAD*-inspired *Not Brand Echh* [1967–1969]), and has Mr. Fantastic declare: "If only we could be like the super heroes in some of these comics magazines, Sue! THEY never seem to worry about money! Life is a BREEZE for them!" (emphasis in the original) (see Figure 8.3). The joke works by appealing to the readers' generic literacy: the Fantastic Four are *of course* superheroes, yet they *also* remain atypical. Here, as elsewhere the individual text exceeds and inflects the genre it belongs to.

Performing Genre

The *Fantastic Four* example also suggests that self-parody does not undermine generic affiliation and can even reaffirm it. This is only superficially paradoxical. To quote Linda Hutcheon, parody is "repetition with a critical distance, which marks difference rather than similarity," while "playing with multiple conventions" (Hutcheon 6;7). Parodies thus replay generic conventions to better establish their singularity. In the conclusion of the same study, Hutcheon quotes approvingly from Robert Burden, in a passage that suggests broader similarities between genres and parody: "[Parody] defines a particular form of historical consciousness, whereby form is created to interrogate itself against significant precedents" (qtd. in Hutcheon 101). In other words, parody, like genre, confers visibility to

Comics Genres: Cracking the Codes 177

Figure 8.3. Stan Lee (w.) and Jack Kirby (i.), *Fantastic Four* no. 9, December 1962. Marvel Comics.

what Gérard Genette calls the "architext": "the relationship of inclusion that links each text to the various types of discourses it belongs to" (Genette 82).

In the *Fantastic Four* example mentioned, the tension between adhesion to the genre and deviation is openly performed for the amusement of the reader. However, I would like to suggest that in the case of any text deliberately positioned within a genre by its creators, that belonging is always performed: writing in the genre involves including references, sending signals and acknowledging expectations. Parodies thus appear as one end of a wide spectrum of imitation and other intertextual relations. Conventions are constantly replayed and performed, though parody emphasizes the singularity of the text more strongly than other performances of the genre.

Conversely, writing in the genre is never naïve. Much has been made of the generic playfulness exhibited in contemporary author-driven popular comics, such as those by Alan Moore or Matt Fraction. Marc Singer has pointed out that while such playfulness has become ubiquitous in popular culture, it has arguably always been present in comics (Singer 47–50). Superman's classic wink to the reader, for instance, is not only a metaleptic device but also a way to underline the convention that played out time and again in the 1950s version of the character (which Eco wrote about in "The Myth of Superman") (see Gordon 150–151). Similarly, horror hosts literally perform genres by functioning as metatextual hucksters, who frequently poke fun at the conventions used in the stories (Round 624–627). Even romance comics, long derided as rigidly formulaic, performs its own conventions in the extreme narrative condensation of its covers.

It is of course possible for readers and critics to assign generic labels retroactively, to works that were not conceived as such. In this case, the notion of performance vanishes, but such examples are usually bracketed away as "precursors" or oddities. Once the genre is established, once the notion of *writing in the genre* emerges (Letourneux 175–216), playfulness and performance become normal modes of engagement with that genre: as we have seen, the early issues of *Fantastic Four* offer a whole spectrum of such performance.

It is tempting to suggest that comics are singular in that regard. For starters, unlike other media, they often comprise a complex and meaning-laden paratext meant to be consumed along with the text itself (as points of comparison, the poster for a movie or the box-cover illustration for video-games are optional paratexts). Comic books, as opposed to graphic novels, are especially rich in that regard, and offer many sites for contradictions, self-parody and displays of self-awareness: Dr. Doom's seriousness is undercut by its use to hawk subscriptions to the magazine, for instance (or see the Ka-Zar cover, Figure 8.2). More crucially perhaps, Jared Gardner argues that comics constantly require their readers to be aware of architextual principles, to make connection and to reflect on them:

> As a form that works with traditionally incommensurate systems of meaning – text and image – to tell its story, it also requires its readers at every turn to make active decisions as to how to read the two in relationship to a larger narrative. (Gardner xi)

As a uniquely dialogic and participative form, one that exhibits its codes and discontinuities at all times, comics offers a fruitful ground for the creation and exhibition of discursive constructs such as genres.

Social Functions

Genres serve as productive taxonomies and efficient, consensual, and often institutionalized architexts. But genres are not only used to talk about the texts themselves, as in the three functions identified by Altman. They also serve as powerful building blocks for cultural hierarchies. In his work on *The Obscure Cities*, Jan Baetens notes that "the age of the emerging graphic novel culture [is] often highly critical of the existing genre classifications and restrictive genre formats," resulting either in parodies or in the avoidance of established formula (Baetens 75). The "existing genre classifications" in this sentence should be understood as referring to "popular genre," since the graphic novel frequently relies on other genres, such as the coming-of-age story or the memoir.[2]

One key difference between legitimate genres and illegitimate ones may be seriality. Though a number of canonical graphic novels were published in chapters or installments (see Baetens and Frey), they tend not to function as cycles or a series; they refuse, in other words, the lingering stigma of what Sainte-Beuve called "industrial literature" and more broadly the association with popular culture. This may be even more pronounced in the North American context, in which the superhero genre played an outsized role in the perception of the medium and appeared to some creators and critics as a force constricting its possibilities. Criticism of the genre could thus serve as a claim for artistic autonomy. In Chris Ware's *Jimmy Corrigan*, for instance, Superman and the superhero genre are ridiculed in-text, even as Ware professes admiration for other elements of comics history. The genre, in this case, is clearly the "bad object" (Altman 113), the stigma of popular culture against which Ware's psychologically complex characters and sophisticated narrative are to be read. Jillian and Mariko Tamakis' *This One Summer* offers an interesting and more nuanced engagement with genre by having the protagonist of their coming-of-age story watch horror movies: the legibility of Spielberg's *Jaws* is contrasted with the complexity of the protagonists' emotional state, but at the same time, the narrative acknowledges the pleasure of such simplicity and the fascination popular films can exert. The range of critical attitudes toward genre can be observed in various author-centric series engaging with romance, from Image's *Twisted Love* (playing within the sandbox while updating the formula) to Vertigo's *Hearthrob* (pushing the formula to unlikely extremes), to the 1970s comix *Young Lust* (attacking the ideological underpinning of the genre).

Taking a different stance, authors such as Charles Burns, Frank Miller, or Michael DeForge have embraced genres in the context of what

---

[2] Several comics authors, wary of the label have in fact produced tongue-in-cheek recipes for aspiring graphic novelists. See for instance Bill Griffith's *Zippy* for April 5, 2015 or Lisa Mandel's *Une Année exemplaire* (2020).

Christopher Pizzino describes as "autoclasm": the refusal of legitimizing discourses by some comics creators. As Pizzino puts it: "The way Burns uses pre-code comics is neither nostalgic nor curatorial; he asserts the direct utility of horror comics, their power to speak meaningfully to the present moment" (Pizzino 137). Indeed, I always qualify my recommendation of *Black Hole* to new readers by warning them that the book relies on body horror. While *This One Summer* gestures towards horror, *Black Hole* embraces it, along the cultural stigma it carries. In all of these examples, genres serve less as categories within the medium than as a way to position their authors, if not the entire medium, in the spectrum of social hierarchies.

Furthermore, and although this is beyond the scope of this essay, genres tend to foster communities. Certainly, other architexts do, the "Marvel zombies" are fans of a specific publisher (Pustz), and in "Platinum Age" discussion groups, dates of publication serve an architextual principle. However, many of these architexts are neatly bounded, or even fully closed. Whether a book is published by Marvel is by and large a binary question, though specific imprints such as the creator-owned Icon may induce some ambiguity. By contrast, genres are amorphous and changing, they are discursive battlegrounds with porous borders. This creates opportunities for idiosyncratic convictions but also for the kind of border-patrolling that matters so much in the creation of communities, by helping define insiders from outsiders.

Limitations: Genres and Other Architexts

Genres thus coexist with other architexts, which fulfill somewhat similar functions. Authors' names, characters, series, publishers, collections, and imprints, to name a few of the most prominent examples, serve as marketing labels and in some cases, at least, shape readers' expectations. The editorial control exercised by publishers can also generate literal blueprints for new authors willing to produce works fitting the norms of these institutions. As many scholars have remarked, it is not uncommon for powerful editors to function as coauthors of the works, in which case the blueprint and the label function in close synergy.

Mike Mignola's *Hellboy* offers a complex example of these interlocking architexts. When Mignola started publishing the series in 1994, *Hellboy* functioned as a slightly idiosyncratic reading of the superhero genre. It followed that blueprint to a large extent, included a recognizable superhero in its cast and the onomastic of the protagonist's name clearly inscribed

Comics Genres: Cracking the Codes

him in the genre. Not unlike Neil Gaiman's *Sandman* (Brayshaw and Mignola), *Hellboy* quickly moved away from the superhero label. The first collected edition foregrounded the gothic elements of the narrative and boasted of a preface by horror writer Robert Bloch. While the film adaptations were widely read in the context of the superhero genre (especially the 2004 and 2008 versions), the comic books carved a specific niche, embracing folk tales and the fantastic in a way that does not neatly align with institutionalized comics genres. Mignola thus occupied an unusual but not entirely novel position as an author – he retained the right to his creation, and his distinctive graphic approach was noted immediately – working in an unusual genre setting. The same could be said of Schuiten and Peeters in Europe, of most of Howard Chaykin's output in the 1980s, and of some of Grant Morrison's work in the US, to mention but a few creators emphatically straddling the divide between auteuristic and popular approaches (Baetens; Costello). However, starting in 1998, Mignola expanded the franchise with *Abe Sapien: Drums of the Dead*, a spin-off story featuring a popular character from the main series. Though Mignola neither wrote nor drew the story, he drew the cover for the one-shot, and his name is the largest on that cover, thanks to a backup *Hellboy* story. In 2002, the franchise expanded more significantly, with a team spin-off, *B.P.R.D.* Not all early issues featured Mignola covers (in 2002–2003, *Hollow Earth* did, but *Dark Waters*, *Night Train*, and the *Soul of Venice* did not), but they all bore the mention "Mignola's B.P.R.D." That mention was dropped in 2004, but Mignola's name remained prominent, on par with that of the other creators, though he was only credited as a plotter. He also drew the covers for all the collected volumes. Furthermore, even with minimal direct involvement from Mignola, the whole series hews close to *Hellboy*: in its narrative mix of pulp tropes, Universal horror movies, nineteenth-century occultism, Lovecraft and superheroes, in its use of colors and even idiosyncratic graphic choices, such as the use of small panels detailing statues and other bas-relief. In this case, the franchise and the author's name work together to delineate a closed architext, albeit one that is sprawling and contains many different flavors. For instance, it is flexible enough to accommodate an artist like Richard Corben, working in his distinctive style, quite unlike Mignola's, for *Hellboy in Mexico*. Like a genre, the Mignola architext functions as a cluster: Mignola's own *Hellboy* stories are its prototype, but ancillary work deviate from this model in a variety of ways. Still, that architext is not *entirely* closed. It can be open through parodies – as shown for instance in Warren Ellis and Stuart Immonen's *Nextwave, Agents of H.A.T.E.* #10

(Marvel, 2007) – and through other works, which reuse some of Mignola's distinctive approach. However, even works that resemble *Hellboy* to some extent, such as Ted Naifeh's *Courtney Crumrin* or Serge Lehman, Fabrice Colin and Gess's *The Chimera Brigade* cannot, by definition, be part of the *Hellboy* architext. Readers may decide to create and use this grouping, for instance, in recommending a book to others, but unlike genres, proprietary architexts are not negotiated.

As a result, these architexts are more profitable to publishers than genres, since they can be protected by copyright or trademarks. DC entertainment, for instance, has a monopoly on Vertigo comics, and Archie cannot be used outside of books published by Archie comics. Such groupings and the expectations they generate cannot be meaningfully extended by competitors the way genres can. Marvel and DC thus promote the Marvel and the DC Universe, respectively, rather than the superhero genre, which they share. Simultaneously, the entertainment industry consolidates around a small – and probably diminishing – number of mega-franchises, constellations of objects produced in a variety of narrative modes and for various types of audiences, in which genres are subsidiary to the franchise rather than alternative modes of engagement. Readers can consume Spider-Man as body horror (*Carnage, USA*; *Spider-Man: Bloodlines*; *Marvel Zombies*), Spider-Man as romance (*Mary Jane*; *Spider-Man Loves Mary Jane*), or as a noir investigator (*Spider-Man: Noir*) and such variations coexist with a constellation of other tweaks on the character for any potential market.

The increasing importance of franchises and massive proprietary architexts is also a transmedia phenomenon, which ensures a high degree of compatibility across media. As we saw earlier, genres are a rough guide to navigating cultural objects across media, but tightly controlled proprietary architexts do not suffer from the same lack of specificity. In other words, for all their usefulness, the current state of the cultural industries tends to turn genres into increasingly subsidiary architexts.

WORKS CITED

Comics

Burns, Charles. *Black Hole*. Pantheon, 2005 (collects *Black Hole* no. 1-12. Kitchen Sink/Fantagraphics, 1995–2004).

Lee, Stan (w.) and Jack Kirby (i.) *Fantastic Four* no. 1-7. Marvel Comics, 1961–1962.

Mignola, Mike et al. *Hellboy*. Dark Horse, 1994 – present.

Comics Genres: Cracking the Codes

Millar, Mark (w.) and Byran Hitch (i.), *The Ultimates*. no. 1-13. Marvel Comics, 2002–2004.

Tamaki, Mariko (w.) and Jillian Tamaki (a). *This One Summer*. First Second Books, 2014.

Waid, Mark (w.) and Andy Kubert (i.), *Ka-Zar* 3d series, no. 4. Marvel Comics, August 1997.

Secondary Sources

Altman, Rick. *Film/Genre*. British Film Institute, 1999.

Anderst, Leah. "'It Both Is and Isn't My Life': Autobiography, Adaptation and Emotion in Fun Home, the Musical." *The Comics of Alison Bechdel*, edited by Janine Utell. University Press of Mississippi, 2019, pp. 105–118.

Baetens, Jan. *Rebuilding Story Worlds: The Obscure Cities by Schuiten and Peeters*. Rutgers University Press, 2020.

Berthou, Benoît. "VI. La bande dessinée: Quelle culture de l'image?" *La bande dessinée : Quelle lecture, quelle culture?*, edited by Benoît Berthou. Éditions de la Bibliothèque publique d'information, 2015. https://doi.org/10.4000/books.bibpompidou.1682.

Brayshaw, Charles and Mike Mignola. "Between Two Worlds: The Mike Mignola Interview." *The Comics Journal*, no. 189, August 1996, pp. 64–90.

Chute, Hillary L. *Graphic Women: Life Narrative and Contemporary Comics*. Columbia University Press, 2010.

Coogan, Peter. *Superhero: The Secret Origin of a Genre*. MonkeyBrain, 2006.

Costello, Brannon. *Neon Visions: The Comics of Howard Chaykin*. Louisiana State University Press, 2017.

Cvetkovich, Ann. "Drawing the Archive in Alison Bechdel's 'Fun Home.'" *Women's Studies Quarterly*, vol. 36, no. 1/2, The Feminist Press at the City University of New York, 2008, pp. 111–128.

Duncan, Randy and Matthew J. Smith. *The Power of Comics: History, Form and Culture*. 2nd ed. Bloomsbury, 2015.

Gardner, Jared. *Projections: Comics and the History of Twenty-First-Century Storytelling*. Stanford University Press, 2012.

Genette, Gérard. *The Architext: An Introduction*. University of California Press, 1992.

Goodrum, Michael D. and Philip Smith. *Printing Terror. American Horror Comics as Cold War Commentary and Critique*. Manchester University Press, 2021.

Gordon, Ian. *Superman: The Persistence of an American Icon*. Rutgers University Press, 2017.

Hague, Ian. *Comics and the Senses: A Multisensory Approach to Comics and Graphic Novels*. Routledge, 2014.

Hatfield, Charles, et al., editors. *The Superhero Reader*. University Press of Mississippi, 2013.

Hatfield, Charles and Bart Beaty, editors. *Comics Studies: A Guidebook*. Rutgers University Press, 2020.

Heer, Jeet and Kent Worcester, editors. *A Comics Studies Reader*. University Press of Mississippi, 2009.

Hutcheon, Linda. *A Theory of Parody: The Teachings of Twentieth-Century Art Forms*. University of Illinois Press, 2000.

Kidman, Shawna. *Comic Books Incorporated: How the Business of Comics Became the Business of Hollywood*. University of California Press, 2019.

Labarre, Nicolas. *Heavy Metal, l'autre Métal Hurlant*. Presses universitaires de Bordeaux, 2017.

Understanding Genres in Comics. Palgrave Macmillan, 2020.

Letourneux, Matthieu. *Fictions à la chaîne: littératures sérielles et culture médiatique*. Éditions du Seuil, 2017.

Licari-Guillaume, Isabelle. "'What Is It with These Brits?': British Culture and the 'British Invasion' Narrative Seen through Letter Columns." *Comicalités. Études de culture graphique*. Université Paris XIII | Villetaneuse – Bobigny – Saint-Denis, April 2021. *journals.openedition.org*, http://journals .openedition.org/comicalites/5585.

Martinez, Nicolas. *Reframing the Western in Bande Dessinée: Translation, Adaptation, Localization*. Cardiff University, March 2020. *orca-mwe.cf.ac. uk*, http://orca-mwe.cf.ac.uk/131912/.

Pizzino, Christopher. *Arresting Development: Comics at the Boundaries of Literature*, 1st ed. University of Texas Press, 2016.

Price, Austin. "Comic Horror: The Work of Junji Ito." *The Comics Journal*, November 2018. www.tcj.com/comic-horror-the-work-of-junji-ito/.

Pustz, Matthew. *Comic Book Culture: Fanboys and True Believers*. University Press of Mississippi, 1999.

Reynolds, Richard. *Super Heroes: A Modern Mythology*. University Press of Mississippi, 1994.

Round, Julia. "Horror Hosts in British Girls' Comics." *The Palgrave Handbook of Contemporary Gothic*, edited by Clive Bloom. Palgrave Macmillan, 2020, pp. 623–642.

Singer, Marc. *Breaking the Frames: Populism and Prestige in Comics Studies*, 1st ed. University of Texas Press, 2018.

Stein, Daniel. "Superhero Comics and the Authorizing Functions of the Comic Book Paratext." *From Comic Strips to Graphic Novels: Contributions to the Theory and History of Graphic Narrative*, edited by Daniel Stein and Jan-Noël Thon. De Gruyter, 2013, pp. 155–189.

Wandtke, Terrence R. *The Comics Scare Returns: The Contemporary Resurgence of Horror Comics*. RIT Press, 2018.

CHAPTER 9

Life Writing in Comics

Shiamin Kwa

In the front matter to *King-Cat Comics and Stories* Number 51, which was published "at last in May 1997," John Porcellino (b. 1968) explained that this issue included what would be "the first of two installments of a big story about the summer of 1986 – which was the summer after [he] graduated from High School" (*Map* 41). This statement indicates the irregularly paced but nonetheless assumed seriality of the practice that Porcellino began when he started self-publishing *King-Cat* in 1989. This zine in which "John" is subject, author, artist, art director, editor, and publisher, is, at the time of this writing, up to issue Number 81.[1] An issue of *King-Cat* usually incorporates prose that is sometimes typed and sometimes hand-written; comics depicting dreams and, events recently occurred, or memories recalled from the near or distant past; letters from readers; lists of various kinds; and other paratextual materials such as tables of contents, forewords, and afterwords. These various forms of expression employed in *King-Cat* generate a kind of unmediated directness between Porcellino and the reader, where the mode of address is constantly modulating; whereas the deictic form of address, "you," a pronoun that has the potential to change depending on who happens to be reading it, is unfailingly treated as stable and continuous. *King-Cat* is a form of life writing that uses the zine format and, in this case, comics featured within the zine, to foreground its aporetic nature. Constantly making the reader switch gears between reading different kinds of information in different forms, *King-Cat* makes the aporetic almost comfortable. The intra- and intertextual dynamics created by Porcellino's life writing practice implicate the reader in an animistic medium of uncertainty, where what the text

---

[1] Because of the vast number of materials that John Porcellino has self-published over the decades, some of which are difficult to access, this essay will focus on materials in two collections of reprints that are readily available in new reissues from Drawn & Quarterly: John Porcellino, *Perfect Example* (Montreal: Drawn & Quarterly, 2005); and Porcellino, *Map of My Heart: The Best of King-Cat Comics & Stories 1996–2002.*

"asks" of the reader shifts in register even in sections of the same page. This kind of reading process challenges traditional linear notions of time and the location of identity within a text, thus suggesting a dynamic communal vision for life writing and, perhaps, for viewing life itself.

The term "life writing" acknowledges the complicated yet often unconsidered distance between the "I" who lived and the "I" who records in the heretofore more commonly used term "autobiography." A scholar of life writing recently put it:

> The relationship between fiction or literature and life is an age-old theme: what happens to life, what happens to "my" life, while I'm narrating it? Is the "I" who does the narrating (regardless in which person "I" am narrating my story, it is always an "I" that is being told) the same "I" as the one that is narrated? The gap between "I" and "I," in fact, that's where life, the real one, the living one, must be taking place. Narrating and living, in fact, mutually exclude each other. While I'm writing I'm living elsewhere, or my "body" at least is living "elsewhere." Literature – auto-biography, life writing – would not only be a substitute for life – a lesser (or, indeed, higher) form of life – it would positively exclude living "as such," if living were to be understood as "being at one with oneself," "mere" being, even less than Dasein (being-there) (Herbrechter 2).

This aporia, or undecidability, between fiction and history thus engineers an outward turn, one that relies on reader participation for its effect where the "distinction between the third and first person pronouns articulated by the act of recording is mitigated by an act of narrative interpretation arranged between the writer and the reader" (Kwa 6). Sarah Kofman noted in her etymological analysis of the term "aporia" that "there can be no aporia, in the true sense of the word, without a transition from a familiar state which affords one every security to a new, and therefore harrowing, state" (21). Life writing in general tends to the aporetic largely through the contradictory way that it assumes an ostensibly uncomplicated position of showing real events as if in real time, often using the present-tense rendering of the writer's retrospective gaze. It cultivates familiarity and then, at certain crucial moments, surprises the reader with a reminder of an insurmountable distance between the reader, the text, and the creator of that text. Paul de Man, writing on autobiography as a kind of "defacement" in 1979 exposed the emptiness of the term by taking pains to define it as:

> Not a genre or mode, but a figure of reading or understanding that occurs, to some degree, in all texts. . .The structure implies differentiation as well as similarity, since both depend on a substitutive exchange that constitutes the

subject. This specular structure is interiorized in a text in which the author declares himself the subject of his own understanding, but this merely makes explicit the wider claim to authorship that takes place whenever a text is stated to be *by* someone and assumed to be understandable to the extent that this is the case. Which amounts to saying that any book with a readable title-page is, to some extent, autobiographical" (922).

The fluctuation between the familiar and the unfamiliar, and the impossibility of broaching a resolution, is constant and is heightened by aspects of Porcellino's zine. In *King-Cat* it is not the title page alone that transmits a "me"ness to the reader, but a whole constellation of documents (what some theorists of life writing are now calling "egodocuments") (Baggerman, Dekker and Mascuch) that collaborate in these transmissions of "me"ness. Events in the past are made to unfurl again into a future that is yet unknowable and unknown to the reader. It is precisely in this disposition towards the future where *King-Cat* offers alternative ways of looking at a life.

The image-text hybrid forms and the paratextual materials that consti- tute *King-Cat* lets the zine maker press the simultaneous presence of incommensurable categories to their absolute limits. Pages are hand- written, hand-drawn, hand-formatted, and laid out, and finally even collated and assembled by hand. Letters from readers written to Porcellino are copied in his own hand. Even when featured stories are presented in typeface, such as *King-Cat* Number 55's feature "Spotlight on: Opossums," the pages are embellished with spot illustrations inserted into the layout (Porcellino *Map*, 96–97; Figure 9.1). In its handmade form, *King-Cat* actively engages with aporetic techniques that demand interpretive blending of time and space from its reader. Moments in time are compressed together on the same page and within the same panel. Authoritative messages from the editor quickly undo the security announced by a title, as when a "Top 40" list only offers thirteen items (Porcellino *Map*, 53). Caption boxes interfere with the time sequences portrayed in the panel, deftly evoking the familiar time markers such as "Later" and "And then" of the comic book tradition; yet, because of their conventionality, such interferences do not intrude entirely but instead encourage readers to establish a blended notion of time, space, and story.[2]

Such devices have been sustained in virtuoso ways, as with Richard McGuire's *Here*, in which the spatial limitations of a room are kinetically

---

[2] For a cognitive perspective on this literary phenomenon see Ralf Schneider and Marcus Hartner, eds., *Blending and the Study of Narrative: Approaches and Applications* (De Gruyter, 2012).

Spotlight on: OPOSSUMS

(Didelphis virginiana)
Family: *Didelphidae*

AKA: Virginia Possum, Texas Possum, Didelphis marsupialis

Only marsupial native to North America

This tree loving creature has both a prehensile tail and opposable "thumbs" on its hind feet

Among the most primitive of living mammals (dating back to the Upper Cretaceous) *(Peterson)*

"Often seen in the beam of auto headlights, or dead along highways" *(Peterson)*

Eye-shine: dull orange *(Peterson)*. Life expectancy: 7+ years

Nocturnal, solitary. Eats fruits, vegetables, nuts, meat, eggs, insects and carrion; however, persimmons, apples and corn are its favorite foods *(Peterson / Great Lakes)*. Martin, Zim and Nelson note that "no available meats are too unsavory for the opossum to eat" *(Wildlife and Plants)*. Ed Dodd further elucidates: "When persimmons are ripe in the Southern woodlands, it's time to go "Possum Hunting." *(Book of Animals)*

Possums are "slow moving, with a sort of ambling gait" *(Great Lakes)* and "may wander widely, especially in fall." *(Peterson)*

The opossum's penis is forked, giving rise to the folk belief that they mate through the nose *(Audubon)*

The male opossum is not tolerated by the female after mating *(Great Lakes)*

Entire litter of up to 14 newborn possums can fit in a teaspoon! After babies emerge from the pouch they often ride "Piggy-back" on the mother, grasping her tail with theirs *(Audubon / Book of Animals)*

Opossum meat is "edible, but oily" and the fur is "saleable, but of little value" *(Peterson)*. *Audubon,* however, notes that opossum meat is considered a delicacy by many.

continued

96

Figure 9.1. John Porcellino, "Spotlight on: Opossums," *Map of My Heart* (Drawn & Quarterly, 2009), p. 96. Copyright John Porcellino. Used with permission from Drawn & Quarterly.

animated by the life forms that inhabit the "same" space over thousands of years. *King-Cat* is less operatic in scope than *Here*, but no less committed to drawing attention to a kind of co-present simultaneity signifying the becalmed aporia that marks Porcellino's work. These devices present an impossible-seeming harmonic at the surface of the text, echoing in form the philosophical questions attending Porcellino's art and writing on the nature of time, the shifting ways that a subject can transform and yet remain essentially the same, and the way that the returning motions of revision and reassembly are the very things that define a person. These are highlighted by Porcellino's narrative metalepsis, a device that John Pier describes as "a paradoxical contamination between the world of the telling and the world of the told" (91) where a narrative voice intrudes and engages with a narrative that should logically exclude them. Most often in Porcellino's comics, it is a narrating "John," just a different version of himself from a different time, who intrudes in the narrative, sometimes even inserting that version into the same panel, and other times inserting text clearly marked as atemporal in the caption box. The effect is less one of contamination, however, than it is an invitation to consider the over-lapping instances that constitute something more akin to possibility than to rejection.

Porcellino does not shy away from engaging with the particulars of uncertainty regarding where the subject is in place or time. Instead, he frequently and enthusiastically takes up this very problem in disparate narratives ranging from Zen koans to retellings of his own dreams and memories, questioning the nature of reality and his comprehension of it. One of the most prominent themes explored in *King-Cat* is Porcellino's experience of and bewilderment by the compression and expansion of time. The comics take pains to highlight its dates of making and dates of recording, and the subject of the comic itself is frequently that of the passage of time. In his introductory essay to Number 51, Porcellino writes in 1997:

> One thing I noticed while working on that big story is how relative time really is. . .the events in the comic as they actually occurred, took place from about June to mid-August of 1986—But when I look back on it now I can't believe it all happened so quickly! When I was seventeen every moment seemed to swell with promise and significance—and at the end of every day there was a measurable progress. Towards what, I don't know, but it was there. Nowadays I find myself saying things like "It's already Friday again?!" and "Is it really May 21st already?!" I'm not sure if it's good or bad, if there's anything I can do about it, or if it's just a natural effect of slowing down and getting older, but here we go (Map 41).

Passages such as this directly address the compression of time engendered specifically by life writing. Porcellino's surprise at the way that time has passed is characterized by his situationality, so that the same event may be understood differently based on where the subject is or what the subject has experienced already.[3] Time seems to move faster in comparison to how he felt in his late teens and early twenties, and it is not just the experience of the passage of time that changes but his understanding of the experiences themselves. This is made all the more striking in the case of *King-Cat,* where the publication history leading up to its currently most accessible version also mirrors and facilitates the backwards appraisals and reconsiderations that are so markedly part of its contents. *Map of My Heart* was published in 2009 and collected materials drawn from six years of *King-Cat* numbering 51 to 61 and self-published and distributed between 1996 to 2002.[4] The 2009 edition had gone out of print in recent years, and was again reissued in October 2021 by its publisher, Drawn & Quarterly. Nested within the issues collected within *Map of My Heart* are comics made in the late 1990s and early 2000s, many of which depict events that occurred in the late 1980s. The pages of the book thus span four decades of Porcellino's life, emphasizing the distance between the writing "I" and the living "I." What's more, the events depicted on their pages gain significance with the years, even when the individual comics are reproduced unaltered, through a series of interventions from the author.

In the introductory essay quoted above, Porcellino was describing the difference between the occurrences of 1986 that he was at that time reconstructing in 1997. Twelve years later, for the 2009 collection *Map of My Heart,* he once again returned to these events, not to alter the words of that essay, nor the original pages themselves, but nonetheless changing their meaning with additional paratext: an introductory comic, and contextualizing and explanatory endnotes appended as back matter. In this way, the paratext mimics how Porcellino himself has changed and been marked by the intervening years. Even more strikingly, the actual story that Porcellino describes in this introductory essay is not included at all in *Map of My Heart,* because it had already been collected in an earlier separate (2005) anthology: *Perfect Example. Perfect Example* had also gone out of print for some years and was reissued again in 2021 by Drawn &

---

[3] In a recent email exchange I had with Porcellino on November 10, 2021, he wrote: "Mostly memory feels like a bunch of stories to me now. Stories I've told myself and stories I've told to others."

[4] Selections from Numbers 1-50 were collected in King-Cat Classix, also reprinted and rereleased in 2021. John Porcellino, *King-Cat Classix* (Montreal: Drawn & Quarterly, 2021).

Life Writing in Comics

Quarterly. This activates a particular kind of metalepsis that is intratextual, and truly requires the reader's engaged participation as invoked by the interruptions and demands of its narrator. The kinds of metaleptic effects typically discussed in literary texts are characterized by an intrusive narrator who occupies a space outside the embedded narrative yet intervenes in it in unexpected and dissonant ways, as in Vladimir Nabokov's *Pale Fire*. It is less common to have the narrator intrude in such a way that it no longer suffices to mark shifts in time within the pages of the text itself, but necessitates a reaching outwards from the text to compare editions or to find a referenced story in a separate volume. This process is native to Porcellino's work and further explored through seriality, processes of republication, collection in other volumes, and changed meanings from the distance of progressive decades.

The 2009 edition of *Map of My Heart* is accompanied by a comic of seven panels that was "written down 3/26/09 drawn a week later." Words are never spoken within the panels themselves, although the panels do depict people interacting; instead, words are limited to an action ("unroll"), words written on articles on the walls of a room, the captions of the panels, and the paratextual (title, place, and time markers) materials that frame the piece. Narrative text is instead located in caption boxes at the top of each panel. Narrative captions in the comics form are "typically distinguished from speech balloons by their frames, background colour, or typography, [and] can also complement, evaluate, or interpret the speech acts presented in the images" (Mikkonen 232). Thierry Groensteen elaborates on the distinction:

> Among all the actions carried out by the characters, there is one that is specifically the act of speaking. The speech act inscribes itself in the chain of actions and reactions that make up the story; it is an integral part of the framework of events. The caption, equivalent to the *voiceover,* enclose[ing] a form of speech, that of the explicit narrator (who can be the principal narrator or the delegated narrator, intra- or extra-diegetic, etc.). Using another code...and reserving a contained space, that of the word balloon, speech is simultaneously at the interior of the image – "it emerges graphically from the mouth of the characters" – and distinct from it. This relative autonomy of verbal statements allows them to be perceived as links in a specific chain, parallel...to those of the images (128).

For the most part, this is true to Porcellino's comics, where caption boxes perform voiceover functions, narrating events from an exterior atemporality that suggests a perspective taken only after the events depicted in the panels. The first panel explains: "During the time I drew many of the comics collected in this book, I was sitting regularly with a Zen buddhist meditation group, and studying with a teacher." It continues into the second and third panel: "we held our sittings at a Unitarian-Universalist church in suburban Chicago/One of my responsibilities with the group was setting up the "Daisan Room" each night before sitting" (Porcellino *Map,* 6). This comic, titled "Map of my Heart" in cursive at the top of the page, shows Porcellino enacting the duties he describes, explaining that a "Daisan" is a face-to-face interview between teacher and student, and the fact that multiple rooms in the church may be used for this purpose. On the second page, he explains that his favorite room is the children's art room, "because [he] loved looking at the drawings and projects displayed on the wall." The last panel shows the title of the volume as it appears in a drawing on a wall in the art room and is accompanied only by two words ("One day:") in the caption (*Map* 7).

The two-page comic made for the 2009 edition deftly makes complex circuits that demonstrate Porcellino's insistence that his reader engage with the passage of time from the very beginning of the book, contesting the false rigor placed between past and present and surface and depth in favor of occupying an animistic suspension where memory and presence are coterminous rather than contradictory. The comics introduce an opportunity to "[open] up the early emphasis on the sequential in understanding strips to consider 'plurivectorial narration' and how its visual and textual arrangement can express an 'emergent causality'" (Laurier 239). His production of the comic for this new edition is already framed so that its temporal positions are clearly marked as distinct moments in time, preventing such specific moments from blending away in the reader's relationship with the surface of the page, where all marks are equally present. It is in the text that the reader engages with the various durations and steps that went into making this comic. Outside the diegesis of the story, Porcellino signs his name, the place (Denver, Colorado), and the notations "Written down 3/26/09" and "Drawn a week later." These notes, with their temporal and spatial specificity, draw attention to the way that such aspects of the comics page typically go unnoted. The time that the comic was conceived is necessarily distinct from the time it was executed, and the actions that it documents are also separated in time again. These gestures raise the reader's awareness of other factors that are not mentioned in the paratext; time elapses in each of these described processes, from the activities described, to recalling them, writing them down, and then drawing them, mark by mark.

These activities and temporalities exist on the page surface, equally present in space and time even though they were not enacted at the same

Life Writing in Comics

times or for the same amounts of time. Likewise, the reader's engagement is also positioned so that simultaneity is taken as a given and challenged by the form itself: "Strictly speaking, the pictorial and the verbal narration in comics cannot be simultaneously perceived...At a given point in time, we either read the writing or look at the image(s) so that text and image are not seamlessly integrated...at best, the verbal and pictorial track are received in virtual simultaneity" (Hescher 117). Hescher connects this reminder of the impossibility of simultaneity to the device of the caption in the comic: "Apart from the differences in the reception of, and the radical semiological difference between, verbal text and images, the question rather is whether or to what extent the narratorial caption script impinges on single images or (an) image sequence(s) in the process of meaning production. By narratorial caption script, I mean the enunciation or voice that usually comes in a caption box or is presented as a discernable block of text, framed or unframed" (117).

Porcellino's captions are usually employed to present information outside the sequence of action within the panels, delivering a retrospectively positioned narrative that incorporates a knowing voice from a vantage point in the actors' future. Groensteen likens this style to voiceover because it so often takes the form of a "reciter [who] does not belong to the fictional world," but this division is muddled by the autobiographical mode (8). Tense is confused in the captions in a story like "I saw where the Root Hog lives." The first caption in the comic is told in the present tense "My parents and I are on our way home from the fen. . ." (Porcellino *Map*, 27). The speech bubbles ooze out of the panel frames on the following page, and the next caption has transitioned to the past tense ("They pulled around the corner and dropped me off in a parking lot") before transitioning into a more distant past in the next caption: "When I was little, this area had been all wild...prairie fields and scattered woods—the place I now stood had been a low, swampy clearing" (Porcellino *Map*, 28, Figure 9.2).

This time, the John depicted in the panel has a different hairstyle from the one in the previous panels, indicating that the image, not simply the caption, is from another time. The following silent panel shows a "present day" John standing at the same spot and contemplating a medical center parking lot instead of the clearing that he remembers, and drew, in the previous panel (Porcellino *Map*, 29). On a later page, the older John actually encounters himself, without the distancing device of the caption but with a thought bubble instead (Figure 9.3). Appearing to view his younger self from behind, he thinks: "I remember standing under this tree,

Figure 9.2. John Porcellino, "They pulled around," *Map of My Heart* (Drawn & Quarterly, 2009), p. 28. Copyright John Porcellino. Used with permission from Drawn & Quarterly.

Life Writing in Comics

looking at the cows" (Porcellino *Map*, 30). The panel is filled with this very image using a framework that Miodrag admiringly argues is particular to comics: a "graphic rendering of language...that presents the most efficacious challenge to the distinction between visual and verbal" (101). The story ends with John remembering his young self being frightened away by an old root hog and then thinking, in a thought bubble: "If I was a millionaire – I'd buy this old farm and keep it just the way it is..." The thought is completed in a caption box at the bottom of the final panel "...and give it to you." Inscribed in the bottom right corner of the panel, within its lines, are the words "Oct – Dec 1996 John P." Although these words are inside the panel, they also occupy a space and time that is distinct from the image and text in the panel (Porcellino *Map*, 33).

This type of seamless presentation is described by Mikkonen as "the multimodal nature of comics [that] allows the invention of forms of complexity...pertaining to the relation between the time of the events and the time of their telling, or the source and perspective of narration, that are not available in the monomodal context of literary narratives" (238–239). Describing Lynda Barry's use of multiframe grids in her own refractive examinations of the past, Miodrag writes that it:

> is a norm invoked in service of conveying narrative information, and not used for what its form in itself contributes. There is no relationship between the story content and the multiframe; the latter is merely utilized as a platform for the former. Barry's standardized four-panel strip is of this type, the regular layout little implicated in aesthetically emphasizing or assisting the narrative content. The decorative type also entails independence of narrative and layout, but here an intricate and elaborate page design serves its own aesthetic ends, rather than supporting the narrative. Primary concern is for the page as a visual unit and narrative breakdown is subordinated to it. Story information is fitted into this totality rather than the page being designed to complement narrative content (222).

However, if we treat not only the comics but their paratexts as a collective body, as an animistic medium rather than as a system of hierarchically discrete parts where form is subordinate to content, we may find equally – or even more – productive ways of understanding the works of artists like Barry and Porcellino. The effects of the captions, title, and dating collaborate with layouts, ornaments on page, and anticipatory reading experiences in the production of a more numinous sense of time that both Barry and Porcellino are determined to enact.

Justin Green, who created the iconic autobiographical comic *Binky Brown Meets the Holy Virgin Mary* in 1972, described his use of comics captions:

Figure 9.3. John Porcellino, "I remember standing under this tree," *Map of My Heart* (Drawn & Quarterly, 2009), p. 30. Copyright John Porcellino. Used with permission from Drawn & Quarterly.

Life Writing in Comics

197

> I felt that what I was doing was very trivial, and I needed to wage my own war. And so I looked within and I don't know if this means anonymity, but I didn't want to present myself as a hero, but rather as a specimen. So the comic form gives you a multifaceted view of doing that. I don't know if you noticed, but old Superman comics have little panels at the top that say later, or soon, next day. Well, I turned that into the narrative voice where I would stack several lines of copy. But then I realized, I'm hiding up there. That's my voice, but I can show something below that either contradicts it or amplifies it. And on top of that, not only do I get to put balloons into the character's mouths, but there are thought balloons. So there is a multidimensional way of being anonymous yet at the same time pushing the story forward. But I never thought – I just thought it would, I guess, biodegrade. [laughter] It's a newsprint. It's been following me around for decades now (Nelson 86).

It is the very ephemerality of comics that Green both pushes against ("I needed to wage my own war") and surrenders to ("I just thought it would. . .biodegrade. It's a newsprint"). Again, the passage of time figures just as heavily as the narratological frames referenced in Green's description. Green's innovation with the caption box moved it away from the more typical stage whispers of "and then" and "later" into stacked lines of complex text that did not just corroborate the images and speech bubbles. Of course the newsprint may biodegrade, but both Green and his reader know that this is not where the actual story, the one that has managed to follow him for decades, exists anyway.

In *The Practice of Everyday Life*, Michel de Certeau focuses on everyday practices that "produce without capitalizing. . .without taking control over time" that include reading, talking, dwelling, and cooking (xx). He writes about how the act of reading is necessarily an act of erosion, where the reader is lost in the act: "the readable transforms itself into the memorable. . .The thin film of writing becomes a movement of strata, a play of spaces. A different world (the reader's) slips into the author's place. This mutation makes the text habitable, like a rented apartment. It transforms another person's property into a space borrowed for a moment by a transient" (xxi). He pauses for a moment during a chapter on "ordinary language," to bring up the historical reconstructions included in the expansive exhibitions of the Shelburne Museum in Burlington, Vermont:

> the display includes innumerable familiar objects, polished, deformed, or made more beautiful by long use; everywhere there are as well the marks of the active hands and laboring or patient bodies for which these things composed the daily circuits, the fascinating presence of absences whose traces were everywhere. At least this village full of abandoned and salvaged objects drew one's attention, through them, to the ordered murmurs of a

hundred past or possible villages, and by means of these imbricated traces one began to dream of countless combinations of existences. (21)

So it is with the autobiographical comics pages that each bear the highly individualistic traces of their authors: Art Spiegelman, Lynda Barry, Robert Crumb, Julie Doucet, Harvey Pekar, Alison Bechdel, Gabrielle Bell, and on and on. As these countless existences tread on leaving their "presence of absences whose traces [are] everywhere," they share the fact that they write their lives with a combination of image and text. The forms they choose to use cannot ultimately be reduced to a consistent set of features and characteristics.

Porcellino's work relies heavily on the backwards glancing narrator of the present, who looks backwards like an Orpheus who cannot help himself. The shades slip away at his glance, skittering this way and that at the slightest threat of being fastened in one place. They know that they are volatile, meant to be so. Paradoxically, Porcellino, for all his raiment of nostalgia, seems not only to recognize this, but to be looking to the past as the material for his stories, but not in order to restore them. Instead, by introducing very many metaleptic moments, he has devised a form of cementing what is yet to be. The insertion of moments from the past, indeed, different temporal moments from the past all within the same presence of the page, is much more concerned with anticipation than preservation. So while it is that the comics he writes impose a plot upon the events that he recalls, Porcellino applies to them the methods of fictional narratives that rely on the structures of beginning, middle, and end. Mark Currie, writing on time and narrative argues that:

> We inhabit the present, which is sandwiched between a fixed past and an open future. But there are some obvious differences. The present for a reader in a fictional narrative is not really the present at all but the past. It is somebody else's present related to us in the past tense. Though it seems like the present, because it is new to us, it is tensed as the past...We are narrated to in the preterite, but we experience the past tense in the present. But because it is the past tense we know that there is a future present, in relation to which the present of the narrative is past (5).

The backwards look in Porcellino's work is knowingly placed there because it provides what Currie calls a "mode of anticipation" (5). In other words, both the reader and the author derive at least some of the pleasure of the text from an anticipation of the way that what has been read will be changed as the story – and alongside it, time, and the reader – progresses. Frank Kermode's description of the sound of the ticking clock (tick-tock) illustrates where we are with respect to time and sequence; "tick" represents the beginning of a narrative and "tock" represents its ending. We inhabit the place in that interval, striving to give meaning to it. Kermode remarks that we tend to think in terms of duration rather than space, "organizing the moment in terms of the end, giving meaning to the interval between *tick* and *tock* because we humanly do not want it to be an indeterminate interval between the *tick* of birth and the *tock* of death" (58).

This focus on the anticipatory possibilities that can be created in Porcellino's works are, practically speaking, reassuring. The reader knows that young John will survive his annihilating depression, because he has survived to write the comic in hand. His unarticulated wish to disappear has obviously not come to pass (Porcellino *Perfect*; Figure 9.4). More than that is the anticipation of the readings that are yet to come. In this way, the unreliability of the narrator actually guarantees his reliability. His artistic practice acknowledges the shifting nature of one's relationship to time; the events shift and transform depending on where one stands. The author proceeds with an acceptance of that fact, leaving occasional marks to show moments at different stages. The back matter of *Map of My Heart* shows yet another metaleptic intrusion now from the distance of several more decades from the *King-Cat* issues collected in the volume. Interspersed with little drawings of Porcellino's beloved cat Maisie, notes contextualize the collection: "When I began drawing the comics contained in this collection, I was living in Denver Colorado. I was 27 years old, engaged to my old sweetheart, Kera, and living my life...My life, which had been so wild and disorderly for years, was shifting before my eyes" (Porcellino *Map*, 287). At the end of *Perfect Example*, Porcellino appends a biography that sketches out events in his life as if, after the lyrical and fragmentary items that the reader has become accustomed to, he ought to provide yet another kind of document for readers to reconsider and recalibrate their understanding of a new, longer, interval between the *tick* and the *tock* presented in these texts. Just like the "Top 40" lists that never seem to produce the complete amount that the title promises, *King-Cat* creates a sense of comfort through its direct acknowledgment of lack. Porcellino makes comics not only aware of the revisions and reconditionings of time, but he seeks to view them for their potential to create something more. On a "Top 40" list containing only 21 items, the 21st item alluringly promises: "and lots more!!" (Porcellino *Map,* 227; Figure 9.5).

Stinging from what he surely felt was unjust rejection, William Blake wrote two letters in quick succession to his patron the Reverend John Trusler in defense of work submitted that had failed to satisfy his patron's specifications, too much lodged in fancy for Trusler's taste. In the second of these letters, dated August 23, 1799, Blake took pains, over three pages

Figure 9.4. John Porcellino, "It seems like nothing really matters," *Perfect Example* (Drawn & Quarterly, 2006), n. pag. Copyright John Porcellino. Used with permission from Drawn & Quarterly.

Life Writing in Comics   201

Figure 9.5. John Porcellino, "King-Cat Top-forty. Winter '00–'01," *Map of My Heart* (Drawn & Quarterly, 2009), p. 227. Copyright John Porcellino. Used with permission from Drawn & Quarterly.

of his idiosyncratically capitalized and punctuated writing, to articulate the inextricable links that existed for him between the world, his personal vision, and his art. Acknowledging the differences of perspective inherent in the world as each person individually perceives it, he declared, therefore, the necessity of regulating his own proportions:

> And I know that This World Is a World of Imagination & Vision I see Every thing I paint In This World, but Every body does not see alike. To the Eyes of a Miser a Guinea is more beautiful than the Sun & a bag worn with the use of Money has more beautiful proportions than a Vine filled with Grapes. The tree which moves some to tears of joy is in the Eyes of others only a Green thing that stands in the way. Some See Nature all Ridicule & Deformity & by these I shall not regulate my proportions, & Some Scarce see Nature at all But to the Eyes of the Man of Imagination Nature is Imagination itself. As a man is So he Sees[5] (702).

Blake's letter is a remarkable document in defense of the "Man of Imagination," extolling the reservoirs of vision available to such men as himself, who is simply painting all the things as he sees them before his eyes. The images rendered in his paintings, though seemingly fantastical to some, represent his perceived world, and, consequently, represent what kind of a man he is.

Blake's reasoning has implications for his reader: what does it mean to be incapable of seeing what a person of imagination can see? What kind of person would that make one who fails to see that same beauty? Blake's letter is especially striking for the pains he takes to emphasize the particularities of each person's capacities with respect to vision. The letter also suggests prescriptive claims that extend beyond the forms in his art. He describes an artistic practice where *seeing* and *making others see* are crucially intertwined acts. So it is with life writing, here in the exemplary works of John Porcellino. His life as he sees it is still, after all, in the making.

WORKS CITED

Comics

Porcellino, John. *King-Cat Classix*. Drawn & Quarterly, 2021.
    Map of My Heart: The Best of King-Cat Comics & Stories 1996–2002. Drawn & Quarterly, 2009.
    Perfect Example. Drawn & Quarterly, 2005.

---

[5] A reproduction of the manuscript held at the British Library is viewable at https://www.bl.uk/collection-items/letters-from-william-blake-to-dr-trusler-august-1799.

Secondary Sources

Baggerman, Arianne, Dekker Rudolf, and Michael Mascuch. *Controlling Time and Shaping the Self: Developments in Autobiographical Writing since the Sixteenth Century*. Brill, 2011.

Blake, William. *The Complete Poetry and Prose of William Blake*. Edited by David V. Erdman. University of California Press, 1982.

Currie, Mark. *About Time: Narrative, Fiction and the Philosophy of Time*. Edinburgh University Press, 2007.

de Certeau, Michel. *The Practice of Everyday Life*. University of California Press, 1984.

de Man, Paul. "Autobiography as De-Facement." *MLN*, vol. 94, no. 5, 1979, pp. 919–930.

Groensteen, Thierry. *Comics and Narration*. Translated by Ann Miller. University of Mississippi Press, 2013.

Herbrechter, Stefan. "Narrating(−)Life – In Lieu of an Introduction." *Narrating Life – Experiments with Human and Animal Bodies in Literature, Science and Art*, edited by Stefan Herbrechter and Elisabeth Friis. Brill, 2016, pp. 1–13.

Hescher, Achim. *Reading Graphic Novels: Genre and Narration*. De Gruyter, 2016.

Mikkonen, Kai. *The Narratology of Comic Art*. Routledge Advances in Comics Studies. Routledge, 2017.

Kermode, Frank. *The Sense of an Ending: Studies in the Theory of Fiction*. Oxford University Press, 2000.

Kofman, Sarah. "Beyond Aporia?" *Post-Structuralist Classics*, edited by Andrew Benjamin. Routledge, 1988, pp. 7–44.

Kwa, Shiamin. *Regarding Frames: Thinking with Comics in the Twenty-First Century*. RIT Press, 2020.

Laurier, Eric. "The Graphic Transcript: Poaching Comic Book Grammar for Inscribing the Visual, Spatial and Temporal Aspects of Action." *Geography Compass*, vol. 8, no. 4, 2014, pp. 235–248.

McGuire, Richard. *Here*. Pantheon, 2014.

Miodrag, Hannah. *Comics and Language: Reimagining Critical Discourse on the Form*. University Press of Mississippi, 2013.

Nelson, Deborah. "Panel: Comics and Autobiography Phoebe Gloeckner, Justin Green, Aline Kominsky-Crumb, Carol Tyler." *Critical Inquiry*, vol. 40, no. 3, 2014, pp. 86–103.

Pier, John. "Metalepsis." *Handbook of Narratology*, edited by Peter Hùhn. De Gruyter, 2009, pp. 190–203.

Schneider, Ralf and Marcus Hartner, eds. *Blending and the Study of Narrative: Approaches and Applications*. De Gruyter, 2012.

CHAPTER 10

Racialines
Interrogating Stereotypes in Comics

Daniel Stein

Comics practitioners routinely identify stereotypes as a constitutive part of the medium. In 1994, Art Spiegelman observed in an essay titled "Little Orphan Annie's Eyeballs":

> *Stereos.* Greek, meaning solid, and *typus*, late Latin, meaning form. The stereotype was invented early in the eighteenth century as a way of making relief-printing plates from paper pulp molds. It's the way newspaper comic plates were made until new technologies overtook the business in the 1960s. So comic strips were literally as well as figuratively generated from stereotypes. (17)

Noting a confluence of production technology and graphic technique – a constitutive process of duplicating images from the same mold of an individually created drawing – Spiegelman understands comics as a medium steeped in stereotype as both technological requirement and aesthetic necessity.

In *Graphic Storytelling and Visual Narrative*, Will Eisner further highlights the centrality of stereotypes in comics: "Its drawings [. . .] depend on the reader's stored memory of experience to visualize an idea or process quickly. This makes necessary the simplification of images into repeatable symbols. Ergo, stereotypes" (11). Comics obviously trade in stereotypes – in simplified, repeatable symbols or, as Scott McCloud suggests, via "amplification through simplification" (30). Yet both Eisner and McCloud underestimate the power of repeatable symbols that are invested in and dependent on popular constructions of race, class, gender, sexuality, and other intersectional identities that shape how and what we see.

Seeing "Race" in Caricature Country

"How do we learn to see?" (22), Sander L. Gilman asks in *Difference and Pathology: Stereotypes of Sexuality, Race, and Madness.* "We learn to perceive

204

in terms of historically determined sets of root-metaphors [that . . .] serve as the categories through which we label and classify the Other" (22). One of these root-metaphors is "race": "In 'seeing' (constructing a representational system for) the Other," Gilman notes, "we search for anatomical signs of difference such as physiognomy and skin color" and position them as the "antithesis of the idealized self's" (25). If seeing "race," in comics and elsewhere, means constructing a representational system rooted in and expressive of an antagonistic sense of difference, this vision also works to establish a non-racialized, idealized, and usually unmarked generic white self. "[C]omics have historically been a loaded, sometimes brutal, means of social discrimination—indeed, a spectacular art of difference" (147), Theresa Tensuan writes; the task is to "dishabituate whiteness," Frederick Luis Aldama holds: to "denaturalize [. . .] it as a seemingly invisible color" ("Unmasking" xii).

Building on these interventions, this chapter turns to the formative years of comics at the turn of the twentieth century, when new technologies enabled mass color printing and facilitated the emergence of new visions of "race," giving rise to a print world of stereotypical depiction where comics offered a rich playing field for the visual imagination and taught Americans to perceive "race" in new ways. "Visual appearances [. . .] became a factor in demonstrating social standing and character," Ian Gordon writes, noting that newspaper comics took part in "creating a national market for visual images" (6–7) in the United States that came to favor individual characters (e.g. Richard Felton Outcault's Yellow Kid and Buster Brown) but continued to pigeonhole black Americans. Early newspaper illustrations by Edward Windsor Kemble, Outcault, and others adapted racial stereotypes from nineteenth-century caricature and related kinds of visual culture into comic form while retaining some of their discriminatory thrust.[1] The cartoonist Frederick Burr Opper even coined a name for the world of the colored supplements in urban newspapers like William Randolph Hearst's *New York Journal* and *Chicago American* or Joseph Pulitzer's *New York World*:

> Colored people and Germans form no small part of the population of Caricature Country. The negroes spent much of their time getting kicked by mules, while the Germans, all of whom have large spectacles and big pipes, fall down a good deal and may be identified by the words, "Vas iss," coming out of their mouths. There is also a good sprinkling of Chinamen, who are always having their pigtails tied to things; and a few Italians, mostly women, who have wonderful adventures while carrying enormous bundles

---

[1] See also Heer: "Racial and ethnic stereotypes grew out of [a] larger tendency to caricature" (n. pag.).

206 DANIEL STEIN

on their heads. The Hebrew residents of Caricature Country [...] have thinned out of late years [...]. This is also true of the Irish dwellers, who at one time formed a large percentage of the population. (Qtd. in Heer n. pag.)

Opper's Caricature Country evokes essentialized ethnic excess and a smorgasbord of stereotypes rather than serious intercultural exchange.[2] It imagines a storyworld where racial and ethnic differences are source material for ribald humor. Absent from this world is the nonethnic, nonracialized norm that allows these stereotypes to work – the "us" against which the comical "them" takes form, the "canvas backdrop against which other ethnicities are measured, seen, evaluated, and examined" (Aldama, "Unmasking" xii).[3] As such, early newspaper comics established an aesthetics of racialized stereotyping that delivered the groundwork for more than a century of constructions of graphic "blackness."

Stereotypes in Comics

In their introduction to *The Blacker the Ink: Constructions of Black Identity in Comics & Sequential Art*, Frances Gateward and John Jennings write: "Comics traffic in stereotypes and fixity. It is one of the attributes at the heart of how the medium deals with representation" (2). But despite their imperative to fix representation, stereotypes also act as "double-edged" entities conveying "negative images" as well as "positive idealizations" (Gilman 25). It is this double function that "make[s] comics and cartoon art a particularly messy medium for representing blackness" (21), Rebecca Wanzo observes.[4] After all, "[r]acist caricature was [...] not a side note to US cartooning's emergence. It was central to it" (7). While Wanzo defines "stereotyping as a subset of caricature" (5), I understand caricature as an expression of stereotype that utilizes its "oxymoronic nature" to "reduce [...] the complexity of a subject to real or imagined excesses" (Wanzo 23). Condensing complexity to create excess is particularly troublesome when

---

[2] Wanzo understands caricature as "reducing people to real and imagined excesses in order to represent something understood as essential about their character" (5). My focus on "blackness" is not meant to marginalize other stereotyped Others. For analysis, see Aldama, *Multicultural*; Ayaka and Hague.

[3] See Saguisag: "These humorous figures not only served to draw a line between 'us' and 'them' but also stirred and satiated white, middle-class curiosity for 'aliens' in their midst" (11).

[4] For Saguisag, "[t]he racist typographies that appeared in the comics meant to repress and ridicule, to highlight the 'inherent' vulgarity and depravity of African Americans. But they also conveyed a fascination with black bodies and culture" (55). We should distinguish between the white fantasies of "blackness" discussed in this chapter and what Howard calls "the black comic strip" created by black creators.

dealing in fictions of "race," as reducing groups of people to readily repeatable graphic features may reinforce notions of racial essentialism.

Gilman defines "stereotyping [a]s a universal means of coping with anxieties engendered by our inability to control the world" (12) and as "part of our way of dealing with the instabilities of our perception of the world" (18). To stereotype is to "project that anxiety onto the Other, externalizing our loss of control. The Other is thus stereotyped, labeled with a set of signs paralleling (or mirroring) our loss of control" (20). We do not have to embrace the psychoanalytical premises of Gilman's words to grasp their usefulness for comics, where projection – especially the interpretive work of filling in the gaps between images and words and between panels and sequences, labeled "closure" by McCloud (63) – is crucial.[5] If sense-making in comics is an "act of projection" and if stereotypes, as "a crude set of mental representations of the world" (Gilman 17), are inscribed into the medium's technology and visual grammar, then unpacking racial stereotypes in comics can illuminate the workings of graphic narrative at large.

The phenomenological questions Gilman raises by foregrounding the "instabilities of our perception" and their psychological implications are most urgent in times of social change. Entering Opper's Caricature Country might have been an entertaining coping mechanism for artists and readers in a rapidly transforming society, where immigration and internal migration created uncertainty about the validity of racialized hierarchies, threatening to loosen what W.E.B. Du Bois famously christened "the color-line" (100), as the latent instability of this line mirrors the instability of the stereotype. "Because there is no real line between self and the Other, an imaginary line must be drawn," Gilman suggests; "so that the illusion of an absolute difference between self and Other is never troubled, this line is as dynamic in its ability to alter itself as is the self" (18).

Gilman's reference to the drawn line, while not directed at graphic storytelling, returns us to questions of visual construction, including the distinction between cartoons and comics in the context of early newspaper comics. Cartoons are single-panel drawings that may or may not contain speech balloons and do not tell an unfolding story. Unlike sequential comics, they do not spatialize time into segments. The difference between cartoon and comic is crucial in terms of representation, Jared Gardner argues: "Single-panel comics [i.e., cartoons] especially lend themselves to

---

[5] See Gardner, *Projections.*

the work of stereotyping. [...] But [...] sequential comics have a unique and contrasting ability to *destabilize* racial stereotype" ("Same" 135). Moreover:

> A single-panel cartoon gag of an ethnic or racial stereotype is contained by its frame; it does the work of stereotyping as the term originally was defined: printing from a fixed mold. It is static and resists ambiguity, directing the reader to very specific ways of reading. [...] But once two panels are put together, narrative is inevitable. [...T]wo radically dissimilar images in different times and space juxtaposed in sequential panels require of their readers the work of imaginatively filling in the time and space that connect them. (136–137)

While single-panel cartoons and sequential comics "rely on stereotype and caricature – on individual characters distilled to iconic characteristics" (136), Gardner proclaims, "the sequential comic is the most powerful [...] medium for embracing the radical consequences of an alterity that disables stereotype and the easy readings of the hegemonic gaze" (147).

Apart from this distinction between the cartoon and the comic strip, another notion of "cartoon" is pertinent here. "When we abstract an image through cartooning, we're not so much eliminating details as we are focusing on specific details," McCloud writes. "By stripping down an image to its essential 'meaning,' an artist can amplify that meaning in a way that realistic art can't" (30). Cartooning, thus, is very much like stereotyping and conducive to the paradox of reductive excess. Yet McCloud's widely cited definition has also been challenged by Brian Cremins, who wonders: "What happens [...] when images of blackness are introduced into McCloud's theoretical framework?" (46). If introducing blackness into the framework means reducing the comic's "*connotative* abilities in favor of a monosemic *denotative* function," as Molotiu holds (160), then simplification entails more than leaving things out and reducing something to its essentials. Indeed, what counts as essential is not so much stored in the image than the result of conventionalized ways of seeing. The meaning of the stereotype derives not just from what is being depicted and what is left out, but also from the depiction's capability to conjure up, adapt, or negate specific readings of "race."

Racialized Lines, or Racialines

How, then, can we grasp the double function of stereotypes as "idealized and ugly typologies" and something that "compels and repels" (Wanzo 5)? One answer to this question lies in the drawn line as "the most undertheorized element in comics scholarship and one that has no neat equivalent in any other narrative form" (Gardner, "Storylines" 53). As I will show, the drawn lines of early US newspaper comics are charged with an expressive force that connotes fictions of "race" for artists and readers alike, and they attain much of their connotative potential from their interaction with colored spaces on the page. While the line is a central element of racial caricature and stereotypical renditions of comical blackness, it is only one of two foundational factors of racialized depiction, as it needs black surfaces to create what I call *racialines*: graphically rendered notions of "race" that emerge from the intersection of the line and the colored spaces it encloses. "When a drop of ink hits a white piece of paper, something happens," Gateward and Jennings maintain. "Is the white paper now blemished by the aesthetically unpleasing dot, or is it made more interesting and nuanced?" (3).

For Gardner, "the graphic enunciation that is the drawn line" suggests "the trace of the hand" ("Storylines" 54) and thus appears as the artist's signature: "the mark of the individual upon the page" (56). This is different from the mechanical process of stereotyping, which only approximates the trace of the artist's hand. This trace is transmitted onto the printing plate before being reproduced and multiplied onto the newspaper page, effectively removing the creator from the creation. The result is an illusion of intimacy between the image and its creator, as well as between the reader and these images, that impacts constructions of "race" and "blackness." If "the line of the artist [is] the handprint of the storyteller" (56), the non-mechanical stereotype serves as a shorthand, capitalizing on the connotative abilities of preconceived and conventionalized assemblages of lines.[6] As a shorthand, it constrains the imagination and inhibits the hand producing the image. In comics invested in racialized depiction, the line always comes with an attitude.

What appears on the page, then, is not just "the flesh-and-blood artist putting pen to paper" (Gardner, "Storylines" 61), whom readers may imagine as they encounter a comic. It is also a particular disposition toward the material that emerges from the loaded lines of racialization. If "the line compels a physical, bodily encounter with an imagined scene of embodied enunciation" (66), the question is whose body is actually imagined. Is it the body of the creator, as Gardner suggests?[7] Is it the body of the reader, whose consumption of the kinds of corporeal contortions found in many

---

[6] Barker defines stereotype as "a shorthand image which fills in gaps in our own knowledge" (196).
[7] Chute maintains: "Marks made on paper by hand are an index of the body" (20).

newspaper comics is also an embodied act? Or is it the (black) bodies depicted on the page and all they connote that the line compels, the stereotypical "blackness" they ostensibly represent? All three options seem possible – from what Hillary Chute calls the "trace of the body of the drawer" (20) to the visual traces of caricatured black bodies created by the artist's corporeal engagement with grotesque forms of "blackness." It is this multiplicity that makes these stereotypes both powerful and messy. By laughing about black bodies on the page, those who perceive themselves as white may feel reassured about their own bodies as the implied norm against which the figures on the page become comically legible. Yet for readers socially constructed as nonwhite, the comic may connote something entirely different, from annoyance at the incongruence between stereotype and lived experience and the realization that someone is poking fun (and making money) at their expense to an awareness of their racialized difference, of being marginalized from the hegemonic norm.[8] Perhaps such racialines made some readers envision the white artist's hand or head (body parts instrumental in the creation of the comic), but probably in a more metaphorical than literal sense, and unlike the bare torsos and bottoms of black children in "pickaninny" representations by artists like Rudolph Dirks, where readers might not necessarily have imagined Dirks's drawing hand while indulging in the children's comical nudity (Figure 10.1).[9] The comic thus at once exposes black bodies and obscures the white body that births these racialized fantasies. It thereby confirms the white body as the point of departure for the standardized, normalized point of view of the narrative while leaving room for some degree of ambiguity, some sense of the color line loosening, through the identical punishment the black and white rascals receive from their respective mothers.

Drawn Lines, Storylines, Color Lines, Lineages

The transition from nineteenth-century caricature to newspaper comics was a foundational process in the history of graphic narrative, when the stereotypical groundwork was laid for the form. This is when the basic

[8] See Kunka: "The reader's engagement with an image, then, is open to debate. Do readers see themselves reflected in caricatures, or are readers distanced from such images?" (278).

[9] See also Saguisag (64–67). Saguisag explains: "The pickaninny's depravity was signaled by his behavior: he engaged in violent acts that brought injury upon himself as well as other pickaninnies, he stole and devoured chickens and watermelons, and he wore ragged clothes or no clothing at all, shamelessly exposing his genitalia and buttocks. The pickaninny was, in other words, a 'child coon'" (56).

Racialines: Interrogating Stereotypes in Comics 211

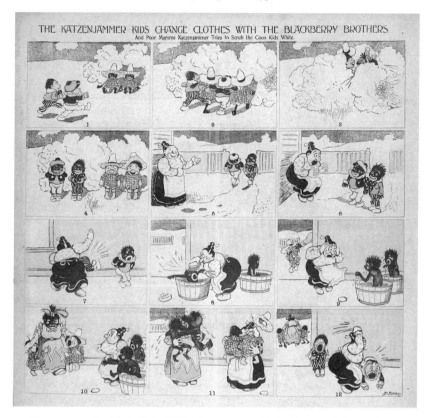

Figure 10.1. Rudolph Dirks, "The Katzenjammer Kids Change Clothes with the Blackberry Brothers," *Chicago American Comic Supplement,* 2 September 1900, p. 2. San Francisco Academy of Comic Art Collection, The Ohio State University, Billy Ireland Cartoon Library and Museum.

narrative apparatus and visual vocabulary of modern comics begins to settle and set the standard for later variants of the medium (comic books, graphic novels, etc.). Contextualizing this moment as the "nadir" of American race relations – "a period of race riots in both northern and southern cities, of an epidemic of brutal lynchings, and of disfranchisement and segregation" – Alan Havig describes this transition as follows: "[I]n the 1890s technological innovation contributed new media of information and amusement; the typecast comic black made an easy transition from older entertainment forms into newspaper color comic sections and onto Victrola cartridges and nickelodeon movie screens" (33).

Figure 10.2. Cover of Edward Windsor Kemble, *Comical Coons* (R. H. Russell, 1898). Emory University, Stuart A. Rose Library, Special Collections.

Lara Saguisag adds: "Cartoonists of the Progressive Era copied typographies that were developed and popularized in late nineteenth-century humor magazines such as *Puck*, *Life*, and *Judge* as well as more 'genteel' publications such as *Harper's Weekly*" (11).[10]

One prominent "coon" illustrator was Edward Windsor Kemble (1861–1933). Kemble was one of the most respected graphic artists of his time, and *Comical Coons* (1898) was one of his popular publications. The cover image presents two stock figures known from the minstrel stage – a rascally black "pickaninny" child and an old devilish uncle playing the banjo (Figure 10.2). The pickaninny's frizzy hair and popping eyes connote the black child's undisciplined yet supposedly funny nature, recalling Harriet Becher Stowe's Topsy from *Uncle Tom's Cabin*.[11] In the visual culture of the time, the old uncle figure frequently signified the antebellum South, romanticized as a paternal space of interracial harmony. Here, he looks demonic, his leering gaze underscoring the ugly anxieties

---

[10] For historical context, see also Banta; Cole; Gambone; Lemons.
[11] Kemble briefly drew cartoons featuring a Topsy character (see Saguisag 58).

Racialines: Interrogating Stereotypes in Comics 213

racist stereotypes sought to address, while the two black kids watching this clownish figure are presented as cute and innocent.

Scholars rightly read such "coon" illustrations as racist artifacts, suggesting that they implemented notions of black inferiority and white supremacy in a society obsessed with the color line. But Jeet Heer's reminder "not to deny the racism or malevolence of the stereotype but rather to link it to the formal practices of the cartoonists" (n. pag.) is crucial. Think of *Kemble's Coons*, published a year before *Comical Coons*. Whereas *Comical Coons* displays stereotypically reductive images of black faces and bodies, *Kemble's Coons* has a softer touch, contains a lesser degree of caricatured excess, and presents its subjects as individual types (some have names) rather than mere stereotypes. This insinuates some degree of identification, or projection, across the color line. Kemble may have drawn single illustrations of his "coons," but he produced them in such large numbers that they enabled a repeated, quasi-serial engagement with these figures. Even if his figures emerged from the mold of "coon" illustration, the very fact that he drew so many of them in different situations and in varying styles might have created room for "forg[ing] a deep identification" (Gardner, "Same" 135) among artist, characters, and audience. What's more, while *Kemble's Coons* presents individual portraits (i.e., single-image sketches), *Comical Coons* collects two-image narratives, the first image setting up the joke, the second providing the spectacularly rendered pun (a mule kicking a cart filled with Professor Pewter and his friends; a mother and her children waiting for Santa Claus to sweep down the chimney as their father is crashing on the floor, spilling the presents). Ironically, the portraits come across as less stereotyped than the double-image skits, complicating the assumption that the gutter provides the images with a greater degree of ambiguity and suggesting that the national market for racial caricature was able to accommodate stylistic variation in stereotyped graphics even from a single artist (Figure 10.3).

Kemble's images seem less rooted in an intimate knowledge of African American life than in a lineage of visually coded racial fantasies, despite the fact that *Kemble's Coons* was subtitled *A Collection of Southern Sketches* and placed its (mostly) black children in pastoral scenery.[12] Nonetheless, these caricatures may have enabled moments of cross-racial identification if we

---

[12] The reference to the Southern sketches suggests a folkloric interest and evokes local color fiction, such as Joel Chandler Harris's *Uncle Remus* publications (some of which Kemble illustrated) as well as writings by African American authors such as Charles Chesnutt.

Figure 10.3. "Ebenezer." From Edward Windsor Kemble, *Kemble's Coons: A Collection of Southern Sketches* (R.H. Russell, 1897). University of Delaware Special Collections.

follow Maaheen Ahmed's conception of the newspaper comic panel "as a contact zone, and as the product of many earlier moments of contacts and molding of stereotypes" (35): as a playground where artists and readers explore their investment in popular constructions of "race."[13] At least, Kemble's creation of multiple "coon" series (*Coontown Calamities, Rag-Time Cadets, Blackberries*) suggests that Americans were willing to invite these characters into their homes (or wherever they read their newspapers).[14] Of course, this invitation was only extended in a mediated form –

[13] See Mitchell: "the dragging or pulling of the drawing instrument, is the performance of desire" (59). Saguisag discerns a "white ambivalence for blacks and black cultural practices: aversion for African Americans was deeply intertwined with feelings of desire and captivation" (55). Maaheen Ahmed takes up Sara Ahmed's discussion of the "contact zone."

[14] Kemble's *Blackberries* and *Rag-Time Cadets* show little interest in investing their characters with humanity. The "Rag-Time Cadets," a troupe of uniformed black "coons," ignore their orders as they are lusting over stereotypically coded food (chicken, watermelon). *Coontown Calamities* may seem less fixed on stereotypes because it is a two-panel cartoon with a limited degree of sequentiality, but its humor is mostly slapstick and its graphic style lacks the nuance of *Kemble's Coons*, ridiculing its black subjects (kids teasing and getting hit by a mule; a mammy telling a child to stick his arm into a tree in search of hidden honey and being kicked in the face when the kid is

Racialines: Interrogating Stereotypes in Comics   215

through the newspaper and as stereotyped "coons" – and the visitors were usually not granted the power of speech. Indeed, many of Kemble's illustrations lack verbal narrative (and thus one characteristic element of comics: the speech balloon); we see his black characters with open mouths in the middle of noisy activities, rendered mute.[15] Readers are compelled to enjoy gazing at black bodies without recognizing that these images cloak the real-life agency of the people they stereotype.

As Kemble was drawing his "coons," newspapers like the *New York Journal* and the *New York World* began to feature comics as part of their Sunday supplements, indicating a larger shift in the commodification of racialized images that would eventually include more individualized depictions of recurring characters in a move toward potentially more complex notions of graphic "blackness." If we recall the similarities between Kemble's illustrations and the basic narrative properties of comics – both heavily invested in caricature – it is no surprise that the cartoonish "coon" figures quickly leaped from illustration into the world of comics. Perhaps the most popular early US-American comics artists was Richard Felton Outcault (1863–1928), whose success was based on the Irish kid character Mickey Dugan, or The Yellow Kid, as he was popularly known by the mid-1890s.[16] Almost every page of the *McFadden's Row of Flats* series featured one or two black characters that recall Kemble's brand of the comical "coon" – signaling that popular entertainment could not do without at least one iconic black (sur)face in a sea of urban characters.

Outcault devoted a whole series to the repertoire of "coon" imagery. *Pore Lil' Mose* ran for a year and a half from 1901 to 1902 in the *New York Herald*. According to Havig, it "was the first comic strip to feature a black person as the central character" and "presented a dual, somewhat contradictory, vision of blacks" by mixing moments of "visual complexity" with instantiations of "the prevailing white stereotype of blacks" (33) that align only imperfectly with the developing setting of the strip (rural South to Northern metropolis).[17] "Pore Lil Mose He Takes a Ride on the Car" is an example of the later, more satirical urban cartoons set in New York City,

---

stung by bees; another mammy hit by a baby "coon" as he and his brother tumble down from a clothesline).

[15] This is different in *Kemble's Coons*, where character speech sometimes appears below a sketch.

[16] On all things Yellow Kid, see Meyer.

[17] Havig observes Outcault's "inconsistent use of racial stereotyping in both the rural and urban Mose cartoons" (35). Saguisag understands Mose as "a liminal figure, at once based on the pickaninny caricature yet also exhibiting characteristics often associated with white childhood" (53), and the strip as a failed attempt to overcome the "marginalization of black characters in the comic supplements" (54).

216   DANIEL STEIN

the place to which Mose, like many African Americans, moved during the Great Migration. It replicates the black face of the neatly dressed picka-ninny (Mose) but focuses on the carnivalesque (more circus-like than explicitly racialized) atmosphere on a street car in a scene of topsy-turvy turbulences instigated by Mose's pet monkey. "Pore Lil' Mose at Coney Island" likewise depicts an urban experience potentially familiar to readers and not primarily aimed at stereotypical excess. Mose and his animal friends play on the beach, buy lemonade, and take a swim, activities that do not directly connote "black" deficiency or inferiority but can still be associated with the deprecating discourse of "black" idleness. The discrep-ancy between these largely happy images and Mose's report to his mother ("I dont like Coney Island, cause its stupid and its bad") adds complexity, making readers wonder, perhaps, whether Mose is telling the truth or trying to conceal the pleasures of urban life. Moreover, they underscore Outcault's "deep-seated ambiguity toward modernization" (Gordon 66).[18]

Two additional installments exemplify Outcault's racialines. The first is titled "Poor Lil' Mose on the 7 Ages" (Figure 10.4). Note the dialect verse on top of the page and the setting, Cottonville, Georgia. Consider further the animalistic depiction of minstrel and "coon"-related figures: the slave mammy, the black rascal child about to "help [him]self to watermelons," the grotesque "coon" lover, the dandy soldier, and the old uncle in his rocking chair. Equally typical are the schoolboy's grin, the oversized mouth signifying animal-likeness and suggesting perpetual happiness, as well as the roasted chicken held up by the mammy figure in the upper right corner. In her reading of this comic, Saguisag notes how the "black male's life cycle is essentially an evolution from one caricature to another" and how "the black female grows up to fulfill sexual and servile roles. She is literally marginalized, reduced to adornments along the borders of the cartoon" (74, 75). It may be true that the final phrase "sans everything" from Shakespeare's *As You Like It* "hints at the shared humanity of blacks and whites" (75), but the question remains whether it complicates the cartoon's investment in racial stereotype. Indeed, these "coons"

---

[18] In the NYC installments, the image is accompanied by a letter in which Mose reports his experiences to his mother, who had remained in the South. Saguisag comments: "While Kemble's nameless characters [in the *Blackberries*] are indistinguishable from one another, Mose is not associated with a 'litter of coons.' He is a distinct individual, the central character and narrator of his own series. While Kemble's little urban dandies constantly return to the countryside, their purported natural habitat, Mose leaves his rural home to explore the city" (73).

Racialines: Interrogating Stereotypes in Comics 217

Figure 10.4. Richard Felton Outcault, "Poor Lil' Mose on the 7 Ages," *New York Herald Comic Supplement*, 3 February 1901, p. 1. San Francisco Academy of Comic Art Collection, The Ohio State University, Billy Ireland Cartoon Library and Museum.

encapsulate the whole range of reductive excess – a segregated universe filled with racially stereotyped characters – even though the degree of graphic stereotyping can vary. (Images 5 and 7 seem less egregiously stereotyped than others.)

The second example is "A True Ghost Story" (Figure 10.5), which Havig reads as "representative of Outcault's crude and largely pointless racial humor" (35). It adapts a popular minstrel routine: the superstitious slave afraid of ghosts. Visual signifiers of comical "blackness" are prominent: bulging eyes, thick lips, bodies twisted into weird poses. The comic mixes popular "coon" imagery with a faux romanticism about the antics of Southern rural black folk. But if Outcault's "coons" were serially published racial caricatures in large panels that presented multiple images, they were technically not yet comic strips because they did not present stories in sequentially arranged panels. Moreover, while they include dialect verse to verbalize what the visual narrative depicts, they render the characters

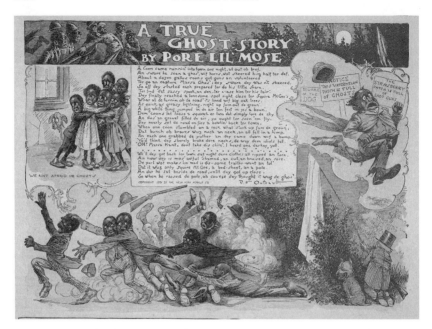

Figure 10.5. Richard Felton Outcault, "A True Ghost Story," *New York Herald*, 28 April 1901. San Francisco Academy of Comic Art Collection, The Ohio State University, Billy Ireland Cartoon Library and Museum.

mute – there are no speech balloons in *Pore Lil' Mose*. Nonetheless, Outcault went beyond the static nature of the single-image cartoon and its relative resistance to racial ambiguity. The images call for a fluid focus from the readers, who must move their eyes across the page to take in the whole panoply of racialized portraiture. Still, there isn't much potential for an evolving narrative; the different parts of the image all tell the same basic story, and it isn't much of a story. All images visualize an already popular repertoire of racial codes and comic moments, and the text accompanying the images does so as well. If there is a small degree of narrative progression – from the "coons" who claim that they are not afraid of ghosts to their frantic fear of the white flag, held up by a cunning white boy hiding behind a bush, and their cowardly flight from the scene of the prank – it is a progression from one familiar story element to the next: the fulfillment of a set course of action, with a sense of racial inferiority as the inevitable outcome, as if to metaphorically ward off the assumed dangers posed by an increasingly multicultural society through Outcault's aesthetically refined treatment of stereotyped stock materials.

Conclusion

Outcault was not the only artist who adapted such materials into comic form. Around the time he was publishing *Pore Lil' Mose*, cartoonists like George Herriman and William Marriner were already producing sequential strips with similar black characters and themes. Herriman's short-lived *Musical Mose* was running in the *New York World*, and Marriner's *Sambo and His Funny Noises* was syndicated by T.C. McClure. Both of these strips featured popular black "coons" as protagonists, but their sequential and serial mode may have enabled more complex responses than Outcault's single-page tableaus. This trend continued with Winsor McCay's *Little Nemo in Slumberland* and culminated in the playful interrogation of the ironies of racial (mis)identification in George Herriman's *Krazy Kat* (1913–1944).[19]

Little Nemo ran from 1905 to 1914 and combined episodic with open-ended forms of serial storytelling. Its central character, little Nemo, goes to bed in every strip to enter a colorful dream world and wake up in the middle of the dream. Every new installment continues the dream, allowing McCay to spin one long adventure story involving Nemo and his best friend Flip. As Saguisag notes, Flip "was perhaps the most visible child-minstrel figure in turn-of-the-century comic supplements"; as he is constantly wearing blackface, he "perpetually acts as the racial Other" and thereby as "Nemo's foil" (71–72). Flip is Nemo's partner-in-crime, a constant presence in Nemo's serial life with whom he discovers the strip's modern dreamscapes. Within these dreamscapes, McCay stages stereotypes of "blackness," for instance, in an episode from 1908 in which he disperses splotches of black across the page (Figure 10.6). Coming upon a lake, the two boys disrobe to their shorts and jump into the water, only to find out that they have suspended themselves in black molasses. Adding color to the boy's bodies, McCay transforms the boys into black pickaninnies. A few moments later, on their way home, they end up covered in flour, which reverses the transformation but still leaves them looking odd. When their cousin sees them, she is "offended and frightened by bodies that represent the 'unnatural' mingling of black and white," as they "evoke miscegenation and the figure of the 'sullied' mixed-race child" (Saguisag 72).

Here, again, we see how racialines resonate in different directions. McCay conceives the strip as a playful comment on the performativity of color, both on a formal level, where adding color (black ink) to a character sparks a racial transformation, and on a metaphorical level, where the artist's trace on the page,

---

[19] On race in *Krazy Kat*, see Amiran; Stein.

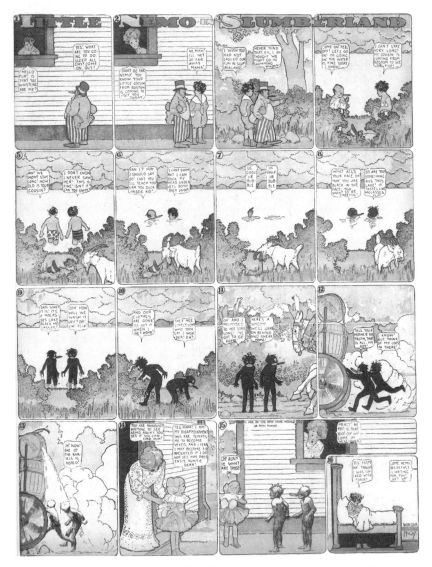

Figure 10.6. Winsor McCay, "Little Nemo in Slumberland", *New York Herald*, 2 August 1908.

the drawn line and colored spaces, reinforces a position of whiteness available to the artist and his white readers. Yet the strip also reveals self-consciousness by highlighting a racialized imagination where the hypervisibility of "blackness" obscures the lives and experiences behind it.[20] This is reinforced by the contentious connection the strip establishes between blackness and sexuality. "The sticky layer makes the children's bodies appear naked yet asexual, expressing a paradoxical view of the relationship between blackness and sexuality," Saguisag notes (but note Flip's phallic cigar!). "On the one hand, the boys' 'exposed' and blackened bodies evoke the notion of blacks' sexual immodesty. On the other hand, the molasses' concealment of their phalli articulates white compulsion to emasculate and desexualize black male bodies" (72). This nakedness is more indicative of modern notions of racialized sexuality – including the brutal de-sexualization through castration and the mutilation of bodies in many race-based lynchings – than of the ability of the line to evoke the artist's body. It seems likely that rather than imagining McCay, readers of the strip would have recalled the many minstrel and blackface illustrations and performances they must have encountered throughout their lives.

The continuing presence and complex legacy of such racialized figures – from Ebony White, the Samboesque sidekick in Eisner's *The Spirit* (1940–1952), and Angelfood McSpade, Robert Crumb's hypersexualized and primitively rendered variant of the Jezebel stereotype in *Zap Comix* #2 (1968), to depictions of nonwhite characters in superhero comics and the shadowy presence of racist imagery in graphic narratives by African American creators[21] – indicates that the fixed mold of the stereotype has proven to be quite durable, even though it now seems to serve increasingly as a historical foil against which more nuanced and more adequate images emerge. Jeremy Love's two-part *Bayou* (2009, 2010) and Ebony Flowers's *Hot Comb* (2019) are only two recent examples of African American artists taking on the task of dismantling racial stereotypes highlighting their social and cultural persistence.

WORKS CITED

Comics

Rudolph, Dirks. "The Katzenjammer Kids Change Clothes with the Blackberry Brothers." *Chicago American Comic Supplement.* 2 September, 1900.
Kemble, Edward W. *Comical Coons.* R.H. Russell, 1898.
  Kemble's Coons: A Collection of Southern Sketches. R.H. Russell, 1897.
McCay, Winsor. "Little Nemo in Slumberland". *New York Herald*, August, 1908.
Outcault, R.F. *Pore Lil Mose: His Letters to His Mammy.* Grand Union Tea Company, 1902.

---

[20] Wanzo suggests: "blackness complicates excess given the hypervisibility of racism in black representational histories" (13).
[21] See, for instance, Creekmur; Hayes; Nama; Rifas; Strömberg; Wanzo; Whaley.

"Poor Lil' Mose on the 7 Ages." *New York Herald Comic Supplement.* February 3, 1901.
"A True Ghost Story." *New York Herald.* April 28, 1901.

Secondary Sources

Ahmed, Maaheen. "Black Boys and Black Girls in Comics: An Affective and Historical Mapping of Intertwined Stereotypes." *The Routledge Companion to Gender and Sexuality in Comic Book Studies.* Edited by Frederick Luis Aldama. Routledge, 2021, pp. 28–41.
Ahmed, Sara. *The Cultural Politics of Emotion.* 2004. Edinburgh University Press, 2014.
Aldama, Frederick Luis, ed. *Multicultural Comics: From Zap to Blue Beetle.* University of Texas Press, 2010.
"Unmasking Whiteness: Re-Spacing the Speculative in Superhero Comics." *Unstable Masks: Whiteness and American Superhero Comics.* Edited by Sean Guynes and Martin Lund. Ohio State University Press, 2020. xi–xvi.
Amiran, Eyal. "George Herriman's Black Sentence: The Legibility of Race in 'Krazy Kat.'" *Mosaic* vol. 33, no. 3, 2000, pp. 57–79.
Austin, Allan W., and Patrick L. Hamilton. *All New, All Different? A History of Race and the American Superhero.* University of Texas Press, 2019.
Ayaka, Carolene, and Ian Hague, ed. *Representing Multiculturalism in Comics and Graphic Novels.* Routledge, 2015.
Banta, Martha. *Barbaric Intercourse: Caricature and the Culture of Conduct, 1841–1936.* University of Chicago Press, 2003.
Barker, Martin. *Comics: Ideology, Power, and the Critics.* Manchester University Press, 1989.
Chute, Hillary L. *Disaster Drawn: Visual Witness, Comics, and Documentary Form.* Harvard University Press, 2016.
Cole, Jean Lee. *How the Other Half Laughs: The Comic Sensibility in American Culture, 1895–1920.* University Press of Mississippi, 2020.
Creekmur, Corey E. "Multiculturalism Meets the Counterculture: Representing Racial Difference in Robert Crumb's Underground Comics." *Representing Multiculturalism in Comics and Graphic Novels*, edited by Carolene Ayaka and Ian Hague. Routledge, 2015, pp. 19–33.
Cremins, Brian. "Bumbazine, Blackness, and the Myth of the Redemptive South in Walt Kelley's *Pogo*." *Comics and the U.S. South*, edited by Brannon Costello and Qiana J. Whitted. University Press of Mississippi, 2012, pp. 29–61.
Du Bois, W.E.B. "The Souls of Black Folk." [1903]. *The Oxford W.E.B. Du Bois Reader*, edited by Eric J. Sundquist. Oxford University Press, 1996. 97–240.
Eisner, Will. *Graphic Storytelling and Visual Narrative.* [1996]. New York: Norton, 2008.
Gambone, Robert L. *Life on the Press: The Popular Art and Illustrations of George Benjamin Luks.* University Press of Mississippi, 2009.

Gardner, Jared. *Projections: Comics and the History of Twenty-First-Century Storytelling*. Stanford University Press, 2012.

"Same Difference: Graphic Alterity in the Work of Gene Luen Yang, Adrian Tomine, and Derek Kirk Kim." *Multicultural Comics: From Zap to Blue Beetle*, edited by Frederick Luis Aldama. University of Texas Press, 2010, pp. 132–147.

"Storylines." *SubStance*, vol 40, no. 1, 2011, pp. 53–69.

Gateward, Frances, and John Jennings. "Introduction: The Sweeter the Christmas." *The Blacker the Ink: Constructions of Black Identity in Comics & Sequential Art*, edited by Frances Gateward and John Jennings. Rutgers University Press, 2015, pp. 1–15.

Gilman, Sander L. *Difference and Pathology: Stereotypes of Sexuality, Race, and Madness*. Cornell University Press, 1985.

Gordon, Ian. *Comics Strips and Consumer Culture 1890–1945*. Smithsonian Institution Press, 1998.

Hayes, David. "Rethinking Ebony White: Race and Representation in Will Eisner's *The Spirit*." *Journal of Popular Culture* vol. 48, no. 2, 2015, pp. 296–312.

Havig, Alan. "Richard F. Outcault's 'Poor Lil' Mose': Variations on the Black Stereotype in American Comic Art." *Journal of American Culture* vol. 11, no. 1, 1988, pp. 33–41.

Heer, Jeet. "Racism as a Stylistic Choice and Other Notes." *The Comics Journal* 14 March 2011. www.tcj.com/racism-as-a-stylistic-choice-and-other-notes/.

Howard, Sheena C. "Brief History of the Black Comic Strip: Past and Present." *Black Comics: Politics of Race and Representation*, edited by Sheena C. Howard and Ronald L. Jackson II. Bloomsbury, 2013, pp. 11–22.

Kunka, Andrew J. "Comics, Race, and Ethnicity." *The Routledge Companion to Comics*, edited by Frank Bramlett, Roy T. Cook, and Aaron Meskin. Routledge, 2017, pp. 275–284.

Lemons, J. Stanley. "Black Stereotypes as Reflected in Popular Culture, 1880–1920." *American Quarterly* vol. 29, no. 1, 1977, pp. 102–116.

McCloud, Scott. *Understanding Comics: The Invisible Art*. [1993]. HarperCollins, 1994.

Meyer, Christina. *Producing Mass Entertainment: The Serial Life of the Yellow Kid*. Ohio State University Press, 2019.

Mitchell, W.J.T. *What Do Pictures Want? The Lives and Loves of Images*. University of Chicago Press, 2005.

Molotiu, Andrei. "Cartooning." *Comics Studies: A Guidebook*, edited by Charles Hatfield and Bart Beaty. Rutgers University Press, 2020, pp. 153–171.

Nama, Adilifu. *Super Black: American Pop Culture and Black Superheroes*. University of Texas Press, 2011.

Rifas, Leonard. "Race and Comix." Multicultural Comics: From Zap to Blue Beetle, edited by Frederick Luis Aldama. University of Texas Press, 2010, pp. 27–38.

Saguisag, Lara. *Incorrigibles and Innocents: Constructing Childhood and Citizenship in Progressive Era Comics*. New Brunswick: Rutgers University Press, 2018.

Spiegelman, Art. "Little Orphan Annie's Eyeballs." *Comix, Essays, Graphics and Scraps: From MAUS to Now.* Raw Books & Graphics, 1999, pp. 17–18.

Stein, Daniel. "The Comic Modernism of George Herriman." *Crossing Boundaries in Graphic Narrative: Essays on Forms, Series and Genres.* Edited by Jake Jakaitis and James F. Wurtz. Jefferson: McFarland, 2012. 40–70.

Strömberg, Fredrik. *Black Images in the Comics: A Visual History.* Fantagraphics, 2003.

Tensuan, Theresa. "Difference." *Comics Studies: A Guidebook*, edited by Charles Hatfield and Bart Beaty. Rutgers University Press, 2020, pp. 138–150.

Wanzo, Rebecca. *The Content of Our Caricature: African American Comic Art and Political Belonging.* New York University Press, 2020.

Whaley, Deborah Elizabeth. *Black Women in Sequence: Re-inking Comics, Graphic Novels, and Anime.* University of Washington Press, 2016.

CHAPTER 11

Women and Comics
Politics and Materialities

Maaheen Ahmed

Women and Comics: A Very Brief History

Women have been present since the earliest days of printed comics as readers and as creators in a variety of roles – artist, editor, colorist, etc. – but their contributions are often overshadowed by the attention accorded to male artists and writers. While comics, at least in the mainstream, seems to be a predominantly male affair, a closer look reveals a far more nuanced picture, confirming the presence of women artists and a strong female readership throughout comics history. Already in Victorian England, the "first comics superstar" Ally Sloper (Sabin), a successful attraction in British newspapers from 1867 to 1913, was mostly drawn by Marie Duval but credit for the character and the drawings was often given exclusively to her husband, Charles Ross (Kunzle). Detailed archival work was only undertaken recently to trace the extent of Duval's contributions (Grennan et al.).[1]

The 2021 exhibition "Ladies First: A Century of Women's Innovations in Comics and Cartoon Art" curated by Caitlin McGurk and Rachel Miller at the Billy Ireland Cartoon Library and Museum captures the diversity of women artists' involvement in all kinds of comics: cartoons and caricatures, zines and graphic novels. In addition to covering different forms and genres, the exhibition also emphasizes the presence of women artists from the earliest days of comics in print culture. Illustrator and caricaturist Nina Allender was active in the Suffragist movement, like Rose O'Neill, creator of the Kewpie Dolls, Edwina Dumm, known for the *Tippie* strips, and Nelly Brinkley, creator of the *Brinkley Girls*. Commercial success did not preclude political commentary and activism;

This chapter is an outcome of the COMICS project funded by the European Research Council (ERC) under the European Union's Horizon 2020 research and innovation program (grant agreement no. 758502).

[1] See the *Marie Duval Archive*: www.marieduval.org

225

both often coexisted since the artists were active in different kinds of genres, from humorous and political cartoons to illustrations for newspapers, advertisements, and books. Political commentary can also unfold within the same space as popular, humorous stories. This is evident in comics such as Jackie Ormes' successful *Torchy Brown* and *Patty Jo n' Ginger* comics and single-panel cartoons from the 1940s and 1950s (Goldstein).

One of the most successful and visible Black women artists of her time, Ormes produced comics with strong Black women and girl protagonists. She countered racist caricature that continued to dominate the representation of Black characters in comics alongside the presence of minstrel tropes in funny animal comics (see Sammond) with stylish drawings and smart jokes. Whereas Torchy Brown appeared as a paper doll printed next to the comic which could be cut out and dressed up, the precocious Patty Jo also figured as a plastic doll, offering young Black girls a rare alternative to the white dolls on market. Mass production fulfilled a crucial political role in countering the dominant order that favored whiteness even though the Patty Jo dolls were a Black version of the Terry Lee dolls, with little changed beyond the color. (For more on racism and stereotyping in comics see Chapter 10.) In our times, Barbara Brandon-Croft's syndicated strip, *Where I'm Coming From*, which began in 1989, continues in this tradition of interweaving humor with strong political commentary on race issues in the US voiced through serial comics characters.

Deborah Whaley's book, *Black Women in Sequence* identifies the first Black female superhero: Butterfly, the alter ego of Marian Michaels, a cabaret singer in Los Angeles, was a secondary character in the *Hell-Rider* comics from the early 1970s. Published by the short-lived Skywald Publications, which could not compete with the more established Marvel and DC Comics on the newsstands, Butterfly symbolizes the fleeting "appearance and disappearance of women of African descent in both independent and mainstream sequential art" (Whaley 7).

Female superheroes in general are vastly outnumbered by their male counterparts. The first female superheroes nevertheless appeared soon after Superman's debut in 1938. The result of a collaboration between psychologist and writer William Moulton Marston and artist Harry Peter, Wonder Woman has had a remarkably long life from her first appearance in 1941. In creating *Wonder Woman*, Marston sought to offer girl comics readers a role model and an alternative to male superheroes (see Lepore; Berlatsky). But *Wonder Woman* was not the only female superhero participating in what is often considered the Golden Age of comics (Brunet and

Davis). Somewhat lesser known and appearing a few months earlier than *Wonder Woman* is June Tarpé Mills' *Miss Fury* (Robbins, *Pretty* 66). As cartoonist and feminist comics historian Trina Robbins points out, *Miss Fury* stood out from most women superheroes through her stylish attire. Mills was not the only women's artist with a keen interest in fashion. Several successful women comics artists maintained close ties to the fashion industry, a trend already evident with the *Brinkley Girls*. Taking over Ethel Hays' *Flapper Fanny* in the late 1920s, Gladys Parker began her *Mopsy* strips a decade later. Parker developed a parallel, successful career as a fashion designer in Hollywood (Robbins, *Pretty* 67).

This connection with fashion remained key in comics for girls and women, which were often but not always made by women artists. *Brenda Starr, Reporter,* created by Dalia Messick (who, like Tarpé Mills, used a male pseudonym, Dale Messick, for signing her comics) in 1940, reinforced the lineup of fashionable comics heroes while also highlighting the rise of a key readership category, adolescents, and their interest in comics about young people without superpowers. The *Archie* comics, beginning with the first Archie story in *Pep* #22 in December 1941, confirmed this trend. Among the many teenage comics published by the successful *Archie* comics publisher, MLJ, is Bill Woggon's *Katy Keene*. Katy Keene made her first appearance in *Wilbur* #5 (an *Archie Comics* publication) in 1949 but soon acquired several titles and a strong fan following that sent in designs for the Katy Keene paper dolls. Paper dolls themselves had already accompanied comic book heroines such as Jackie Ormes' Torchy Brown and Patsy Walker, who appeared in 1944 and was drawn by Ruth Atkinson. *Patsy Walker* had a long comics career and Atkinson herself was prolific and created other successful titles such as *Millie the Model*.

These humor and fashion comics, like romance comics, the key genres for girl readers, would not survive the 1970s and the 1980s. While attempts were made to revive comics such as *Katy Keene* by Barbara Rausch, such experiments were rarely successful, not necessarily because of a lack of readership but because of a lack of interest from publishers and bookstores (see Robbins, *Girls* 107). As this very brief overview has tried to show, the historical oversight regarding the role of women comics creators often goes hand in hand with an ignorance of female readerships and the comics made for them. (See Chapter 14 on comics readers and fans.)

As space for women in the comics mainstream became increasingly limited, the 1960s and 1970s witnessed a new movement in comics: the underground (see also Kirtley, *Typical Girls*). Countering the restrictions and infantilization of comics imposed by the Comics Code, the movement was concurrent with second-wave feminism and resulted in several activist comics that critiqued misogynist tendencies in society at large and the comics world in particular. Starting out at the underground paper, *East Village Other*, for which she would eventually close her clothes shop, Robbins drew comic strips for the underground feminist newspaper *It Ain't Me Babe* and edited a comics anthology, *It Ain't Me Babe: Women's Liberation* in 1970, featuring only women artists. This was the beginning of several women's underground publications, including *Wimmen's Comix*, published by a collective that included Robbins, Aline Kominsky-Crumb, Lee Marrs, Melinda Gebbie, and Shary Flenniken.

Active in underground comics and women's rights movements, Robbins has played a key role in highlighting the role of women comics artists and comics for women. While her focus has essentially been on North American artists, Nicola Streeten and Cath Tate have written a history of women cartoonists and illustrators in Britain that reaches back to the 1760s. Streeten is also author of a critical overview of feminist comics in the UK. Together with fellow artist and scholar, Sarah Lightman, Streeten founded the women's comics-making community, Laydeez Do Comics, based in the UK and with chapters all over the world. Both Streeten and Robbins exemplify the multifaceted nature of women's comics work: their activities extend from making comics that can speak to and for women, to actively reversing the tendency of overlooking women's contributions to comics history and their prominence as comics readers and makers.

In many ways, the underground movement, which bridged the personal and the collective through making space for autobiographical and socially engaged stories, laid the seeds for the trends we encounter in the graphic novel today. *Wimmen's Comix*, for instance, was where Aline Kominsky-Crumb published her first autobiographical comic (Robbins, *Girls* 91). Autobiographical and autofictional stories are a dominant genre for the graphic novel and many of these graphic novels are made by women (see, for instance, Chute; Chaney; and Chapter 9 on life writing). Before turning to female graphic novelists, however, one more role involving several women deserves special attention because it transformed the kinds of comics published: editors.

Numerous women editors have contributed towards shaping comics history. Notable editors include Flo Steinberg at Marvel Comics, who began as a secretary for Stan Lee and went on to edit one of the earliest underground comic books, *Big Apple Comix*. Denise Loubert founded

Renegade Press after her divorce from Dave Sim, with whom she had launched Aardvark press. Although Renegade was short-lived, it published diverse alternative comics such as Bob Burden's *Flaming Carrot*, Max Collins and Terry Beatty's *Ms. Tree*, Bob Woggon's *Vicki Valentine*, and Arn Saba's (now Katherine Collins) *Neil the Horse*. Loubert also tried to revive romance comics with a twist through the *Renegade Romance* comics. As part of the Friends of Lulu collective, Loubert edited the manual, *How to Get Girls (Into Your Store): A Friends of Lulu Retailer Handbook* (1997) with contributions by Amy Goetz, Liz Schiller, and Neil Gaiman.

Perhaps the most famous female editor is Karen Berger, who helped launch DC Comics' Vertigo imprint, which transformed the mainstream comics scene by including projects such as Gaiman's *Sandman* and Alan Moore's *V for Vendetta*. She was briefly succeeded by Shelly Bond, who had been Berger's assistant editor and had worked on the Vertigo imprint for more than two decades. Recently, Marvel editor Sana Amanat came under the spotlight for introducing a new Ms. Marvel, Kamala Khan, a Pakistani-American teenager from New Jersey.

A recent exhibition by Trina Robbins and Kim Munson, titled *Women in Comics: Looking Forward and Back*, which traveled from the Society of Illustrators in New York to Rome and Naples, celebrated women artists from the 1970s to the present. It also projected the 2014 documentary, *She Makes Comics*, which features artists, editors, and other comics professionals as well as members of fan communities. The exhibition covers the artists' role in activism but also mainstream comics before capturing the diverse artworks by contemporary women artists. Both Lynda Barry and Ebony Flowers were part of this exhibition, with Barry being part of the "Ladies of the 80s" section and Flowers included in the "Diverse Voices in Contemporary Comics" section. In contrast to the brief intertwined history of women and comics presented earlier, in which many women artists produced both commercial and political comics and cartoons, both Barry and Flowers are best known for their graphic novel work.

In comparison to the dominant comics genre of the superhero, the graphic novel has attracted numerous international women creators and readers. Girlhood is a recurrent theme in these works that have a strong penchant for autobiographical and autofictional stories: the list is long and includes Marjane Satrapi's *Persepolis*, Lynda Barry's *One! Hundred! Demons!*, Phoebe Gloeckner's *Diary of a Young Girl*, and Alison Bechdel's *Fun Home*. All four books are discussed in detail in Hillary Chute's *Graphic Women: Life Narrative and Contemporary* Comics. In her introduction, Chute offers a long list of contemporary women artists making comics (1). For Chute, "(s)ome of today's most riveting feminist cultural production is in the form of accessible yet edgy graphic narratives" (2). *My Favorite Thing Is Monsters*, which we encountered in the introduction, is very much situated in this trend but it also expands on it and suggests the possible future forms of comics and graphic novels by women artists. It does so through experimentation with the scope of the graphic novel and through drawing connections with comics and popular culture on one hand and through reworking – literally breathing life into – the fine arts on the other. Like *My Favorite Thing is Monsters* and the works Chute examines, both Flowers and Weng Pixin experiment with different aspects of comics and graphic novels to offer stories that are simultaneously personal and collective. Part of this effect is created through interweaving codes of mass media with layers of signification and narrative devices that insist on rereading and relooking. Another part of the effect is created through the ambiguous positioning of the artists, suggesting that the comics are autobiographical while simultaneously unsettling such assumptions.

Chute describes the power of the graphic narratives she discusses as follows: "Against a valorisation of absence and aporia, graphic narratives assert the value of presence, however complex and contingent" (2). She emphasizes how each artist activates new kinds of materialities, connected to but also going beyond comics devices, from surface textures to archives. This chapter focuses on three material aspects to channel its readings: found images (Barry), hair (Flowers), and symbolic threads connecting generations (Pixin).

Found Images: Lynda Barry's Comics and Life Handbooks

Originally published online on *Salon.com*, Lynda Barry's *One! Hundred! Demons!* is named after a painting exercise by the sixteenth-century Zen monk Hakuin Ekaku and announces itself as "a book of autofictionalbiography." In Barry's work, autobiography and fiction are as inextricable as the acts of interrogating the comics form, remembering through comics and teaching comics. In this graphic novel, Barry visualizes her own monsters and ends with instructions to encourage her readers to do the same. The one hundred demons exercise takes the form of free painting. The artist is encouraged to follow the strokes of the brush to see which demons emerge forth.

The frontispiece imitating Japanese woodcuts (*ukiyo-e*) is dominated by a multiple-eyed demon who is pregnant with a demon baby and surges above the troubled waters that Barry's monkey avatar cheerfully tries to

Women and Comics: Politics and Materialities 231

navigate in a boat. The frontispiece contains a false, unreadable table of contents, beginning with an introduction and a chapter on "selfhood." The actual table of contents is a list of chapters bearing the names of different demons. These range from "Head Lice and My Worst Boyfriend" and "Lost Worlds" to the more abstract "Resilience," "Common Scents," and "Lost and Found." Most of these sections, like all of Barry's books, are connected to childhood in general and her own childhood memories. "Lost and Found," for instance, is both about classified advertisements and the unwanted transition from childhood to adolescence. These stories are interspersed with richly collaged pages that combine drawings, watercolors, comics panels, photographs, fragments of textile, glitter, and numerous objects, as can be seen in the double spread for "Dancing" (Figure 11.1). "Head Lice and My Worst Boyfriend" ends with a page full of irregular beige checks. As in the double spread preceding the story, a small colorful origami cootie moves towards a heart with the word "cootie," both of which are placed in this closing double spread in a frame made of jagged-edged cloth fragments. Such pages preceding and ending the chapters can be seen as spaces where Barry attempts to resolve the issues personified by individual demons to move on to the next ones.

Chute likens Barry's intense collage work, which generally shuns blank spaces, to the Pattern and Decoration movement that emerged in the US around the mid-1970s (Chute 110). This feminist art movement involved artists such as Valerie Jaudon, Joyce Kozloff, Robert Kushner and Miriam Schapiro. Inspired by the decorative arts and ornaments, the artists challenged the relegation of such art to domestic and feminine realms. Their works celebrated repetitive, all-over patterns and bright colors. In bringing forms of image-making that were often denied a space in art museums, Pattern and Decoration reshuffled the boundaries between high and low arts. Barry's books accomplish similar work. As Chute points out, "[t]he three-dimensional aspect captured in *One Hundred Demons* evokes both artists' book and children's pop-up books, juxtaposing and rendering unstable, in this aspect as elsewhere, the discernable line between childhood and adulthood" (112). In unsettling categories, between works for children and adults, between the popular and the fine arts, Barry also tests the limits of the comics medium: although her works are generally categorized as comics and graphic novels, books such as *Cruddy* and *The Good Times Are Killing Me* are closer to illustrated diaries whereas *Syllabus* and *Making Comics* can be considered as comics-making manuals.

Teasing out the implications of the rich, material dimension of Barry's art, Chute elaborates on Barry's acts of "wrinkling" through her collages as

Figure 11.1. Lynda Barry, "Dancing," *One! Hundred! Demons!* (Drawn & Quarterly, 2015), n. pag. Copyright Lynda Barry. Used with kind permission from Drawn & Quarterly.

"a subjective, bodily ruffling of the smooth, objective [...] surface of a printed page" (Chute 112). The collages generate a dynamic nexus of subjective and objective impulses not only through the contrast between the printed page and the material chosen and pasted by Barry but also by

Figure 11.1. (cont.)

the very nature of those materials, which do not always stem from Barry's hand. Even the drawings are drawn by diverse hands. For Susan Kirtley, who introduces Barry as an "image-wrangler" in her book *Lynda Barry: Girlhood through the Looking Glass*, Barry's "collages imply a broader story, rather than an individual one, and utilize the remains of childhood, in particular, to build a connection, rather than to shine insight into one individual's experience" (181). This is especially the case in *What It Is,* in which Barry freely incorporated material from the archives of an elementary school teacher, Doris Mitchell, who had kept her students' assignments. Barry regularly combines her own images and a variety of found images, including: images that she finds in her imagination; images that she cuts out; and images by her students that were thrown away, gifted to her, or left over from her classes. These found images are a means of unpacking and surpassing the tension between idea and form and sometimes also bypassing paralyzing self-judgments.

While collages of found images remain at the margins of works such as *One! Hundred! Demons!,* where they frame the beginnings and the ends of the short stories, they are central to comics manuals such as *Syllabus.* Despite the variations in image-making techniques, all of Barry's books share the obsession of tracking down images. She describes the aim of her class, "What it is: manually shifting the image" as follows: "I was trying to understand how images travel between people, how they move through time, and if there was a way to use writing and picture making to figure out more about how images work" (*Syllabus* 49). Notably, all images that Barry incorporates in her books become comics images of sorts. They are, to use Colin Beineke's term comicitous, because they acquire comics-like qualities through functioning not alone but in conjunction with the words and the potential thoughts or stories that they are a part of (Beineke).

Situated between the public and the private, the collages also have a collective, relational quality that is similar to comics themselves. As Barry explains in an interview: "So where's the comic? The comic is somewhere between the person who made it and the person who's looking at it. It's a relationship" (Misemer and Barry 174, see also Chapter 1 on comics drawing). Flowers' *Hot Comb* and Pixin's *Let's Not Talk Anymore* offer different takes on the relational aspect of comics: while Pixin interweaves and reconnects five generations of young women in her own matriline, Flowers connects her stories – such as "Hot Comb" which tells us about her first perm – with experiences of other women whom she has not necessarily known herself as in the case of "My Lil' Sister Lena."

Herstories through Hair: Ebony Flowers' Hot Comb

In her acknowledgments, Flowers thanks Barry for having "taught me how to discover the writing in the drawing and the drawing in the writing" (182). Flowers uses a fluid, playful style for her graphic novel *Hot Comb,*

Women and Comics: Politics and Materialities

which combines eight slice-of-life stories with parodic advertisements for products for Black hair. In contrast to Barry's intense, colorful pages, however, Flowers relies on black, white, and washes in shades of grey. Varying drawing styles and handwriting, she embraces dynamic combinations of words and images, with the words often spilling out of the confines of the word balloons. Her lines are light and energetic and the layout is equally varied and rhythmic. The hair product advertisements interspersed between each story exemplify Flowers' holistic combination of images with the visual facet or iconicity of the written word.

Flowers explains that "My Lil' Sister Lena" was drawn "in a process that mimicked free writing. Whenever I wasn't sure of how the story would proceed, I drew individual scenes from multiple perspectives on index cards. I also worked out some of the main character's life and mannerisms using my daily drawing and writing practices (McNamara)." She also maintains some doubt about the autobiographical nature of the stories. Although "My Lil' Sister Lena" is written in an autobiographical mode, it is "inspired by my memories of playing softball as well as my friend's dissertation that examined the experiences of black women who play collegiate sports like soccer, swimming, and field hockey" (McNamara). It tells the story of Flowers' sister Lena, an eager softball player and the only Black girl on her high school team, the Tennessee Cougars. The Cougars are successful enough to travel across the country for tournaments. Swimming together after one such tournament, Lena's teammates realize that her hair changes from tight curls to longer curls when wet. This starts a collective obsession with Lena's hair with the other girls seizing every opportunity to touch it. This unwanted attention makes Lena start pulling hair. Although she ends up quitting the softball team and the sport altogether and tries to follow therapy, she does not succeed in curing the compulsive act.

The Cougars' team cheer bookends the story, serving as both introduction and conclusion. While Lena actively participates in the cheer with her teammates at the beginning of the story, the bold, loud words of the cheer at the end of the story alternate with panels showing Lena pulling out a strand of hair and the momentary relief she felt afterwards (109).

Very early in the story, with Lena's first swim with her team, her curly hair becomes a protagonist in its own right (96–97, Figure 11.2). The change unfolds over two pages as the white girls see nothing but Lena's hair and insist on touching it; repeatedly Lena's own voice is silenced and her body, and her very being, disappears under her hair, which is pulled in opposing directions by the girls who remain unmoved by Lena's distress. Flowers alternates with diary-like handwritten entries, through which the

236 MAAHEEN AHMED

Figure 11.2. Ebony Flowers, 'My Lil Sister Lena' in *Hot Comb* (Drawn & Quarterly, 2019), pp. 96–97. Copyright Ebony Flowers. Used with kind permission from Drawn & Quarterly.

Women and Comics: Politics and Materialities 237

Figure 11.2. (*cont.*)

I-narrator tells Lena's story, and panels with word balloons, which bring parts of Lena's experiences to life. Both are contained within a hand-drawn, slightly irregular page-sized frame. In an image at the bottom of the page, Lena, partly cut off by the frame, pulls at two strands which serve as uneven lines for the following description: "Lena had long shiny black coils"(96). What was qualified as "good hair" became the source of despair. Incorporating a dynamic layout, combining comics panels with journal pages, Flowers captures both the narrator's perspective and Lena's distressing realization that her teammates were only interested in marveling about her hair than in listening to her. The playful cartoony style ironically highlights the cruelty of the situation and also encourages the reader to empathize with Lena through the story's layers of immediacy and authenticity. Hair becomes a place where racial aggression and trauma unfolds in most of the stories in *Hot Comb*. In stories such as "My Lil' Sister Lena," the trauma remains unresolved. Other stories such as "The Lady on the Train" emphasizes the recurrent, everyday nature of racial aggression. The ads punctuating the stories serve as ironic intermezzos reflecting on the capitalization of anxieties connected to Black hair.

"*Hot Comb* is like a masterclass in how to make comics," concludes John Seven in his review of the graphic novel for *The Beat*. This is because, "[t]he narratives in *Hot Comb* make the point. The characters make the point. You learn through the experience. You learn through empathy." *Hot Comb*, then, teaches without being a manual, through sensitively conveying personal stories of exclusion and resilience.

Writing about Barry's *What It Is* and *Syllabus*, Eszter Szép suggests "repositioning the line not as a trace or a product but as an active partner to the vulnerable drawer" (54). The drawn line, as Szép reminds us, remains undertheorized especially because it resists transposition to narrative concepts (see also Chapter 1 on drawing; Gardner). In focusing on vulnerability, Szép emphasizes the many moments of hesitation and despair that can be implied in the act of drawing and which Barry often visualizes and provides tips to overcome.

Beyond vulnerability, Barry, Flowers, and Pixin give visual form to different kinds of materiality: be it regarding childhood, its memories, images and objects (Barry), or the polysemous role of hair, signifying racialized and racist personal experiences and mechanisms of othering (Flowers), or a small caterpillar that flits in and out of the lives of the young girls and the diverse objects they create in Pixin's *Let's Not Talk Anymore*. Like the books discussed before, *Let's Not Talk Anymore* is also very much about resilience as it interweaves the stories of five generations of women, stories that are very personal, especially through the matrilineal connections with the artist, but that are in reality often imagined to make up for the women's silences and missing stories.

Threading Generations: Weng Pixin's Let's Not Talk Anymore

A story that winds across five generations of women, Pixin's semi-autobiographical *Let's Not Talk Anymore* opens with her great grandmother's separation from her mother in 1908 to to take up a job as a domestic worker.. It continues into 2032, when we encounter Pixin's imaginary daughter, Rita who, like every other girl in the graphic novel, is fifteen years old, at the threshold of leaving childhood and entering adulthood.

The cover shows the five girls connected through a vegetal-decorative form that bends along the five bodies from the back to the front flap of the book, blossoming at the end (which is paradoxically the front flap), next to Rita, who sits drawing. Every girl in the graphic novel takes part in some kind of creative activity, which is often a source of comfort and escape from their problems and traumas. The creative activities range from the miniature baskets woven by Pixin's great-great-grandmother, Kuān, to Mèi, Pixin's great-grandmother's patchwork sewing, to the paintings and drawings made by Pixin's mother, Bīng, Pixin's alter-ego Bǐ and Rita. Rita and her friend Solar also make *Ojos de Dios* talismans for each other. In highlighting these creative activities, many of which unfold in the domestic space, Pixin draws attention to the artistic and personal value of such work, similar to Patterns and Decorations, mentioned earlier. Like Barry, Pixin deftly interweaves collages into her graphic novels. While collage has a much stronger presence in Pixin's earlier book, *Sweet Time*, it alternates with painted images on many of the pages separating the different stories in *Let's Not Talk Anymore*. Collage also plays a subtle but meaningful role on almost every page in the book: in lieu of white gutters, Pixin's panels are connected through colored strips or tape that gently overlap. Like Barry, Pixin avoids white spaces, patching up gaps with abstract forms that often have feminine connotations through their decorative nature.

The childhood and teenage memories portrayed avoid nostalgia and focus on relationships, from strong bonds to dysfunctional or frictional relationships, especially between mothers and daughters. Kuān's separation from her mother and from their home in South China at the age of fifteen, especially their tearful final goodbye, is especially moving. The last we see of Kuān's mother is a tiny figure curled up in the fields and surrounded by darkness. Pixin frequently resorts to abstraction, often through blurring images, or through dramatic zoom-outs or close-ups to open up a layered symbolic space, similar to the patched-up gutters: the abstraction generated through changes in perspective situates the very personal moment into a more universal context. The abstracted moments contribute to the pace and rhythm of the stories, forcing the reader to pause and reconsider what is being shown and how it connects to what they have read so far. Such spaces also help calibrate the mood of the story. Sometimes, for instance, they generate a necessary distance from especially painful moments in the story. When the young girl Kuān takes care of tells her about a nightmare she had and asks what Kuān's mother would have told her, there is silence for two panels. The first one reproduces Kuān's final embrace with her mother in which both child and mother form one body. The second one is a blurred version of the first, without clear outlines of the figures and only masses of color (Figure 11.3). This brief insight into Kuān's thoughts activates the affective power of memories, almost unbearably moving and painful in this case, while also pointing towards their fleeting, immaterial, and even indefinable nature.

Figure 11.3. Weng Pixin, *Let's Not Talk Anymore* (Drawn & Quarterly, 2021). Copyright Weng Pixin. Used with kind permission from Drawn & Quarterly.

Women and Comics: Politics and Materialities 241

Memories in graphic form are an especially successful graphic novel genre. Many such memoirs, such as Bechdel's *Fun Home* and some of Lynda Barry's books engage with the medium of photography, playing on its contrasts with drawing. Instead of incorporating actual photographs, Bechdel draws them, in a realistic style with crosshatching that contrasts with the stylized, cartoony drawings used to narrate the story. Pixin also draws and paints a few photographs but opts for less realistic and varied styles. Perhaps the most important painted photograph is the one of Bīng's parents, who separated when Bīng was fifteen. The photo is eaten into by a caterpillar, creating a hole between her parents' faces. It nevertheless reappears intact when Rita and her friend flip through Rita's family album which bears the ironic title, "Sweet Memories." The insect itself weaves another thread, like the creative activities and the familial ties linking the five girls.

"If I have a choice, I will choose to be a butterfly in my next life," Kuān thinks to herself, playing with a caterpillar, "so life will be fleeting and painless." The final pages of the graphic novel show Rita greeting a butterfly, which flies across ten pages and is only interrupted towards the end by a picture of a smiling, adult Bīng, taken six years after the stories about her, in 1978, followed by the author description and photograph of Pixin on the next page, right behind her mother's. These butterfly pages imitate the now obsolete form of moving picture books: the butterfly flits from flower to flower as the pages are turned. Like the moving picture books, the image is without sound. This reflects on the silences that underly *Let's Not Talk Anymore*. It is easy to imagine how many of the uncomfortable moments portrayed in the graphic novel – Bīng's fights with her choleric mother, Mèi, the young Mèi's abuse at the hands of her adopted mother's boyfriend, Kuān's tearful parting from her mother – were never talked about. In filling those silences with images and stories, Pixin also re-performs the act of piecing together women's stories, herstories that are often excluded from dominant narratives. We learn more about the unsaid in Pixin's matrilineal story through Rita, who reminds us that Kuān never talked about her past: "She did not have the pleasure of telling *anyone* what her favorite flowers were (it was the Chrysanthemums). She grew to quiet her voice, just so she could survive." By adding the name of Kuān's favorite flower, Rita reenacts the work of the entire graphic novel: filling in the silences and piecing together missing information through all available resources, both factual and imaginary.

Coda

Towards the end of *Syllabus*, Barry pastes a handwritten quote from Marion Milner: "Instead of trying to force myself into doing what I imagined I ought to be doing, I began to inquire into what I *was* doing" (194). Barry's, Flowers' and Pixin's graphic novels are all the result of inquiries into how the comics medium can be used for telling stories, in particular women's stories and girlhoods.

As we saw earlier in this chapter, the famous feminist slogan "the personal is political" acquires new dimensions in women's comics work. Many of the early twentieth-century women artists introduced here engaged in political activism through their art. In comics of the underground, activism played a major role. In our contemporary era of the graphic novel, we see the political stances acquire newer, ever more sophisticated forms, narrating womanhood and girlhood in layered and innovative ways.

WORKS CITED

Comics

Barry, Lynda. *Syllabus: Notes from an Accidental Professor*. Drawn & Quarterly, 2014.
  One! Hundred! Demons! Drawn & Quarterly, 2019.
  What It Is. Drawn & Quarterly, 2019.
  Making Comics. Drawn & Quarterly, 2019.
Flowers, Ebony. *Hot Comb*. Drawn & Quarterly, 2019.
Pixin, Weng. *Let's Not Talk Anymore*. Drawn & Quarterly, 2021.

Secondary Sources

Beineke, Colin. "On Comicity." *Inks*, vol. 1, no. 2, 2017, pp. 226–253.
Berlatsky, Noah. *Wonder Woman: Bondage and Feminism in the Marston/Peter Comics, 1941–1948*. Rutgers University Press, 2017.
Brunet, Peyton and Blair Davis. *Comic Book Women: Characters, Creators and Cultures in the Golden Age*. University of Texas Press, 2022.
Chaney, Michael A., ed. *Graphic Subjects: Critical Essays on Autobiography and Graphic Novels*. University of Wisconsin Press, 2011.
Chute, Hillary L. *Graphic Women: Life Narrative and Contemporary Comics*. Columbia University Press, 2010.
Gardner, Jared. "Storylines" *Substance*, vol. 124, 2010, pp. 53–69.
Goldstein, Nancy. *Jackie Ormes: The First African-American Woman Cartoonist*. University of Michigan Press, 2019.

Grennan, Simon, Sabin, Roger, and Julian Waite. *Marie Duval: Maverick Victorian Cartoonist*. Manchester University Press, 2020.

Kirtley, Susan. *Lynda Barry: Girlhood through the Looking Glass*. University Press of Mississippi, 2012.

Typical Girls: The Rhetoric of Womanhood in Comic Strips. Ohio State University Press, 2021.

Kunzle, David. "Marie Duval: A Caricaturist Rediscovered. *Women's Art Journal*, vol. 7, no. 1, 1989, pp. 26–31.

Lepore, Jill. *The Secret History of Wonder Woman*. Vintage Books, 2014.

McNamara, Nathan Scott and Ebony Flowers. "A Place Where Past, Present, and Future Come Together: Ebony Flowers on *Hot Comb*." *Los Angeles Review of Books*, 13 July 2019. https://blog.lareviewofbooks.org/interviews/space-past-present-future-come-together-ebony-flowers-hot-comb/ Accessed 3 August 2022.

Misemer, Leah and Lynda Barry. "Teaching the Unthinkable Image: An Interview with Lynda Barry." *With Great Power Comes Great Pedagogy: Teaching, Learning and Comics*. Edited by Susan Kirtley, Antero Garcia, and Peter E. Carlson. University Press of Mississippi, 2020, pp. 168–184.

Robbins, Trina. *From Girls to Grrrlz: A History of Women's Comics from Teens to Zines*. Chronicle Books, 1999.

Pretty in Ink: North American Women Artists, 1896–2013. Fantagraphics, 2013.

Last Girl Standing. Fantagraphics, 2017.

Sabin, Roger. "Ally Sloper: The First Comics Superstar?" *Image [&] Narrative*, vol. 4, no. 1, 2003, www.imageandnarrative.be/inarchive/graphicnovel/rogersabin.htm. Accessed 3 August 2022.

Sammond, Nicholas. *Birth of an Industry: Blackface Minstrelsy and the Rise of American Animation*. Duke University Press, 2015.

Streeten, Nicola. *UK Feminist Comics and Cartoons: A Critical Survey*. Palgrave, 2020.

Streeten, Nicola and Cath Tate. *The Inking Woman: 250 Years of British Women Cartoon and Comic Artists*. Myriad Editions, 2018.

Szép, Eszter. *Comics and the Body: Reading, Drawing and Vulnerability*. Ohio State University Press, 2020.

Whaley, Deborah E. *Black Women in Sequence: Re-inking Comics, Graphic Novels, and Anime*. University of Washington Press, 2015.

CHAPTER 12

Comics at the Limits of Narration

Erwin Dejasse

Reviews of comics – in print, on radio, television or online media – often focus mainly, if not entirely, on the story. It is quite common to read reviews that ignore the specificity of comics and are therefore not any different from reviews of novels, movies, or TV series. Thierry Groensteen claims that "the inherent imperialism of the narrative form always over-shadows the elements comprising the work"[1] (Groensteen, "Fictions" 17). The "imperialism of the narrative" shapes the reception of the works and affects discourses on comics, from mainstream media to specialist magazines and even academic publications. It is highly revealing that today the term "graphic novel" (see Chapter 3) is commonly used to label longform comics that supposedly counter the tenets of mass culture. The use of the word "novel" suggests that these creations are only a form of literature which, consequently, narrows the scope of analysis and appreciation.

Critics are often somewhat helpless when they face comics that are challenging to describe in narrative terms. One recent tendency that radically questions the "imperialism of the narrative" is incarnated by abstract comics. Unsurprisingly, these works are not bestsellers and are rarely discussed in mainstream media. They require us to rethink our assumptions and critical tools. The overwhelming majority of abstract comics are issued by alternative publishers[2] reacting to mainstream publishing policies deemed as too formulaic. Alternative comics publishers are driven by the ambition to rethink the subjects, aesthetics and narrative structures of comics. I argue elsewhere that they are characterized by a "quest for new affordances of comics" (Dejasse).

---

[1] "l'impérialisme intrinsèque de la forme récit qui récupère à son profit l'ensemble des éléments composant l'œuvre"

[2] For instance, the abstract comics of Ibn Al Rabin published in *Bile Noire* (issues 13 to 16, Atrabile, 2003–2005), *Petit Trait* by Alex Baladi (L'Association, 2008), *Skyface Sensrmap* by Brenna Murphy (Floating World Comics, 2012), *978* by Pascal Matthey (La Cinquième Couche, 2013) or *LOTO* by Alexis Beauclair (Matière, 2019).

Moreover, we cannot fully understand what abstract comics are if we do not take into account a range of publications that often fall under the "alternative" umbrella; self-published volumes with no ISBN or archiving and with very limited distribution networks, are a hidden but fundamental part of contemporary comics history. Such self-published comics – small press comics, minicomics, fanzines, or simply zines – offer a space where cartoonists are free to experiment and test the limits of comics without necessarily worrying about profitability.

Abstract comics were introduced in 2009 with the anthology *Abstract Comics* published by the alternative comics publisher Fantagraphics and edited by comics artist and scholar Andrei Molotiu. The book brought together cartoonists from different countries who were engaging in similar experiments without necessarily influencing each other. In addition to connecting isolated experiments in comics, the anthology also encouraged artists making abstract comics to continue their efforts. These include Tim Gaze and Kym Tabulo, who describes discovering Molotiu's book as a "real moment of enlightenment" showing the direction in which she could develop her work as an abstract visual artist (Tabulo, *Paul Klee*).

A reader for whom comics must first tell a story based on a succession of events and reaching some kind of conclusion will probably be confused by abstract comics and regard them as pointless exercises in style. According to Hans Robert Jauss' reception theory, readers have the possibility to accept or refuse any literary experience. Jauss also coined the notion "horizon of expectations" to emphasize how reader expectations depend upon their interests, desires, needs, or experiences. These observations can easily be applied to media beyond literature, including comics. Since for most readers "good comics" are, above all, those that tell "good stories," appreciating abstract comics implies setting aside the "imperialism of the narrative" and therefore shifting the "horizon of expectations."

Abstract Comics and Music

A possible approach to abstract comics is to ascribe them qualities commonly associated with other media. According to its blurb, *Abstract Comics* brings "the art of comics [. . .] closer than it, or any other visual art, has yet come to the condition of instrumental music." Although such links with music appear to be evident, it is worth questioning whether they express deeper connections between abstract comics and music or whether they are simply metaphors.

It is noteworthy that comics artists themselves often highlight the musical connections in their works. Some works in *Abstract Comics* have titles that use musical vocabulary: *Viral Suite, Border Suite, Color Sonnet*. Another artist Rosaire Appel (who is not published in *Abstract Comics*) establishes an organic link between music and her abstract comics. Music is part of the creative process because the artist considers her comics as means to produce creations akin to visual music. Fascinated by sheet music, she uses it as raw material, as in *soundtrack/s* (Figure 12.1), a self-published artists' book in the form of a saddle stitched booklet: "I listen, later I draw. How might something invisible – sound – look? [...] These pages call for visual listening." Before Appel, the similarities between comics and musical scores had already been highlighted by Chris Ware and Jean-Christophe Menu, two creators strongly tied with the alternative movement as their own works are driven by the "quest for new affordances of comics." Comics and scores produce a flow that accompanies the reader eyes when scanning a sequence of signs. Even when she does not make comics directly on the basis of scores, the pleasure the reader can feel in front of Appel's work is intimately linked with the production of such a flow (Figure 12.2).

Raphaël Baroni underlines characteristics of music that are similar to abstract comics: they are "likely to arouse various feelings or reveries but, finally, only refer to themselves." As abstract comics do not provide access to a "story" by converting visual forms into representations, the reader is left with a more or less complex set of lines, forms, and colors – including balloons, captions, and frames – that neither seek to represent nor imitate anything. The non-representational forms unfolding within panels (for panels are always implicit in comics), make the rhythmic dimension of the medium much more obvious than in comics that are mimetic, where the "attention is primarily captured by the plot and consequently focused on the [figurative] content of each panel" (Groensteen *Comics,* 135).

Asserting that figurative comics are nonnarrative may appear self-evident. The full picture, however, is more complex. According to Jan Baetens, "the difficulty of narrativization should not be equated with the absence of narrativity" ("Abstraction" 96). Terms such as story, plot, or narration are part of our everyday language and are highly polysemous; their respective meanings tend to overlap and it is somehow risky, if not impossible, to provide a very strict definition of these terms. Thus, I will focus on the concept of plot provided by Baroni. He redefines the plot "not as the structure of the story told, but as a dynamic form that depends on a progression through phases of tension and resolution." By

Comics at the Limits of Narration 247

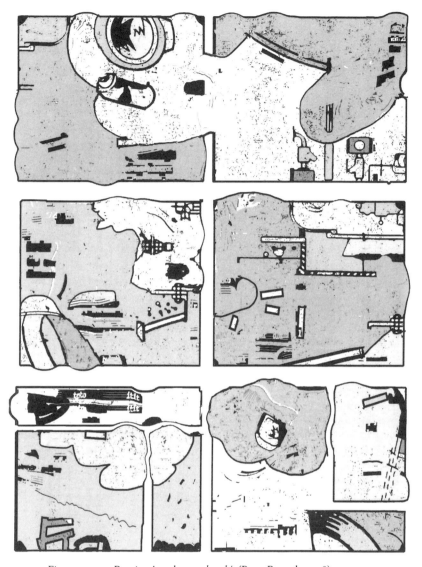

Figure 12.1. Rosaire Appel, *soundtrack/s* (Press Rappel, 2018), n. pag.

highlighting suspense, climax, denouement, and dramatic effects in compositions by Johann Sebastian Bach and Charlie Mingus, Baroni brings music closer to "storytelling media." In his *Cello Suite no. 1 in G major* (BWV 1007), Bach "dramatizes" the melodic line by using a rising

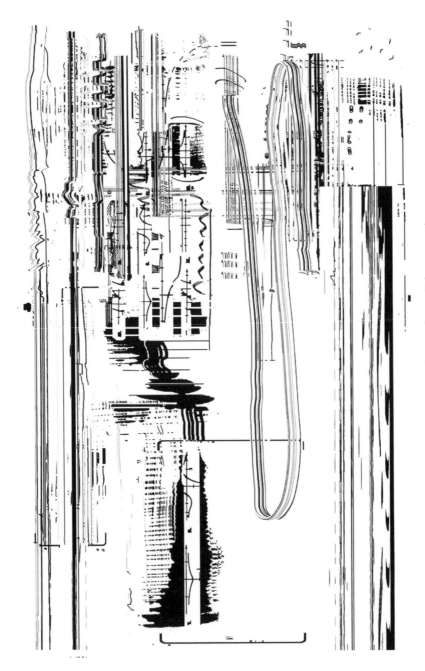

Figure 12.2. Rosaire Appel, *Perturbation* (Adverse, 2019), n. pag.

Comics at the Limits of Narration

chromatic figure before unpacking a series of more or less dissonant notes with a succession of arpeggios. Mingus's *Pithecanthropus Erectus* is described as one of the most "narrative" works from modern jazz repertoire where "the growing tension is accompanied by an increase in volume and tempo; the whole culminates in a shattering, chaotic noise before falling again in the starting theme."

Turning the pages of Molotiu's book, the reader – in this case more of a viewer – will immediately feel similar rises and falls, tensions and resolutions without necessarily analyzing the devices producing such effects. The three-page comic *The Panic* drawn by Andrei Molotiu, shows, against a dark backdrop, fluorescent yellow forms with orange punctuations. The first page conforms to a regular layout – a layout where all the frames have the same size (Groensteen *System*, 93–97) – with six square panels arranged in three tiers. The second page also begins with a tier with two square frames but the lower two-thirds are occupied by one big square image breaking the regularity of page 1 (Figure 12.3). The third page shows two square panels in the middle tier above and below a tier with an image that fills the entire width of the page. Changes in frame size are a fundamental part of the rhythmic perception of the pages. This perception is also dependent on the forms inside the frames. Here, Molotiu plays with their density: on the first page, the colored forms nearly saturate the space of each panel. In the big image on the second page, on the contrary, these forms are less pervasive as they are falling apart, giving more space to the black background. The first page is the locus of a tension that is extended by the repetition of the equally sized images until the denouement – the "visual explosion" on the second page – and concluded, on the third page, by a resolution where the forms are less and less present inside the frames.

The reading/viewing experience is enriched by color changes beginning on the second page, almost coinciding with the appearance of the grey-blue parts that contrast with the yellow ones. I have deliberately chosen a work where the unfolding of the "plot" stays relatively simple and relatable. Despite the absence of representative elements, *The Panic* is reflective of Antonio Altarriba's sentence – "transformation is the oxygen of comics"[3] – (36) as Molotiu produces variations in three main elements: the colors, the size of the frames and the density of forms in each of them. Nevertheless, as the anthology shows, cartoonists use many other techniques to render the plot more dynamic, often by introducing other types of variation: the shape of the frames, the graphic styles, the size of the

---

[3] "Le changement est l'oxygène de la bande dessinée".

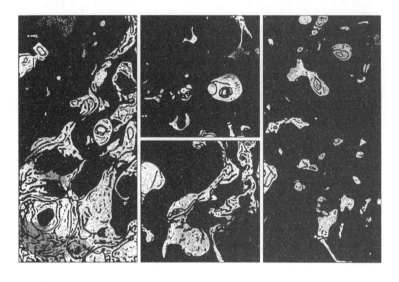

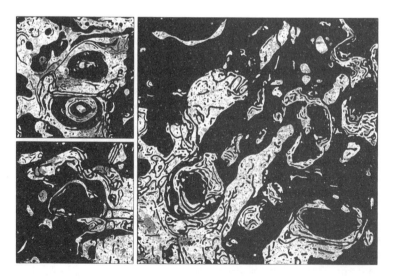

Figure 12.3. Andrei Molotiu, *The Panic*. From Andrei Molotiu. *Abstract Comics. The Anthology* (Fantagraphics, 2009), n. pag.

gutters or the spaces between the panels or in the textures, by using different pictorial techniques or introducing collages... Balloons and captions, when they do appear, lose their semiotic function to become components of these "visual melodies."

Molotiu's book clearly shows that the rejection of figurative drawing does not automatically imply a rejection of narration as long as it is not used in the narrow sense of the word, of a story that should necessarily refer to our tangible world. As mentioned in the introduction, "the formal elements of comics [. . .], even in the absence of a (verbal) story, can create a feeling of sequential drive, the sheer rhythm of the narrative or the rise and fall of a story arc" (Molotiu). If the narrative dimension is undoubtedly connected to sequentiality, it has also much to do with the internal dynamics of the images. To better understand these dynamics, we can turn to a 1954 text by poet and artist Henri Michaux on an exhibition of abstract paintings by Paul Klee. The title, *Adventures of Lines*, is very indicative of his singular perception of the works. He does not only emphasize the musical dimension of Klee's work but anthropomorphizes the lines by giving them actions, feelings, and psychological depth: lines "have a walk," others are "travelers," "penetrating" or "allusive"; "A line is waiting. A line is hoping. A line thinks about a face" (113–117). Michaux's text is both a poetry exercise and a critical review but it shows eloquently that even a single abstract image can be narrative.

In one of her abstract comics, Kym Tabulo pays tribute to Paul Klee, an artist she describes as one of her main sources of inspiration. *What Would Paul Klee Say?* uses nonfigurative motives that evoke Klee's abstract works. Each of Tabulo's panels conserves its dynamism: the lines are whirling arabesques. Klee famously stated that "a line is a dot that went for a walk," highlighting the viewer's role in recreating, with her eyes, the path of the artist's hand. The eye of the reader/viewer scans the images from left to right producing a flow that is superimposed on the internal dynamic of the images; each panel is "over-dynamized" by its inscription in a sequence.

Since abstract comics break away from representation and are not constrained by the imperative to produce a story in the narrowest sense of the term, they are, much more than "figurative" comics, able to question the devices and even rethink principles such as sequentiality that are often regarded as essential features of comics. As Pierre Fresnault-Deruelle has pointed out, comics are both linear and tabular: the reader has the opportunity to both consider each panel in a fixed sequence and, at the same time, to look at each page as a visual unity. With abstract comics, the author's wish to emphasize the tabular dimension is no longer conditional upon the necessity to produce a comprehensible narrative. Tim Gaze's untitled pages in Molotiu's anthology (Figure 12.4) generate a crisis of comics sequentiality by breaking up the frames and making linear readings impossible. Baroni explains that in a music track, "the *energy* or the *strength* of the plot directs the attention of the audience towards a possible resolution" but that sometimes there is no resolution. This is the case with Gaze's comics: the tension is permanent and does not reach a denouement. Gaze's pages are saturated with chaotic black lines and patches that recall noise music. An anonymous online comment confirms, "Really feeling these noise" (*sic.*).

Poetry Comics

Often assimilated with music, abstract comics also have strong connections with poetry. Rosaire Appel and Tim Gaze – to name only two artists – are multidisciplinary creators who are making abstract comics and poetry. Appel has published an artists' book called *wordless (poems)* that contains abstract drawings that sometimes look like cursive script although they do not directly refer to anything. As she explains on her website: "Between writing (language) and drawing is another area, an open, uncodified territory that has not yet been fully explored." When Appel uses the word uncodified, she reverses the current trends in comics analysis according to which comics are a hyper-codified medium, a complex set of codes and devices that work together to produce meaning.

Poetry comics have acquired prominence as a relatively recent tendency in the quest for new affordances of comics. The word "poetry" is as broad as "story" or "narrative" and can hardly be reduced to a single definition. It is often used when speaking about comics that leave room for ambiguity and where the production of emotion is at least as important as the understanding of the story. This also includes figurative works such as the creations of Bianca Stone whose books often bear the subtitle of "poetry comics." Again, such a term appears as an open invitation to the reader to shift their horizon of expectations.

Figurative comics are not necessarily less polysemous or more unequivocal than abstract comics. As Jan Baetens points out, "the reader is confronted with an opaque materiality paradoxically highlighted by the figurative dimension of the drawings" (97). According to Stone, the images "are not there to translate what is already there" ("Notes" 211). Building on *On Pictures and the Words That Fail Them* by the art historian James

Figure 12.4. Tim Gaze, untitled. From Andrei Molotiu. *Abstract Comics. The Anthology* (Fantagraphics, 2009), n. pag.

Elkins, Charles Hatfield develops a reflection on Jack Kirby's comics that echoes Stone's statement:

> There is a fundamental tension in such drawing between the very picture-ness of the pictures and their compelling narrative function. Picture-ness is hard to describe, for, as James Elkins argues, pictures "are always partly nonsemiotic," that is, outside or in excess of narrative and linguistic structures. Indeed, the pleasure and provocation they offer reside in precisely that. [...] To ignore such qualities is to ignore pictures: "Parts of pictures are disorderly, unpredictably irrational, inconsistently inconsistent, and ill suited to stories of symbols or visual narratives; we tend to ignore those aspects in favor of readily retrievable meanings." (65)

These issues are reflected in the dichotomy between iconic signs and plastic signs proposed by the Groupe µ, a Belgian interdisciplinary group mostly known for its research on visual semiotics. An iconic sign is "what is represented" whereas a plastic sign is "how it is represented." The two types are closely interlinked: an image is always an iconic sign and a plastic sign at the same time. While discourses on comics largely emphasize the former, poetry comics such as Bianca Stone's call for greater attention to be paid to the latter.

Unlike abstract comics, poetry comics do not necessarily reject all references to reality. The reader/viewer perceives the images as both iconic signs and plastic signs, meaning that they simultaneously appreciate their representational qualities and the graphiation underpinning them. Graphiation is a concept forged by Philippe Marion to designate, in comics, the act of producing a graphic trace, a mark of subjectivity. The agent responsible for this trace is the graphiator. Marion states that "the comics reader-viewer is encouraged to connect his gaze with the graphiator's gesture; it is through incorporating the graphiator's trace that the reader-viewer can construct the message" (35–36)[4]. Every reader participates in such an experience when they open a comic book: being exposed to a bunch of lines that could stir up a vast and rich range of feelings. Even before having any idea of the fictional content, they would see the comics in their hand as joyful, uncomfortable, boring, questioning, exciting, repulsing... Making one's eyes coincide with the graphiator's gesture concerns not only the images but also the design of the letters, speech balloons and panel frames that, especially when they are handmade, can be

---

[4] "[L]e lecteur-spectateur de BD est appelé à mettre son regard en coïncidence avec le geste du graphiateur; c'est en épousant l'empreinte graphique du celui-ci qu'il peut participer au message."

Comics at the Limits of Narration

considered as plastic signs. According to Marion, all of these elements are "extensions of the same graphic impetus" (41).

On the nineth page of *Because You Love You Come Apart* from the collection *Poetry Comics from the Book of Hours*, we can see a hot air balloon floating above a lunar landscape of hills in the first panel and, in the second panel, a young woman in a bra and pajamas sitting on a sofa or on a mattress covered with several motives, including two small screaming horses, in front of a shelf with toy figures. The speech balloons stemming from the woman's mouth declare: "You are gruesome. Hungry. / At the edge of the earth." These words are complemented by the captions under the second panel: "Where the dead wait / From a babble in the ground / In a vortex of quilts" (Figure 12.5). The "imperialism of the narrative" has no role in this poetry comic, semantic vagueness rules instead. The absence of univocal meaning also gives more room for subjective interpretation as Stone states: "[the images] are there to seamlessly interact and allow the readers the space to feel and create meaning on their own" ("Notes", 211). The freedom given to the reader can be connected to a certain kind of pleasure they can take from reading such a work.

Bianca Stone began writing poetry before making comics: "For me, poetry is always first and foremost. Honoring the words is the most important aspect of making a poetry comic. Text will always lead the images" (Schmuhl). Indeed, the written elements in Stone's comics function as poems on their own building on the rhythm of the phrases, the choice of words and their acoustic dimensions, and the feeling of strangeness produced by the verbal images, such as "a vortex of quilts." As with her words, Stone creates powerful and disconcerting pictures by freely associating disparate elements; their weirdness is further emphasized by the juxtaposition of diverse scales, producing a collage effect reminiscent of surrealist paintings. "In my work I prefer to have the images move away from literal illustration of what the text is saying," Stone claims (Dueben). The texts participate in the ambiguity of the message. To a certain extent, this claim contradicts theoretical assumptions that texts and images are complementary entities in comics that collaborate to create meaning, as proposed by Groensteen when analyzing the function of the verbal in *System of Comics* (127–134). In contrast, Stone builds up a "third entity" that arises from the friction between images and texts.

Alexander Rothman's creations are similarly driven by the desire to test the possible dialogues that can be generated between written and graphic elements. In a short essay, he states: "So what is poetry? I understand it as the purest example of a form where the medium is language." Based on

Figure 12.5. Bianca Stone, *Poetry Comics from the Book of Hours* (Pleiades Press, 2016), n. pag.

this, he asks himself "How do I solve this creative problem with language?" or "What else can language do?" in order to "harvest" its "expressive potential" ("Comics Poetry"). "Language" here means the codes that are commonly associated with comics: the page divided into panels and frames, the presence of texts and – when required – balloons and captions. Rothman does not think that these elements should be used exclusively to tell a story; he rather sees them as devices to test. The "Exercises" section on his website presents a series of attempts to take over the space of a regular layout of four or six frames, with drawings and often texts. Improvisation seems to play a strong role, especially regarding the motives in each frame that do not appear to be semantically connected to each other, such as a crouched man, an overripe fruit, a tree trunk, and a pair of scissors. Rothman points out that seeing "two or more images next to each other [trigger] some semiotic impulse in our minds [that] can't help but connect them."

He reconnects with the automatic writing which the Surrealists had employed alongside their strategies of creating art through fortuitous juxtapositions. Improvisation also characterizes music such as jazz. Music is everywhere in Rothman's work, directly when he draws singers or musicians playing, and indirectly when he plays on the rhythmic dimension of his comics. For example, on the first page of *Taking Time, Keeping Time*, he punctuates each of the four identically sized panels with a balloon, three of which have a metronome drawn inside them; these graphic elements emphasize the basic beat established by the regular layout.

Poetry comics open a space that brings together very different works sharing a common rejection of the story in favor of semantic ambiguity. While Rothman uses the canonical devices of comics as a template, Mita Mahato's poetry comics deviate so much from familiar comics devices that their allegiance to the medium is questionable and established through her use of labels such as poetry comics or even comixed poetry. Speech balloons are rather rare and she associates texts with images in very unconventional ways. Frames are usually absent and it is often difficult to mentally isolate each panel; this reinforces the perception of the page as a visual unity. The use of various pictorial techniques sometimes enriched with collages give them a "visual immediacy" and encourages their appreciation as visual matter or "plastic signs." *It's All Over and Other Poems on Animals* presents a series of uncoated paper sheets folded into fourths, showing monochrome silhouettes against a background of geometrical forms and accompanied with a short sentence infinitely repeated and ignoring the spaces between the words such as "THELAST TIMEISAWYOUTHELASTTIMEISAWYOU," "IT'SALLOVERIT' SALLOVER," "FROMTIMETOTIMEFROMTIMETOTIME," or "SOSORRYSOSORRY."

As with poetry comics by Stone or Rothman, readers might be tempted to think that Mahato's *It's All Over* deliberately plays with semantic vagueness and the friction between images and texts. However, a look at some of Mahato's other works as well as her posts on social networks provide an additional layer of meaning. They show her commitment against global warming: she has, for instance, conceived educational comics for the Seattle Climate Health Action Team in which she explains the impact of climate change on health and how to prevent further harm. This casts new light on the title *It's All Over* and on the phrases that cover the animals, expressing her fear of species extinction and the accompanying feeling of guilt. Although poetry comics do not produce a story that can be summarized or paraphrased, paratexts sometimes add additional layers of meaning.

This is the case with Renee French's *h day*, a wordless comic consisting of two series of images; most of the double-pages show a simple line drawing on the left against a blank background and a more complex composition in grey scale within a square frame on the right (Figure 12.6). The reader/viewer can appreciate the plasticity of the images, the rhythm produced by the alternation of two different graphic styles or the flow generated by the succession of the images. According to Barbara Postema, "the division of the work into something like chapters – the so-called 'stages' – adds another layer of narrative by implying a progression" (287) like a symphony in six movements. The text on the back cover mentions that the artist "illustrates her struggles with migraine headaches and Argentine ant infestation." Such clarification invites a rethinking of the meaning of the images. Among others, the reader associates the monstruous deformation of the character's head on the left page with the pain suffered by the author and the small black bugs on the right pages with Argentinian ants. One would think that in order to represent the pain produced by the migraine, French would have chosen to saturate the space of the page with lines. She relies, on the contrary, on a minimalist device without words – claiming, "I hate words as they make things too explicit" (Goldberg) – to preserve its polysemy. French offers not a literal testimony but a sensitive translation of a life experience built on the visionary power of each image and on the sequentiality of the images. The text on the back cover states that *h day* can be read "as an oblique autobiography." An autobiography that is not based on facts but that expresses French's emotions. *h day* demonstrates that moving away from representation does not rule out personal testimony. Kym Tabulo, whose abstract comics are even more detached from representation, asserts:

> My works could be related to autobiographical sequential artworks, for example, those graphic novels that record the time and emotions in an artist's life. Though not intentionally autobiographical it clearly does portray some candid and cautions echoes of emotional life. ("Abstract Sequential," 148)

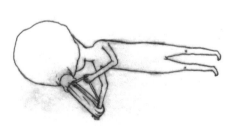

Figure 12.6. Renée French, *h day* (Picture Box, 2010), n. pag.

Intermediality

If the works analyzed in this chapter have several features that set them apart from the typical understanding of comics, this has much to do with the careers of the artists. Kym Tabulo, for example, describes abstract painting, and in particular Paul Klee, as the bedrock on which she has built her future works. She feels that being an abstract artist in the twenty-first century is an uncomfortable position because abstraction is deeply rooted in twentieth-century avant-gardes to the extent that pursuing this avenue would be like redoing what has already been done. The discovery of *Snake*, an installation by visual artist Sidney Nolan, combined with Shaun Tan's wordless comics *The Arrival* and Molotiu's anthology, opened up a new field for Tabulo, where she could create works at the crossroads of different media (*Art*). Among others, she has introduced processes from visual arts into the field of comics, such as "gallery comics," that is, works conceived to be both printed in books and displayed in exhibition spaces while rejecting hierarchical tendencies between the two approaches. Rosaire Appel, for her part, describes her path as follows: "I started with poetry, moved to painting [. . .], then to fiction writing, to photography – and then back to drawing, both analog and digital, and to making books" (Yaniv). Her predilection for self-made booklets owes as much to zine traditions as to artists' books.

Appel's and Tabulo's testimonies are not isolated cases; other authors mentioned here have also engaged with several media. Some of them were first comics creators who had been nourished by external influences whereas others, coming from different media and art traditions, have incorporated comics into their practices. This is another illustration of the "quest for new affordances of comics" that drives alternative, small press or self-publishing spheres. Considering comics as a component of a more global artistic project is an approach that was quite marginal in the twentieth century and has only emerged in the last few decades. In order to fully understand the recent evolution of comics, we need to take their relationships with other media into account. In other words, they must be considered from an intermedial perspective, an approach that Éric Méchoulan summarizes as follows: "We must account for a plurality of relations which are constitutive of a 'medium' but, above all, [acknowledge] that a medium is never separated from other media. On the contrary, it is in connection with other media that a medium is formed."[5]

The limits between media are very difficult if not impossible to establish; there are always borderline cases. In 2006, in the second issue of the short-lived, alternative comics magazine *L'Éprouvette*, editors Jean-Christophe Menu and Christian Rosset imagined a section titled "Progressive Erosion of Boundaries" – retitled "Transgressive Explosion of Boundaries" in the next issue – in which they presented works that placed comics in dialogue with other art forms, creations lying at the intersection of several media. The influences claimed by creators whose work has been considered here are very telling. Bianca Stone mentions: "*Peanuts*, Edward Gorey, Maira Kalman, Joe Brainard, *Swamp Thing*, *Batman* comics, Ralph Steadman, Scott McCloud's books on comics, Marlene Dumas, Henry Darger, to name a few" (Dueben). She creates works that are unambiguously comics but also creations commonly associated with other media such as the references cited by Tim Gaze: collage books and decalcomania paintings by Max Ernst, Henri Michaux's tachiste sequential work, and some Art Brut works. Regarding the references that are not commonly associated with comics, they are – to borrow a neologism forged by Colin Beineke – "comicitous." This means that they present specific features that are commonly associated with comics – for example, the plurality of images, their sequentiality or the division of the space in frames. In the introduction to his anthology, Molotiu mentions and reproduces works by abstract visual artists – El Lissitzky, Wassily Kandinsky, Willem de Kooning, among others – that show obvious similarities with the abstract comics brought together in the book. An intermedial study entails taking into account what Jean-Christophe Menu has christened the "*corpus hors-champ de la bande dessinée*" to describe "an entire corpus of works that undoubtedly belong to the field [of comics] but is not integrated into its History, and is therefore not recognized as an integral part of the field" (432).

Besides confirming the need to study comics from an intermedial perspective, works that resist the "imperialism of the narrative" bring to

---

[5] 'Nous [devons] prendre en compte une pluralité de relations constitutive du "média", mais surtout [que] ce média n'est jamais séparé d'autres médias. C'est au contraire dans la relation aux autres médias qu'un média est constitué'.

light alternative ways of apprehending comics of all types, including those where all devices seem to be put to the service of a story. Here too, the reader-viewer has the opportunity to appreciate the singularity of graphiation, the particular rhythm and flow, to contemplate the page as a plastic unity, to appreciate the ambiguity of meaning or the blurring of figuration, developing, ultimately, an awareness that there is poetry in "storytelling comics" and abstraction in "visual comics."

WORKS CITED

Comics

Appel, Rosaire. *wordlesss* (poems). Self-Published 2013.
    Soundtrack/s. Press Rappel, 2018.
    Perturbations. Adverse, 2019.
French, Renée. *h day*. Picture Box, 2010.
Gaze, Tim. *100 Scenes. A Graphic Novel*. Asemic, 2010.
Mahato, Mita. *It's All Over and Other Poems on Animals*. [Self-Published], 2020.
Molotiu, Andrei. *Abstract Comics: The Anthology*. Fantagraphics, 2009.
Stone, Bianca. *Poetry Comics from the Book of Hours*. Pleiades Press, 2016.
Tabulo, Kym. *What Would Paul Klee Say?* [Self-Published] 2016.

Secondary Sources

Altarriba, Alberto. "Propositions pour une analyse spécifique du récit en bande dessinée." *Bande Dessinée, récit et modernité. Colloque de Cerisy, 1–11 Août 1987*, edited by Thierry Groensteen. Futuropolis, 1988, pp. 25–44.
Baetens, Jan. "Abstraction in Comics." *SubStance*, vol. 40, no. 124, 2011, pp. 94–113.
Baroni, Raphaël. "Tensions et résolutions: Musicalité de l'intrigue ou intrigue musicale?." *Cahiers de narratologie. Analyse et théorie narrative*, no. 21, 2011. https://doi.org/https://doi.org/10.4000/narratologie.6390
Beineke, Colin. "On Comicity." *Inks: The Journal of the Comics Studies Society*, vol. 1, no. 2, 2017, pp. 226–253.
Dejasse, Erwin. "Art Brut and Alternative Comics: Reciprocal Sympathies." *Études Francophones*, vol. 32, 2022, pp. 197–220.
Dueben, Alex. "A Bianca Stone Interview." *The Comics Journal*, 18 September 2021. www.tcj.com/a-bianca-stone-interview/
Fresnault-Deruelle, Pierre. "From Linear to Tabular (1976)." *The French Comics Theory Reader*, edited by Bart Beaty and Ann Miller. Leuven University Press, 2014, pp. 121–138.
Goldberg, Myla. *Renee French "H Day" Part 2. Interview by Myla Goldberg. Youtube*, 2010 www.youtube.com/watch?v=bPghC2GqMTc
Groensteen, Thierry. *Comics and Narration*. University Press of Mississippi, 2018.

"Fictions sans frontières." *La Transécriture: Pour une théorie de l'adaptation*, edited by André Gaudreault and Thierry Groensteen. Nota Bene, 1998, pp. 9–29.

The System of Comics. University Press of Mississippi, 2009.

Groupe μ. *Traité visuel du signe*. Seuil, 1992.

Hatfield, Charles. *Hand of Fire: The Comics Art of Jack Kirby*. University Press of Mississippi, 2012.

Isabelinho, Domingos. "Monthly Stumblings # 14: Tim Gaze." *The Hooded Utilitarian*, 8 March 2012. www.hoodedutilitarian.com/2012/03/monthly-stumblings-14-tim-gaze

Jauss, Hans Robert. *Toward an Aesthetic of Reception*. University of Minnesota Press, 1982.

Marion, Philippe. *Traces en cases: Travail graphique, figuration narrative et participation du lecteur*. Academia, 1993.

Méchoulan, Éric. "Intermédialité, ou comment penser les transmissions." *Fabula / Les Colloques: Création, intermédialité, dispositif*, 5 March 2017. www.fabula .org/colloques/document4278.php

Menu, Jean-Christophe. *La bande dessinée et son double: Langage et marges de la bande dessinée*. L'Association, 2011.

Michaux, Henri. *Passages (1937–1963)*. Gallimard, 1998.

Postema, Barbara. "Adding Up to What? Degrees of Narration and Abstraction in Wordless Comics." *Abstraction and Comics / Bande dessinée et abstraction*, edited by Aarnoud Rommens et al. Presses Universitaires de Liège / La 5e Couche, 2019, pp. 284–298.

Rothman, Alexander. *Alexander Rothman*, https://versequential.com/.

"What Is Comics Poetry?" *Solrad. The Online Literary Magazine for Comics*, 4 March 2020. https://solrad.co/what-is-comics-poetry-an-essay-by-alexan der-rothman

Schmul, Elizabeth. "On 'Poetry Comics from The Book of Hours': An Interview with Bianca Stone." *Michigan Quarterly Review*, May 2016. https://sites.lsa .umich.edu/mqr/2016/01/on-poetry-comics-from-the-book-of-hours-an-interview-with-bianca-stone/

Stone, Bianca. "Notes on Time and Poetry Comics." *Abstraction and Comics/ Bande dessinée et abstraction*, edited by Aarnoud Rommens et al. Presses Universitaires de Liège / La 5e Couche, 2019, pp. 210–228.

Tabulo, Kym. *The Art of Abstract Comics*. Pecha Kucha, 5 September 2016. www .pechakucha.com/presentations/the-art-of-abstract-comics

"Abstract Sequential Art: An Artists Insight." *Abstraction and Comics / Bande dessinée et abstraction*, edited by Aarnoud Rommens et al. Presses Universitaires de Liège / La 5e Couche, 2019, pp. 147–165.

Yaniv, Etty. "Rosaire Appel – Cajoling Sound and Image [Interview]." *Art Spiel. Reflections on the Work of Contemporary Artists*, 29 June 2018. https://artspiel .org/rosaire-appel-cajoling-sound-and-image/

PART III

Uses

CHAPTER 13

Comics and Their Archives

Benoît Crucifix

In his 2011 graphic novel *The Great Northern Brotherhood of Canadian Cartoonists*, Seth offers his readers a virtual tour of an imaginary national society of affiliated cartoonists: the brotherhood is a patchwork of hobbyist clubs, private societies, and cultural institutions.[1] One of its major (fictional) achievements – set in the late 1960s – is the establishment of the grand G.N.B.C.C. Archive, located in the remotest and most Northern corners of Canada in an igloo-designed architecture concealing stacks of safely preserved unique comics in a climate-controlled environment (Figure 13.1). Seth's witty portrayal of an imaginary archive is tacitly set against the history of disregard for popular media within nation-wide archival policies and institutional heritage programs. It pays tribute to, while gently mocking, the postwar emergence of comics fandom and its networks of individual collectors, readers' clubs, and amateur societies, by imagining what would have happened if they had succeeded in building some kind of collective archival institution. Even though older comics have now found their way in national libraries and in dedicated collections from Columbus, Ohio, to Angoulême, France, the archival fantasy of a comprehensive record of past comics is a common one for a medium that was long deemed unworthy of preservation efforts. But if the history of the G.N.B.C.C. is one told in terms of its greatest and best, this veneer of bombast and grandiloquence laid on by an unreliable narrative voice ultimately conceals loss, disinterest, and failure. The description made of the archive matches this ambiguous tone: it struggles with lack of funding, its infrastructure is in thorough need of an upgrade, and its staff cannot keep up with the cataloguing of its passing members' donations. Seth's

---

This article is an outcome of the COMICS project funded by the European Research Council (ERC) under the European Union's Horizon 2020 research and innovation program (grant agreement no. 758502).

[1] For a close-reading of Seth's works in terms of metafiction and historiography, see Marrone's *Forging the Past*.

Figure 13.1. *The Great Northern Brotherhood of Canadian Cartoonists* (Drawn & Quarterly, 2011), p. 103. Copyright Seth. Used with permission from Drawn & Quarterly.

archival imaginary addresses issues of access, relevance, and sustainability. The icy setting of the G.N.B.C.C. archive, along with its multiple safe vaults, might further recall the Svalbard Global Seed Vault, a seed bank for the preservation of crop diversity located on an Arctic archipelago and launched in 2008. Even though crop cultures and popular print heritage follow different preservation needs and logics, the analogy strengthens the notion that the preservation of comics heritage is not only about keeping the past but also about enabling future uses. The very idea of a remote, hardly accessible archive of comics and popular print artifacts, however, seems like an outdated model when lined against today's digital archives, with their global reach and their seemingly immediate availability and reusability.

If this fictional archive offers a nostalgic look back at old libraries, their card catalogues, and associated furniture, Seth's graphic novel evidences the processes of selection and organization of archives, as they mediate access and meaning, and stresses the demands, constraints, human work, financial costs, and material infrastructures needed to assemble and maintain archives, as they are subject to changing conditions. Altogether, this nostalgic undertone prongs us to think historically about comics and "their" archives. What kind of archives have been envisioned for comics? How does a medium long considered throwaway popular culture survive through time? What is the relation of comics culture to archives and institutions of memory? How have collecting practices defined the ways in which the history of comics is written? How have comics navigated the archival turn and its digital ramifications? This is not just about the capsizing change in cultural status that comics have undergone over the past decades, shifting "from disposable to durable" (Jenkins 2). This shift is itself inseparable from sweeping global changes in terms of archives, preservation concerns, cultural memory, and heritage industries, accelerated by the emergence and rapid spread of digital technologies. It is not just that comics are moving into archives – designating collections of documents and the institutions that house them – but also that the very notion of the "archive" has been unsettled by the expansion of the concept beyond its usual perimeters.

Just as comics studies was emerging as a new research field, "the archive" was being redefined as a capacious and tendentious theoretical concept across the humanities and a new keyword in fields such as trauma and memory studies, postcolonial theory, performance and installation art, histories of surveillance and governance.[2] If the expanded notion of the "archive" and its metaphorical usage raised some skeptical eyebrows among archivists and curators used to assemble and handle actual archives, the digital realm did effectively popularize gestures of archiving, of sorting out through a mass of information, of curating personal selections out of vast online databases. Privileging iterative and serial modes of distribution and reproduction, digital culture has unsettled the relationship to cultural memory as it becomes less of a record of cultural production than "an archive to be plundered, an original to be memorized, copied and manipulated" (De Kosnik 4). Diminishing the role of traditional gatekeepers of cultural memory while opening a field for commercializing and datamining archives and their uses, digital media have accelerated the democratization of cultural access initiated by nineteenth-century cultural industries

---

[2] Daniel Stein offers a useful and concise survey of the main theoretical trends around "the archive" in "What's in an Archive?," while Elizabeth Yale offers a "state of the discipline" from a historical perspective. For an archival sciences perspective, see also Cook.

and heightened tensions between copyright ownership and advocacy for cultural commons, between an overload of available archives and anxieties about their fragility.

Comics make for a compelling and multivalent case study to capture shifting notions around archives as they relate to popular culture and other historically "low" media. Precisely because comics were not part of canonical culture, they raise questions about preservation and archiving that, under the impulse of digitization, have now moved front stage. The preservation of comics has for a large part depended on and been shaped by readers, collectors, and fans; as well as commercial initiatives resulting from the professionalization of its fandom. As such, comics archives cannot be dissociated from their history as commodities of popular seriality (see Chapter 2 on Comics, Media Culture and Seriality) and from the particular work of preservation performed by their audiences (see Chapter 14 on Readers and Fans). This makes for a situation where the categories and roles of archiving, reading, and making seem to be ceaselessly crisscrossing. Comics require us to adopt a holistic approach to archives and this chapter proposes to disentangle some of their multiple relationships, at different levels of articulations.

How (Not) to Preserve Comics?

The cultural memory of comics and their preservation cannot be considered without its necessary corollaries: forgetting, neglect, erasure, loss.[3] It takes a social and cultural shift in perception to perceive loss as such and to trigger the impulse for preservation (Lowenthal). Understanding the relationship of comics to archival status requires us to appreciate their origins in popular print culture, marked by disposability and ephemerality. In a 1955 essay about comics, popular literature, and the middlebrow, the New York intellectual Leslie Fiedler stated that "the articles of popular culture are made, not to be treasured, but to be thrown away; a paperback book is like a disposable diaper or a paper milk container." Contrasting paperbacks with the "calf-bound volumes of another day," he opposed the disposability of mass culture to the durability of canonical culture, further suggesting that "its very mode of existence challenges the concept of a library, private or public" (124–125). If this statement calls for many nuances, it rightly highlights the relationship between material format and preservation as indicative of a work's desired circulation, and the tacit assumptions about

---

[3] For an in-depth discussion of comics and cultural legitimacy, see Christopher Pizzino's landmark *Arresting Development*.

the ephemerality and obsolescence of these productions, often meant to be replaced and succeeded by their next installment. These assumptions were integrated by producers who did not see economic interest or profit in maintaining extant archives, outside of those necessary to sustain commercial strategies of licensing and merchandising, and sometimes precluded the possibilities of future iterations and rediscoveries. A subsequent chunk of historical documents and archives related to comics culture – from original art to professional records – has simply not been kept, or remains undisclosed, leaving contemporary historians with a cipher of dispersed traces.

In the years running up to Fiedler's article, libraries and their custodians were not oblivious to comics, as the timely debates around comics and juvenile delinquency stirred a variety of professional concerns among youth services librarians (Tilley). These debates touched mostly on contemporary changes and on the educational role of public and school libraries, as comic books were primarily seen and understood as children's culture. Archival approaches to comics were furthermore sparse and perfunctory. As suggested by Jenny Robb, curator at the Billy Ireland Cartoon Library & Museum, comics were not completely absent from archival institutions but "for most of the 20th century, librarians – both public and academic – shunned the idea of spending precious financial, staff, or space resources on collecting, preserving, and cataloging comics and cartoons" ("Librarians" 71). Comics were sporadically found in storage but without resources for indexing, cataloging, and "making them discoverable or accessible," they remained invisible, only waiting for later moments of rediscovery (73). Cultural loss is sometimes harder to identify and describe when it is the result of neglect and disinterest rather than that of deliberate destruction, according to philosopher Judith Schlanger (22–23). While ample attention has been devoted to moral panic and comic book burnings, we do not yet fully grasp the effects of a more passive but also more widespread marginalization of comics within archives and libraries with existing collections, such as the lack of information on the history of these collections.

A wholesale shift in conceptions around comics and archives, rewiring popular culture as an item for preservation, slowly unfolded over the 1960s and 1970s, amidst social and countercultural upheavals that shook university campuses, thanks to new networks of comics fandom and the emergence of popular culture studies on academic agendas. If, at the time Fiedler's article came out, there already was a fan-addict club around EC comics (initiated by the editors themselves), the "second wave" of fans in those years, finding affective and commercial value in old comic books, had a solid and long-lasting influence on the consolidation of comics fandom networks around shared practices of collection, authorization, and exchange (Beaty 154). Strengthened by this grassroots movement and by the general public visibility of pop culture, comics gradually integrated a range of university libraries and archives, often based on donated collections from affiliated scholars or alumni, with the help of skilled librarians advocating their cause. Randall Scott, at Michigan State University Libraries in East Lansing, and a bit later, Lucy Caswell, at the Ohio State University in Columbus, established the basis for what have now become the two main hubs for comics archives in the US, alongside a series of other university libraries.[4]

Any discussion of these changes in the 1960s and 1970s would be incomplete without briefly mentioning the case of Bill Blackbeard's unique archival enterprise. Remembered as "the man who saved comics", Harvey, ("Bill"), Blackbeard founded the San Francisco Academy of Comic Art (SFACA) in July 1969, a nonprofit institution collecting the bound newspaper volumes that public libraries in the US were discarding in favor of their microfilm versions. From these volumes, he assembled and maintained an exhaustive collection of newspaper comics over three decades, until it was loaded into six semitrucks and moved over to OSU in 1998 (Robb, "Blackbeard" 254). Contrasting with contemporary collectors of cartoon original art such as Mort Walker or Erwin D. Swann (Scully), Blackbeard's collection is not only important for the heritage and legacy it now constitutes, but because it directly grew in response to changing policies of preservation and access within US libraries and thus situates collecting within broader cultural and technological transformations. The postwar boom in publishing indeed challenged libraries with an unprecedented amount of documents to collect and sparked institutions to consider how they could collaborate and pool resources across a nationwide network (Marcum and Schonfeld 14–32). Microfilming offered the promise of precious gains in storage space by miniaturizing and compressing records. This format change, however, erased the material specificities of original size, proportions, texture, and color that were crucial for understanding the Sunday comics pages. Blackbeard tried to position the SFACA within a network of interlibrary exchanges, but remained a rather quirky, highly personal and financially precarious enterprise. His collection

---

[4] See Robb's chapter for a description of their foundational role and for a more exhaustive presentation of comics archives around the world.

was not indexed according to standards, nor did Blackbeard write a guide or catalog of its holdings (McCrory 141). Blackbeard's recovery of the newspaper volumes discarded by public libraries was meant to allow for ways of accessing, reading, and using the archives that were not in tune with the new styles of information management.

In salvaging these paper volumes, Blackbeard emphasized the importance of the original materiality of newspaper comics, not only as visual culture but as objects to handle, manipulate, touch, perhaps even smell. This sensorial and affective engagement with archives as a form of embodied historical knowledge is perhaps best described by quoting from *The Comics*, one of the first books on newspaper comics published in 1947, in which Coulton Waugh invited his readers to visit the Newspaper Room of the New York Public Library: "the way to really understand the old comics is to lug out the musty newspaper volumes and have a look at them, even if you crack a few vertebrae doing it" (16). This physical handling of newspapers was increasingly being replaced in the 1970s by the surrogate experience of accessing newspapers on microfilm readers, entangled with new managerial views on library spaces and their uses. To implement this tactile approach to comics history, Blackbeard perhaps paradoxically intervened into the very materiality of these newspapers. Relying on damaged volumes, whose spines had been cut for microfilming, Blackbeard, his wife Barbara, and their peers clipped out series of comic strips to organize them into what he described as "files," borrowing the language of records, stored into metal cabinets. The gesture of cutting-out is a telling act of selection, uprooting the comics from their immediate paratext and from the publication context of the newspaper. It also allowed for further circulations and new uses, most notably in supporting a range of reprint initiatives with which Blackbeard was involved, but also more simply for access in the study room of the academy or for mailing out Xeroxed reproductions (Figure 13.2) – a circulation network that sometimes drew this "rogue archivist" *avant la lettre* into copyright squabbles.[5] This community archive, rooted in fandom, would have a long-term impact on the later rediscovery of newspaper comics in the graphic novel and on the historical fascination of cartoonists like Art Spiegelman, Trina Robbins, Chris Ware, and others (Crucifix).

---

[5] Blackbeard's role as director of the archive is targeted by the copyright holders of Percy Crosby's *Skippy*, vigilant about the kind of circulations that the SFACA was facilitating; letter from Joan Crosby Tibbetts to Bill Blackbeard, July 24, 1978; Billy Ireland Cartoon Library and Museum, SFACA collection, Box 23, "Academy Papers" file.

Figure 13.2. Xeroxed reproduction of a 1926 comic strip by Milt Gross, sent out by Bill Blackbeard to Art Spiegelman in 1982 for possible inclusion in *RAW*. Handwritten caption reads: "originals on *very* aged paper—sorry about graininess…" Billy Ireland Cartoon Library & Museum, Art Spiegelman and Françoise Mouly collection.

Scrapbooks, Long Boxes, Hardcovers, and .cbr

If "in the United States, the bond between comics and their storage and reproduction media has been precarious from the very start," as Alexander Starre puts it (550) and as we have just seen, the role of fans and dedicated consumers has always been crucial in performing preservation efforts, even if only for private pleasures or collective exchanges. The impulse for preserving comics has originated in grassroots initiatives more than in institutional policies. But as enterprises in popular seriality, comics producers and makers have always heavily relied on their readers and audiences and one can trace a feedback loop between the production of serial desires, the cultivation of dedicated audiences, the gaps and vagaries of serial narratives, and the archival impulse to hold on to past installments of a beloved title (Gardner, *Projections* 173).

If the 1960s are again an important turning point, as "comics became collectible – that is, sought after for preservation by fans of the medium – for the first time" (Pustz 15), this view privileges comic books over cartoons and newspaper comics, which had been collected by readers – that is, clipped and preserved in bound albums – since at least the nineteenth century. In fact, the comic book originally emerged as a format based on the reprinting of syndicated comic strips, only to be quickly highjacked for the dissemination of new stories (Gabilliet, *Of Comics and Men* 10). Newspaper readers regularly clipped out favorite images and pasted them within blank albums specifically produced for that purpose. As Ellen Gruber Garvey argues, scrapbook makers engaged in "performing archivalness, acts and gestures of preservation," as "they express the will to save, organize, and transmit knowledge through a homemade archive"

(20). Scrutinizing the story papers of antebellum America, Jared Gardner has shown the kinship between the development of serial fictions, the inclusion of images and graphic narratives, and the friendship albums and scrapbooks of the time: the layout in story papers often "serves as an invitation to recirculate the images in private albums," taking into account the most common scrapbook formats of the time (Gardner, "Antebellum" 46). In the first half of the twenty-first century, with the emergence of the syndicated comic strip, scrapbooks were further used by readers to consign endlessly evolving serials into cheap homemade albums, to be reread privately or shared in domestic circles. As Garvey suggests, the clipping scrapbook "leads towards the understanding that items can be detached from their original sources while keeping connected to them via identifiable format and typeface" (21). The premise was of course shared by press syndicates, who strived to see their comic strips circulate in as many newspaper titles as possible, while always retaining their copyright notice within the border of the panels. When Blackbeard took up the scissors, he set forth the same archival gestures that newspaper readers of comics had been performing beforehand, while tracking the different versions of syndicated comic strips across various local newspapers. Even if they are completely different objects as a commercial publishing phenomenon, the reprints of newspaper comics in the 1970s, and later in the 2000s, perform a similar sense of archival record by compiling serial comic strips over time, sometimes more randomly garnered depending on availability, or appended with extra documents. And indeed, reprints today are in the US designated as "archival reprints" or "archival collections." (The term took on "official" status with its inclusion as a specific category for the Eisner Awards in 1993.)

While newspaper readers were creating homemade books of their favorite comics, the emergence of comic books also quickly led to various "second-hand" activities of swapping, trading, and collecting copies as means of overcoming their ephemerality. As early as the late 1930s, a used books seller in Concordia, Kansas, tried to remediate comic books' limited durability by introducing "modifications that included brown tape and extra staples along the spines" (Gearino 15). This kind of material intervention would later become obsolete with the "professionalization of the comics collecting market," fixing down collecting practices based above all on the pristine conditions of preservation and giving more and more place to the financial value of old comic books, strengthened by "the explosive growth of a network of comic book specialty stores as well as by the creation of the *Overstreet Comic Book Price Guide*" (Beaty 10). While visits to the comic book shop were undoubtedly rhythmed by weekly releases, they also crucially provided access to back issues and lengthened the shelf life of ephemeral titles. The comic book store instituted practices of collecting, structured around price guides, back issues, long boxes, mylar bags, and distilled a set of archival gestures particular to comic book culture (Pustz). By contrast with the gestures of cutting and handling that have defined the preservation of comic strips (and which are arguably more identified with the feminized sphere of the domestic space), the gendered habits of slabbing, trading, and speculating in comic book culture, where material condition and commercial value are key, have produced a context where "touch is taboo" (Hague 95). At its peak in the 1980s and 1990s, comic book collecting ultimately had less to do with the long-term preservation aims of archivists than with the short-term logics of speculative financial traders (Beaty 180).

By slowing down the obsolescence of comics, stores nevertheless participated in the transformation of comic book culture, the consolidation of dedicated fan communities, the production of historically reflexive narratives for knowing audiences. Accordingly, mainstream comics publishers have developed an approach that caters to niche audiences' archival knowledge: memory has become a central creative force spanned around the editorial monitoring of serial continuity, requiring publishers to develop a cohesive management of "narrative memory" (Méon), as the reprints and anthologies produced in this context are meant to back up the unfurling of serial continuity (see chapter 2). This might lead to all sorts of tug-of-war relationships between producers and audiences, as Baetens and Frey remark in the context of European comics, and which may count even more strongly in the US: "fans see themselves as much the guardians of a series' authenticity as the copyright holders themselves, and the force of their conviction is an important actor in the continuation network" (Baetens and Frey 219). The vocabulary used to describe a serial product's relationship to its own history often borrows the language of heritage. We can find a striking example of that usage in a series of volumes that called upon the archival fantasy of the "vault" to present materials from the history of superheroes comic book publishing, with titles such as *The Marvel Vault* and *The DC Vault*. These package volumes relied on a trademarked "museum-in-a-book" format presenting "rare collectibles" and "plastic-encased archival gems" (Thomas and Sanderson). Their digitally reproduced facsimile contents elevate sketches, original art pages, unpublished documents, rare comic books to "museum" status in a typically nostalgic fashion that has become widespread in the comics publishing field (Gabilliet, "Facsimile"). And as Stein suggests in his analysis of the "museum-in-a-book" format, these titles might "usher in the ossification of what used to be a lively culture of interaction and immersion in a thriving serial genre" (*Authorizing* 245). The title reference of the "vault" is telling in this regard, and further speaks volumes about the relationship to archives: the "vault" serves to both allude to otherwise inaccessible private collections and to obscure their actual compositions, as these large publishing companies "are notoriously opaque when it comes to their in-house archives" (Stein, *Authorizing* 242). This vault imaginary summons readers' and fans' memories, aligned on proprietary transmedial storyworlds, while cultivating the mystery around what the purported vault actually holds. If the vault aggregates notions of value (both cultural and financial), rarity, and long-time preservation, it is also a form of control on its own historiography and a strategic containment of its items against unauthorized and undesired uses.

These complex relationships to the archive in comics appear perhaps even more strongly in the digital realm. As Darren Wershler and Kalervo Sinervo argue in a compelling analysis of Marvel's approach to digital distribution of its products, the publisher's "patchy" history of archiving its own materials has everything to do with its efforts in "building and maintaining a media empire" based on transmedial proliferation and circulation, at the expense of storage, continuity, and preservation (190–191). Relying on cloud storage and authorized access, Marvel ensures that its digital catalog remains "a walled garden," as users can access copies without exactly owning their purchases, "mak[ing] it possible to maintain centralized control of intellectual property, expand rapidly, and maintain uniformity through inexpensive methods of access and translation" (191–192). While large publishing companies and brands use digital media formats to assert control over their productions, the Web has also spawned a network of "rogue archivists" (De Kosnik) who more or less willingly flout legal restraints to distribute comics scans (see also Chapter 5 on digital comics). As Sinervo shows in another study, these unauthorized practices of sharing, framed as piracy by media industries, have never posed a serious threat to the industry nor offered a lucrative business for its actors. This particular situation has allowed for comics scanning to become primarily a matter of niche audience participation, or an exercise in what Sinervo describes after Foucault "author function" as an "audience function," and the performance of "a specific kind of preservation" (Sinervo 229). This archival commitment is also at work with the construction and maintenance of online archives assembled from scans of public domain, out-of-commerce or orphan works, making available the wide mass of lesser-known comic book titles produced by publishers who were driven out of business or stopped putting out comics after the introduction of the Comics Code Authority. To best serve their aims, comic book scanners have developed an archive file (such as .cbr or .cbz) facilitating not only the on-screen reading of comic books, but also easily allowing for additions, modifications, selections, appropriations, and remixing. In such files, one often finds information by which scanners affix their signature – in the form of logos, pseudonyms – and disclose part of the restoration process: in this example of a romance comic hosted on the Digital Comics Museum, one finds an acknowledgment of the original state of the paper copy, ripped and scribbled, of its collector (as identified by the portrait on the upper right corner) and the index card used to reference its contents, and of the crew who performed the scanning and digital "restoration" of the file (Figure 13.3). This visual example serves well to illustrate the more general point that preservation and transmission do not unfold in a vacuum, but are inseparable from particular reproduction media, alongside particular social practices, habitual gestures, sites, legal and material constraints: whatever is kept from the past offers a new version reframed as a historical object, as much as it is inevitably ripped from its original context and functioning.

Graphic Reproduction and Drawn Documents

The archiving and preservation of comics, as we have seen, is entangled with matters of materiality and reproduction. If these concerns are not unique to comics, their specific relevance to stakeholders in the field has everything to do with the particular make-up of comics as a medium that is based on drawing – imbued with trace, mark, presence, gesture – while being solidly anchored in the history of mass print reproduction – dominated by notions of seriality, sequence, duplicate, and the multiple. Cartooning has usually meant drawing for reproduction, and for an economy that privileges repeated acts of reproduction (see Chapter 1 on comics drawing). This raises specific issues at the level of preservation. For instance, if comics original art was primarily considered in functional terms (as a preparatory stage in the production process, and afterward as something to be discarded or gifted away more often than preciously kept), its newfound financial value has completely shifted its place in the hierarchies of value, as it now tends to obscure, in heritage discourses, the importance of other documents along the chain. Besides issues of

Comics and Their Archives 279

Figure 13.3. First and last page of a .cbr file containing scans of *True Love Problems and Advice Illustrated* no. 13 (1949), hosted online at the Digital Comics Museum.

Figure 13.3. (*cont.*)

Comics and Their Archives

conservation, medium specificity further raises complex questions about the archival work that comics do, or rather are thought to do, as they force us to reconsider the "productive tension" between archive and style in comics memory (Ahmed and Crucifix 3).

As drawn artifacts, comics do not share the same relationship to historicity and archival status as do photography and film, their birth companions, which were at least partly understood along the lines of mechanical objectivity, as technical means for recording and documenting the world. The development of cartooning both derived from mass-printing reproduction and its technical requirements and evolved in response to the verisimilitude of photography and its growing place in newspapers and periodicals. The indexicality of drawing in comics inevitably refers to a drawing hand, as trace of a particular gesture, pointing to a visible mark that is nevertheless "effaced in print" (Gardner, "Storylines" 66). Hillary Chute's *Disaster Drawn* explores at length the implications of this indexicality for the relationship of drawing to history in documentary comics, and particularly for narratives of witnessing and testimony (20). As Chute suggests in her reading of Art Spiegelman's *Maus*, the "comics form literalizes the work of archiving: selecting, sorting, and containing in boxes" (192). Indeed, graphic non-fiction most visibly displays its use of historical archives, as cartoonists rework and reproduce visual documents in their comics while offering drawn accounts as a form of witnessing. The development of graphic memoirs (see Chapter 9 on life writing) and documentary comics has run parallel to the growing visibility and accessibility of public and personal archives, as well as the central role of family pictures in these engagements with post-memory (Hirsch). From Alison Bechdel's *Fun Home* to Carol Tyler's *Soldier's Heart* or Nora Krug's *Heimat*, many cartoonists have relied on photographic archives of various sorts to compose their graphic memoirs which frequently echo the formats and forms of personal and public records, family scrapbooks, private diaries, and photo albums – making visible the archives that they draw from and producing what Ann Cvetkovich influentially called an "archive of feelings."

This marked use of archival documents in graphic non-fiction as well as the insistence on the presence of the hand-drawn trace should nevertheless not erase the longer history of reference-based drawing in comics. Jack Jackson's early historical work *Comanche Moon*, as Josh Kopin compellingly argues, is based on swipes of historical paintings and other documents "in order to make visual arguments about the past through reconstruction and verisimilitude" (38), embodying a completely different way of using the archive than the tendency of visually highlighting the authenticity of iconic documents in contemporary graphic nonfiction. Jackson's practice of selecting and quoting from popular references serve to implement a sense of distance that ultimately strengthens a "method of public history" (Kopin 45). This drawing approach connects to a long-learned tradition, as cartoonists, with objectives perhaps different from Jackson's historiographic aims, have always assembled reference files to sustain their drawing practice, cutting out relevant images from newspapers and magazines, taking photographic references, clipping favorite fragments from comics – a whole economy of clipping that appears very clear when one reads the biography of Milton Caniff (Harvey, *Meanwhile*), for instance. Copying has been and remains ubiquitous in comics making, as a fundamentally iterative drawing process that is often preceded by practices of collecting images and archiving them for future reuse.

The practice is sometimes described as "swiping," a term vernacular to the comics industry to identify forms of copying and debate their status as knowing allusions or unethical plagiarism; and which today increasingly lends itself to creative uses meant to saliently quote from comics archives (Crucifix). Swiping is coeval with its filing media, from the hanging folders and their metallic furniture of yesteryear to the commercial catalogues of copyright-free images or today's corporate-owned online databases of images: the legal constraints and commercial opportunities are here narrowly intertwined with the management of collections and the uses that are made thereof. The digital expansion of archives has dramatically amplified acts of reproduction and collection, as readers and makers are able to easily (although not always legally) access large amounts of existing comics in digitized formats. Many comics produced today are hence directly assembled by copy-paste, sampling, remixing, by extensive forms of redrawing and copying older comics – with very different creators as Ilan Manouach, Robert Sikoryak, or Samplerman as prominent exponents of this "uncreative" approach.

The ubiquitous presence of archives and archival elements in contemporary graphic novels – whether as documents, as fictional or autobiographical reflections on collecting and on amassing "stuff" (Jenkins), or as basis for creative reuse and remaking – lends some weight to Jared Gardner's suggestion that comics is "closer to the archive than to traditional narrative forms," based on the "excess data" that is always at hand in comics. Comics, always made of multiple images distributed on a given space and in time, tend to offer "a visual archive for the reader's necessary work of rereading, resorting, and reframing" (*Projections* 177). The emphasis on reading is here crucial, as it foregrounds skills and practices geared to the exploration of "excess data" and suited for navigating the visual and archival overabundance of our digital era. Some kind of "rereading, resorting, and reframing" comics are a key part of comics reading – a temporal excess always hanging in balance with the "lack" of time, compressed by fast reading, seriality, or the easiness to simply "scan" pages at a glance (Baetens); this helps explain the medium-specificity of different archival engagements with comics.

Conclusion

Navigating this "excess data" is similarly the core task of comics studies as it struggles to define and construct its object of knowledge and to delineate its history. Comics scholars have become increasingly aware of the gaps and erasures that define the archives we rely on. Eddie Campbell's study of early sports cartooning had to cope with Blackbeard's trimmed selections and particular blind spots, paradoxically turning to the digitized archives of microfilmed newspapers in order to complement its corpus. Margaret Galvan has highlighted the complexities and problems that come with archiving and indexing an all-women periodical that adopted rotating editorial coordination and was founded on collective and collaborative efforts. Simon Grennan, Roger Sabin, and Julian Waite have assembled an online archive to allow for the public rediscovery of the nineteenth-century cartoonist Marie Duval, whose name had been almost erased from comics memory. These various examples do not only display a fascinating understanding of existing archives and of the complexities of their history. In a landmark study of new media's historicity, Lisa Gitelman referred to the "data of culture" to designate the "archivable bits or irreducible pieces of modern culture that seem archivable under prevailing and evolving knowledge structures, and that thus suggest, demand, or defy preservation" (10). In doing so, she underlines the inextricability of history, or "our sense of history," from its inscriptive media, that is from "our experience of inscription" (21). As a medium that holds a precarious relationship to archives as well as a complex relation to inscription, comics will continue to raise compelling questions about archives, preservation, and transmission.

WORKS CITED
Comics

Seth. *The G.N.B Double C: The Great Northern Brotherhood of Canadian Cartoonists*. Drawn and Quarterly, 2011.

Secondary Sources

Ahmed, Maaheen, and Benoît Crucifix. "Introduction: Untaming Comics Memory." *Comics Memory: Archives and Styles*, edited by Maaheen Ahmed and Benoît Crucifix. Palgrave, 2018, pp. 1–12.

Baetens, Jan. "Reading Comics in Time." *New Readings*, vol. 18, 2022, pp. 1–13.

Baetens, Jan, and Hugo Frey. "Continued Comics: The New 'Blake and Mortimer' as an Example of Continuation in European Series." *The Edinburgh Companion to Contemporary Narrative Theories*, edited by Zara Dinnen and Robyn Warhol. Edinburgh University Press, 2018, pp. 215–226.

Beaty, Bart. *Comics versus Art*. Toronto University Press, 2012.

Campbell, Eddie. *The Goat Getters: Jack Johnson, the Fight of the Century, and How a Bunch of Raucous Cartoonists Reinvented Comics*. IDW/The Ohio State University Press, 2018.

Chute, Hillary L. *Disaster Drawn: Visual Witness, Comics, and Documentary Form*. The Belknap Press of Harvard University Press, 2016.

Cook, Terry. "The Archive(s) Is a Foreign Country: Historians, Archivists, and the Changing Archival Landscape." *The American Archivist*, vol. 74, no. 2, 2011, pp. 600–632.

Crucifix, Benoît. *Drawing from the Archives: Comics' Memory in the Contemporary Graphic Novel*. Cambridge University Press, 2023.

Cvetkovich, Ann. "Drawing the Archive in Alison Bechdel's Fun Home." *Women's Studies Quarterly*, vol. 31, no. 1/2, 2008, pp. 111–128.

De Kosnik, Abigail. *Rogue Archives: Digital Cultural Memory and Media Fandom*. The MIT Press, 2016.

Fiedler, Leslie. "The Middle against Both Ends." *Arguing Comics: Literary Masters on a Popular Medium*, edited by Jeet Heer and Kent Worcester. University Press of Mississippi, 2004, pp. 123–133.

Gabilliet, Jean-Paul. *Of Comics and Men: A Cultural History of American Comic Books*. Translated by Bart Beaty and Nick Nguyen, University Press of Mississippi, 2010.

"Reading Facsimile Reproductions of Original Artwork: The Comics Fan as Connoisseur." *Image [&] Narrative*, vol. 17, no. 4, 2016, pp. 16–25.

Galvan, Margaret. "Archiving Wimmen: Collectives, Networks, and Comix." *Australian Feminist Studies*, vol. 32, no. 91–92, 2017, pp. 22–40.

Gardner, Jared. "Antebellum Popular Serialities and the Transatlantic Birth of 'American' Comics." *Media of Serial Narrative*, edited by Frank Kelleter. The Ohio State University Press, 2017, pp. 37–52.

Projections: Comics and the History of Twenty-First-Century Storytelling. Stanford University Press, 2012.

"Storylines." *SubStance*, vol. 40, no. 1, 2011, pp. 53–69.

Garvey, Ellen Gruber. *Writing with Scissors: American Scrapbooks from the Civil War to the Harlem Renaissance*. Oxford University Press, 2013.

Gearino, Dan. *Comic Shop: The Retail Mavericks Who Gave Us a New Geek Culture*. Swallow Press/Ohio University Press, 2017.

Gitelman, Lisa. *Always Already New: Media, History, and the Data of Culture*. The MIT Press, 2006.

Grennan, Simon, et al. *Marie Duval: Maverick Victorian Cartoonist*. Manchester University Press, 2020.

Hague, Ian. *Comics and the Senses: A Multisensory Approach to Comics and Graphic Novels*. Routledge, 2014.

Harvey, Robert C. "Bill Blackbeard, The Man Who Saved Comics, Dead at 84." *The Comics Journal*, April 2011. www.tcj.com/bill-blackbeard-1926-2011/
Meanwhile . . .: A Biography of Milton Caniff, Creator of Terry and the Pirates and Steve Canyon. Fantagraphics Books, 2007.

Hirsch, Marianne. "Family Pictures: Maus, Mourning, and Post-Memory." *Discourse*, vol. 15, no. 2, 1992, pp. 3–29.

Jenkins, Henry. *Comics and Stuff*. New York University Press, 2020.

Kopin, Joshua Abraham. "'With Apologies to The Old Masters': Jack Jackson's Citational Practice and the History of Comic Book History." *Inks: The Journal of the Comics Studies Society*, vol. 3, no. 1, 2019, pp. 27–47.

Lowenthal, David. *The Past Is a Foreign Country – Revisited*. Cambridge University Press, 2013.

Marcum, Deanna, and Roger C. Schonfeld. *Along Came Google: A History of Library Digitization*. Princeton University Press, 2021.

Marrone, Daniel. *Forging the Past: Seth and the Art of Memory*. University Press of Mississippi, 2016.

McCrory, Amy. "Archiving Newspaper Comic Strips: The San Francisco Academy of Comic Art Collection." *Archival Issues*, vol. 27, no. 2, 2002, pp. 137–150.

Méon, Jean-Matthieu. "Sons and Grandsons of Origins: Narrative Memory in Mainstream Superhero Publishing." *Comics Memory: Archives and Styles*, edited by Maaheen Ahmed and Benoît Crucifix. Palgrave, 2019.

Pustz, Matthew. *Comic Book Culture: Fanboys and True Believers*. University Press of Mississippi, 1999.

Robb, Jenny E. "Bill Blackbeard: The Collector Who Rescued the Comics." *The Journal of American Culture*, vol. 32, no. 3, 2009, pp. 244–256.

"The Librarians and Archivists." *The Secret Origins of Comics Studies*, edited by Matthew J. Smith and Randy Duncan. Routledge, 2017, pp. 71–88.

Schlanger, Judith E. *Présence des œuvres perdues*. Hermann, 2010.

Scully, Richard. "A Serious Matter. Erwin D. Swann (1906–1973) and the Collection of Caricature and Cartoon." *Journal of the History of Collections*, vol. 27, no. 1, 2015, pp. 111–122.

Sinervo, Kalervo A. "Pirates and Publishers. Comics Scanning and the Audience Function." *The Comics World: Comic Books, Graphic Novels, and Their Publics*, edited by Benjamin Woo and Jeremy Stoll, University Press of Mississippi, 2021, pp. 208–233.

Starre, Alexander. "American Comics Anthologies: Mediality – Canonization – Transnationalism." *Transnational American Studies*, edited by Udo J. Hebel. Winter, 2012, pp. 541–560.

Stein, Daniel. *Authorizing Superhero Comics: On the Evolution of a Popular Serial Genre*. Ohio State University Press, 2021.

"What's in an Archive? Cursory Observations and Serendipitous Reflections." *Anglia*, vol. 138, no. 3, September 2020, pp. 337–354. https://doi.org/10.1515/ang-2020-0033

Thomas, Roy, and Peter Sanderson. *The Marvel Vault: A Museum-in-a-Book with Rare Collectibles from the World of Marvel*. Marvel, 2007.

Tilley, Carol L. *Of Nightingales and Supermen: How Youth Services Librarians Responded to Comics Between the Years 1938 and 1955*. Indiana University, 2007.

Waugh, Coulton. *The Comics*. Macmillan, 1947.

Wershler, Darren, and Kalervo A. Sinervo. "Marvel and the Form of Motion Comics." *Make Ours Marvel: Media Convergence and a Comics Universe*, edited by Matt Yockey. University of Texas Press, 2017, pp. 187–206.

Yale, Elizabeth. "The History of Archives: The State of the Discipline." *Book History*, vol. 18, 2015, pp. 332–359.

CHAPTER 14

Readers and Fans
Lived Comics Cultures

Mel Gibson

This chapter expands on some of the different practices, interactions, and preferences of readers and fans as part of their lived comics cultures, for, as Benjamin Woo argues, "[a]n adequate understanding of the readers of comic books and graphic novels must extend beyond reader-text relationships to comprise contexts of reception" (125). Engagement with the medium has taken various forms, from casual readership and sharing titles among friendship groups in childhood through to being a collector. Further, the chapter looks at how readers, both historically and today, have accessed their comics in varied formats and across many genres in Britain and the USA, linking their lived experience with production. In looking into these issues, the chapter touches upon several different publishers, genres, and titles, including DC and Marvel comics as well as British girls' comics and what might be considered cult publications because of their popularity and lasting impact on the comics scene, such as *2000 AD* (1977–to date).

Reading comics and participating in fandom intersects with both age and gender, which this chapter adopts as lenses to look at constructions of childhood and comics reading. This includes the common practice of parents throwing out childhood comics and the way that authority figures have historically considered reading comics to be a bad habit that should be repressed, which sometimes also served to make it an attractive activity to young people who came to consider comics reading subversive.

Beyond simply involving reading comics, fandom can incorporate a range of other activities as part of an enhanced commitment to the medium. For example, fandom may involve face-to-face and online activities including attending conventions and events, writing fanfiction,[1] or

---

[1] Fanfiction is unauthorized fictional writing based on an existing work of fiction written in an amateur capacity by someone identifying as a fan.

287

participating in cosplay,[2] all of which serve to build communities and networks. This means that lived comics cultures encompass physical and virtual venues such as social media, comics conventions, bookstores, comic shops and libraries, revealing connections between comics distribution practices and communities.

A final aspect of the chapter relates to how fan and reader interactions in these spaces and participation in activities often vary according to gender. Indeed, it can be argued that comics reading and collecting has been heavily gendered from the ends of both production and reception. It touches on how women might be excluded as comics readers, the ways that boys and girls were historically offered comics from gender-specific genres, and why memories of reading comics might be forgotten.

Historical Publishing Patterns and Reading Behaviors

Publishing and distribution practices create specific reader expectations and behaviors. These can change over time and according to location, even within comics cultures where there are shared elements, such as those in the USA and Britain.

In Britain, the dominant comics culture in the mid-twentieth century and onwards was that surrounding the weekly children's comic. These titles were divided into several genres along age and gendered lines, including girls' titles, comics for boys, nursery comics for the very young, and humor (see Figure 14.1). All were anthologies,[3] although the former two were distinctive as they contained story arcs lasting for twelve or more weeks with each weekly episode ending on a cliffhanger until the narrative finished completely.[4] The publishers staggered stories in the periodicals so that they did not finish simultaneously, thus ensuring ongoing reader commitment to the title. That this was effective is suggested by a comment made by one of my interviewees when talking about their memories of comics from forty years earlier, "I don't remember the stories, just wanting to know what happened next" (Gibson, "What You Read" 153).

---

[2] Cosplay, or the practice of appearing in costume as a fictional character, is a popular practice within various fandoms, including superhero fandom (McGunnigle 144–145).

[3] This meant that they contained a number of ongoing stories that ran simultaneously, rather than being focused on one at a time.

[4] Each of these titles was accompanied by an annual, a durable hardback volume aimed at the Christmas market that reflected the content of the weekly titles through includion of short stand-alone stories about the same characters, using the same creators.

Readers and Fans: Lived Comics Cultures 289

Figure 14.1. A selection of British weekly comics and annuals.

These comics were sold via newsagents' shops and people would typically have a weekly order in place, usually for delivery at home. Comics were often shared with other family members, most typically siblings or cousins, but also, sometimes, parents and grandparents. In work I have done on childhood memories about comics, readers often reported a great deal of anticipation of the next edition, both because of the narrative structure and the way in which comics were delivered (Gibson, *Remembered Reading* 127). Sharing had an additional impact on the comics reading experience as there could be a family "pecking order" of who got to read first, and some readers' accounts said there were fights between family members when the comics arrived (Gibson, *Remembered Reading* 128). It also meant that reading would be, in some ways, a communal activity which could be intergenerational, building a family-based comics culture.

Beyond the home, comics would be swapped in school, creating peer networks through shared cultural capital. In this lived comics culture, collecting was not necessarily a primary activity (Gibson, "What You Read" 157). There were multiple readers for every copy sold due to the practices of swapping and sharing, as noted by George Pumphrey in the early 1960s. There was second-hand trade in these titles, but not through specialist shops, which started to appear in the late 1960s. Rather, one would buy bundles of comics from jumble sales, market stalls, or school fairs (Gibson, "What You Read" 157). This was a low-key reading community that did not typically subscribe to the fervor of fandom but was a very significant part of children's culture.

In contrast, in the USA of the same period, the dominant comics culture was based around serial publications in monthly single issues, also known as "floppies," published by a group of companies that came to be dominated by the "Big Two," Marvel and DC Comics. These titles tend to focus on a single narrative, sometimes with a supporting story, although there were some anthologies with what Julia Round calls a "series host. . . a character who bookends a nonsequential group of stories that are unrelated except in their theme" (128–129). Initially these narratives were self-contained ones featuring the same cast of characters. Over time, however, narratives became increasingly long and complex, especially, though not exclusively, at Marvel. This meant that if readers did not have a deep knowledge of narrative history, the comics were inaccessible, resulting in a focus on continuity in USA comics culture. Simultaneously, publishers became more focused on a single genre, that of the superhero comic.

Initially comics were sold via newsstands and general stores to a mass audience, but the slow growth of direct marketing to specialty comic retailers throughout the 1970s meant that by the early 1980s, sales were largely to a devoted clientele who had standing orders or subscriptions at a specific location and made a potentially sizable economic commitment to comics lasting into adulthood.[5] This was a major change in comics culture. Having a specific location for sales and interaction (shops, conventions), Woo argues, came from both economic rationalization and the desire for safety, given the sometimes-derisory cultural depictions of comic fans. It also resulted, as Woo stated, in "an ever more insular subculture" (127).

Woo's analysis of specialist comic shops shows how they function as spaces for interaction, communities based around social and subcultural capital, and competitive arenas for flaunting deep knowledge of comics. This reflects how, as Woo stated, "'competent' reception depends on a set of skills, knowledges and dispositions that is learnt from other participants in a taste culture" (128). This form of fandom, partly driven by continuity, plus a growing emphasis on being a collector, remains a dominant form of lived comics culture.

Thus, physical locations combined with publishing practices created a different dominant form of community in the USA, as compared to Britain.[6] This difference between comics cultures is further reinforced by various practices, including specialist shops selling comics in sealed bags, collectors seeking professional grading regarding the condition of comics,[7] and even, as comics became increasingly seen as investments in the 1990s, getting them "slabbed," encased in an unopenable plastic shell that rendered them unreadable. Developing a personal, "valuable" collection contrasts starkly with the informal community circulation of comics through swapping and sharing.

There is an overlap with Britain in that specialist shops also opened there in the late 1960s. These shops were central to a comics culture that formed a parallel universe to that of British children's comics. Although the range of material specialist shops carried changed over time, they did

---

[5] In the USA, direct marketing to specialist shops bypassed newsstand distributors who returned all unsold merchandise. Making comics unreturnable (and heavily discounted for the benefit of the retailers) meant that the distributor's financial risks were considerably lower.

[6] While there are major collectors and academics, expertise, fandom, and collection are not generally the dominant discourses around British comics.

[7] Comic book grading is the process of determining the grade or condition of a book, which directly influences its value. There are eight major grades, shown here in descending order:
Mint (MT)
Near Mint (NM)
Very Fine (VF)
Fine (FN)
Very Good (VG)
Good (GD)
Fair (FA)
Poor (PO)

Figure 14.2. Advertising poster for London shop, 'Dark They Were and Golden Eyed' created by Bryan Talbot (1979). Reproduced with kind permission from Bryan Talbot.

not usually sell British comics, which continued to be sold in newsagents' shops and supermarkets. Instead, they sold comics from the USA and adopted a similar rationale for engaging with comics as Woo describes. For instance, London shop "Dark They Were and Golden Eyed" (c.1969–1981) was one of the earliest major British comic shops and nurtured a growing and active comics fandom (see Figure 14.2). Staff there were involved with organizing the British Comic Art Convention (known as Comicon) from 1968–1981, which began as a social event enabling enthusiasts to share their expertise but later became more focused on professional guests and comic dealers. In addition, the store had a duplicator, a predecessor of the photocopier, which clients used to make print copies of their personal fanzines and comics for distribution. This lived comics culture involved supporting the development of events and networks through sharing all kinds of resources.

I would add that reading comics from the USA in Britain had an additional emotional charge, in part because of the differences in production outlined earlier. To a reader used to British comics, a monthly single issue focused on a single character or groups of characters, in ongoing narratives and in full color (the latter was rare in British comics) was a source of excitement. Further, these titles also offered additional information about who created these comics, in contrast to British publications. This alerted readers and fans to the possibility of becoming professional creators and of the range of roles existing in comics publishing. That fans do become creators, either in an amateur or professional capacity, represents another aspect of lived comics cultures.

Cultures of Control: Young Readers and Their Comics

This chapter now turns to titles specifically aimed at young readers and looks at what might be at stake in their engagement with comic cultures as readers. While the medium is, of course, capable of addressing any subject or genre for readers of any age, perceptions about who comics are for, particularly from the point of view of adult authority figures, can determine what content is considered suitable. For example, if adults decide comics are only suitable for the youngest readers, and a dominant cultural discourse states that children are innocent and in need of protection, comics content will reflect that discourse. Teenagers, in contrast, may be the subject of different dominant cultural discourses, ones that argue that they are easily influenced, impulsive, and rebellious, and so are considered potentially dangerous or deviant. In this case, any comics produced in the light of this discourse will ensure that these tendencies are not encouraged.

As seen through the lens of adult authority figures, then, to enjoy reading a comic was to indulge in a bad habit that might have two kinds of impact. One was educational, as it was assumed that comics were not demanding to read and that engaging with them would have an impact on literacy. The second, as the dominant discourses mentioned above suggest, was that reading comics might undermine morality. In summary, reading comics was seen as engaging with a poor-quality mass medium considered crude and violent and, it was feared, could make its readers crude and violent too.

These assumptions about comics and their supposed impact on young readers were central to national anti-comics campaigns. The most notable participant and a driving force in the anti-comics campaign in the USA was Fredric Wertham, whose *Seduction of the Innocent* (see Figure 14.3)

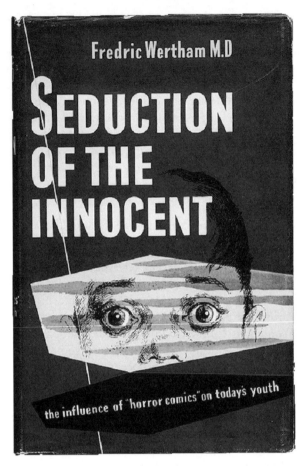

Figure 14.3. Cover image of *Seduction of the Innocent* (Wertham, 1954).

argued for limitations on the sale of comics to children because he thought that comics encouraged juvenile delinquency. This claim has been heavily contested by many comics scholars, including Carol Tilley. The American anti-comics campaign had international repercussions, which have been discussed by John A. Lent and others, and Martin Barker has analyzed the impact of the British campaign. These campaigns were influenced by a media effects discourse that assumed that children or young people were blank slates, easily led astray, without agency, incapable of thinking for themselves, and therefore in need of protection from texts containing material considered subversive or otherwise problematic. To control the texts, in effect, was considered a way of controlling the child. These hostile responses to young people reading comics can be characterized as moral panics. Rather than seeing problematic behavior in young people as related to issues like the experience of inequality, poverty, and racism, these cultures blamed comics, so attempting to deflect attention away for the need for social change.[8]

Many readers, as I have argued elsewhere, were conscious of the ways that they and their reading matter were problematized; this could imbue reading comics and participating in comics cultures with a subversive charge (Gibson, *Remembered Reading*). Reading comics considered unsuitable can, therefore, be seen as a form of resistance to social norms, whether that charge comes from a perception of comics as a working-class medium, or as containing adult content. I have noted that reading forbidden comics in friends' homes gave an illicit thrill to reading them and built peer communities (Gibson, "What you read"). This idea of comics reading as subversive constructs the practice as an "other" to reading for educational purposes, or of reading text-only materials labelled as "classics" for instance.

Gendered Production, Gendered Reading

In addition to segmenting readers according to their age, publishers also created comics according to what they considered appropriate gendered interests. This too was a means of controlling and molding children and young people. This could unfold at the level of genre: romance comics target female readers with the intention of directing girls towards heteronormativity, while superhero titles were intended for male readers, encouraging the emulation of hegemonic masculinity. Regarding the former, Trina Robbins talks about the historical dominance of romance in mainstream comics for girls and young women in the USA (see also Chapter 11 on women and comics history).

This is not to say that readers limit their reading according to publishers' audience segmentation or respond in predictable ways to content. All the same, such publishing practices had three main consequences in terms of lived experience of comics cultures. Firstly, female engagement in comics fandom historically tended to be less prevalent, and, secondly, materials coded as female were typically considered to be of lower value or significance. Female readers were, if not directly excluded, certainly discouraged

---

[8] Other media were also the subject of media panics, such as rock and roll music and television.

from participating. The third consequence was a male sense of ownership of medium and practices, which is discussed later.

To offer a more detailed example of gendered comics reading, girls in Britain during the mid- to late twentieth century were offered comics that featured girls as central characters in all stories. While titles for preteens such as *Bunty* (1958–2001) might include school stories, mysteries, rags-to-riches narratives, sport (from netball and gymnastics to other female-coded physical activity), and animal-related tales (about horse-riding, for instance), titles for slightly older female readers, such as *Jackie* (1964–1993), contained romances, indicating how publishers cross-cut age and gender. British publications of the 1950s and earlier were aimed at less well-defined age ranges, so a title like *Girl* (1951–1964) incorporated career-based stories about nurses, air hostesses, and other service and care professions, alongside school stories, autobiographies of famous women (from saints to scientists), and even comic strips about cookery.

However, in both earlier and later cases the reader was directed along a specific trajectory towards a heteronormative womanhood, usually via an aspirational middle-class model of girlhood. This was, for instance, demonstrated in the romance narratives in *Jackie* (1964–1993), although as Barker discusses, the form romance took throughout the life of the title changed, with disillusionment with romance starting to appear in later editions (Comics). Finally, it was assumed that there would be a shift to reading women's magazines, thus uncoupling comics from womanhood as part of lived culture. I have argued that this makes female readers more likely to have forgotten their memories of childhood comics reading, as the cultural coding of comics as male creates an extra barrier to recollection (Gibson, "Memories"). If comics are for boys, one might think that as a girl one could not have read them. Dominant discourses, then, overwhelm personal memory. Further, the idea of girls' cultures as lesser, embarrassing, or even a guilty and secret pleasure, as discussed by Janice Radway in relation to adult women's reading of romance novels, can serve to create a reluctance to remember that becomes habitual.

The titles aimed at boys followed different trajectories. Whilst the format was similar to girls' titles, the content was different. There were sports stories, just as in the girls' titles, for instance, but they were about soccer, athletics, and boxing. They also incorporated other genres, such as adventure, science fiction, and war stories. One could theoretically grow out of these titles and for some parents disposing of childhood comics was a symbolic act emphasizing that their child was becoming older and should seek more appropriate entertainment. However, many males continued engaging with these titles into adulthood, creating a comics culture that encompassed a collector's market for readers of boys' comics, although small in comparison to that for American comics. Indeed, destruction of a collection could act as a spur to purchases as an adult to reconstruct aspects of youthful lived experience. Until recently the same kind of market for old comics did not exist of girls' titles, although female readers reported similar memories of destruction (Gibson, *Remembered Reading*). In contrast to the disconnect between comics and womanhood, there was continuity from boyhood into adult masculinity in relation to comics.

Further, alongside the boys' and girls' titles lay a raft of humor anthology comics, of which the longest lived is *The Beano* (1938–date), where the stories were usually short and self-contained weekly tales, rather than offering a narrative arc that extended over weeks. The stories featured the same main characters presented in funny situations that were slightly different, but generally repetitive. There was a subversive and anarchic aspect to them and authority figures, despite being back in control at the end of the story, were undermined, belittled, and resisted throughout it. The humor comics were often perceived as for boys, despite including girl characters and being read by some girls. Again, this is linked to constructions of gender, and assumptions about appropriate subject matter, where humor is typically coded male.

This linking of humor and male readers is evident in the case of humor comic *Viz* (1979–to date) (see Figure 14.4). This publication created a sense of continuity for older comics readers, in that it was intended to appeal to adults. The creators had clearly understood and enjoyed the anarchy of the children's titles and built on them by incorporating profanity and toilet humor, satirical versions of news stories, and a hefty dose of surrealism – all styles of humor that are typically coded male in British culture. This title also serves as an example of how readers embedded in a specific genre extended their role in comic cultures by becoming creators.

As a final example of gendering in British comics, I now turn to the anthology comic *2000 AD* (1977–date). Like *Viz* (1979–date), it can be seen as a cult title that had mainstream appeal, although in this case the subject matter was initially focused on recycling and adapting existing science fiction sources (another male-coded and male-dominated genre). The comic also functioned as parody, had a cynical form of gritty humor, and incorporated anti-authoritarian elements by subverting authority figures and making such characters extremely violent, as embodied by one of the title's best-known characters, Judge Dredd (see Figure 14.5). The title attracted a devoted, largely male, readership who continued to

Figure 14.4. Cover of *Viz* Number 273 (March 2018) showing their usual irreverent view of popular culture and the world in general.

read it into adulthood and developed expertise regarding narratives and creators, meaning that the fandom surrounding the title had a lot in common with that of superhero comics. This has led, among some fans, to an insistence on policing the content and critiquing any changes to ensure that the magazine stays in line with both their extensive knowledge and youthful memories of the title.

As with *Viz* (1979–date), many of the creators involved in *2000 AD* (1977–date) had started as fans. In the latter case, their engagement with comics fandom is evident in the influence of American comics, especially superhero titles, on *2000 AD* (1977–date) despite the subversive twists they made to that genre. When the title became popular in America and British creators were brought to the notice of DC Comics and other companies, parts of that professional (and fan) community began to work on the more

Readers and Fans: Lived Comics Cultures

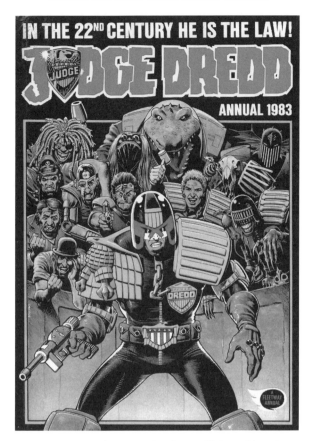

Figure 14.5. The cover of *Judge Dredd Annual* (1983).

lucrative American titles. This arguably helped to revitalize comics in the 1980s via, for instance, Alan Moore's work on *Swamp Thing* (1984–1987) and *Watchmen* (1986–1987). In both these examples, lived comics cultures led readers into being creators. It is noteworthy that these are typically male creators, confirming the many ways in which fandom and gender intersect.

Gender, Age, and Contemporary Shifts in Reading Practices and Comics Cultures

From the previous sections it is apparent that the publication, circulation, and distribution of print comics have an impact upon lived comics cultures, something that newer publishing practices also indicate. For example, publication via various platforms and apps, such as ComiXology, is increasing and attracts younger readers. Aaron Kashtan argues that digital reading is the future of comics and that the physical single issue will no longer be the core publishing product in the dominant superhero comics genre (80–81). Reading digitally has a significant impact upon comics cultures, because, as described by Adrienne Resha, digital access enables readers to explore historical iterations of characters and titles and engage with the letters pages that helped create comics communities and stimulate fandom, in addition to the possibility of reading contemporary titles and tracing their interactions with printed matter. This means that comics continuity becomes available to everyone who is interested and does not entail developing expertise through collecting.

Another change in reading patterns is eschewing monthly comics and the subscription model and instead waiting for the publication of trade paperbacks. Trade paperbacks collect five or six issues of a series and incorporate one or more story arcs. This necessitates a different pattern and rhythm of reading. Further, while part of a series, a trade paperback can also be read as a self-contained volume like a graphic novel, which offers easier access to any given series for new readers. This, too, has triggered a change in lived comics cultures in that short bursts of intense reading combined with participation in online discussions has become a typical practice, like that of a reading group, but open to a broad spectrum of reader commitment that can incorporate both casual reading and fandom. That participants may have differing levels of commitment is unimportant if they have read the texts and want to discuss them, so creating more equal access to texts and community, another move away from the more traditional model of fandom.

In terms of spaces and locales that are part of lived comics cultures, trade paperbacks are sold in traditional bookshops as well as specialist ones. Along with graphic novels, they are the most common format found in libraries, as they are comparatively durable and are the right size and shape to fit on normal bookshelves, so enabling them to be stored and promoted effectively. Consequently, a wider audience may access the medium via graphic novels and trade paperbacks acquired in non-specialist settings. This is, in a sense, a resurgence of a previous form of lived comics culture, that of the physical accessibility of the medium to the casual reader.

As discussed by Charlotte Fabricius, there is growing evidence from academics that trade paperback sales are increasing alongside digital ones, although figures for these sales are not always released by major companies.[9] Fabricius argues that the newer formats allow readers to engage on their own terms, something she sees as especially important for female readers of traditionally male-coded genres, with her key example being the superhero comic. In effect, they enable one to be a fan and part of a community, but without having to experience antagonistic gatekeeping from those elements of fandom who see reading, owning, and collecting monthly comics as a gold standard, so positioning themselves and their approaches as readers and fans as "authentic" and "valuable" while denigrating younger, female, and ethnically diverse readers and their modes of engagement with lived comics cultures. However, as the sale of monthly comics remains key to publishing decisions at Marvel and DC Comics, these older aspects of comics culture are validated, along with the behaviors that accompany them, despite aggregate sales giving a different picture of what is popular.

Fabricius also flags that since the 2010s there has been a rise in shorter runs of titles and limited series (described by Freeman and Taylor-Ashfield as low-stake access for new comics audiences). However, she notes that this emphasis on shorter runs may result, as Suzanne Scott has also argued, in the marginalization of titles taking those forms by hardcore comics fans, leading to the exclusion of those who read them.

Another shift in publication is an increase in rebooting (restarting) a title. This started as a response to the cultural dominance of long and complex narratives and has become a key device in superhero comics continuity since the 1985 DC Comics crossover event "Crisis on Infinite Earths." Rebooting updates old characters for new audiences which means that there is no need for readers to have extensive historical knowledge. This again suggests a decentering of the continuity and expertise that is otherwise key to lived comics cultures and an enabling of other forms of commitment and engagement.

So, while the emergence of different formats changes the lived experience of readership and fandom, there is also resistance to such potential. Tensions can arise between newer comics cultures and older ones, with members of the latter trying to exclude those from the former. Reading limited series, for instance, may be seen by fans who celebrate extensive continuity as showing a lack of commitment to comics culture. Similarly, a reboot may create "legacy characters," which are new (and often younger) versions of original characters (Davis 196) as is the case with the current

---

[9] Including Matthew Freeman and Charlotte Taylor-Ashfield, Carolyn Cocca, Christopher M. Cox, and Jill Pantozzi.

302 MEL GIBSON

Ms. Marvel, Kamala Khan. Such characters may be dismissed as anomalous deviations from the characters that members of older comics cultures consider original. Hence productive differences that new iterations of characters might offer run the risk of being rejected.

Tensions around Gender in Relation to Making Comics and Participating in Fandom

In terms of historical lived experience, as earlier sections suggest, to be a female fan does not as readily lead into being a creator as being a male fan does. A female creator is much more likely to have to deal with exclusionary tactics and sexism, as discussed, for instance, by Nicola Streeten in her research on feminist comics and cartooning in Britain. Nevertheless, there are increasing numbers of female creators, both professional and amateur. This has been partly generated by the publication and distribution of *shōjo* manga in English since the late 1980s, especially by publishers like Viz Media and Tokyopop, another example of a comics culture that has emerged due to shifts in publishing practices.[10] It is also a response to the growth of graphic novels and to the flourishing of memoirs in comic form. In both cases, gender is less significant in determining access, both as reader and maker.

This change in gender representation can also be linked to practices within fandom that connect making and reading, such as cosplay and fanfiction. This shift in comics culture is embodied in some comics, such as *Ms. Marvel*, where the central character is part of a diverse fan community, writes fanfiction, and creates her own costume, referencing her passion for the original version of the character. These actions effectively endorse and encourage cosplay and fan practices by readers (Wilson and Alphona, *No, Generation*).

Nevertheless, the feeling of being unwelcome in some comics cultures, especially those established around long-term readership and expertise, persists for many girls and women. This is confirmed by Stephanie Orme who begins by stating that media portrayals of comic book fandom continue to position it as a masculine space despite increasing numbers of female participants in comics cultures. Orme points out that 40–50% of US comic shops users are female and offers convention reports

---

[10] *Shōjo* manga are Japanese comics aimed at a teen female demographic and covering a very wide range of genres, from science fiction to historical drama, but also focus on emotions and relationships. For more on manga see Chapter 4.

from San Diego Comic-Con and New York Comic-Con indicating a similar split.

However, despite the increasing presence of women, "[s]tereotypical representations of what a comic book reader looks like and acts like, gendered language, such as fan*boy*, that codes geek culture as something belonging to men, and marketing campaigns that continue to alienate female fans, all contribute to the prevailing narrative that women who enjoy comic books are abnormal or perhaps even not 'true' fans" (Orme 403). To address this issue, there are comics events that are very consciously marketed as family and female friendly, such as UK-based Thought Bubble and The Lakes International Comic Art Festival. Their rationale suggests that other events might not have the same approach, again pointing to the durable masculine stereotype of comics culture.

Orme's interviews with women comic fans flagged up a self-consciousness about their fandom outside of comics, but also within comics culture given assumptions about a male "norm" and the anticipation, or direct experience, of being patronized or stigmatized. Consequently, Orme reports that online communities and social media were important to them, as engagement there meant physical comic book shops and face-to-face events could be bypassed. This is also suggested by Trisha L. Crawshaw's research, which points out that while many specialist comic shops today aim to attract those from excluded demographics (i.e., anyone other than a white male), some remain less welcoming.

The debates around gender, then, tend to be about representation within comics, on the one hand, and who specific genres of comics, or, indeed, the whole medium is for, on the other. From the point of view of some fans, the answer is solely themselves. One of the most visible of these attempts at policing comics cultures is ComicsGate. This was a backlash against diversity in comics and among comic creators, readers, and fans. Inspired by a similar movement in the gaming community, GamerGate, it coincided with Marvel VP David Gabriel saying during a retailer event "[w]hat we heard was that people didn't want any more diversity. They didn't want female characters out there. That's what we heard, whether we believe that or not" (Griepp).

Gabriel's comments were seen by Beth Elderkin and others as attempting to blame declining sales on readers rather than publishing practices, but ComicsGaters saw them as confirming their view that diversity was undermining comics. They consequently attacked readers they saw as representing diversity, especially women, who they labelled "fake geek girls."

304   MEL GIBSON

However, this was not simply name-calling, as their actions extended into harassment and threats, sometimes in the form of doxing.[11]

Another aspect of this attempted expulsion of female and other "unwanted" fans, was that ComicsGaters considered what they saw as nontraditional audiences as being irrelevant to the medium's continued existence. This refutation of diversity as economically irrelevant can also be read as a means of ensuring that no move towards it could occur in comics culture. Here, then, one part of comics culture attempted to control the whole culture at the levels of fandom, community, publishing, and content.

Conclusion

This chapter has touched upon some of the many factors that are significant within lived comics cultures and explored some of the practices, interactions, and preferences that appear among fans and readers. It has flagged up a selection of the ways that production, distribution, and circulation practices have an impact upon reader and fan behavior by offering thumbnail sketches of specific genres and titles in both Britain and the USA.

In discussing how age and comics can be intertwined and what that means in terms of comics content, the chapter indicates that comic readership has been seen as potentially problematic by authority figures. In effect, children's comics are a sector in which comics cultures have, historically, been policed by people external to the culture. In this case, theories about media effects have dominated understandings of the medium, leading , for instance, to moral panics.

The chapter has, in addition, noted how younger, female, and otherwise diverse fans may be unwelcome in what has become the dominant comics culture, based on long-term readership and expertise around continuity in relation to superhero comics. Representatives of this culture, claiming ownership of the medium, can feel undermined by recent publishing practices that decenter their long-developed skills and understandings, something weaponized by extreme fans in actively resisting change to what they consider their culture.

However, what the chapter also shows is that many comics cultures exist, and have existed, in relation to English-language comics. They often

---

[11] Doxing or doxxing is the act of publicly revealing private personal information about an individual or organization online and can be a vehicle for revenge of perceived slights.

Readers and Fans: Lived Comics Cultures 305

have little in common beyond the desire to engage with an aspect of the medium and encompass numerous modes of engagement, ranging from collecting to making creative responses to texts. These cultures will continue to diversify as readers find new and original ways of responding to what comics offer.

WORKS CITED

Comics

2000 AD. IPC/Fleetway/Rebellion, 1977–date.
The Beano. DC Thomson, 1938–date.
Bunty. DC Thomson, 1958–2001.
Girl. Hulton Press, 1951–1964.
Jackie. DC Thomson, 1964–1993.
Moore, Alan. *Swamp Thing*. DC Comics, 1983–1987.
Moore, Alan and Dave Gibbons. *Watchmen*. DC Comics, 1986–1987.
Viz. Self-published/Dennis Publishing, 1979–date.
Wilson, G. Willow and Adrian Alphona. *Ms. Marvel Vol. 1: No Normal*. Marvel, 2014.
Wilson, G. Willow et al., *Ms. Marvel Vol. 2: Generation Why*. Marvel, 2015.

Secondary Sources

Barker, Martin. *A Haunt of Fears: The Strange History of the British Horror Comics Campaign*. University Press of Mississippi, 1984.
 Comics: Ideology, Power and the Critics. Manchester University Press, 1989.
Cocca, Carolyn. *Superwomen: Gender, Power, and Representation*. Bloomsbury Academic, 2016.
Cox, Christopher M. "Ms. Marvel, Tumblr, and the Industrial Logics of Identity in Digital Spaces." *Transformative Works and Cultures*, vol. 27, 2018, n.pag. https://doi.org/10.3983/twc.2018.1195. Accessed 21 August 2021.
Crawshaw, Trisha L. "Truth, Justice, Boobs: Gender in Comic Book Culture." *Gender and the Media: Women's Places*, edited by Marcia Texler Segal and Vasilikie Demos. Emerald, 2018, pp. 89–103. www.emerald.com/insight/publication/doi/10.1108/S1529-2126201826. Accessed 21 August 2021.
Davis, Blair. "Bare Chests, Silver Tiaras, and Removable Afros: The Visual Design of Black Comic Book Superheroes." *The Blacker the Ink: Constructions of Black Identity in Comics and Sequential Art*, edited by Frances K. Gateward and John Jennings. Rutgers University Press, 2015, pp. 193–212.
Elderkin, Beth. "Marvel VP of Sales Blames Women and Diversity for Sales Slump." *Gizmodo*, 2017. https://gizmodo.com/marvel-vp-blames-women-and-diversity-for-sales-slump-1793921500. Accessed 31 August 2021.

Fabricius, Charlotte Johanne. Super-Girls: Girlhood and Agency in Contemporary Superhero Comics. 2021. University of Southern Denmark. PhD thesis.

Freeman, Matthew, and Charlotte Taylor-Ashfield. "'I Read Comics from a Feministic Point of View': Conceptualizing the Transmedia Ethos of the Captain Marvel Fan 235 Community." *The Journal of Fandom Studies*, vol. 5, no. 3, 2017, pp. 317–335. doi.org/10.1386/jfs.5.3.317_1. Accessed 21 August 2021.

Gibson, Mel. "'It's All Come Flooding Back': Memories of Childhood Comics." *Comics Memory: Archives and Styles*, edited by Maheen Ahmed and Benoît Crucifix. Palgrave, 2018, pp. 37–56.

Remembered Reading: Memory, Comics and Post-War Constructions of British Girlhood. University of Leuven Press, 2015.

"What You Read and Where You Read It, How You Get It, How You Keep It: Children, Comics and Historical Cultural Practice." *Popular Narrative Media*, vol. 1, no. 2, 2008, pp. 151–167.

Goodrum, Michael D. et al. *Gender and the Superhero Narrative.* University Press of Mississippi, 2018.

Griepp, Milton. "Marvel's David Gabriel on the 2016 Market Shift." *ICv2*, 2017, https://icv2.com/articles/news/view/37152/marvels-david-gabriel-2016-mar ketshift. Accessed 21 August 2021.

Kashtan, Aaron. *Between Pen and Pixel: Comics, Materiality, and the Book of the Future.* Ohio State University Press, 2018.

Lent, John A, ed. *Pulp Demons: International Dimensions of the Postwar Anticomics Campaign.* Fairleigh Dickinson University Press, 1999.

McGunnigle, Christopher. "Rule 63: Genderswapping in Female Superhero Cosplay". *Gender and the Superhero Narrative*, edited by Michael D Goodrum, Tara Prescott, and Philip Smith. University Press of Mississippi, 2018, pp 144–179.

Orme, Stephanie. "Femininity and Fandom: The Dual-Stigmatisation of Female Comic Book Fans." *Journal of Graphic Novels and Comics*, vol. 7, no. 4, 2016, pp. 403–416. doi.org/10.1080/21504857.2016.1219958

Pantozzi, Jill. "Young Women Are the Fastest Growing Demographic According to New Comics Retailer Survey." *The Mary Sue*, 2014, themarysue.com/ youngwomen-comic-demographic-growing/. Accessed 21 August 2021.

Pumphrey, George H. *What Children Think of Their Comics.* Epworth Press, 1964.

Radway, Janice. *Reading the Romance.* University of North Carolina Press, 1984.

Resha, Adrienne. "The Blue Age of Comic Books." *Inks: The Journal of the Comics Studies Society*, vol. 4, no. 1, 2020, pp. 66–81.

Robbins, Trina. *From Girls to Grrrlz.* Chronicle Books, 1999.

Round, Julia. *Gothic for Girls: Misty and British Comics.* University Press of Mississippi, 2019.

Scott, Suzanne. "Fangirls in Refrigerators: The Politics of (in)Visibility in Comic Book Culture." *Transformative Works and Cultures*, vol. 13, 2012, n.pag. doi .org/10.3983/twc.2013.0460. Accessed 21 August 2021.

Streeten, Nicola. *UK Feminist Cartoon and Comics: A Critical Survey*. Palgrave Macmillan, 2020.

Tilley, Carol L. "Seducing the Innocent: Fredric Wertham and the Falsifications That Helped Condemn Comics." *Information & Culture*, vol. 47, no. 4, 2012, pp. 383–413. *JSTOR*, www.jstor.org/stable/43737440.

Wertham, Fredric. *Seduction of the Innocent*. Rinehart & Co., 1954.

Woo, Benjamin. "The Android's Dungeon: Comic-Bookstores, Cultural Spaces, and the Social Practices of Audiences." *Journal of Graphic Novels & Comics*, vol. 2, no. 2, 2011, pp. 125–136. doi.org/10.1080/21504857.2011.602699

CHAPTER 15

Comics in the Museum

Kim Munson

Exhibitions focusing on art from comics, graphic novels, and related pop culture topics have been appearing more regularly in museums, collecting institutions, and university galleries. It is not unusual to see work on the walls celebrating Marvel superheroes, the art of Robert Crumb or Art Spiegelman, or group shows on themes like graphic medicine or climate change. However, interest in comics from exhibiting institutions is not new and has ebbed and flowed with the whims and controversies of the art world since at least the 1930s.

Exhibitions often reflect the cultural interests and biases of the institutions and curators that organize them. Driven by these interests and biases, exhibits have an internal logic, shaped in response to the questions raised by a previous exhibit elsewhere, ideas brought forward by a new book, or by an exhibition obligation to a collector. Some artists – for example Milton Caniff, Will Eisner, Art Spiegelman, and Chris Ware – recognized the benefits of exhibits and advocated for them throughout their careers. As we examine a few key moments in exhibition history, we will see that artists are often the most passionate advocates for exhibitions as a means of celebrating the comics art form and as a different way to share their work with the public.

The First Comics Exhibitions

It is difficult to pinpoint exactly when the exhibition of comics began. Historian and curator Brian Walker opens his essay *Substance and Shadow: The Art of the Cartoon* with the earliest known drawing of cartoons on public display, *Cartoon #1, Substance and Shadow* by John Leech of *Punch* magazine, July 1843 (Figure 15.1). The drawings hanging on the walls were patterns for tapestries, called cartoons at the time. Leech's use of

Much of this chapter has been adapted from my 2020 Eisner-nominated book *Comic Art in Museums*.

Figure 15.1. The first modern use of "cartoon." John Leech (1817–1864). "CARTOON, No 1: Substance and Shadow." *Punch*, July 1843. The Ohio State University, Billy Ireland Cartoon Library & Museum.

"Cartoon" in his caption is widely considered to be the first modern use of the term. Walker puts the image in context:

> Nine years after the Houses of Parliament in London were destroyed by fire in 1834, a competitive exhibition of preliminary design drawings (traditional cartoons) for the historical murals in the New Palace of Westminster was held as the construction concluded. *Punch* magazine, founded in 1841, satirized the competition by publishing its own submissions under the title "Mr. Punch's cartoons." The first of the series by John Leech, "Cartoon, No. 1," contrasted the government's lavish spending with the plight of its citizens. Accompanying the cartoon was the comment, "The poor ask for bread and the philanthropy of the state accords an exhibition" (Munson, *Comic Art* 23.)

Punch was quickly followed in the US by *Puck* (1877), *Judge* (1881), and *Life* (1883), all magazines that featured cartoons in their pages. Public interest in magazine cartoons and political commentary continued through the exhibits in the early 1930s. These were often small displays culled from an individual's collection or thematic group shows.

One example of this type of show is *Contemporary Cartoons: An Exhibition of Original Drawings at the Huntington Library* (1937, San Marino, CA) an exhibition marking Isabel Simeral Johnson's donation to the library of her large collection of political cartoons from 1815 to the New Deal era. Johnson, who had a degree from the University of Chicago and a Ph.D. from Columbia, wrote about comics history for several publications, including the Huntington's exhibit brochure, touching on cave art, Egypt, and Pompeii as comics ancestors in her essay (*Contemporary*, 5).

Larger institutions gave space to comics as well. The Whitney Museum of American Art (New York), for example, displayed cartoons by Thomas Nast along with other drawings and paintings from their permanent collection in an exhibition in March 1932.[1] The Museum of Modern Art included four frames from the Disney cartoon *Three Little Wolves* in their 1936 show *Fantastic Art, Dada*.

In 1939 the Metropolitan Museum of Art purchased a production painting created for a scene in *Snow White and the Seven Dwarfs*, which they credited to Walt Disney. It was a close-up of two vultures craning their necks to watch as the wicked witch falls to her death at the end of the

---

[1] This is the first show listed in the Whitney's online exhibition history: *An Exhibition of Provincial Paintings of the 19th Century: Audubon Prints, Colored Lithographs, Thomas Nast Cartoons Selected from The Permanent Collection*, March 8–30, 1932.

film.[2] The work was a composite (often known as a cel set-up): a painted animation cel with an original background piece behind it. Drawings like these sold in art galleries for around $200. Disney assigned people who were between tasks at the studio to assemble these composites so he would not have to lay them off between projects.

According to Frank S. Nugent of *The New York Times*, Disney objected to the museum crediting this artwork solely to himself, stating that it was the result of work by many craftsmen at the studio. In response to Disney's self-deprecating remarks, the museum defended its decision. "Whether Disney appreciates it or not," stated Harry B. Welhe, the museum's curator of painting, "his animals have become part of the literature of our age... this painting is a splendid moment of arrested motion" (Nugent, 1939). Welhe also took a larger view of the labor represented in this composite, comparing the coordinated workmanship on *Snow White* to paintings created by the workshops of masters like "Rubens, Rembrandt, and Cranach" who added a few strokes and signed their names to paintings that were chiefly made by other artists in their studio. This workshop idea has continued into the present day, as museums continue to credit "the lone genius" for collaborative work, particularly in the case of comics, which are often created by a team including the penciler (usually the artist credited), writers, inkers, letterers, and colorists.

One of the pioneers of comic art exhibitions, Milton Caniff – the creator of *Terry and the Pirates* and *Steve Canyon* – got his start with a 1939 art exhibit in his hometown at the Dayton Art Institute (Ohio). *Terry* was one of the most successful strips in the US, and Caniff was riding a tide of public popularity. In his epic Caniff biography *Meanwhile...*, Robert C. Harvey explains how this show came about:

> Dwight Young, the publisher of the *Dayton Journal-Herald*, took an almost paternal pleasure in running *Terry and the Pirates*. He was pleased by Caniff's showering his journalistic alma mater with special drawings for community projects, and he also noticed the evolution of the cartoonist's graphic style. As the shadows deepened in *Terry*'s panels, it seemed to Young that the strip had crossed the line from cartoon drawings to representational art... Some of the individual panels were virtually paintings in black and white. As a director of the Dayton Art Institute, Young arranged for the Institute to mount a special exhibit of the work of Dayton's now famous hometown boy (323.)

---

[2] The Met included this piece in the exhibit and catalog *Inspiring Walt Disney: The Animation of French Decorative Arts*, on view December 6, 2021–March 6, 2022, touring to the Wallace Collection, London later in 2022 and the Huntington Library Art Museum, San Marino, CA, in 2023.

Caniff threw himself into the project, thrilled to have this kind of artistic recognition and the opportunity to celebrate his success with his parents, with whom he remained close. He was also eager to promote *Terry* and recognized the positive publicity an exhibition could bring. Ultimately, he provided more work than the expected selection of original strips, including "preliminary studies for drawings in the strip, as well as several oil paintings of Mongol tribesmen and other Oriental subjects" (Harvey, 324).

The Dayton show was quickly followed by a 1940 exhibit of some of his reference drawings of Asian subjects at the Julian Levy Gallery, an upscale commercial gallery in New York. The show at the Levy Gallery attracted attention from the national media, including articles in Newsweek and LIFE magazine. The success of these two exhibitions inspired Caniff to actively design and promote exhibits himself. He organized *The Art of Terry and the Pirates*, which toured around the US from 1944 to 1946. Caniff was an adviser on the important 1942 exhibition, *The Comic Strip: Its Ancient and Honorable Lineage and Present Significance*, organized by the female magazine illustrator Jessie Gillespie Willing for the American Institute of Graphic Arts (AIGA) at the National Arts Club in New York (Figure 15.2). Inspired by how clearly information was conveyed by Mayan panels she studied while researching an art project, Willing's exhibit was of an unprecedented scope and scale for a comics show up to that point. Drawing on the collection of the rare books department of the New York Public Library, the exhibit included copies of cave paintings, Japanese scrolls, Mayan panels, Egyptian tomb paintings, medieval manuscripts, fifteenth-century block books, art by Bruegel, Holbein, Cranach, Hogarth, Töepffer, Doré, and Cruikshank. There were comic strips by prewar comics innovators like Outcault and McCay and strips by contemporary stars like Rube Goldberg, Ernie Bushmiller, Al Capp, Chester Gould, and Frank King. It was the first known show to include examples of comic books such as *Funnies on Parade, Famous Funnies, Picture Stories from the Bible, Superman*, and the very first issue of *Wonder Woman* (DC #1, Summer Issue). Caniff's *Terry and the Pirates* was voted the audience favorite of the show. The exhibit generated a lot of media interest. Cartoonists and curators appeared on several New York area TV talk shows, and the publisher M.C. Gaines wrote an in-depth article about it for *Print* magazine. The show toured to eighteen cities in the US but had to cancel its planned European tour because of transportation issues due to the war.

In 1946, Caniff said goodbye to *Terry* and shifted his attention to *Steve Canyon*. He joined the newly formed National Cartoonists Society (NCS) as their treasurer, and quickly became the chairman of the Exhibit

Figure 15.2. Program cover for the first comics exhibit to display comics with their historical ancestors, *The Comic Strip: Its Ancient and Honorable Lineage and Present Significance* (1942). Cover drawing: Fred Cooper. Courtesy of AIGA Design Archives. AIGA, the professional association for design, 222 Broadway, New York, NY 10038. www.aiga.org.

Committee. He organized the first exhibit of work by NCS members in 1947. Through the NCS, Caniff was directly involved in several key shows. In 1949, the NCS undertook a multicity national tour to promote US Savings Bonds. They traveled the country in a United Airlines Dreamliner painted with their characters, which began in Washington DC at the Library of Congress, with the gala opening of the touring exhibit *20,000 Years of the Comics*.

Two milestone exhibitions of comics took place in 1951: *American Cartooning*, an exhibition of primarily NCS members was shown at the Metropolitan Museum of Art (NY). *I Exposição Internacional de Historias em Quadrinhos*, the first known international exhibition and conference, was organized by Alvaro de Moya and a group of Brazilian intellectuals who studied the similarities between cinema, literature, and comics. De Moya wrote to cartoonists he admired in the US and elsewhere, asking for pages of art with the promise of a comics show in Brazil, which came to fruition at the Centro Cultura e Progresso, São Paulo, on June 18, 1951.

American Cartooning displayed the work of 265 cartoonists showing everything from *Little Nemo* to *Howdy Doody*. The NCS committee, chaired by Otto Soglow (*The Little King*), wanted to show at least one piece by every member that submitted artwork to the committee. The art critics that covered the Met regularly wanted the curators to help select art with more of a critical eye. For example, in the review "Pooh to Art" in the August 14, 1951, issue of *Harper's Magazine*, Mr. Harper opined: "In that room there were hundreds of drawings. It was as though every boy in the eighth grade had been asked to show their stamp collection and the teacher decided she had to exhibit all of them or some boy's feelings would be hurt." Despite their complaints about specific content in the show, all of the critics had a lot to say about the importance of comics and of good drawing. Not one of them said that comics did not belong at the Met. It was a real step forward for the recognition of comics as art.

Pop Art, Transatlantic Exchanges and the Rise of Independent Institutions (1960s–1970s)

The NCS continued with a busy exhibition schedule in the 1960s. In 1963, they launched *Cavalcade of Comics*, a show made up of laminated tear sheets, original strips, and character drawings that were displayed at the 1964 New York World's Fair. For *Comic Art Goes Pop!*, a 1965 gala art auction for the United Service Organizations (a charity serving on-duty US military members and their families), NCS members lampooned their own work in pop-art-style paintings. After the auction, these "pop art" pieces were displayed at the World's Fair in the Top of the Fair restaurant. When the Fair concluded, *Cavalcade* continued to tour, appearing at the Smithsonian in 1966, at Lever House (NY) in 1971, and then touring the US into the 1980s.

Across the Atlantic in Paris, French intellectuals that closely studied US and European comics formed several fan clubs in the 60s to advance comics as "the ninth art" and to celebrate the art form they had loved since childhood. SOCERLID (Société civile d'études et de recherches des littératures dessinées), the best known club, was founded by Claude Moliterni (one of the founders of the Angoulême Festival) and Pierre Couperie, an historian, who were joined by key members, including David Pascal (the bridge between SOCERLID and the NCS), Édouard François, Proto Destefanis, the author/historian Maurice Horn (another US connection), filmmaker Alain Resnais, press tycoons Pierre Lazareff and Paul Winkler, and *Asterix* creator René Goscinny.[3] The group published the fanzine *Phenix*, and produced several exhibitions at the French Society of Photography. The breakthrough show they are best known for is *Bande dessinée et figuration narrative* organized at the Musée des Arts Decoratifs, Paris (1967). Outraged by the use of comics imagery and idioms in Pop Art, particularly the works of Roy Lichtenstein, the curators set out to prove that real comics drawings were better by showing large photographic blow ups of comics panels so they could be seen in a comparative format. The show generated a lot of positive press, and the museum extended its run. *Bande dessinée et figuration narrative* continued to tour from 1967 to 1971.[4]

---

[3] There is an exciting exchange of newly published research on the topic of French comics groups of the 1960s, their influential interactions with the NCS, their exhibitions, and publications (see Munson "How the French"). Antoine Sausverd explains the genesis of the 1967 Musée des Arts Decoratifs show and how it was organized (see English translation in Munson, *Comic Art*); *The Journal of Comics and Culture* published a special edition about the response to French comics published in the US and to US comics in France (vol. 5, 2020); *La Crypte Tonique #6. Du prive au publique* by Phillipe Capart uncovers the history of 1960s French comics clubs (2021; English translation forthcoming).

[4] Herdeg's *The Art of the Comic Strip* has a very detailed bibliography of shows up to 1972. It lists all the locations *Bande dessinée et figuration narrative* visited following the Musée des Arts Décoratifs: the Maison de la Culture de Nevers; Stadstbibliotheek van Antwerpen; Musées Royaux d'Art et d'Histoire, Bruxelles; Puteaux; Akademie der Künste, Berlin; Théâtre de l'Ouest Parisien; Rencontres de Chateuvallon; and Andersonin Taidemuseo Helsinki. It also mentions comics exhibits organized around the same time in Canada, France, Italy, Spain, Brazil, Sweden, Belgium, Germany, Argentina, Switzerland, the United Kingdom, and Japan.

In the US, there was a renewed interest in showing comic art by museums and university galleries following the Pop Art craze and the rise of the underground comix movement. Many of these were large survey shows that took historical and intellectual inspiration from Jules Feiffer's *The Great Comic Book Heroes* (1965) and the widely read English translation of the *Bande dessinée et figuration narrative* catalog, *A History of the Comic Strip* by Pierre Couperie and Maurice Horn (1968). Unlike the Paris show, they did not show pop art style reproductions and opted for original comic art drawings instead. These exhibitions tried to show a range of works from comics history mostly from the US, from Töpffer and Outcault, to syndicated strips, mainstream superhero comics, and the new undergrounds. At these shows, the comics drawings were neatly framed and hung in a line at eye level on neutral walls, a more respectful treatment than the hastily tacked up shows of the 1930s and 1940s. See, for instance, the exhibit design of *The Collection of Jerome K. Muller*, a Southern California collector and dealer whose two-hundred-piece survey show toured mid-sized museums and university galleries from 1972 to 1979 (Figure 15.3).

Other significant exhibits at this time include Judith O'Sullivan's *The Art of the Comic Strip* at the University of Maryland (1971), which was circulated by the Smithsonian and received rave reviews from John Canaday of the *New York Times* and *The Nation's* art critic Lawrence Alloway. Maurice Horn, a participant in *Bande dessinée et figuration narrative*, curated his own show, *Seventy-five Years of the Comics*, at the New York Cultural Center in 1971. *Comics as an Art Form* was organized by Peter L. Myer for the University of Nevada, Las Vegas, which included a symposium with Will Eisner, Jack Kirby, Charles Schulz, and Harvey Kurtzman (1970, toured to Colorado Springs Fine Arts Center). Cartoonist and collector Jerry Robinson displayed the jewels of his collection at the Graham Gallery in New York (1972).

The Phonus Balonus Show of Really Heavy Stuff, the first formal museum exhibit to focus exclusively on underground comix, was organized by Bhob Stewart for the Corcoran Gallery of Art's Dupont Circle location in 1969, featuring art by Vaughn Bode, Robert Crumb, Kim Deitch, Larry Hama, Jay Lynch, Spain Rodriguez, Gilbert Shelton, Art Spiegelman, John Thompson, and Skip Williamson. Many of these artists joined Jack Kirby's *New Gods* in their first international appearance, *Aaargh! A Celebration of Comics*, a show of original comic art at the Institute of Contemporary Art in London (1970).

The 1970s also saw the rise of independent institutions led by artists and collectors. Mort Walker, the creator of the long-running newspaper

Comics in the Museum

Figure 15.3. Typical exhibit design for comics exhibits in the 1970s. Exhibition view of *The Cartoon Show: Collection of Jerome K. Muller* at the Bowers Museum, Santa Ana, CA. 1976. Courtesy of the Bowers Museum.

strips *Beetle Bailey* and *Hi and Lois*, founded the Museum of Cartoon Art in Greenwich, CT (1974), the first museum solely dedicated to comics and animation with a schedule of public events, active members, a collection, and an education program. The museum was the first to produce a retrospective of Jack Kirby (1975), the history of *Looney Tunes* and Warner Animation (1980), and *Women and the Comics* (guest curated by Trina Robbins, based on her book with cat yronwoode, 1985). In 1996, the museum moved to Boca Raton, Florida, changing its name to the International Museum of Cartoon Art. After the Florida museum closed due to financial problems, there was an effort to reopen it as an attraction in the Empire State Building in Manhattan. That endeavor failed, and Mort Walker donated his entire collection to the Billy Ireland Cartoon Library and Museum at the Ohio State University.

Taking inspiration from Walker in 1984, Troubador Press publisher Malcolm Whyte founded the Cartoon Art Museum in San Franciscso with a large grant from Charles Schulz, where it has maintained an active and innovative event and exhibition schedule. It officially opened in 1988 with *Drawn to Excellence: Masters of Cartoon Art*, then continued with a number of groundbreaking shows, including the first known US show to focus exclusively on Black cartoonists, *Black Ink: African American Showcase* (1992, with a spotlight on Jackie Ormes), *Visions of the Floating World* (1992, an extensive survey of manga), *Electronic Comics and Computer Art* (1991, first museum show to include Pixar), plus multiple shows celebrating different aspects of the underground comix scene, and of the art of Edward Gorey.[5]

Sometimes exhibitions dialogue with other exhibitions, with one responding to or building on another. This is true of two of the best known, and most controversial comics-related exhibits in the US, the 1990 exhibit *High and Low: Modern Art, Popular Culture* at the Museum of Modern Art, NY, and *Masters of American Comics*, presented jointly by the Hammer Museum and the Museum of Contemporary Art, Los Angeles (2005–2006).[6]

The tale of these two shows begins with *The Comic Art Show*, a wide-ranging exhibit encompassing the new wave of Pop Art spilling out from the streets and subways of the East Village (such as Keith Haring), classic comic art, new comics drawn for *Raw* magazine, 1960s pop art, animation, and graffiti. It was curated by John Carlin and Sheena Wagstaff who, in 1983, were graduate students in the Independent Study Program at the Whitney Museum (see also Munson, "Revisiting"). The creative group that came together because of this show – Carlin, Wagstaff, Spiegelman, Brian Walker, and Ann Philbin – would come back together to organize *Masters of American Comics* after Philbin was named Director of the Hammer Museum in Los Angeles.

In the 1980s, the New York museums, particularly MOMA, were under increasing pressure to become more inclusive, to pay attention to how their

---

[5] *Comic Art in Museums* includes the essay, "Exhibitions at the Museum of Cartoon Art: A Personal Recollection" by comics historian and curator Brian Walker, Mort's son and former director of the museum. Elsewhere I have discussed Whyte's extensive relationship with the underground cartoonists in San Francisco, the founding of the museum, and exhibits of note during the first ten years when he was the museum's director (Munson, "Collaborative"). Whyte is a nationally known specialist on the art of Gorey. His most recent book is *Gorey Secrets: Artistic and Literary Inspirations Behind Divers Books by Edward Gorey* (2021).

[6] After MOMA, *High and Low* toured to the Chicago Art Institute and the Museum of Contemporary Art, Los Angeles. *Masters of American Comics* continued from Los Angeles to the Milwaukee Art Museum (where it was reformatted into one exhibit) and to the New York area where it was shown at the Jewish Contemporary Museum (New York) and the Newark Museum (New Jersey).

Comics in the Museum

curatorial and collecting choices privileged selected groups, and to spread attention to a more diverse group. The Guerrilla Girls pointed out the lack of opportunities for women and asked if women "had to be naked" to be on the walls of the Metropolitan Museum. "Histories of the Tribal and the Modern," a 1985 essay by the anthropologist James Clifford criticizing MOMA's exhibit *Primitivism in Twentieth Century Art: Affinity of the Tribal and the Modern* started a debate about colonialism and how the art of different cultures is shown.

When Kirk Varnedoe became the Museum of Modern Art's new director of Painting and Sculpture in 1988, the museum was still considered the temple of Modernism. Its hallways were literally dark, so visitors could contemplate Modernist masterpieces by Pollack, Rothko, and de Kooning as they hung on the walls in pools of light. The 1990 exhibition *High & Low: Modern Art, Popular Culture* curated by Varnedoe and Adam Gopnik, art critic for *The New Yorker*, was meant to turn a new page and bring MOMA from abstraction and connoisseurship into the era of postmodernism. The show focused on the creative cross-pollination between modern art and popular culture, specifically comics, caricature, graffiti, and advertising. Controversy ensued as soon as the show was announced. Critics felt that the show went too far in the move away from Modernism (Hilton Kramer, who loved the status quo) or not far enough by focusing on such a limited sample of popular culture (Arthur Danto, who thought the exclusion of cinema was a missed opportunity). Art Spiegelman primarily thought MOMA was still stuck in the past, saying in his 1990 *Artforum* review "Oh Roy, your dead high art is built on dead low art! The real political, sexual, and formal energy in living popular culture passes you by. Maybe that's [*sob*] why you are championed by museums."

Gopnik's detailed catalog essay on comics and their entwined relationship with fine art was highly praised, but the exhibit design seemed to undercut the curator's good intentions by paying minimal attention to the comic art in the display, which made it look like nothing but source material for Pop Art paintings. This angered cartoonists and fans, who felt that comics had made a respectful return to museums with the survey shows of the 70s and thought this was a setback. For example, the curators wanted to display the heroic-scale paintings of Phillip Guston with the underground comix of Robert Crumb because of some shared imagery, like the bean-shaped cyclops character Crumb borrowed from Guston and featured on the front and back covers of *Weirdo* #7 (1983). The *High and Low* exhibit included *Weirdo* in a display case of Crumb comics along with two or three framed pages of Crumb's cover art, but they were completely overwhelmed by the monumental paintings of Guston, some of which were as long as one hundred inches. In the eyes of comics fans and advocates, this problem of scale accentuated the feeling that comics were secondary to the paintings on display.

In response to *High and Low*, comics creators and fans were motivated to educate and engage the museum world on how comics work and the best ways to meaningfully display them. In 1992, after Robert Storr organized a show of work from Spiegelman's Pulitzer Prize–winning *Maus* at MOMA, Spiegelman refused to sell pages from *Maus* to the museum, explaining that at that time they had no concrete plan to collect or show comics, and this would be "equivalent to burying it in a vault" (Juno, 1997). He recognized that he had to teach curators that there was more to a good comic than nice drawing and he began to invite curators to his studio for "Comics 101."

Ann Philbin, who had seen *The Comic Art Show* as a graduate student, stayed in touch with Carlin and Spiegelman, inviting them to curate comics shows at the Drawing Center in NY. When she became director of the Hammer Museum in Los Angeles, she invited Carlin, Spiegelman, and Walker to respond to *High and Low* with the comics show they had always dreamed of.

Masters of American Comics was split between two influential fine art museums, with Winsor McCay, Lyonel Feininger, George Herriman, E. C. Segar, Frank King, Chester Gould, Milton Caniff, and Charles Schulz representing the evolution of the comic strip at the Hammer Museum near UCLA in Westwood, and Will Eisner, Jack Kirby, Harvey Kurtzman, R. Crumb, Art Spiegelman, Gary Panter, and Chris Ware representing the evolution of the comic book at the Museum of Contemporary Art, Los Angeles, across town in the financial district. The curators diligently found the best-known examples of artwork by these fifteen renowned cartoonists, who each got their own mini gallery within the show. The show provoked controversy among critics and fans because it stated the goal of creating a canon, and then excluded all women and people of color except for George Herriman.[7]

---

[7] George Herriman, the genius behind the influential and beloved comic strip *Krazy Kat* is an interesting case. Throughout his career, everyone thought he was white, to the point of nicknaming him "the Greek" to account for his curly hair and swarthy complexion. He was actually African American, born to a prominent Creole family that hid its racial identity in the dangerous days of Reconstruction after the US Civil War. See Tisserand.

Figure 15.4. Postcard design for *She Draws Comics: 100 Years of America's Women Cartoonists,* a show of all women cartoonists organized by Trina Robbins in rebuttal to the all-male *Masters of American Comics* exhibit. Museum of Comic and Cartoon Art, NY (now part of the Society of Illustrators). May 20–November 6, 2006. Courtesy of Trina Robbins.

Comics herstorian, collector, and retired cartoonist Trina Robbins, who responded to sexism in the underground comix era by producing the first ever comic completely written and drawn by women (*It Ain't Me Babe: Women's Liberation*, 1970), advocated for women on two fronts. First, she gave presentations on deserving women at both the Hammer in LA and at the Jewish Museum in NY during the run of *Masters*. Second, she organized *She Draws Comics* at the Museum of Comic and Cartoon Art (Figure 15.4), an exhibition of women comics artists from Nell Brinkley (1910) to Alison Bechdel (2005) as a direct rebuttal to the all-male *Masters* show when it appeared in New York.[8]

After Masters: Exhibit Trends

Since the controversy incited by the *Masters* exhibit, more shows focusing on women and people of color have been produced. Some well-reviewed

---

[8] *Ain't Me Babe: Women's Liberation* was originally published by Ronald Turner for Last Gasp. The entire comic was recently reproduced in *The Complete Wimmen's Comix* anthology, edited by Robbins in 2016. See also, *Pretty in Ink: North American Women Cartoonists 1896–2013,* her most recent herstory of women cartoonists.

recent exhibits include *Drawn to Purpose: American Women Illustrators and Cartoonists* at the Library of Congress (2018) and *Beyond the Black Panther: Visions of Afrofuturism in American Comics* at Michigan State University (2021–2022). Robbins herself has continued to curate and loan artwork to exhibitions, most recently showing over a hundred artworks from her collection in *Women in Comics*, displayed in New York at the Society of Illustrators, and in Italy at the Palazzo Merulana in Rome and the Foqus Corte dell'Arte in Naples (with Kim Munson, 2020–21).

Another influential and lasting contribution *Masters* made to the forward momentum of comics was its elegant and meticulously detailed catalog, published by Yale University Press. The catalog is packed with lush images showing every brushstroke and remnant of the comics production process, influencing the look of reproductions in many exhibit catalogs to follow. In *Comic Art in Museums: An Overview*, Kitchen Sink Press publisher, cartoonist, and curator Denis Kitchen explains the catalog's influence as follows:

> It reproduced the originals as they actually appeared, showing white-out, paste-overs, marginal notes, smudges, etc., instead of the sanitized versions always shown in prior books and even earlier art museum catalogs about comics. That set the general approach John Lind and I used for *Underground Classics* and the current *Eisner Centennial* catalog, though we prefer text that is less academic in approach and more broadly accessible. The importance of a strong catalog must be stressed. Thousands of individuals may see an exhibit in person and enjoy the maximum experience, but years later all that is left long after the exhibit is over is the catalogue and it must stand as the historic and educational tool (Munson Comic Art, 17.)

The *Masters* catalog is a sophisticated volume that takes comic art seriously, with a detailed historical essay by Carlin and knowledgeable commentary on the fifteen comics artists. The fidelity of the reproductions is a recognition of the unique position comic art has as both a part of the production process and art on its own.

Another reason the scholarly nature of the *Masters* catalog is important is its timing, which coincided with the growth of comics studies in academia. Following books like McCloud's *Understanding Comics*, methods of storytelling and narrative in comics have been a frequent topic of academic papers, analyzing how the eye moves through the page and how part of the story is filled in by the reader, especially between panels. Concepts like these have informed exhibitions, enabling curators to help the viewer better understand the close relationship between image and text and the construction of comics narratives.

Comics in the Museum 323

Figure 15.5. *The Bible Illuminated: R. Crumb's Book of Genesis* displays all 200 pages of Genesis in order. Installation view at the Hammer Museum, Los Angeles. October 24, 2009–February 7, 2010. Photo by Brian Forrest, courtesy of the Hammer Museum.

Figuring out how much to show can be a bit of a challenge. It's a rule of thumb in exhibition design classes that the viewer will tire of reading standing up in the gallery after about 250 words, but in comics exhibitions they sometimes encounter entire books on the wall, as is the case with R. Crumb's *Genesis Illustrated* (almost 200 pages, shown in Los Angeles, Portland (OR), Columbus (OH), Brunswick (ME), San Jose (CA), Seattle, Paris, and the 55th Venice Biennale, see Figure 15.5), Art Spiegelman's *Maus* (shown in its entirety in his *Co-Mix* retrospective in Paris, Cologne, Vancouver, New York, Toronto), and Carol Tyler's 2016 exhibit, *Pages and Progress*, which featured the pages of her collected graphic novel *Soldier's Heart* fluttering from a clothesline (Meyer Gallery, University of Cincinnati, Ohio). When Denis Kitchen curates exhibits of underground comix or of the work of veteran masters like Will Eisner and Harvey Kurtzman, he selects two-page stories, cover art, or five to six pages that represent an important story arc, so the visitor can appreciate the artist's storytelling skills without being overwhelmed.

Some exhibits have taken comics outside of the book altogether, showing panels and digital images specifically for exhibition, arranged in a way

324 KIM MUNSON

that lets the visitor decide on the narrative. These "gallery comics" have long been of interest to British author and curator Paul Gravett, who has experimented with this concept several times, notably in the 2010 exhibit *Hypercomics: The Shape of Comics to Come* at the Pump House Gallery in Battersea Park. This type of experimentation is the perfect fit with the gradual movement of museums away from a model based on collections and connoisseurship to one that promotes more diversity and visitor interaction. Since the 1970s, museums have been criticized for being elitist, privileging "high art" that they considered worthy of attention and preservation and dismissing "low or mass art" like comics and most popular culture. Now, as museums strive to stay relevant with a visually oriented, plugged-in audience, they will continue to find new ways to communicate with this audience through the comics medium.

WORKS CITED

Comics Exhibitions and Catalogues

AAARGH! Bumper Souvenir Catalogue (Exhibition booklet: December 31, 1970–February 6, 1971). Institute of Contemporary Arts, 1970.

Beyond the Black Panther: Visions of Afrofuturism in American Comics (exhibition, February 1, 2021–April 30, 2022). Michigan State University Museum 2021. www.museum.msu.edu/?exhibition=beyond-the-black-panther-visions-of-afro futurism-in-american-comics Accessed 11/19/21.

"Black Ink: African American Cartoonist Showcase" (exhibition catalog: February 5–May 16). 1992. Cartoon Art Museum, 1992

Carlin, John, Paul Karasik and Brian Walker, eds. *Masters of American Comics*. Hammer Museum and the Museum of Contemporary Art/Yale University Press, 2005.

Carlin, John and Sheena Wagstaff. *The Comic Art Show: Cartoons and Paintings in Popular Culture*. Whitney Museum of American Art, 1983.

Claremont, Chris et al. *Marvel Universe of Superheroes* (exhibit catalog). Verlag für moderne Kunst, 2019.

Contemporary Cartoons: An Exhibition of Original Drawings by American Artists at the Huntington Library March-April (exhibit brochure). The Huntington Library, 1937.

Horn, Maurice. *75 Years of the Comics* (exhibition catalog: September 8–November 7, New York Cultural Center). Boston Book & Art Publisher, 1971.

Muller, Jerome K. 1976. *The Cartoon Show: Original Works by 100 Outstanding American Cartoonists Selected for the Jerome K. Muller Collection* (exhibition booklet: February 28–April 4), Bowers Museum, 1976.

Myer, Peter L. ed. *The Comics as an Art Form* (exhibition booklet: March 29–April 24). University of Nevada Art Gallery, 1970.

O'Sullivan, Judith. *The Art of the Comic Strip* (exhibition catalog: April 1–May 9). University of Maryland Art Gallery, 1971.

Stewart, Bohb. *The Phonus Balonus Show of Some Really Heavy Stuff* (exhibition booklet, May 20–June 15). Corcoran Museum of Art, 1969.

Spiegelman, Art. *Co-Mix: A Retrospective of Comics, Graphics, and Scraps (exhibition catalog)*. Drawn and Quarterly, 2013.

Tyler, Carol. *Pages and Progress* (Video and exhibit photos). *Neuroticraven.com*, 2018. www.neuroticraven.com/blog/2018/1/22/carol-tylers-pages-progress Accessed January, 8, 2022.

Varnedoe, Kirk and Adam Gopnik. *High and Low: Modern Art, Popular Culture*. Museum of Modern Art, 1990.

Secondary Sources

Burchard, Wolf. *Inspiring Walt Disney: The Animation of French Decorative Arts*. Metropolitan Museum of Art, 2021.

Capart, Philippe. *Du privé au public*. La Crypte Tonique #16. La Crypte Tonique, 2021.

Cavalcade of American Comics (newsprint program). The Newspaper Comics Council, 1963.

Couperie, Pierre and Maurice Horn. *A History of the Comic Strip*. Crown Publishers, 1968.

"Drawn to Purpose: American Women Illustrators and Cartoonists" (exhibition November 18, 2017–October 20, 2018). *Library of Congress*, University Press of Mississippi, 2017.

Gaines, M. C. "Narrative Illustration: The Story of the Comics." *Print: A Quarterly Journal of the Graphic Arts*, vol. 3, no. 2, 1942, pp. 25–38.

Gravett, Paul. *Comics Art*. Tate Publishing, 2013.

"Fourth Estate: Terry and the Pirates Storm New York Gallery in New Adventure." Newsweek, vol. XIV, no. 25, p. 48.

Harper, Mr. "After Hours: Pooh to Art." *Harper's Magazine*. August, 1951, p. 14.

Harvey, Robert C. *Meanwhile: A Biography of Milton Caniff*. Fantagraphics Books, 2007.

Herdeg, Walter and David Pascal. *Comics: The Art of the Comic Strip*. The Graphis Press, 1972.

Juno, Andrea. "Art Spiegelman." *Art Spiegelman Conversations*, edited by Joseph Witek. University Press of Mississippi, 1997, pp. 163–190.

Munson, Kim. "Revisiting The Comic Art Show." *International Journal of Comic Art*, vol. 14, no. 2, 2012, pp. 264–288.

"A Collaborative Journey: Malcolm Whyte, Troubador Press, and the Cartoon Art Museum, San Francisco." *International Journal of Comic Art*, vol. 18, no. 2, 2016, pp. 61–110.

"How the French Kickstarted the Acceptance of Comics as an Art Form in the US: The Books and Exhibitions of Maurice Horn." *International Journal of Comic Art*, vol. 18, no. 2, 2016, pp. 111–155.

Comic Art in Museums. University Press of Mississippi, 2020.

"Viewing R. Crumb: Circles of Influence in Fine Art Museums." *The Comics of R. Crumb: Underground in the Art Museum,* edited by Daniel Worden. University Press of Mississippi, 2021, pp. 232–252.

"Women in Comics Photo Grid (New York)." *Neuroticraven.com.* 2021. www .neuroticraven.com/blog/2020/5/20/women-in-comics-photo-grid Accessed January, 8, 2022.

Nugent, Frank S. "Disney Is Now Art – But He Wonders: That Picture in the Museum Is Not All His, He Reveals." *The New York Times.* February 26, 1939.

Robbins, Trina. "Women and the Comics." *Cartoonist Profiles* , no. 64, December 1985, pp. 40–45.

Pretty in Ink: North American Women Cartoonists 1896–2013. Fantagraphics Books, 2013.

Robbins, Trina, ed. *The Complete Wimmen's Comix.* Fantagraphics Books, 2016.

Robbins, Trina and Catherine Yronwode. *Women and the Comics.* Eclipse Comics, 1985.

Serrell, Beverly. *Exhibit Labels: An Interpretive Approach.* Rowman and Littlefield, 2015.

Spiegelman, Art. "High Art Lowdown": This Review Is Not Sponsored by AT&T)." *Artforum,* December, 1990.

Tisserand, Michael. *Krazy: George Herriman, A Life in Black and White.* HarperCollins, 2010.

CHAPTER 16

Comics in Libraries

Joe Sutliff Sanders

Comic books rarely made an appearance in US public or school libraries before the 1990s, but for a kind of book that so rarely appeared, they had an extraordinary presence. Although librarians of the mid-twentieth century seldom allowed comic books or even the mention of comic books into their libraries, they spent a great deal of time writing about comics. Those writings provide an opportunity to think about comics as cultural objects with contested meanings. Tracing how librarians talked about comic books helps us understand both comics and the adult cultural gatekeepers who resisted them. The resulting history hints at how librarians understood themselves, their role in children's reading, and the threat that they convinced themselves that comic books presented not only to children, not only to books, but also to librarianship.

Four writers, two of them working together, are inevitable to the task of understanding what comic books meant to American librarians in the mid-twentieth century. The first of these are Allen Ellis and Doug Highsmith, who in 2000 published a survey of professional librarians' thoughts on comic books. Ellis and Highsmith used the then-new capability of electronic databases to scour the published literature to put together the best overview possible at the time with clear observations about the patterns emerging. For instance, they note that the published conversation between librarians in the 1940s and 1950s was "fraught with 'anti-comic books' writings – articles, books, and essays that categorized comic books as nothing more than ephemeral trash" (22). During this period, they find, there was little to no suggestion that comic books could support reading, meaning that comics were "considered to be unworthy of inclusion in

---

The author gratefully acknowledges the Baldwin Library of Historical Children's Literature at the University of Florida, the Billy Ireland Cartoon Library & Museum at the Ohio State University, and the Stephen O. Murray and Keelung Hong Special Collections at Michigan State University, without which this research would not have been possible.

327

library collections, be they public, school, or academic" (22). They do, however, point to a significant number of library articles on comics that were "mixed or neutral" and even the rare article that they found to be positive (29). Ellis and Highsmith's major contribution, then, is to demonstrate that the conversation about comics in professional librarian discourse in the mid-century (and indeed they continue their survey until the late century) was largely negative, though more complicated than it might first appear.

Ellis and Highsmith also provide an introduction to some of the major refrains and characters of the mid-century debate about comics, and perhaps the most colorful and significant of those characters, at least until the mid-1950s, was Sterling North. By 1940, North had published multiple books and established a career as a journalist, rising to the position of Literary Editor for the *Chicago Daily News*. Later in his career, North would see one of his books adapted into a film by Walt Disney and another win a Newbery Honor, but in May of 1940, his name became familiar to librarians across the country when his article "A National Disgrace" was published in the *News* and almost immediately reprinted widely and at length. Indeed, today finding a copy of the original is difficult, but finding a reprint is simple. As late as 1944, even people who publicly disagreed with North, such as Harvey Zorbaugh, reproduced much of North's essay: for many years, any conversation about comics began with North's highly quotable screed. North noted with alarm the sudden popularity of comics, their staggering sales, their "voluptuous females in scanty attire, blazing machine guns," the poor printing and hasty art, and "their hypodermic injection of sex and murder [that] make the child impatient with better, though quieter, stories." All of these, North claimed, combined to incite "a cultural slaughter of the innocents" (qtd. in Zorbaugh 193–194). Ellis and Highsmith found in their 2000 survey that "A National Disgrace" "set the tone for the attitude of America's cultural elite toward the infant art form" (21), engendering "a striking sameness among library literature's criticism of comic books" in which librarians echoed North and one another (26–27). The major themes of librarian criticism in the mid-century emerge in North and, as Ellis and Highsmith demonstrate, remain remarkably consistent for more than a decade.

Amy Kiste Nyberg, the third writer key for understanding the place of comics in libraries in the mid-twentieth century, is a communications historian with an essay and full-length book on the largely negative history of adult reactions to children reading comics. Nyberg finds that opponents of comics repeatedly returned to one idea, an idea implicit in Sterling North's famous essay. Comics, these educators warned, "prevented children from developing an appreciation for better literature" ("Poisoning" 174). Comics were not just a distraction but the opposite of literature, and "once a child grew accustomed to a diet of comic books, his taste was ruined for other types of reading" (174). As a result, cultural gatekeepers of the period argued for going to war with comic books by insisting on the value of good literature. Nyberg traces the influence of North's article and argues that two key ideas emerged. The first was the danger that comics posed to children, and the second was that "the solution to the problem of comic-book reading was to substitute 'good' children's literature as an 'antidote' to the comic-book poison" (172). As educators took up the banner offered by North, Nyberg makes a key claim that explains how the problem of comics, literature, and cultural gatekeepers would be structured for decades to come. For educators, children's reading time was a finite resource, and every time that children read comics, they were choosing *not* to read literature. It was the role of educators, then, to determine why children liked comics and to help them see that they must forego comics in favor of "better literature" (175).

These vocal opponents of comics were not simply the custodians of the books being ignored as children turned to comics; their professional identity rested on those books and the right to tell children what to read. "[B]y the time the comic book made its debut," Nyberg argues, "the supervision of children's reading had been largely given over to teachers and professional librarians in public and school libraries" (*Seal* 18–19). In later years, Anne Lundin would demonstrate that this shift in authority over children's reading dated back to the evolution of the children's department and the librarians in charge of it in the late nineteenth and early twentieth centuries (2, 13). The real problem, Nyberg argues, was not simply that librarians stood for good books, not simply that they understood comics as competing with literature in a zero-sum game for attention, not even simply that librarians defined themselves according to their allegiance to traditional books, but that comic books *allowed children to skirt librarians' authority* over what children read. In the mid-century, "comic books were widely available at grocery stores, news stands, and corner drug stores" (1), venues in which librarians had no jurisdiction. The established forms and formats of children's literature were published by presses who understood libraries as their chief markets, meaning that librarians influenced and in some cases directed children's reading material from conception through editing, publication, review, distribution, and purchase. Comic books, however, not part of the traditional market, "were selected and purchased by children themselves, often without the direct supervision of adults." Further, after children bought comics, they circulated their purchases in a marketplace of friends and neighbors over which no adults had jurisdiction ("Poisoning" 169). Such reading represented a threat to librarians' claim to a professional identity.

The final writer whose work is inevitable to an understanding of comics and mid-century libraries is Carol Tilley, a Library and Information Sciences specialist with multiple essays and an important unpublished dissertation that have had significant impact on the ongoing conversation. Tilley confirms and enriches the ideas advanced by Ellis, Highsmith, and Nyberg but draws from a richer pool of evidence than does the first study and a body of evidence more specific to librarians than does Nyberg. Tilley further argues that librarians defined themselves as champions of *morality*, a perception that combined with the existential threat of comics to motivate librarians in ways that were unique to that profession. At the time that comic books exploded across the country, children's librarians still often tended to "perpetuate Victorian concerns about literary and moral value" (*Nightingales* 31). For the most part, Tilley takes such concerns at face value, suggesting that librarians of the time "genuinely seemed to have the best interests of young people in mind," but their investment in the moral value of reading combined with their sense of themselves as the best-informed arbiters of reading selection meant that "many youth services librarians still viewed themselves as the pivotal figures standing between children and books" (199). From her position within librarianship, Tilley notes multiple contradictions within the field at the time, including a marked hypocrisy as librarians preached against censorship but made censorship of comics a regular practice (Tilley and Bahnmaier 60). Further, she notes within librarians' own history of the field that whatever the profession's public stance on privileging children's emerging tastes or combatting censorship, "librarians worked to suppress, not protect, comics, perhaps indicating the profession's continuing belief that guarding children against lowbrow culture and its poor morals trumped broader professional commitments" (*Nightingales* 10). Although adult gatekeepers in general scorned comic books, librarians had a unique history and self-definition that routinely led them to insist that they were obliged to privilege more traditional forms of literature over comics and to use their reading rooms to promote literature to the exclusion of comics.

These four writers provide a vision of libraries in the mid-century that can support any number of further investigations, but for now, two points are especially important. The first is that librarians in general perceived comic books as the opposite of literature. Children could read comics *or* they could read real books, the sorts of book that US librarians had already been celebrating for decades through major awards such as the Caldecott and Newbery. The second point arises from the first: librarians perceived themselves as the agents of great literature, so they felt themselves to be the natural enemy of comics. Further, because of their professional identification with literature, librarians saw comic books as a threat to themselves professionally. Awards such as the Caldecott and Newbery did more than lift up good books; they also confirmed to publishers, teachers, parents, and librarians themselves that American librarians, who bestowed the awards, were best positioned to connect the right child with the right book. Comics, which circumvented the space of libraries and the selection of librarians, appeared to librarians as a threat to the books and profession they had cultivated since the nineteenth century.

However, the relationship between books, librarians, and comics took a surprising turn when comics publishers responded to librarians' animosity not by challenging their professional authority but by making overtures to literature. Tilley has explored a compelling, focused example of this strategy in her analysis of experiments from 1935 to 1946 by National Comics – the publisher of *Superman*, a publisher today known as DC Comics – evidently designed "to encourage children and young adults to read books other than comics" ("'Superman'" 251). Through a letter directly from Superman to his readers, editorial notes with recommended children's books, and even reviews for traditional books published inside the front cover of popular titles, National directed its readers to the kinds of books that librarians championed, and it did so explicitly, across multiple titles, for months in a row. Tilley even considers testimony from mid-century librarians and finds that the direct appeal of Superman to children had measurable success in helping get recommended books into the hands of children: "Superman said, 'Read,'" she argues, "and young people did" (262).

A closer look at those elements reveals not just that comics publishers were publicly friendly to literature but that they understood that librarians were a key opponent whom they needed to mollify. Consider, for example, several reviews that ran monthly in National Comics titles beginning in 1942. These reviews usually appeared on the inside front covers, which are themselves rich areas for analysis: the lower-left column tells children about other National comics they ought to be buying, the top left introduces a panel of experts on childhood and literature who advised

332   JOE SUTLIFF SANDERS

the publisher, and the bottom right contains a secret message from a DC character for children who had sent off for a special decoder, but the lion's share of the space is given over to "Good Books Worth Reading," a column by Josette Frank of the Child Study Association of America. Frank was a key and vocal ally for comics and a member of National's Editorial Advisory Board, and she repeatedly addressed librarians to make the case that comics were reasonable literature for young people. In an essay for *The Journal of Educational Sociology*, she combatted several of the main arguments made in library journals, and she even compared the genres of comics to the genres of literature, asking librarians to look past the comics format to the familiar content. "Any librarian," she soothed, "will at once recognize here the categories that have always been prime favorites on the children's book shelves" ("What's in the Comics?" 215). A decade later, in her book *Your Child's Reading Today*, she responded bluntly to librarians' central claim against comics: "The fallacy in our approach to the whole subject of comics lies in our *either-or* attitude – the fear that children will read *either* books *or* comics. This fear is not justified" (246).

Her review column made this argument assiduously. By placing reviews for more traditional literature, the kinds of books that librarians feared would lose out to comic books, inside a comic book, alongside a message from Superman, a list of other comics to read, and the names of adult authorities who endorsed the very comic book in front of them, Frank was telling librarians, children, and parents that comics and literature could absolutely coexist. Further, Frank put money down that she was right: in late 1942, she launched a contest for comics-reading children who would write reviews about select books. Beginning with the January 1943 issues, National awarded five dollars to children such as Miriam Sandberg of New York City, who reviewed *Lassie Come Home* or, in the following month, Ronald Langley of Otwell, Arkansas, who reviewed Covelle Newcomb's *Black Fire*. The books children were invited to review came from lists selected, Frank was careful to note, by librarians, including "Irene Smith, Superintendent of Work with Children, Brooklyn Public Library"[1] and "Grace E. Cartmell, Supt. of Work with Children, of the Queensboro Public Library".[2] Frank repeatedly assured readers that these librarians had found that children in their libraries loved these books, and she encouraged children to go find these books *in libraries*. Frank's own reviews

---

[1] See, e.g., *Adventure Comics* no. 80, November 1942.
[2] See, e.g., *Adventure Comics* no. 79, October 1942.

occasionally suggested that children might like to buy a copy of a recommended book at a newsstand,[3] but she was much more likely to encourage children to find the books she reviewed at libraries.[4] Frank's columns, whether they featured her own writing or the winning reviews submitted by children around the country, were carefully designed to argue that comics and traditional books could happily live alongside one another, that children who read comics were good readers of good books, and that comics posed no threat to librarians, who could find in comics another venue for directing children's reading.

The adults invested in defending comic books used similar strategies for making the case that comics were not the enemy of librarians and literature, with arguments that were sometimes indirect and sometimes very direct indeed. The May 1960 issue of *Superman's Girlfriend Lois Lane* offered a regular column of letters from readers, still a fairly new innovation in comic books.[5] A letter by Holly Hart, of Chicago, heads the nine letters printed that month, and although most of the letters complain, criticize, or offer corrections, Hart praises the February issue. She notes, "We are studying short stories in school and the technique used in your story reminded [me] greatly of the writing craft used in that classic story, 'The Necklace.' Your writer deserves a Pulitzer Prize!" (np). If we assume that there were more than nine letters from which to choose, Hart's letter – and its placement at the top of the column – seems to indicate that the editors were very interested in having readers think of their serial in terms relevant to literature and its institutional study. Considering the hairsplitting arguments and indignant outrage of most of the other letters, even the praise seems less valuable to the editors, who did not select letters based on how positive they were, than the comparison with literature. A year earlier, various comics published by National, including *Lois Lane*, ran an even more explicit appeal to libraries: a full-page public service advertisement on the inside front cover (see Figure 16.1). The advertisement took the form of a comic strip titled "The Magic Card!" in which a group of teens are happily spread out across a middle-class living room consulting items they have borrowed from the public library. Two boys compare a remote control with a diagram in a book, two girls work on a costume using "swell designs" from another book, and a boy and girl

---

[3] See, e.g., *Adventure Comics* no. 77, August 1942.
[4] See, e.g., *Adventure Comics* no. 78 and no. 81, September and December 1942.
[5] Although *Real Fact Comics* printed readers' letters in the July 1946 issue, the first regular letters column in a DC comic began in *Superman* no. 124, which had a cover date of September 1958 (Cowsill, et al. 91).

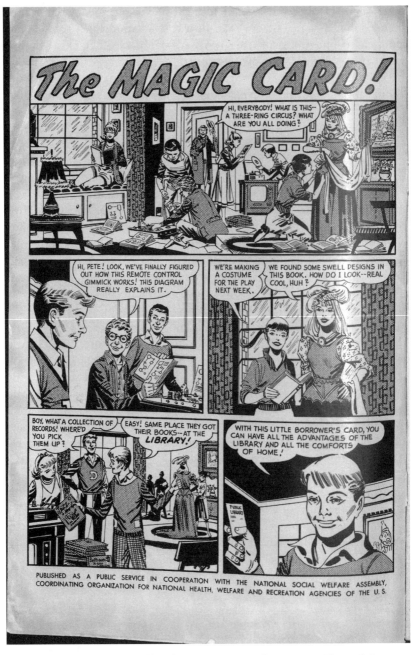

Figure 16.1. *Superman's Girlfriend Lois Lane* no. 7, February 1959. National Comics. Inside front cover.

connect over records they found at the "same place they got their books – at the library!" The ad takes a nuanced approach, not exactly arguing for literature but self-improvement, intellectual inquiry, and hobbies that would keep children at home. The "magic" library card, National told children (and adults peeking over their shoulders), was a key to "all the advantages of the library and all the comforts of home!" These paratextual materials became venues for comic books to signal that although libraries saw comics as a threat, comics were eager for a truce.

Comic books also made space for that argument in the stories themselves. A story of Tawky Tawny, the talking, bipedal tiger, in *Captain Marvel Adventures* # 126, November 1951, shows the loveable tiger growing steadily weary of his regular job giving tours at a museum. He works all day, comes home to put in time on his book manuscript, and feels that wealth and fame will never come to him. He turns to silly, gaudy publicity stunts and earns fame that is immediate but also, he realizes with the help of his friend Captain Marvel, fleeting. "Now I understand," he soliloquizes, "What I got before was cheap notoriety, not true fame! The fickle crowd has already forgotten me!" The next day, his friend brings a group of scientists to consider Tawny's manuscript, and they dub it "A work of patient, plodding genius! We'll publish it and Mr. Tawny's fame will never tarnish for a thousand years!" (Figure 16.2). Tawny thanks his friend, declaring that "True fame comes from doing important and worthwhile things! This book was my claim to fame all the time and I didn't know it!" Obviously, Tawny's re-commitment to his book is a reaffirmation of the importance and lasting value of books with proper covers published by teams of experts. Less obviously, Tawny's rejection of "cheap," flashy, popular acclaim bears significant similarities with the complaints librarians made about comic books. The transitory nature of the fame that Tawny outgrows mirrors the ephemeral pleasures of comics, subtly accepting and even reproducing the arguments of librarians that comics were to be left behind as quickly as possible for the "patient, plodding genius" of the real books that could be found in libraries.

Comics of the period even went so far as to embed literary references into their stories, with varying levels of commitment, virtually from the very beginning. The March 1937 issue of *Famous Funnies*, for example, featured Jerry Iger's strip *Bobby*, with a title banner sporting young Bobby himself coyly reciting, "To be or not to be[,] that is the question?" In the August–September 1951 issue of *Walt Disney's Mickey Mouse*, Goofy and Mickey star in "The Ruby Eye of Homar-Guy-Am," a playful allusion to *Rubáiyát of Omar Khayyám*. Disney continued the silliness with Moby

Figure 16.2. "Mr. Tawny's Fight for Fame." Originally published in *Captain Marvel Adventures* no. 126, November 1951. Fawcett Comics.

Duck, introduced in *Donald Duck* # 112, March 1967. In each of these instances, the reference means little to the story: Bobby's extradiegetic recitation is a foreshadowing of the gag at the end of the strip; Goofy and Mickey do seek a ruby, but not one associated with anyone by the invented name; and Moby Duck lives at sea but is in fact a duck, not even an especially large one, and he is marked by ginger hair, not white. Still, there is some element of humor embedded in each of these references, an element that rewards readers who catch the references, bypassing or confusing readers who do not. Elsewhere, the references are more meaningful to the story, as in the June–August 1958 issue of *Walt Disney's Uncle Scrooge*, in which the boys are trying to get Scrooge to relax and enjoy nature. As part of their efforts, they read to him from *The King of the Golden River*, John Ruskin's classic Victorian fable published in 1851 and reprinted well into the twentieth century. In a Gandy Goose story published in *Paul Terry's Mighty Mouse Comics* (April 1953), Gandy

Comics in Libraries

and his friend obtain a movie camera and enthusiastically apply themselves to producing great film. Gandy's friend relies extensively on Shakespeare, delivering Hamlet's "To be or not to be," *Julius Caesar*'s "I come to bury Caesar, not to praise him" (upon which Gandy exclaims, "That's from another play"), *Macbeth*'s "Lay on MacDuff," and *Richard III*'s "My kingdom for a horse." These examples rarely give extended attention to any particular text, and often the literary references exist only to signal literariness – Gandy Goose's film aspires to a certain level of dignity, Scrooge's story is calm and dreamlike rather than energizing – but they take for granted an ability to recognize literature, even if that recognition is trivial.

One comic book series incorporated literary references into an original story world both frequently and gracefully. Most readers today will know Walt Kelly's *Pogo*, featuring Pogo the Possum, Albert Alligator, Howland Owl, "Churchy" LaFemme, and the other residents of Kelly's lushly illustrated swamp, as a comic strip published in newspapers and distributed nationally through the third quarter of the century. However, Pogo premiered in a comic book, and by the end of 1949, when Kelly began publishing the comic book *Pogo the Possum* through Dell Comics, the cast had taken on the appearances and habits now familiar. From that first issue, Kelly was already finding ways to fold in allusions. In the story "The End of the Rainbow," the friends go looking for treasure they think will be revealed where the rainbow touches ground. In a parallel plot, fireworks are being set off elsewhere in the swamp, and when the treasure-seekers see one of the fireworks go up, they mistake it for a rainbow. As the dialogue unfolds across one panel, Albert says, "My heart leap!" Howland exclaims, "Oop!" and Rackety Coon concludes, "An' I behole a rainbow in the sky" (Figure 16.3). The reference is of course to Wordsworth's "My Heart Leaps Up," whose opening reads, "My heart leaps up when I behold/A rainbow in the sky." The literary callouts continue in the second issue, in the story "The Gingerbread Cure," as Howland and Albert hatch a scheme to trick Pogo. Albert pretends to be ill, striking dramatic poses and shedding a tear. He recites in one panel, "When I am dead, my dearest,/ Sing no sad songs for me;/Plant thou no roses at my head,/Nor shady cypress tree:", continuing in the next panel with, "Be the green grass above me/With showers and dewdrops wet;/And if thou wilt, ree-member,/And if thou wilt, forget!" Here, Albert quotes the opening lines of Christina Rosetti's "When I Am Dead, My Dearest" verbatim (with the exception of his exaggerated "ree-member"), even maintaining nearly all the punctuation and line breaks. In both examples, the allusion is more than a signal of

Figure 16.3. *Pogo Possum* no. 1, October–December, 1949. Dell.

literariness. Both are playful, with the animals' dialect transforming Wordsworth and Albert's over-acting turning Rosetti's poem into sentimental melodrama. The references are submerged enough to fit into the diegetic world but foreign enough to signal that they are allusions, allowing readers unfamiliar with the originals to follow the story while remaining alert to another text hovering just off-panel.

Pogo Possum also brings those texts into the comics themselves. The fifth issue, the May–July number from 1951, uses a six-panel silent strip inside the front cover (Figure 16.4). In it, Howland rests against a tree, laughing at something he reads as Pogo approaches. Howland holds the text up to display the cover of Pogo's own comic book, much to Pogo's delight. Pogo struts off, but the moment he is gone, Howland reveals that he was using the comic book to hide a more traditional book, and in the final panel, Howland goes back to laughing at what he was really reading: Shakespeare. The humor of the strip comes from its direct inversion of the standard fearful fantasy of librarians, that comics would come between readers and literature: here the prankster is pretending to flatter his friend while secretly reading what he prefers. Indeed, Shakespeare literally comes

Comics in Libraries

Figure 16.4. *Pogo Possum* no. 5, May–July 1951. Dell.

340 JOE SUTLIFF SANDERS

between Howland and the comic book. It also reinforces and plays with the lofty cultural position of Shakespeare, as it is the bespectacled owl who reads the Bard, implying that a sharp mind is required to understand him. However, the strip suggests that Shakespeare is not simply an author to be admired as literary: he is in fact very funny – a high compliment from a funny animals comic.

This mixture of admiration and delight in the literary continues in a final example from the following issue, the July–September number, in a story titled "The Howl and the Pussy Cat." The story opens with Pogo promising to read Edward Lear's "The Owl and the Pussy-Cat," bound in a thick volume larger than Pogo's head, to two "chilluns," a frog and bird listening attentively. As Pogo reads the words of the poem, the font in his word balloons shifts from its usual sans serif to an elegant, italicized font. When the frog interrupts to object to the absurdity of the poem, Pogo reprimands it with an appeal to "a fierce ol' poetic license," and the bird scolds, "Hush now and learn somethin' with that fat punkin' head of you'rn" (9). The opening of the story, then, establishes the poem as authoritative, coming from a massive book, inspiring elegant speech, and somehow pregnant with knowledge that the youth would do well to absorb. It also, though, treats the poem playfully. Playfulness is inevitable with Kelly's bizarre dialect – a northeastern American's caricature of rural Georgia patois – and it is difficult to take seriously the admonition to use "that fat punkin' head of you'rn" as the measured advice of an educator. As Pogo returns to reading the poem, Howland and Churchy the turtle arrive and argue with him over its interpretation. Howland insists that he is the descendant of the owl in the poem, and Churchy, to everyone's surprise including his own, argues that he is a descendant of the cat. Albert arrives to propose that the only way to determine the truth of the claim is to have Howland and Churchy act out the poem as Pogo reads it again, "An' if ol' Churchy act ee-nough like a cat – then he's it!" (13) Over the next few pages, the owl and turtle/cat pretend to be in love, immediately squabble and push one another into the water, drag a pig into the story, and generally add one layer of absurdity upon another to Lear's nonsense poem. Albert admires their acting prowess, but, Pogo adds, "they is actin' somethin' elsen what they s'pose to" (16). Throughout, the characters and the written poem tug authority back and forth, until Pogo runs out of lines to read because the book from which he is reading is missing a page. Unable to appeal to book or author, the animals settle in to watch the argument between owl, turtle, and pig unfold to see how the story ends. "They is givin' it a obvious endin'," Pogo observes, "but I guess that's as good a way to wind up as any" (18). The comic book story thus cites, respects, interrogates, expands, and ultimately exceeds the original literary text. The engagement with literature is fond, critical, and creative.

In some instances, these olive branches that comics extended to librarians seem flatly driven by self-interest; in others they might be organic. The paratextual elements – the establishment of advisory boards, reviews with explicit reminders to borrow great books from libraries, selection of fan letters, interior advertisement for the riches to be found at libraries – are difficult to read as anything other than comics publishers trying to make peace with their loudest and most powerful enemy. Even Tawky Tawny's story of the value of "patient, plodding" books over celebrity feels too didactic to be utterly genuine. Many of the off-hand references work some middle ground, taking advantage of a pun based on a reference to high literature for a story idea or gag. *Pogo Possum* may well have had an eye toward pleasing cultural authorities with its carnivalesque reinventions, but the stories that resulted imagine a relationship between literature and comics that is less patronizing, more collaborative. The level of self-interest in the many, many examples of comic books referencing libraries and literature may have varied, but the antipathy between libraries and comics was entirely one sided. Comics creators and publishers were delighted to imagine their wares as part of a continuum of reading that children would perform over their lives, and the reading of comics would be enriched, not threatened, by the reading of the sorts of books that libraries championed. Librarians had only to look in comics to find that they had a potential ally.

The problem, of course, was that very few librarians were willing to look inside a comic book; Tawny, Mickey, Donald, Scrooge, and Pogo could include all the references they liked, but librarians were unlikely to know. Some librarians, such as Esther Baker, publishing in *Illinois Libraries* in 1952, were content to find a compromise with comics. Baker calls comics a "ten-cent menace" (399), a reminder of the threat that the purchase price of comics posed to librarians' right to choose reading for children. However, she then goes on at length about how librarians can leverage children's enthusiasm for comics to improve their reading, especially poor readers. She suggests three specific areas of improvement: understanding the mechanics of reading (as long as children are forced to read the dialog instead of just the pictures), understanding "an author's ideas" (399), and exercising discrimination in reading based on a wide exposure to different kinds of reading. Indeed, Baker implies that comics offer a path for librarians back into the position of arbiter of good reading: "The student with reading difficulty is probably already a comic reader, so comics alone are not the solution to his problem. The key to the improvement of his reading ability is the comics plus help and guidance" (400). Louise Seaman Bechtel, the first head of a juvenile book department at a major US publisher, made a strong late career in part on the popularity of her public talks against comic books, but at a speech delivered at the public library in the tiny town of Katonah, New York, she suggested that comics had the ability to "lure [children] back to a library," provided that the library also had "plenty of other kinds of books about" (12).

Some evidence exists that librarians did use comics as a way to, as Bechtel put it, "lure" children back to libraries, and that evidence may be more eloquent than it first appears. Ellis and Highsmith and Tilley have noted a broad pattern of librarians publishing lists of books to wean children off of comics and onto real literature. They note that as early as the 1940s, "Displays were created to compare comic books with 'real' book alternatives; children's librarians learned from their charges what comics they liked and suggested comparable children's books based on similar elements" (29). Such efforts suggest a willingness on librarians' part to be guided by children's tastes, if only so that the librarians could then be better positioned to guide those same children back to real literature. Tilley recalls librarians of the period who "published lists of books intended to wean young readers away from superheroes, vicious criminals, and talking ducks" (191). Even in these marginally conciliatory moments, though, librarians jealously monitored the right to determine what qualified as good literature and guarded their role as arbiters of good taste.

An especially unsubtle example comes from the Soulard Branch of the public library system in St. Louis, Missouri. As the children's librarian there, Charlotte D. Conover, wrote to report in the June 1941 issue of the *Wilson Library Bulletin*, she and her team had "gathered two collections of books" whose appeal, they felt, rested on similar characteristics to those found in comic books. The books found in those collections, though, were "children's books which we approve and regularly purchase, and are several steps up from the other variety." To advertise these collections, the librarians strategically placed signs announcing a collection of "Funny Books," a mid-century synonym for comic books, and another collection of "Heroes and Supermen." Conover recalls that boys habitually approached the children's librarians, "gasp[ing] incredulously, 'Do you really have SUPERMAN?'" Conover met such joyous requests with a didactic, "No, but what do you think of Robin Hood and Baron Munchausen and Paul Bunyan? Aren't they Supermen?" (qtd. in Kunitz 846–847). This librarian's strategy was purposely to deceive children,

Comics in Libraries 343

luring them in, as Bechtel might put it, with comics, only to preach at them, insisting on a loftier literature, while crushing their delight.

The 1950s saw all this heightened rhetoric reach its peak with Frederik Wertham, the Estes Kefauver Senate hearings, and the Comics Code Authority,[6] after which librarians fell strangely silent on the subject of comic books until the 1970s. Ellis and Highsmith find that from 1956 until 1969, librarians published nothing at all about comics, and even after 1969, the articles were infrequent and innocuous. "Suddenly," Ellis and Highsmith write, "the great comics 'debate' seemed dead" (30). That silence might have come about because the Code assuaged librarian fears. Alternatively, it might have been the result of librarians having spent their outrage in the previous years. It might have resulted from the precipitous drop in comics sales – whether that drop came about because of the loss of quality following the Code, the retraction of the market, or the encroaching popularity of television. Whatever the reason, the role that comics played in the imagination of librarians was no longer vital. Still, from the birth of the form until the establishment of the Code, the space that comics occupied in libraries was one that allowed librarians to galvanize themselves, to rally around a certain concept of literature, and to define themselves and their books in opposition to comic books. The fact that comics were never invested in stealing attention from literature no longer mattered, but then, it never had in the first place.

The trajectory of librarian conversations on comics moves from mostly antagonistic in the 1940s to largely absent in the 1960s, tentatively affirmative in the 1970s, and, today, almost universally positive. Emily C. Horner's 2004 survey of seven youth-services library departments and the librarians who tended them found that every single one had a graphic novels collection. By the time of her interviews, the opinion had swung so completely that several of her participants "said that they didn't feel that the presence of graphic novels in their library collections needed to be justified; they asked, 'why not?' rather than 'why?'" (20). As Gwen Athene Tarbox puts it in her recent study of the intersection of children's literature and comic books, children of the new century "can access comics for free and can borrow graphic novels and manga from school media centers and public libraries" (8). Indeed, the distribution of comics has shifted such

---

[6] On which subjects see Nyberg's *Seal of Approval* as well as Tilley's game-changing essay "Seducing the Innocent."

that although few children have access to a brick-and-mortar comics specialty shops, they are very likely to have access to graphic novel collections through libraries (46). Finally, after decades as serving as the foil to real literature and the bogeyman to librarians' authority, comics have a consistent physical presence in American libraries.

WORKS CITED

Comics

Captain Marvel Adventures, no. 126, November 1951.
Donald Duck, no. 112, March 1967.
Famous Funnies, no. 32, March 1937.
Pogo Possum, no. 1 October–December 1949.
Pogo Possum, no. 2 April–June 1950.
Pogo Possum, no. 5. May–July 1951.
Pogo Possum, no. 6 July–September 1951.
Superman's Girlfriend Lois Lane, no. 7, February 1959.
Superman's Girlfriend Lois Lane, no. 17. May 1960.
Walt Disney's Mickey Mouse, no. 343, August–September 1951.
Walt Disney's Uncle Scrooge, no. 22. June–August 1958.

Secondary Literature

Baker, Esther. "Contribution of Comics to Education." *Illinois Libraries*, vol. 34, 1952, pp. 399–401.
Bechtel, Louise Seaman. "Talk for Katonah Library, October 16, 1944. Adventures in a Library." Unpublished manuscript. Baldwin Libraries, University of Florida.
Cowsill, Alan et al. *DC Comics Year by Year: A Visual Chronicle*. DK, 2010.
Ellis, Allen and Doug Highsmith. "About Face: Comic Books in Library Literature." *Serials Review*, vol. 26, no. 2, 2000, pp. 21–43.
Frank, Josette. "What's in the Comics?" *The Journal of Educational Sociology*, vol. 18, no. 4, December 1944, pp. 214–222.
   Your Child's Reading Today. Doubleday, Inc., 1954.
Horner, Emily C. *Librarians' Attitudes and Perspectives Regarding Graphic Novels*. Unpublished master's thesis, University of North Carolina at Chapel Hill, 2004.
Kunitz, Stanley J. "The Comic Menace." *Wilson Library Bulletin*, vol. 15, June 1941, pp. 846–847.
Lundin, Anne. *Constructing the Canon of Children's Literature: Beyond Library Walls and Ivory Towers*. Routledge, 2004.
Nyberg, Amy Kiste. "Poisoning Children's Culture: Comics and Their Critics." *Scorned Literature: Essays on the History and Criticism of Popular Mass-*

Produced Fiction in America, edited by Lydia Cushman Schurman and Deidre Johnson. Greenwood Press, 2002, pp. 167–186.

Seal of Approval: The History of the Comics Code. University Press of Mississippi, 1998.

Paul Terry's Mighty Mouse Comics. No. 40, April 1953.

Tarbox, Gwen Athene. *Children's and Young Adult Comics.* Bloomsbury Academic, 2020.

Tilley, Carol L. Of Nightingales and Supermen: How Youth Services Librarians Responded to Comics between the Years of 1938 and 1955. Unpublished doctoral thesis, University of Indiana, 2007.

"Seducing the Innocent: Fredric Wertham and the Falsifications That Helped Condemn Comics." *Information & Culture*, vol. 47, no. 4, 2012, pp. 383–413.

"'Superman Says, 'Read!'" National Comics and Reading Promotion." *Children's Literature in Education*, vol. 44, no. 3, 2013, pp. 251–263.

Tilley, Carol and Sara Bahnmaier. "The Secret Life of Comics: Socializing and Seriality." *The Serials Librarian*, vol. 74, 2018, pp. 54–64.

Zorbaugh, Harvey. Editorial. *The Journal of Educational Sociology*, vol. 18, no. 4, Dec. 1944, pp. 193–194.

CHAPTER 17

"Educationally Occupied"
Learning with Comics

Susan Kirtley

I have found the effect of comic books to be first of all anti-educational. They interfere with education in the larger sense. For a child, education is not merely a question of learning, but is a part of mental health. They do not "learn" only in school; they learn also during play, from entertainment and in social life with adults and with other children. To take large chunks of time out of a child's lifetime during which he is not positively, that is, educationally, occupied–means to interfere with his healthful mental growth.

Fredric Wertham, *Seduction of the Innocent*, 89

While some critics, like the infamous Fredric Wertham in the 1950s,[1] decried comics as anti-educational dross that corrupted youth and robbed them of the opportunity to engage in enriching learning opportunities, comics have experienced something of a renaissance in classrooms over the past few years. In fact, a closer examination of comics history reveals that despite any bad publicity, comics have actually enjoyed a rather long tradition as educational tools, from Will Eisner's work with *PS Magazine* to help the military train and inform soldiers, to *Martin Luther King and The Montgomery Story*'s treatise on nonviolent protesting, to Art Spiegelman's graphic memoir *Maus* providing important insight into one survivor's experience of the Holocaust. In his book, *Graphic Encounters: Comics as Sponsors of Multimodal Literacy*, Dale Jacobs explains:

> Since their inception in the early 1930s, comics have been one of the central kinds of texts in the literate lives of both children and adults. . .comics have

---

[1] While Wertham is most known for his stance on comics as presented in *Seduction of the Innocent*, scholars point out that over the course of his career, Wertham came to a more nuanced perspective on the form as presented in his book *The World of Fanzines: A Special Form of Communication* (Carbondale: Southern Illinois University Press, 1973). Bart Beaty notes that "the book bore little resemblance to his other works except that it built on earlier statements that violence represented the antithesis of communication" (189) and "although he was unwilling to recant his earlier position on comic books" (190) Wertham "regarded fanzines as a positive counterforce to the mass media" (190).

346

been used by for-profit companies, creators, critics, not-for-profit educational groups, churches, schools, parents' groups, and libraries to sponsor particular kinds of multimodal and alphabetic based literacies. (210)

Building on that lengthy tradition, comics are finding even broader representation and roles in educational settings today, and these innovations are being explored in various, overlapping scholarly communities, including comics studies, pedagogical theory, and even in more mainstream venues. In our book *With Great Power Comes Great Pedagogy: Teaching, Learning, and Comic Books*, my colleagues Peter Carlson, Antero Garcia, and I noted that currently, as more educators are embracing comics in their classrooms, scholars are taking notice, articulating and sharing the newest developments in comics pedagogy. Presently, the majority of scholarship focusing on comics in education centers around the following themes: teaching with comics, teaching about comics, and teaching through creating and producing comics as a way of processing and communicating information (*With Great Power* 12). This chapter will explore these interrelated approaches in turn, examining the ways in which comics can be used in various learning contexts, demonstrating how educators, academics, and creators can work together to understand how comics might be used to encourage visual literacy and multimodal thinking for students.

In an increasingly visual and digital world, more and more educators stress the importance of approaching curriculum development from a multimodal perspective, a mindset that acknowledges the rapidly changing modes for communication that students are being called to comprehend and, ultimately, use. But what, exactly, should educators understand about multimodality? According to *College Composition and Communication*:

Multimodality refers to the various resources – among them image, signs, document design, and graphics – that authors tap to create meaning in all kinds of texts. Multimodality reminds us of the richness of all texts, and of the many ways we create meaning. Interestingly, small children – mixing drawing, colors, letters, and layout – seem to compose multimodally almost "naturally." It may be that engaging in the same kind of "multimodal play" would benefit many composers: it is often through such play that we see alternative ways of seeing and of making meaning. (506)

In incorporating multimodality into our pedagogy, teachers can embrace the many ways that individuals think and process information – in image and text. And, significantly, Dale Jacobs contends that comics can act as key "sponsors" of this sort of multimodal literacy. Jacobs notes that "by examining comics as multimodal texts and reading comics as an exercise of

348   SUSAN KIRTLEY

multiliteracies or multimodal literacies, we can shed light not only on the literate practices that surround all multimodal texts and the ways in which engagement with such texts can and should affect our thinking about them" (9). However, before delving into the specifics of the ways comics can and should be used in classrooms, it is useful to briefly address the sometimes fraught history of comics in education which informs contemporary pedagogy.

A Checkered Past: A Historical Perspective on Comics in Education

Although comics have struggled with a bad reputation for many years, they were incredibly popular reading material in the 1940s, when, according to a study of the time by W. W. D. Sones, "95 per cent of children 8 to 14 years old, inclusive, and 65 per cent of the 15- to 18-year-olds read comic magazines" (233). Given their widespread popularity, it wasn't surprising that comics made their way into classrooms in the 1940s and scholars, eager to study this trend, followed. (For more on the mixed reception of comics in the 1940s, see Chapter 15.) In his piece "Comics in Education," award-winning comics artist and teacher Gene Yang notes of the past that "Educators lined up on both sides of the debate" with some touting comics as exceptional instructional texts and others denouncing their value. It wasn't long before the doubters found a profoundly influential voice in the form of Dr. Fredric Wertham, who, through his (now largely debunked[2]) research, his book *Seduction of the Innocent*, and his testimony before the Senate, inspired a swift and expansive backlash against comics in society and in schools, a reaction that ultimately resulted in the creation of the Comics Code Authority in 1954, the group established by publishers that censored and limited the content of mainstream comics. Yang reports, "America – and the American educational establishment – had gotten Wertham's message: comics were bad for children. Scholarship on the educational value of comics effectively stopped." While a few daring teachers openly brought comics into the classrooms over the intervening years (or at least only a few publicly admitted to doing so), it wasn't until Art Spiegelman's *Maus* received a Pulitzer in 1992 and heralded a new understanding of comics as "serious art" that "comics began gaining ground in the world of education" (Yang, "Comics in Education"). Since the publication of *Maus*, a flurry of comics on various issues and subjects,

---

[2] See the work of Carol Tilley and Amy Kiste Nyberg.

some serious and some not, have similarly found widespread acclaim, and, consequently, scholarship on comics has flourished over the past thirty years, as has the acceptance of comics in education, which has led, concomitantly, to a resurgent interest and discussion of comics in education. But why, after all this fuss, should we enter into the fray and teach with comics?

Teaching with Comics: Rationale and Context

In *Unflattening*, comics creator and scholar Nick Sousanis makes the point that "In relying on text as the primary means of formulating understanding, what stands outside its linear structure is dismissed. Labeled irrational – no more conceivable than the notion of upwards to a flatlander – the visual provides expression where words fail. What have we been missing? And what can be made visible when we work in a form that is not only *about*, but is also the thing itself?" (59). Indeed, what has been missing when school curriculums ignore or denigrate the visual in favor of a narrow understanding of text-based literacy? Even in their earliest years, students bring a keen but often unexamined knowledge of visual rhetoric with them into classrooms. And though they may be unsure of the culture and language of the academy, they have experienced many years of reading the signs and symbols of our image-based culture. The interpretation of visual culture belongs not only to scholars; again, students also come to the academy with advanced skills in translating the signs, symbols, and images that bombard them every day. Instructors have the ability to draw on this expertise, incorporating the exploration of image and text into our own teaching through comic art, helping students construct powerful arguments through text and image.

Furthermore, I would argue that to be fully literate in today's society, one must be able to read the symbols that surround us. This is not always a comfortable idea for those of us trained to focus primarily on text, yet as I look to the future I want my students to be not only consumers, but also producers of visual, image-based communication. Examining the relationship between the words and pictures of comic art allows students to draw on their "insider" knowledge as they negotiate the challenges of succeeding in school. According to Gail Hawisher and her colleagues, "people often acquire and develop the literacies they need in places other than the classroom where, often, instructors tend to limit literacy activities to the narrow bandwidth of conventional written English" (670). Using comics in classrooms allows students to employ (and improve) their own skills with visual literacy.

Educators are quick to point out that comics can encourage critical thinking, engage multiple intelligences, enhance visual and multimodal literacy, and, quite frankly, inspire passionate readers with great storytelling. In her article "Multigenre, Multiple Intelligences, and Transcendentalism," Colleen Ruggieri argues that incorporating comic art into the curriculum for her 11th grade American Literature class transformed her students' experience of the texts she assigned, claiming that "By reading comic books, my students were able to...interpret social commentaries, make connections with works they'd studied in class" promoting further considerations of language, self and society (61). Clearly, in Ruggieri's experience, reading comic art encouraged the students to read and respond in powerful ways.

Based on his own work in the classroom, Gene Yang argues for several of what he terms the "strengths of comics in education," including that comic art is "motivating," "visual," "permanent," "intermediary," and "popular," and that these advantages can be "harnessed in practically any subject and at practically any grade levels." Yang believes that graphic narratives encourage reluctant readers, help provide "an intimate, emotional connection" with texts, and invite students to slow down their reading process. He continues, explaining that comic art can also "serve as an intermediate step to difficult disciplines and concepts" while drawing on themes, characters, and media that are enormously popular. In *The Narratology of Comic Art*, Kai Mikkonen illustrated this concept as he reflected on the importance of comics in his own literacy development, remembering: "I first learned to read by reading comics with my father when I was around 5 or 6 years old. For all I know, my father never read comics by himself, except perhaps when browsing comic strips in his morning newspaper, but he wanted to teach me how to read. That's why we ended up reading my comic books" (2). For Mikkonen, learning to read with his father and comic art are inextricably linked. Sean Howe also reflected on the allure of comics for engaging with readers, arguing:

> A comic book's inclusion of visual information is probably the major reason for its intellectual ghettoization, the idea being that words are harder earned than pictures. Conversely, images can invite the reader to reflect, to slow down, in a way that pure text never will. There is, intrinsically, a greater sensory relation to the characters and setting, an almost guaranteed involvement. Nothing tops comic books for the mysterious one-two punch of active engagement and submissive escape. When you get right down to it, *that's* the common thread of an art form. (*Give Our Regards to the Atom Smashers*, x).

Even though graphic narratives are often associated with an easier form of reading and associated with children's picture books, comic art is, in fact, incredibly sophisticated, as it invites the reader into the meaning-making process, slowing down and filling in the gaps and gutters and making sense of multiple tracks of information, including the images, the narrative text, and the intradiegetic details contained in each panel.

For those who are looking to begin incorporating comics into K-12 classes immediately, there are some fantastic and practical guidebooks that provide lesson plans and resources, such as *Using Graphic Novels in the Classroom Grade 4–8* (Teacher Created Resources, 2010) by Melissa Hart and *Teaching Graphic Novels: Practical Strategies for the Secondary ELA Classroom* by Katie Moninall (Maupin House, 2013).[3] For those teaching in colleges and universities, *The Power of Comics: History, Form, and Culture*, edited by Randy Duncan and Matthew J. Smith (Bloomsbury, 2014), would be an excellent textbook in a comics history course, while *A Comics Studies Reader*, edited by Jeet Heer and Kent Worcester (UPM, 2009) collects key thinking from prominent scholars. *Teaching the Graphic Novel*, edited by Stephen E. Tabachnick (MLA, 2009) would work well for university educators looking to bring comics into their classrooms across the disciplines and provides information on understanding comics before digging into different types of courses, important creators, and various themes and issues. And most anyone teaching comics at any level would want to take a look at Scott McCloud's *Understanding Comics* (HarperCollins, 1994), a foundational text that has been critiqued and built upon, but remains a touchstone for scholars. University classrooms would also undoubtedly want to examine additional considerations of the unique affordances of the comic form in works such as *The System of Comics* (University Press of Mississippi, 2007) by Thierry Groensteen, *Comics and Language* (University Press of Mississippi, 2013) by Hannag Miodrag, and *Narrative Structure in Comics: Making Sense of Fragments* (RIT Press, 2013) by Barbara Postema. While these texts provide very useful introductions and ideas for educators looking for hands-on guidance, it is also beneficial to consider in more detail how instructors can use comics in diverse ways, such as taking advantage of comics as a window into other disciplines and subjects.

---

[3] Additional resources for K-12 instructors include: *The Graphic Novel Classroom: POWerful Teaching and Learning with Images* by Maureen Bakis (Thousand Oaks, 2014), and *Teaching Graphic Novels: Building Literacy and Comprehension* (Prufrock Press, 2014) by Ryan J. Novak.

Teaching With *Comics*

Comics have been cropping up on classroom reading lists alongside more traditional text-based narratives with increasing frequency in recent years. However, in *The Greatest Comic Book of All Time*, Bart Beaty and Benjamin Woo assert that "In reality, only an extremely small smattering" of comic art "is chosen for academic study" (5). And, just as some comic books appear more often in academic scholarship, it would also appear that there are several texts that appear more frequently in classrooms, including *Maus* by Art Spiegelman, *Persepolis* by Marjane Satrapi, and the *March* trilogy by John Lewis, Andrew Aydin, and Nate Powell.

Thus, it would appear that, as these particular texts might suggest, the most common role of comics in classrooms is alongside more traditional, text-based works as another way of understanding and exploring other subjects, such as reading *Maus* in a history class or *March* in a social studies course. This approach offers another window, another lens or way of seeing the subject matter, and one that might inspire more enthusiasm from students. Educators are able to invoke comic art's popularity and even novelty when presented alongside more traditional text-based narratives to encourage excitement for subjects such as history, English, psychology, art, gender studies, studies of race and ethnicity, and disability studies, just to name a few.

Comic art is, by nature, interdisciplinary, and as a hybrid form that blends text and image, its study necessarily draws from different perspectives. Thus, this boundary crossing is particularly well-suited to teaching across departments and subject matters. In fact, comics pedagogy draws from various perspectives and diverse ways of seeing, resisting the compartmentalization of knowledge, and even the very structure of educational institutions. Some scholars have indicated that the interdisciplinary nature of the field can create challenges, as Charles Hatfield does in his piece on "Indiscipline: Or the Condition of Comics Studies," in which he argues that "comics studies has no disciplinary status in the traditional sense, that is, no clear, cohesive, and self-contained disciplinary identity." However, the fact of this essential interdisciplinary approach also offers opportunities for, as Alison Friedow et al. explain, "interdisciplinary pedagogy as a practice...can enhance disciplinary knowledge, rather than [being] forged in opposition to it." Therefore, rather than acting against a singular tradition or discipline, comics can enrich the understanding of various fields and subjects. For example, an American history class might read a nonfiction comic on civil rights like *Martin Luther King and the*

Montgomery Story or a science class could read *Climate Changed: A Personal Journey through the Science*. Reading these comics alongside traditional, text-based narratives engages multiple intelligences and has the potential to excite students by allowing them additional ways to see and understand the concepts under discussion.

As educators recognize their value, including graphic narratives alongside other texts in a number of subjects and at a variety of grades and levels is becoming more and more common in classrooms, and subsequently, more accepted in school settings. Graphic narratives enter into the educational conversation and shine like the facets of a prism, dividing the various subjects and topics in new ways while illuminating multiple aspects for closer examination. Comic art encourages reader participation and engagement across the curriculum.

Teaching About *Comics*

Even though the academy has frequently dismissed comics along with other forms of popular culture, recent developments suggest that comics studies has finally arrived as a distinct field of study welcomed in academic circles. University presses regularly publish books devoted to comics and peer-reviewed academic journals focusing on comics and graphic narratives, such as *Inks: The Journal of the Comics Studies Society* and *ImageText*, are thriving. The Modern Language Association maintains a Forum for Comics and Graphic Narratives, and the International Comic Arts Forum and Comics Studies Society represent just two of the rising number of scholarly societies devoted to comics scholarship. And this scholarly interest in comics is appearing in classrooms as well, as courses on comics are now being offered on many college campuses, with some universities boasting comics studies programs and degrees.[4]

Comics studies programs help provide a stable foundation for comics scholars, opportunities for students, and important connections with the comics community. As comics are interdisciplinary, so are the class offerings, with some classes focusing on the scholarly study of graphic narratives, such as "The History of Comics" and "Comics Theory." Other courses focus more narrowly on subjects such as "Editorial Cartoons" or "Autobiographical Comics." World language departments might offer

---

[4] Portland State University, San Francisco State University, the University of Oregon, the Center for Cartoon Studies in Vermont, the University of Calgary, and the University of East Anglia all offer degree programs in comics, and even more schools are offering individual courses on comics.

classes on "Manga" or "Franco-Belgian Comics," and a sociology department could present a course on "Comics and the City," while a "Representations of Mental Illness in Comics" could be a popular course in a Psychology department. Still other classes take a more practical, hands-on approach to comics creation, with courses on "Comics Writing," "Comics Editing," or "Drawing Comics." The options are ever-evolving and growing.

While the development of these comics programs is encouraging and provides visibility and constancy for comics scholarship, there are, of course, challenges for fledgling comics studies programs. The interdisciplinary nature of comics, as previously indicated, also makes it difficult to find a home within heavily departmentalized educational institutions. In the attempt to legitimize comics studies within "the ivory tower," it may be necessary to forge a new path and a new place in the university. Some comics programs develop inside English departments, while others take up residence in art or film, but as an interdisciplinary effort, comics works against the traditional organization of the university and its "silos" of learning. Gregory Steirer maintains, "without the ability to position itself in relation to existing disciplinary formations, comics studies thus risks 'ghettoizing' itself within the academy" (263). The story of comics *programs* offering degrees as part of programs within colleges and universities, as opposed to a few comics-related courses sprinkled throughout the curriculum, is still very much being written. Regardless, most courses focusing primarily on comics currently reside at community colleges and four-year colleges and universities, rather than in the K-12 curriculum. For the majority of students and educators, comic art is primarily embedded within other subject areas, rather than the focus of the study itself.

Teaching Through *Comics Creation*

One of the most exciting developments in comics pedagogy is an emphasis on making comics, both as a way of presenting information on a variety of subjects and as a method of processing information and thinking through ideas. In more and more classes across various disciplines, students are being asked to create their own comics. This trend is inspiring exciting work by teachers and students, but also suffers a bit from language challenges, as the vocabulary surrounding comics creation in classrooms is very much in development. For example, in his book, *The Sketchnote Handbook*, Mike Rohde proposes using "sketchnotes," notes that use both text and image, and his term has taken off with various authors and educators, including Nichole Carter. Emily Mills prefers to focus on "visual notetaking," while in his book *Cartooning: Philosophy and Practice*, renowned comics creator Ivan Brunetti prefers the more traditional term "cartooning." For her part, Lynda Barry references "finding the image" in her many heuristic workbooks focusing on comics creation, including, *Picture This, What It Is, Syllabus*, and *Making Comics*. Sunni Brown calls her process "doodling" or "making spontaneous marks (with your mind and body) to help yourself think" (*The Doodle Revolution* 11).

Although Sunni Brown's *The Doodle Revolution* doesn't reference comics exactly and the author finds the word "drawing" "too loaded" (8), the book does argue strongly for the impact of pairing text and image for thinking and communicating in a variety of settings. Brown argues that, as a culture, "We aren't being taught about visual language...We have false beliefs about visual language...There is significant impact from our ignorance of visual language...Visual language is native to everyone...And we can't afford not to learn it" (xvii). Brown maintains that doodling helps us think, noting that "what's really happening is that a doodler is engaging in deep and necessary information processing" (11). The process offers three primary gifts: "power," "performance," and "pleasure" (17) and can be refined into a more focused "infodoodle" that both inspires thinking and documents the results for individuals as well as larger groups in spaces such as workplaces or educational settings (see Figure 17.1).

The book and philosophy have been well-received, particularly in professional settings, as evidenced by Brown's popularity as a commentator on CNN, her TED talk, and her work leading workshops for various corporations, but a search of peer-reviewed, academic scholarship on education suggests that the term "doodling," at least as envisaged by Brown, hasn't yet taken off as recognized vocabulary in many classrooms, or at least in scholarly discussions of comics pedagogy.

The term "sketchnoting," as outlined by Mike Rohde, has gained more traction in educational circles, and Rohde notes that the practice "engages your whole mind" (27). Rohde explains, "Dual Coding Theory, proposed in the 1970s by Allan Paivo, suggests that the brain processes information using two primary channels: verbal and visual" (27, see Figure 17.2.)

Extrapolating on the dual coding theory, Rohde posits that sketchnoting "activates verbal and visual modes to capture concepts. Your whole brain is absorbed in hearing, synthesizing, and seizing ideas...When your brain codes verbal and visual concepts together, it's also building a visual map of what you are hearing, seeing, and thinking" (28–29). Rohde's focus on

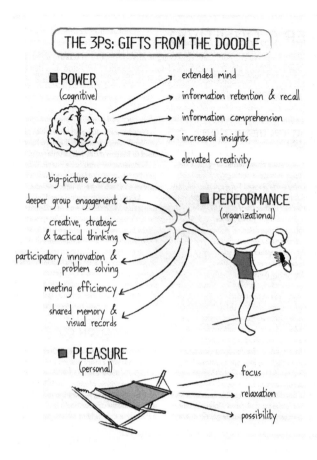

Figure 17.1. Sunni Brown, *The Doodle Revolution*, Penguin, 2015, p. 17. Used with permission from @SunniBrown.com

sketchnoting as a superior form of comprehension to more traditional methods inspired a number of scholarly pieces, including "A Multimodal Approach to Visual Thinking: The Scientific Sketchnote" (2019) by Fernández-Fontecha et al., "From Sketchnotes to Think-Alouds: Addressing the Challenges of the Social Studies Text" (2017) by Jennifer Altieri, "Sketchnoting: An Analog Skill in a Digital Age" (2013) by Robert Dimeo, and, especially, the comprehensive book *Sketchnoting in the Classroom: A Practical Guide to Deepen Student Learning* (2019) by Nichole Carter.

"Educationally Occupied": Learning with Comics   357

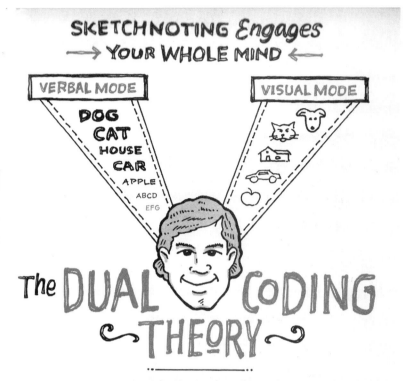

Figure 17.2. Mike Rohde, *The Sketchnote Handbook*. Peachpit Press, 2012, p. 27.

Carter presents a thorough rationale as well as incredibly detailed instructions for incorporating sketchnoting into classes across disciplines and age ranges. Carter explains that, as instructors, "Brains also love visuals, and they need connections for what they learn. The more connections, the deeper the learning. If we deliver information in only one specific way, we are neglecting other brain functions" (25); thus, educators are doing a disservice to our students if we neglect the visual. Furthermore, she urges instructors to take an active role in incorporating sketchnoting into classrooms: "Teachers need to model the process of sketchnoting with their students to create a culture of acceptance; brain-based research shows that the more we offer these types of immersive multimodal learning options for students, the higher the retention rate and the more brain connections will be made" (34). Sketchnoting must become an ordinary part of the classroom experience, not an anomaly but a regular occurrence. Ultimately, Carter advocates for incorporating sketchnotes both as a boon to critical thinking as well as a multimodal method of communication, pointing out that students will be able to: "synthesize information, sometimes from multiple sources, and then communicate their knowledge in a creative way in which they choose their platform" (36–37).

Emily Mills shares Carter's enthusiasm for the potential of incorporating visual and verbal modes in fostering critical thinking, but, once again, she chooses slightly different terminology in her book *The Art of Visual Notetaking: An Interactive Guide to Visual Communication and Sketchnoting*, in which she, too, outlines her process for visual notetaking in a heuristic workbook. However, Mills argues forcefully that "visual notes are not doodles" (11) contesting that her approach is anything but "absentminded" (11), but rather "one of the best ways to learn" (13, see Figure 17.3). The book, designed like a workshop, has many lessons that could usefully be adapted and taught to students.

Although Ivan Brunetti focuses his book *Cartooning: Philosophy and Practice* on creating cartoons as a discipline in and of itself, rather than as a teaching tool, his ideas and exercises can usefully be adapted into a variety of classrooms ranging in age and subject. Brunetti argues that cartooning is "a translation of how we experience, structure, and remember the world" (8) and his book provides a detailed breakdown of his own cartooning class, including the required materials, rules and regulations, and weekly exercises. This approach could be used as a textbook or template for a "Cartooning" or "Making Comics" class, but again, numerous activities could also be included as meaning-making and thinking exercises in other classrooms. For instance, in the section entitled "Week 2," Brunetti focuses on "Single-Panel" cartoons, using his adaptation of *The Catcher in the Rye* as an example. Brunetti carefully explicates his own process of adapting the novel into a single-panel cartoon, showing the progression of his thinking. This activity would certainly prove engaging for a literature

Figure 17.3. Emily Mills, *The Art of Visual Notetaking: An Interactive Guide to Visual Communication and Sketchnoting*, Quarto Publishing Group, 2019, p. 11.

class, as students of any age could be invited to distill the essence of the book into a single scene, thus challenging them to consider the most important ideas of the text and how they might communicate them.

Lynda Barry credits Ivan Brunetti with inspiring her recent work, which also focuses on comics creation, although her approach is much more philosophical in nature, asking readers to reflect on the ways in which drawing and writing are connected, both to one another and to the thinking process. Barry recorded her teaching and learning journey in a series of heuristic workbooks, including *What It Is* (2008), *Picture This* (2010), *Syllabus* (2014), and *Making Comics* (2019), which document her work as an "Associate Professor of Interdisciplinary Creativity" at the University of Wisconsin. In *Making Comics*, Barry remarks: "I wondered if I could teach what I knew about the power of comics as a way of seeing and being in the world and transmitting our experience of it...We draw before we are taught. We also sing, dance, build things, act, and make up stories long before we are given any deliberate instruction beyond exposure to the people around us doing things" (14–15). In her series of books, Barry offers many exercises that, like Brunetti, stress the importance of creating comics as meaning-making activities that can be adapted in a wide range of classroom settings.

One of the most delightful and intellectual ruminations on comics in education comes in the book *Unflattening* by Nick Sousanis. The book, published in 2015 by Harvard University Press, was originally developed as Sousanis's dissertation, a lushly illustrated meditation on the importance of incorporating text *and* image into pedagogy, the form itself carrying the argument. Sousanis notes the power of drawing as a way of thinking, explaining:

> Drawing, as Masaki Suwa and Barbara Tversky suggest, is a means of orchestrating a conversation with yourself. Putting thoughts down allows us to step outside ourselves and tap into our visual system and our ability to see in relation. We thus extend our thinking – distributing it between conception and perception – engaging both simultaneously. We draw not to transcribe ideas from our heads but to generate them in search of greater understanding. (79)

Furthermore, Sousanis argues that pairing drawing with text results in even greater insights: "Perhaps, in comics, this amphibious language of juxtapositions and fragments – we have such a form. A means to capture and convey our thoughts, in all their tangled complexity, and a vehicle well-suited for explorations to come" (67). *Unflattening* does not offer activities or ideas for classroom use, although Sousanis has written on this elsewhere,[5] but instead provides a thoughtful reflection on the ways in which traditional education practices have limited our understanding, and that of our students, and how incorporating comics represents more than simply bringing in a fun activity. Inviting students to read and think and compose comics signifies a new, more inclusive, more expansive pedagogy, encouraging students to engage with both visual and verbal modes.

Conclusion

Comic art, with its long and often unacknowledged history in education, is enjoying renewed popularity and respect in schools. However, it is important to recognize that schools are often dominated by high-stakes testing and teachers are being forced to do more with ever-dwindling resources. And while this unfortunate curricular context seems likely to continue for the foreseeable future, I would argue that comics can offer students and educators innovative ways of questioning, communicating, and thinking through ideas, and allows for exploration outside of the strictures of

[5] See Sousanis's website www.spinweaveandcut.com.

competency exams. Comic art invites us to imagine not just the current reality but what *is possible*, and provides opportunities for educators to excite our students about learning across the disciplines. Graphic narratives possess a rich history and practice worthy of study as a field in and of itself. And, of course, comics can act as new ways of thinking and communicating, allowing students to process and present knowledge in new ways, enhancing visual literacy and multiple modes and intelligences. Contrary to any of Dr. Wertham's outdated admonitions, comic art can, and should, "educationally occupy" spaces in our classrooms. Educators can find inspiration from colleagues, students, and creators and consider how we might use comics to invite innovative methods for reflecting, exploring, and connecting.

WORKS CITED

Comics

Barry, Lynda. *Making Comics*. Drawn & Quarterly, 2019.
    Picture This: The Near-Sighted Monkey Book. Drawn & Quarterly, 2010.
    Syllabus. Drawn & Quarterly, 2014.
    What It Is. Drawn & Quarterly, 2008.
Lewis, John, Aydin, Andrew and Nate Powell. *March Trilogy*. Top Shelf, 2016.
Satrapi, Marjane. *Persepolis I & II*. Random House, 2008.
Sousanis, Nick. *Unflattening*. Harvard University Press, 2015.
Spiegelman, Art. *The Complete Maus*. Pantheon, 1996.
Squarzoni, Phillipe. *Climate Changed: A Personal Journey through the Science*. Abrams, 2014.

Secondary Sources

Altieri, Jennifer L. "From Sketchnotes to Think-Alouds: Addressing the Challenges of Social Studies Text." *Social Studies and the Young Learner*, vol. 30, no. 1, 2017, pp. 8–12.
Bakis, Maureen. *The Graphic Novel Classroom: POWerful Teaching and Learning with Images*. Thousand Corwin, 2014.
Beaty, Bart. *Fredric Wertham and the Critique of Mass Culture : A Re-Examination of the Critic Whose Congressional Testimony Sparked the Comics Code*. University Press of Mississippi, 2005.
Beaty, Bart and Benjamin Woo. *The Greatest Comic Book of All Time: Symbolic Capital and the Field of American Comic Books*. Palgrave Macmillan, 2016.
Bennett, Marek. "Multiple Intelligences & Comics." www.nd.gov/cte/crn/elementary/docs/multiple_intelligences_comic.pdf. Accessed 10 August 2018.
Brown, Sunni. *The Doodle Revolution*. Penguin, 2015.
Brunetti, Ivan. *Cartooning: Philosophy and Practice*. Yale University Press, 2011.

Carter, Nichole. *Sketchnoting in the Classroom : A Practical Guide to Deepen Student Learning*. ISTE, 2019.

College Composition and Communication, vol. 65, no. 3, February 2014.

Dimeo, Robert. "Sketchnoting: An Analog Skill in a Digital Age." *Computers & Society*, vol. 46, no. 3, 2013, pp. 9–16.

Duncan, Randy and Matthew J. Smith, eds. *The Power of Comics: History, Form, and Culture*. Bloomsbury, 2014.

Fernández-Fontecha, Almudena, O'Halloran, Kay L., Tan, Sabine and Peter Wignell. "A Multimodal Approach to Visual Thinking: The Scientific Sketchnote." *Visual Communication*, vol. 18, no. 1, 2019, pp. 5–29.

Friedow, Alison, Blankenship, Erin E., Green, Jennifer L. and Walter W. Stroup. "Learning Interdisciplinary Pedagogies." *Pedagogy: Critical Approaches to Teaching Literature, Language, Composition, and Culture*, vol. 12, no. 3, 2012, pp. 405–424.

Hatfield, Charles. "Indiscipline, or, The Condition of Comics Studies." *Transatlantica* no. 1, 2010. http://transatlantica.revues.org/4933

Hawisher, Gail, & Cynthia Selfe with Brittney Moraski and Melissa Pearson. "Becoming Literate in the Information Age: Cultural Ecologies and the Literacies of Technology." *College Composition and Communication*, vol. 55, no. 4, 2004, pp. 642–692.

Heer, Jeet and Kent Worcester, eds. *Arguing Comics: Literary Masters on a Popular Medium*. University Press of Mississippi, 2004.

eds. *A Comics Studies Reader*. University Press of Mississippi, 2009.

Howe, Sean. *Give Our Regards to the Atom Smashers*. Pantheon, 2004.

Jacobs, Dale. *Graphic Encounters: Comics as Sponsors of Multimodal Literacy*. Bloomsbury Academic, 2013.

Kirtley, Susan, Antero Garcia and Peter Carlson, eds. *With Great Power Comes Great Pedagogy: Teaching, Learning, and Comic Books*. University Press of Mississippi, 2020.

Mikkonen, Kai. *The Narratology of Comic Art*. Routledge, 2019.

Mills, Emily. *The Art of Visual Notetaking: An Interactive Guide to Visual Communication and Sketchnoting*. Quarto Publishing Group, 2019.

Moninall, Katie. *Teaching Graphic Novels: Practical Strategies for the Secondary ELA Classroom*. Maupin House, 2013.

Moulton Marston, William. *American Scholar: The Journal of Phi Beta Kappa*. Winter, 1943.

The New London Group. "A Pedagogy of Multiliteracies: Designing Social Futures." *Harvard Educational Review*, vol. 66, no. 1, 1996, pp. 60–93.

Novak, Ryan. *Teaching Graphic Novels: Building Literacy and Comprehension*. Prufrock Press, 2014.

Nyberg, Amy Kiste. *Seal of Approval: The History of the Comics Code*. University Press of Mississippi, 1998.

Resnick, Benton and Hassler, Alfred (writers) Barry, Sy (artist). "Martin Luther King and the Montgomery Story." *Social Welfare History Image Portal*. https://images.socialwelfare.library.v

Rohde, Mike. *The Sketchnote Handbook*. Peachpit Press, 2012.

Ruggieri, Colleen. "Multigenre, Multiple Intelligences, and Transcendentalism." *English Journal*, vol. 92, no. 2, 2002, pp. 60–68.

Sones, W. W. D. "The Comics and Instructional Method." *The Journal of Educational Sociology*, vol. 18, no. 4, December 1944, pp. 232–240.

Tabachnick, Stephen, ed. *Teaching the Graphic Novel*. MLA, 2009.

Tilley, Carol. "Seducing the Innocent: Fredric Wertham and the Falsifications that Helped Condemn Comics." *Information & Culture: A Journal of History*, vol. 47, no. 4, 2012, pp. 383–413.

Troutman, Philip. "Interdisciplinary Teaching: Comics Studies and Research Writing Pedagogy." *Graphic Novels and Comics in the Classroom: Essays on the Educational Power of Sequential Art*, edited by Carrye Kay Syma and Robert G. Weiner. Macfarland and Co., 2013, pp. 120–132.

Wertham, Fredric. *Seduction of the Innocent*. Rinehart, 1954.

The World of Fanzines: A Special Form of Communication. Southern Illinois University Press, 1973.

Yang, Gene. "Comics in Education." www.geneyang.com/comicsedu/history.html.

Further Reading

While the *Companion* strives to give a comprehensive account of the major topics and trajectories in comics scholarship, this further reading list reflects the rich scope and diversity of comics scholarship, expanding on aspects introduced in the volume and incorporating perspectives that could not be covered.[1]

Comics History

Baetens, Jan, Frey, Hugo, and Tabachnick, Stephen E., eds. *The Cambridge History of the Graphic Novel*. Cambridge University Press, 2018.

Barker, Martin. *A Haunt of Fears*. Pluto Press, 1984.

Beronä, David A. *Wordless Books: The Original Graphic Novels*. Abrams, 2008.

Gabilliet, Jean-Paul. *Of Comics and Men: A Cultural History of American Comic Books*. Translated by Bart Beaty and Nick Nguyen. University Press of Mississippi, 2010.

Gibson, Mel. *Remembered Reading: Memory, Comics and Post-War Constructions of British Girlhood*. Leuven University Press, 2015.

Gordon, Ian. *Comic Strips and Consumer Culture 1890–1945*. Smithsonian Institution Press, 1998.

Hajdu, David. *The Ten Cent Plague: The Great Comic Book Scare and How It Changed America*. Picador, 2008.

Kennedy, Martha. *Drawn to Purpose: American Women Illustrators and Cartoonists*. University Press of Mississippi, 2018.

Kirtley, Susan. *Typical Girls: The Rhetoric of Womanhood in Comic Strips*. Ohio State University Press, 2021.

Kunzle, David. *History of the Comic Strip, Volume 1, The Early Comic Strip: Narrative Strips and Picture Stories in the European Broadsheet from c. 1450 to 1825*. University of California Press, 1973.

History of the Comic Strip Volume 2, The Nineteenth Century. University of California Press, 1990.

---

[1] For a concise overview of comics criticism see Julia Round, Rikke P. Cortsen, and Maaheen Ahmed, *Comics and Graphic Novels* (Bloomsbury, 2022).

Father of the Comic Strip: Rodolphe Töpffer. University Press of Mississippi, 2007.

Rebirth of the English Comic Strip: A Kaleidoscope, 1847–1870. University Press of Mississippi, 2021.

Mainardi, Patricia. *Another World: Nineteenth-Century Illustrated Print Culture.* Yale University, 2017.

Mazur, Dan, and Danner, Alexander. *Comics: A Global History, 1968 to the Present.* Thames & Hudson, 2014.

Nadel, Dan. *Art Out of Time: Unknown Comics Visionaries, 1900–1969.* Abrams, 2006.

Art In Time: Unknown Comic Book Adventures, 1940–1980. Abrams, 2010.

It's Life as I See It. Black Cartoonists in Chicago, 1940–1980. New York Review Comics, 2021.

Nyberg, Amy Kiste. *Seal of Approval: The History of the Comics Code.* University Press of Mississippi, 1998.

Pustz, Matthew, ed. *Comic Books and American Cultural History: An Anthology.* Continuum, 2012.

Robbins, Trina. *Pretty in Ink: North American Women Artists, 1896–2013.* Fantagraphics, 2013.

Roeder, Katherine. *Wide Awake in Slumberland: Fantasy, Mass Culture, and Modernism in the Art of Winsor McCay.* University Press of Mississippi, 2014.

Round, Julia. *Gothic for Girls: Misty and British Comics.* University Press of Mississippi, 2019.

Sabin, Roger. *Comics, Comix and Graphic Novels: A History of Comic Art.* Phaidon Press, 1996.

Tisserand, Michael. *Krazy. George Herriman: A Life in Black and White.* HarperCollins, 2016

Wright, Bradford W. *Comic Book Nation: The Transformation of Youth Culture in America.* Johns Hopkins University Press, 2003.

Comics Theory and Criticism

Alaniz, José. *Death, Disability, and the Superhero: The Silver Age and Beyond.* University Press of Mississippi, 2014.

Aldama, Frederick Luis, ed. *Multicultural Comics: From Zap to Blue Beetle.* University of Texas Press, 2011.

Baetens, Jan and Hugo Frey. *The Graphic Novel: An Introduction.* Cambridge University Press, 2014.

Barker, Martin. *Comics: Ideology, Power and the Critics.* Manchester University Press, 1989.

Beaty, Bart. *Comics Versus Art.* University of Toronto Press, 2012.

Beaty, Bart and Woo, Benjamin. *The Greatest Comic Book of All Time.* Palgrave Pivot, 2016.

Bramlett, Frank, ed. *Linguistics and the Study of Comics.* Palgrave Macmillan, 2012.

Further Reading

Brienza, Casey. *Global Manga: The Cultural Production of 'Japanese' Comics without Japan*. Routledge, 2015.

Brown, Matthew J., Duncan, Randy and Matthew J. Smith, eds. *More Critical Approaches to Comics: Theories and Methods*. Routledge, 2019.

Bukatman, Scott. *The Poetics of Slumberland: Animated Spirits and the Animating Spirit*. University of California Press, 2012.

Chaney, Michael A., ed. *Graphic Subjects: Critical Essays on Autobiography and Graphic Novels*. University of Wisconsin Press, 2011.

Chute, Hillary L. *Disaster Drawn: Visual Witness, Comics and Documentary Form*. Harvard University Press, 2016.

Chute, Hillary L. and Patrick Jagoda, eds. *Comics & Media. A Critical Inquiry Special Issue*. University of Chicago Press, 2014.

Cohn, Neil. *The Visual Language of Comics: Introduction to the Structure and Cognition of Sequential Images*. Bloomsbury Academic, 2013.

Cremins, Brian and Brannon Costello, eds. *The Other 80s: Reframing Comics' Crucial Decade*. Louisiana State University Press, 2021.

Curtis, Neil. *Sovereignty and Superheroes*. Manchester University Press, 2016.

Denson, Shane, Meyer, Christina and Daniel Stein, eds. *Transnational Perspectives on Graphic Narratives: Comics at the Crossroads*. Bloomsbury.2013.

Dorfman, Ariel and Mattelart, Armand. *How to Read Donald Duck: Imperialist Ideology in the Disney Comic*. International General, 1976.

Dunst, Alexander, Laubrock, Jochen and Janina Wildfeuer, eds. *Empirical Comics Research: Digital, Multimodal and Cognitive Methods*. Routledge, 2018.

Eisner, Will. *Comics and Sequential Art*. Poorhouse Press, 1985.

Fawaz, Ramzi and Darieck Scott, eds. *Queer about Comics. An* American Literature *Special Issue*. Duke University Press, 2018.

García, Santiago. *On the Graphic Novel*. Translated by Bruce Campbell. University Press of Mississippi, 2015.

Gardner, Jared. *Projections: Comics and the History of Twenty-first-century Storytelling*. Stanford University Press, 2012.

Gavaler, Chris. *The Comics Form: The Art of Sequenced Images*. Bloomsbury, 2022.

Giddens, Thomas, ed. *Critical Directions in Comics Studies*. University Press of Mississippi, 2020.

Goggin, Joyce and Dan Hassler-Forest, eds. *The Rise and Reason of Comics and Graphic Literature: Essays on the Form*. McFarland, 2010.

Grennan, Simon. *A Theory of Narrative Drawing*. Palgrave Macmillan, 2017.
Thinking about Drawing. Bloomsbury, 2022.

Groensteen, Thierry. *The System of Comics*. Translated by Bart Beaty and Nick Nguyen. University Press of Mississippi, 2009.
Comics and Narration. Translated by Ann Miller. University Press of Mississippi, 2013.

Hague, Ian. *Comics and the Senses: A Multisensory Approach to Comics and Graphic Novels*. Routledge, 2014.

Hatfield, Charles. *Alternative Comics: An Emerging Literature*. University Press of Mississippi, 2005.

Further Reading

Hatfield, Charles, Heer, Jeet and Kent Worcester, eds. *The Superhero Reader*. University Press of Mississippi, 2013.

Hoberek, Andrew. *Considering Watchmen: Poetics, Property, Politics*. Rutgers University Press, 2015.

Howard, Sheena C. *Black Comics: Politics of Race and Representation*. Bloomsbury, 2013.

Heer, Jeet and Kent Worchester, eds. *Arguing Comics: Literary Masters on a Popular Medium*. University Press of Mississippi, 2004.

Karasik, Paul and Newgarden, Mark. *How to Read Nancy: the Elements of Comics in Three Easy Panels*. Fantagraphics Books, 2017.

Kashtan, Aaron. *Between Pen and Pixel: Comics, Materiality, and the Book of the Future*. Ohio State University Press, 2018.

Kukkonen, Karin. *Contemporary Comics Storytelling*. University of Nebraska Press, 2013.

Kwa, Shiamin. *Regarding Frames: Thinking with Comics in the Twenty-First Century*. RIT Press, 2020.

McCloud, Scott. *Understanding Comics: The Invisible Art*. Kitchen Sink Press, 1993.

   Reinventing Comics: How Imagination and Technology Are Revolutionizing an Art Form. Paradox Press, 2000.

Meyer, Christina. *Producing Mass Entertainment: The Serial Life of the Yellow Kid*. Ohio State University Press, 2019.

Mickwitz, Nina. *Documentary Comics: Graphic Truth-Telling in a Skeptical Age*. Palgrave Macmillan, 2016.

Mikkonen, Kai. *The Narratology of Comic Art*. Routledge, 2017.

Miller, Ann. *Reading Bande dessinée: Critical Approaches to French-Language Comic Strip*. Intellect, 2007.

Miller, Ann and Bart Beaty, eds. *The French Comics Theory Reader*. Leuven University Press, 2014.

Miodrag, Hannah. *Comics and Language: Reimagining Critical Discourse on the Form*. University Press of Mississippi, 2013.

Pizzino, Christopher. *Arresting Development: Comics at the Boundaries of Literature*. University of Texas Press, 2016.

Postema, Benoît. *Narrative Structure in Comics: Making Sense of Fragments*. RIT Press, 2013.

Sabin, Roger. "Framing Pre-1914 Comics." *Framing [in] Comics and Cartoons: Essays on Aesthetics, History and Mediality*, edited by Johannes C. P. Schmid and Christian A. Bachmann. Ch. A Bachmann Verlag, 2021, pp. 123–136.

Singer, Marc. *Breaking the Frames: Populism and Prestige in Comics Studies*. University of Texas Press, 2019.

Smith, Matthew J. and Randy Duncan, eds. *Critical Approaches to Comics: Theories and Methods*. Routledge, 2012.

Smolderen, Thierry. *The Origins of Comics: From William Hogarth to Winsor McCay*. 2000. Translated by Bart Beaty and Nick Nguyen. University Press of Mississippi, 2014.

Stein, Daniel. *Authorizing Superheroes: On the Evolution of a Popular Serial Genre.* Ohio State University Press, 2021.

Sousanis, Nick. *Unflattening.* Harvard University Press, 2015.

Wanzo, Rebecca. *The Content of Our Caricature: African American Comic Art and Political Belonging.* NYU Press, 2020.

Wertham, Fredric. *The World of Fanzines: A Special Form of Communication.* Southern Illinois University Press, 1973.

Whitted, Qiana J. *EC Comics: Race, Shock, and Social Protest.* Rutgers University Press, 2019.

Williams, Paul. *Dreaming the Graphic Novel: The Novelization of Comics.* Rutgers University Press, 2020.

Witek, Joseph. *Comic Books as History: The Narrative Art of Jack Jackson, Art Spiegelman and Harvey Pekar.* University Press of Mississippi, 1989.

Index

Titles of published works are indicated in *italics*, and refer to comics unless otherwise indicated. Page numbers in *italics* indicate figures. References to notes are indicated by "*n*" (e.g., "39*n*1" indicates note 1 on page 39).

"Seventy-five Years of the Comics" (exhibition), 316
"20,000 Years of the Comics" (exhibition), 314
25 Images de la passion d'un homme, 66
2, 113
2000 AD, 287, *289*, 297–299
   see also Judge Dredd

À la recherche du temps perdu [Remembrance of Things Past] (novel), 146, 149
"Aaargh!!! A Celebration of Comics" (exhibition), 316
Aardvark-Vanaheim, 229
Abe Sapien: Drums of the Dead, 181
abstract comics, 157, 244–252, 261
Abstract Comics: The Anthology: 1967–2009 (book), 245–246, 249–251, 252, *253*, 260, 261
Ace Drummond (film serial), 135, 136–137
Action Comics, 48, 54, 56, 172
A.D.: New Orleans After the Deluge, 78
Adlard, Charlie, 63
adolescents (teenagers), 77, 227, 293
   see also young adults
adult readers, 1, 4, 5, 66, 71
   continuity with childhood, 291, 296–297
   and graphic novels, 63, 69, 74, 76
   manga for, 84, 85, 90
   see also young adults
The Adventures of Batman (animated television series), 139
Adventures of Captain Marvel (film serial), 137
Adventures of Dr. Festus [Le Docteur Festus], 4
The Adventures of Jodelle, 69
The Adventures of Phoebe Zeit-Geist, 69
The Adventures of Superboy (animated television series), 138
The Adventures of Superman (radio series), 175
Adventures of Superman (television series), 138

agency, 94, 114–117, 115*n*13
   see also readers: engagement
Ahmed, Maaheen, 214
Akira, 85
Aldama, Frederick Luis, 205
Alice's Adventures in Wonderland (novel), 6
Allender, Nina, 225
Ally Sloper, 225
Ally Sloper: A Moral Lesson, 65
Ally Sloper's Half Holiday, 1
Altarriba, Antonio, 249
Alter Ego (fanzine), 176
alternative comics, 73
alternative publishers, 244
   see also independent publishers; small presses; *and names of individual publishers*
Altman, Rick, 166–167
Alyn, Kirk, 137
Amanat, Sana, 229
Amazing Man, 50
The Amazing Spider-Man, 55*n*1
American Born Chinese, 77, 78
"American Cartooning" (exhibition), 314
American Splendor, 75
Anand, Narasimhan, 32
animation, 134, 137
   in digital comics, 112, 115
anime, 10, 82
animistic medium, 185, 192, 195
Une année exemplaire, 179*n*2
Annihilation, 58
anthology comics, 48–50, 54, 288*n*3, 288
anti-comics campaigns, 67, 293–295
Appel, Rosaire, 246, *247*, 248, 252, 260
Aquaman, 138–139
Archie, 56, 182, 227
Archie Comics, 56, 59, 182

Index

Archies, the (musical group), 59
Archipelago, 113
architexts, 50, 58, 177, 178, 180–182
archives, 267–283
    rogue, 118, 277
    see also preservation of comics
Argon Zark, 107
The Arrival, 260
Arrow (television series), 139
The Art of Pho, 108
"The Art of Terry and the Pirates" (exhibition), 312
"The Art of the Comic Strip" (exhibition), 316
The Art of Visual Notetaking (book), 358, *359*
"Art Spiegelman's Co-Mix: A Retrospective" (exhibition), 323
As You Like It (play), 216
Asterix, 173
Astonishing X-Men, 140
Astro Boy, 87
Atkinson, Ruth, 227
audio in digital comics, 112, 115
augmented reality (AR) comics, 112, 113
Auster, Paul, 155
The Authority, 169
authors, 107–109, 117
autobiography (life writing), 186–187, 190, 198, 202
    see also graphic memoirs; graphic novels: memoirs/autobiographies
autoclasm, 180
autofiction, 147, 228, 229
autographics, 11
autonomy, creative, 73, 74, 179
The Avengers, 57, 138
Avengers, the, 46, 57, 126, 138, 140, 171
Avengers: Infinity War Prelude, 140
Aydin, Andrew, 141, 352
Azumanga Daioh, 89

B.P.R.D., 181
Bach, Johann Sebastian, 247–249
Badajos, Ed, 69
Baetens, Jan, 11–13, 63–64, 78, 179, 246, 252, 276
Baker, Matt, 67
Bakhtin, Mikhail, 39
Balak (Yves Bigerel), 112, 116
"Bande dessinée et figuration narrative" (exhibition), 145n4, 315
Bandette, 78
Barbarella, 69
Barefoot Gen [*Hadashi no Gen*], 84, 88–90
Barker, Martin, 209n6, 294, 296
Baronet Books, 71

Baroni, Raphaël, 246–249, 252
Barry, Lynda
    artistic strategies, 195, 198, 230–234, 238, 241, 242, 355, 359
    Cruddy, 231
    exhibitions featuring, 229
    The Good Times Are Killing Me, 231
    influence, 234
    Making Comics, 231, 355, 359
    One! Hundred! Demons!, 73, 229–231, 232, 234
    Picture This, 355, 359
    recognition, 78, 229
    Syllabus: Notes from an Accidental Professor, 78, 231, 234, 238, 242, 355, 359
    What It Is, 234, 238, 355, 359
Bartier, Pierre, 69
Batman, 50, 172
    as brand, 58
    comic books, 50, 57
    digital comics, 107
    film and television adaptations, 59, 137, 139, 169
    graphic novels, 58, 74, 75
Batman (film), 59, 139
Batman (film serial), 137, 169
Batman (television series), 139, 169
Batman: Digital Justice, 107
Batman: The Dark Knight Returns, 58, 74, 75
Baudry, Julien, 105–106
Bayou, 78, 221
The Beano, 297
Beaton, Kate, 107, 141
Beatty, Terry, 229
Beaty, Bart, 2, 346n1, 96–97, 352
Bechdel, Alison, 78, 198
    Fun Home, 1–2, 78, 171, 229, 241, 281
Beckett, Samuel, 157
Beetle Bailey, 317
Beineke, Colin, 234, 261
Bell, Gabrielle, 198
Berger, Karen, 229
Bergs, André, 113
Berthou, Benoît, 168
Berusaiyu no Bara [*The Rose of Versailles*], 86n6, 86, 91
Betty Boop (animated cartoon series), 137
"Beyond the Black Panther: Visions of Afrofuturism in American Comics" (exhibition), 322
"The Bible Illuminated: R. Crumb's Book of Genesis" (exhibition), 323, *323*
Big Apple Comix, 228
Big Baby: Curse of the Molemen, 76
Billy Ireland Cartoon Library and Museum, 317

Index 371

Binky Brown Meets the Holy Virgin Mary, 70, 195
Bishōjo Senshi Sērā Mūn [Sailor Moon], 84, 86, 90–91
Black Americans (African Americans), 205, 206n4, 214n13, 221, 318
Black Hole, 180
"Black Ink: African American Showcase" (exhibition), 318
Black Lightning (television series), 139
Black Panther, 140
Blackbeard, Bill, 129, 272–273, 273n5, 274, 275, 283
Blackberries, 214, 214n14, 216n18
Blackmark, 70, 71
blackness, 206, 209, 210, 215, 217, 219, 220–221, 221n20
Blake, William, 2, 199–202
Bloch, Robert, 181
Blondie, 131, 134, 137
Blondie (television series), 137
Bloodstar, 70
Blue Bolt, 50
The Boat, 112–113
Bobby, 335
Bochořáková-Dittrichová, Helena, 66
Bolland, Brian, 298
Bolter, Jay, 138
Bond, Shelly, 229
Boob McNutt, 131
The Book of Genesis Illustrated by R. Crumb, 146, 323, 323
bookstores, 57, 70, 74, 76, 77, 82, 300
Bowers Museum, 317
boys love genre [shōnen'ai, yaoi], 94
braiding (tressage), 13–14
Brake, Laurel, 37
Brandon-Croft, Barbara, 226
Breccia, Alberto, 145n4
Brenda Starr, Reporter, 227
Brick Bradford, 51
Bringing Up Father, 51, 125
Bringing Up Father (film), 135
Brinkley, Nelly, 225
The Brinkley Girls, 225, 227
Britain, 288–293, 291n6, 294, 295–298
British Comic Art Convention (Comicon), 292
Brown, Sunni, 355, 356
The Brownies, 125
Brunetti, Ivan, 355, 358–359
Buck Rogers, 46, 53
Buck Rogers (film serial), 135
Buck Rogers (television series), 137
Buddha, 82
The Building [L'immeuble], 113, 113
Building Stories, 78, 110

Bunty, 289, 296
Burden, Robert (Bob), 176, 229
Burns, Charles, 76, 179–180
Burt, Stephanie, 10
Burton, Tim, 59, 139
Bushmiller, Ernie, 10
Buster Brown, 46, 51, 132, 205
Butterfly, 226
Byrd, Ralph, 135

The Cage, 152
Campbell, Eddie, 283
Camus, Albert, 1
Caniff, Milton, 131, 282, 308, 311–314
CAPA-alpha (Amateur Press Association), 68n2
Cape, Jonathan, 66
Captain America, 137, 138, 139, 140
Captain America (film serial), 137
Captain America (television series), 139
Captain America: First Vengeance, 140
Captain Marvel, 137, 335, 336
Captain Marvel Adventures, 335, 336
caricature, 206, 206n2, 226
"Caricature Country", 205–206, 207
Carlin, John, 318, 320, 322
Carlson, Peter, 347
Carnage, USA, 182
Carter, Nichole, 355, 356–358
"Cartoon, No. 1. Substance and Shadow" (cartoon), 308–310, 309
Cartoon Art Museum, 317–318
"The Cartoon Show: The Collection of Jerome K. Muller" (exhibition), 316, 317
cartooning, 278, 281, 358
see also drawing
cartoons, 126–127, 207–208, 274, 308–310
The Case of the Winking Buddha, 67
Casterman, 97
The Castle [Das Schloss] (novel), 149
Caswell, Lucy, 272
"Cavalcade of Comics" (exhibition), 314, 315
.cbr files, 278, 279
.cbz files, 278
CD-ROMs, 107
Cello Suite No. 1 in G Major (Johann Sebastian Bach), 247–249
censorship, 330
see also Comics Code Authority
Certeau, Michel de, 197–198
Cham (Charles Amédée de Noé), 65, 156–157
character development, strategies for, 56–60, 126, 139
Charyn, Jerome, 144n3
Le Château: D'après F. Kafka [The Castle: After F. Kafka], 149, 150, 151

Index

372

Chaykin, Howard, 181
Chesnutt, Charles, 213n12
Chicago American (newspaper), 205, *211*
Chicago Tribune (newspaper), *9*
Childhood [*Z Mého Dětství*], 66
children
  association with comics, 3–4
  comics as obstacle to appreciation of literature
    by, 329, 331
  graphic novels for, 77
  impact of comics on education of, 346
  literature for, 6, 329–330
  see also young people
"Children's Corner" (newspaper section), 3–4
The Chimera Brigade, 182
China, 27, 32
Chute, Hillary, 63, 209n7, 210, 229–232, 281
Citizen 13660, 67, *68*
City of Glass (novel), 155
City of Glass: The Graphic Novel, 155
Civil War, 58
Claremont, Chris, 55–56
Classics Illustrated, 138, 144, 144n3
clear line (*ligne claire*), 28, 149
"Click and Drag" (webcomic episode), 111
*Climate Changed: A Personal Journey through the
    Science*, 353
Clowes, Daniel, 65n1, 73
Coe, Sue, 76
Cole, Jack, 3
Colette, Sidonie-Gabrielle, 1
Colin, Fabrice, 182
collage, 231–234, 239
Collins, Katherine (Arn Saba), 229
Collins, Max, 229
color line, 207, 210, 213
color printing, 129, 205
Comanche Moon, 281–282
Comeau, Joey, 107
"Comic Art Goes Pop!" (auction), 314–315
"The Comic Art Show" (exhibition), 318, 320
comic books, 290
  appeal in Britain of, 293
  collectibility, 274, 275–276
  crossover series, 57
  emergence of medium, 131, 274
  film and television adaptations, 132, 137,
    138–140
  as financial investments, 276, 291
  grading, 291n7, 291
  influence of comic-strip conventions, 131
  multimodality, 132
  parallel series, 56, 58
  paratextual aspects, 178
  publication dynamics, 46, 48

of reprinted comic strips, 125, 131, 274
and seriality, 46, 48–50, 54–56, 276
and serialization, 46, 90, 99
strategies for brand development, 56–60
comic shops, 303
  in Britain, 290, 291–292
  in the United States, 71, 275–276, 290, 291,
    291n5, 302, 343
"The Comic Strip: Its Ancient and Honorable
    Lineage and Present Significance"
    (exhibition), 312, *313*
comic strips
  compared with cartoons, 208
  film and television adaptations, 132–138
  influence of conventions on comic books, 131
  multimodality, 127–131
  in newspapers, 31, 51–54, 65, 127–129, 219
  publication dynamics, 46, 48
  reprint collections, 65, 125, 275
  reprinted in comic books, 125, 131, 274
  and seriality, 46, 51
  serials, 46, 51, 53–54
  series, 46, 51–53
  weekday *v.* Sunday, 127–129
Comical Coons, 212–213, *212*
comicitous features, 234, 261
Comicon (British Comic Art Convention), 292
comics
  change in cultural status, 269, 271
  codification of medium, 252, 256–257
  collecting of, 274, 275–276, 291
  definition, 27, 31, 102–104, 105
  emergence of medium, 26–27, 37, 40, 211
  exchange of, 118, 290, 330
  genealogy, 27, 31
  "growing up" narrative, 1, 74, 76
  multimodality, 3, 125–141, 178, 195, 347–348
  network aspects, 13–14, 114–115, 116
  subversive aspects, 8, 74, 94, 287, 295, 297
  and tension between high and low culture, 2,
    5–6
  see also abstract comics; alternative comics;
    anthology comics; comic books; comic
    strips; digital comics; documentary
    comics; gallery comics; girls' comics;
    graphic memoirs; graphic novels; nursery
    comics; poetry comics; underground
    comix
"Comics as an Art Form" (exhibition), 316
Comics Code Authority, 278, 343, 348
  Comics Code, 70, 71, 173, 228, 343
  see also censorship
comics studies, 283, 322, 352, 353–354
ComicsGate, 303–304
comics, underground, *see* underground comix

Index

ComiXology, 109, 110, 116, 117n14, 141, 300
The Complete Maus, 107
Conard, Sébastien, 157–163, *159*
"Contemporary Cartoons: An Exhibition of Original Drawings at the Huntington Library" (exhibition), 310
A Contract with God and Other Tenement Stories, 71, *72*
conventions, 287, 291, 292, 302–303
  see also events
Coogan, Peter, 172, 173–174
Coontown Calamities, 214n14, 214
Cooper, Fred, *313*
Coover, Colleen, 78
copying (swiping), 282
Corben, Richard, 70, 181
cosplay, 85, 287, 288n2, 302
Coughan, David, 155
Couperie, Pierre, 315, 316
Courtney Crumrin, 182
Crabbe, Buster, 135, 136
Crawshaw, Trisha L., 303
creative autonomy, 73, 74, 179
creator credits, 293
creators, 293, 298–299, 311
  female, 229–230, 302
  self-publishing, 73
  see also artists; authors
Creepshow, 140
Cremins, Brian, 208
crime genre, 67
Crisis on Infinite Earths, 57, 301
Crosby, Percy, 137, 273n5
crossover series, 57
crowdfunding, 109, 117
Crowquill, Alfred, 65
Crucifix, Benoît, 115
Cruddy, 231
Cruikshank, George, 65, 126
Crumb, Robert, 2, 146, 198, 221, 319–320, 323, *323*
cummings, e. e., 5
Currie, Mark, 198
Cvetkovich, Ann, 281

Dagwood, 134
Daniels, Ezra Claytan, 108
Daredevil, 74
Daredevil (television series), 139
The Dark Knight Returns, 58, 74, 75
"Dark They Were and Golden Eyed" (shop), 292, *292*
Dayton Art Institute, 311
DC Comics
  involvement in film and television adaptations, 138–139

publishing strategy, 56, 57–59, 73–74, 77, 140, 182, 290, 301, 333n5
shared narrative universe, 57, 182
use of British creators, 299
  see also National Comics; Vertigo Comics
The DC Vault (book), 276–277
DC's Legends of Tomorrow (television series), 139
De Kosnik, Abigail, 118
De Seve, Mike, 113
The Defenders (television series), 139
DeForge, Michael, 179–180
Delany, Samuel L., 2–3
Delitoon, 109
Dell Comics, 337
Dennis the Menace (television series), 137
Deprez, Olivier, 149, *150*, *151*
Destefanis, Proto, 315
Destiny: A Novel in Pictures, 66
Di Paola, Lorenzo, 103
Diary of a Young Girl, 229
Dick Tracy, 131
Dick Tracy (film serials), 135, 136
Dick Tracy (films), 137
Dick Tracy (television series), 137
digital archives, 268, 269–270, 277–278
digital comics, 102–119, 126, 141
Digital Comics Museum, 278, *279*
digital graphic novels, 78–79
digital storage media, 105, 118
  see also CD-ROMs
direct-market system, 71, 73, 290, 291n5
Dirks, Rudolph, 127, 210, *211*
Disney, 59, 126
Disney, Walt, 310–311
Disney+, 140
disposability of popular culture, 270–271
Dispossession, 149, 153–156, *154*, *157*
A Distant Neighborhood [*Harukana Machi e*], 96–97, *98*
Ditko, Steve, 26, 55n1, 57, 69
Dixie Dugan, 131
Dr. Doom, 175, 178
Doctor Strange (television series), 139
documentary comics, 281
dolls, 225, 226, 227
Donald Duck, 336
Donner, Richard, 139
The Doodle Revolution (book), 355, *356*
doodling, 355, *356*
Doré, Gustave, 65
Dotter of Her Father's Eyes, 78
Doubleday, 75
Doucet, Julie, 198
12 La Douce, 113
Doyle, Richard, 127

Index

Dozo, Björn-Olav, 115
Dragon Ball, 84
Drake, Arnold, 67
drawing
  forms of, 25–27, 31
  indexicality, 281
  styles, 27–28, 37–39
  use of media in the production of, 33–35
  as way of thinking, 360
  see also cartooning
Drawn & Quarterly, 190, 191
"Drawn to Excellence: Masters of Cartoon Art" (exhibition), 318
"Drawn to Purpose: American Women Illustrators and Cartoonists" (exhibition), 322
Dream of the Rarebit Fiend, 129, 133
Dream of the Rarebit Fiend (film), 133
Drnaso, Nick, 78
Du Bois, W. E. B., 207
dual coding theory, 355, *357*
Dumm, Edwina, 225
Duval, Marie, 37–39, *38*, 65, 225, 283
Dylan, Bob, 147*n*7

East Village Other, 228
EC Comics, 48, 50, 69, 140, 271
Eclipse Comics, 71–73
Eco, Umberto, 51, 53, 178
education, 1, 78, 346–361
Eerie, 131
egodocuments, 187
Eisner, Will, 13, 14, 71, *72*, 131, 138, 204, 221, 308, 316, 346
Eisner Awards, 275
Elderkin, Beth, 303
Electricomics, 109
"Electronic Comics and Computer Art" (exhibition), 318
Eliot, T. S., 5
Elkins, James, 254
Ella Cinders, 131
Ellis, Allen, 327–328, 342, 343
Ellis, Warren, 181–182
L'Éprouvette (magazine), 261
Everett, Bill, 175
Evergreen Review, 69
exhibitions, 225, 229, 308–324

Faber & Faber, 77
Fabricius, Charlotte, 300–301
Famous Funnies, 125, 131, 335
fan communities, 55, 85, 117, 118, 180, 271–272, 288, 315
  access to, 301, 302–304
  see also fans; readers

fanfiction, 287*n*1, 287, 302
fans, 302–305
  as consumers, 71, 74
  engagement with comics narratives, 55, 56, 140
  role in maintenance of narrative continuity, 276, 298
  role in preservation of comics, 270, 274
  see also fan communities; readers
Fantagraphics, 245
"Fantastic Art, Dada, Surrealism" (exhibition), 310
The Fantastic Four, 131, 168, 173–176, *177*, 177, 178
Fantastic Four (animated television series), 138
fanzines (zines), 176, 245, 315, 346*n*1
Farazmand, Reza, 107
Fawcett Publications, 67, 68
Feiffer, Jules, 316
The Feitlebaum Family, 274
Felski, Rita, 10–11
female creators, 229–230, 302
female fans, 302–304
female readers, 295, 296, 301
feminism, 228, 230, 231, 242
  see also suffragism
Fernandez, Margarita Molina, 113
Ferris, Emil, 14–16, *15*
Fiedler, Leslie, 270
Filipino Food, 69
film serials, 135–137, 169
Filmation Associates, 138
films (movies), 41–42, 127
  adaptations of comics, 42, 59–60, 85, 126, 132–137, 139–140, 169
  museum exhibits based on, 310–311
  documentaries, 229
  multimodality, 132–137, 139–140
  transmedia perspectives, 60, 168
The First Kingdom, *70*, 71
First Second Books, 77
Flaming Carrot, 229
Flapper Fanny, 227
The Flash (television series), 139
Flash Gordon, 54, 131
Flash Gordon (television series), 137
Flash Gordon's Trip to Mars (film serial), *136*, 136, 140
Fleischer, Dave, 137
Flenniken, Shary, 227
floppies, *see* comic books
Flowers, Ebony, 221, 229, 230, 234–238, *236*, 242
Forest, Jean-Claude, 69
Foucault, Michel, 277
fo(u)r watt, 157–163, *159*
Foxy Grandpa, 125, 132

Index

Fraction, Matt, 177
Fradon, Ramona, 138
France, 147, 168, 315n3
  see also Francophone comics (*bandes dessinées*)
franchises, 182
François, Édouard, 315
Francophone comics (*bandes dessinées*), 31, 32
  see also France
Frank, Josette, 332–333
Frankenstein (novel), 166, 175
Freeman, Don, 67
Freeman, Matthew, 301
French, Renée, 258–259, *259*
Fresnault-Deruelle, Pierre, 13, 251
Frey, Hugo, 11–13, 63–64, 276
Friedow, Alison, 352
Friends of Lulu, 229
fumetti (Italian comics), 31
Fun Home, 1–2, 78, 171, 229, 241, 281
Funny Page (film), 134–135
The Further Fattening Adventures of Pudge, Girl Blimp, 70
Fury, Nick, 60

Gabriel, David, 303
Gaiman, Neil, 145, 181, 229
Gaines, M. C., 312
gallery comics, 260, 324
Galvan, Margaret, 283
GamerGate, 303
Gandy Goose, 336–337
Garcia, Antero, 347
Gardner, Jared, 178, 207–208, 209, 275, 282
Garrick, David, 40
Garvey, Ellen Gruber, 274, 275
Gateward, Frances, 206, 209
Gavaler, Chris, 31
Gaze, Tim, 245, *251*, 252, 261
Gebbie, Melinda, 228
gekiga, 84, 85, 90
gender, 288
  manga and, 85, 91
  segmentation of readers according to, 295–299
Genette, Gérard, 13, 50, 177
genre, 48–50, 150–151, 166–182
  boys' love', 94
  crime, 67
  horror genre, 50, 67, 92, 131, 171, 178, 180
  humor genre, 288, 297
  pornography, 169
  romance, 28, 50, 178, 179, 227, 229, 295
  science fiction, 297
  superhero, *see* superhero genre
  western, 169, 171
Gerber, Steve, 73n3

Gertie the Dinosaur (animated film), 133
Gess, Fabrice, 182
Ghetti, Lorenzo, 112
Ghost World, 73
Gibbons, Dave, 74
Gillis, Peter, 107
Gillray, James, 126
Gilman, Sander L., 204–205, 207
Girl, 296
girls' comics, 288, 295, 296
Gitelman, Lisa, 283
Gloeckner, Phoebe, 229
Gods' Man, 66
Goethe, Johann Wolfgang von, 4
Goetz, Amy, 229
Goldberg, Rube, 50, 51
The Good Times Are Killing Me, 231
Goodbrey, Daniel Merlin, 113
Goodwin, Archie, *70*, 71
Goofy, 335
Gopnik, Adam, 319
Gordon, Ian, 104, 205
Gorey, Edward, 318
Goscinny, René, 315
Gould, Chester, 131
grammatextuality, 12–13
Grantray-Lawrence Animation, 138
graphiation, 16, 254–255
The Graphic Canon (books), 146
graphic memoirs, 11, 171, 179, 240–241, 281, 302
  see also graphic novels: memoirs/autobiographies
graphic non-fiction, 281, 282
  see also documentary comics; graphic memoirs;
      graphic novels: memoirs/autobiographies
graphic novels, 1–2, 32, 57, 63–64, 67–79,
      179n2, 302
  adult readers and, 63, 69, 74, 76
  archival elements in, 282
  definitions, 64
  digital, 78–79
  emergence of term, 68–69
  female creators and, 229–230
  and genre, 179
  implications of term, 244
  in libraries, 74, 300, 343–344
  literary aspects, 144–145
  memoirs/autobiographies, 11, 147, 228, 229,
      230, 241, 258
  see also graphic memoirs
  online, 78–79
  precursors, 65–67
  and seriality, 179
  for young people, 77
Graphix, 77
Gravett, Paul, 323–324

Index

Gray, Harold, 131
The Great Northern Brotherhood of Canadian Cartoonists, 267–269, *268*
Green, Justin, 70, 195–197
Grennan, Simon, 149, 153–156, *154*, 157, 283
Griffith, Bill, 179*n*2
Groensteen, Thierry, 13–14, 82, 191, 193, 244, 255
Gross, Milt, *274*
Groupe μ, 254
Grove Press, 69
Grusin, Richard, 138
Guardians of the Galaxy Prelude, 140
Guibert, Simon, 107
guided view, 116, 126
Gulacy, Paul, 73
Gurewitch, Nicholas, 107
Gurihiru, 77
Guston, Phillip, 319–320
Guts, 77
gutters, 13, 26, 127, 213, 249–251

h day, 258, *259*
Hadashi no Gen [*Barefoot Gen*], 84, 88–90
Hague, Ian, 31
Hall, Radclyffe, 2
Hamlet (play), 335
Hammer Museum, 318, 320, *323*
Hanna-Barbera, 138
Hanshaw, Julian, 108
Happy Hooligan, 127
Happy Hooligan (film), 132
Haring, Keith, 318
Hark! A Vagrant, 107, 141
Harold Teen, 135
Harper's Weekly (magazine), 212
Harris, Joel Chandler, 213*n*12
Harukana Machi e [*A Distant Neighborhood*], 96–97, *98*
Harvey, Robert C., 311
Hatfield, Charles, 2, 73, 252–254, 352
Havig, Alan, 211, 215, 215*n*17, 217
Hawisher, Gail, 349
Hays, Ethel, 227
Hear the Sound of My Feet Walking.. Drown the Sound of My Voice Talking.., 70
Hearst, William Randolph, 205
The Heart of Juliet Jones, 53
Heartstopper, 86
Heartthrobs, 179
Heck, Don, 138
Heer, Jeet, 205*n*1, 213
Heimat, 281
Hell-Rider, 226
Hellboy, 180–182

Herbrechter, Stefan, 186
Here, 113–114, 187–189
Herriman, George, 5–8, *7*, 41–42, *52*, 131, 219, 320*n*7
Hescher, Achim, 193
Heuet, Stéphane, 146, 149
Hi and Lois, 317
"High & Low: Modern Art and Popular Culture" (exhibition), 318*n*6, *318*, 319–320
Highsmith, Doug, 327–328, 342, 343
Histoire d'Albert, 4, 4–5, 14
Histoire de la Sainte Russie, 65
Histoire de M. Cryptogame [*Mr. Cryptogame*], 4
Histoire de Monsieur Jabot, 65
Hobo Lobo of Hamelin, 111
Hogan's Alley, 47–48, 65, 127, *128*
Hogarth, Burne, *70*, 71
Hogarth, William, 5, 36–37, 40
Holkins, Jerry, 141
Hollingsworth, Alvin, 131
Homestuck, 117
Hopalong Cassidy, 59
Horn, Maurice, 315, 316
Horne, Emily, 107
Horner, Emily C., 343
horror, 50, 67, 92, 131, 171, 178, 180
hosting platforms, 109, 110, 116, 117*n*14, 141, 300
    see also platform economy
Hot Comb, 221, 234–238, *236*
Hotspur, 289
House of Secrets, 167–168
How to Commit Suicide in South Africa, 76
How to Get Girls (Into Your Store): A Friends of Lulu Retailer Handbook (booklet), 229
Howard, Sheena C., 206*n*4
Howe, Sean, 350
"The Howl and the Pussy Cat" (story), 340–341
Hugo, Victor, 156
Hulk (film), 140
Hulk, the, 138, *139*, 140, 172
Human Torch, the, 175
humor, 288, 297
Hussie, Andrew, 117
Hutcheon, Linda, 176
Huynh, Matt, 112–113
Hyde, Laurence, 67
hypercomics, 112, 113
"Hypercomics: The Shape of Comics to Come" (exhibition), 323–324

"I Saw Where the Root Hog Lives" (story), 193–195

Index

377

Icon Comics, 180
iconicity, 104*n*2
"If This Be My Destiny...!" (story), 55*n*1
Iger, Jerry, 335
Ikeda, Riyoko, 86*n*6, 86
Image Comics, 179
image libraries, 282
imagetext, 2, 99
immersion, 114–117, 115*n*13
L'immeuble [*The Building*], *113*, 113
Immonen, Stuart, 181–182
Impressions de voyage de Monsieur Boniface, 65
In the Shadow of No Towers, 78
The Incredible Hulk, 138
The Incredible Hulk (television series), 139
The Incredibles (film), 168
independent publishers, 71–73
   see also alternative publishers; small presses
indicia (pictorial runes), 26, 83, 83*n*4
Indiegogo, 109
Infocomics, 107
Instagram, 112, 141
intellectual property, 73, 270, 273, 273*n*5
interactivity, 114
   see also narrative agency
intermediality, 148–149, 260–261
International Museum of Cartoon Art, 317
Invasion of the Elvis Zombies, 76
Iron Fist (television series), 139
Iron Man, 57, 138
Iser, Wolfgang, 115
It Ain't Me Babe (newspaper), 228
It Ain't Me Babe: Women's Liberation, 228, 321, 321*n*8
It Rhymes with Lust, 67
It Shouldn't Happen, 67
Itō, Junji, 92, 166
It's All Over and Other Poems on Animals, 257–258
Izneo, 109, 110, 116

Jack Survives, 76
Jackie, *289*, 296
Jackson, Jack, 281–282
Jackson, Samuel L., 60
Jacobs, Dale, 346–348
James, Henry, 1
Janguru Taitei [*Kimba, the White Lion*], 88
Japan, 27, 32, 41, 84–87
   see also manga
Jaudon, Valerie, 231
Jauss, Hans Robert, 245
Jennings, John, 206, 209
Jessica Jones (television series), 139
Jimbo, 76

Jimmy Corrigan: The Smartest Kid on Earth, 11–13, *12*, 14, 73, 78, 179
Joe Palooka, 131
Joe Palooka (films), 137
Joe Palooka (television series), 137
John Caldigate, 149, 153–155, 157
John Lecrocheur, 107
Johnson, Isabel Simeral, 310
Johnson, R. Kikuo, 28
Jonathan Cape, 66
Joyce, James, 1
Judge (magazine), 212, 310
Judge Dredd, 297, *299*
Judy, or the London Serio-Comic Journal (magazine), *38*
Julien Levy Gallery, 312
Julius Caesar (play), 337
Jungle Jim (film serial), 135
Jungle Jim (films), 137
Jungle Jim (television series), 137
Justice League of America, the, 46, 57, 126, 173
juvenile delinquency, 293, 294
   see also moral panics

kabuki, 41
Kafka, Franz, 149
Kane, Gil, *70*, 71
Karasik, Paul, 8, 155
Kashtan, Aaron, 110, 300
Katchor, Ben, 78
Katsushika, Hokusai, 35, *36*, 42
Katy Keene, 227
Katz, Jack, *70*, 71
The Katzenjammer Kids, 127, 132, 134, *211*
Kawano, Naoko, 77
Ka-Zar, 173, 178
Ka-Zar, *174*
Kaze to Ki no Uta [*The Poem of Wind and Trees*], 94–96, *95*
Kelly, Walt, 337–341
Kemble, Edward Windsor, 205, 212*n*11, 212–215, 213*n*12, 214*n*14, *214*, 216*n*18
Kemble's Coons: A Collection of Southern Sketches, 213*n*12, 213, *214*, 215*n*15
Kermode, Frank, 198–199
Kewpie Dolls, 225
Khan, Kamala (Ms. Marvel), 1, 229, 302
Kick, Russ, 146
Kickstarter, 109
Kidman, Shawna, 168
Killing and Dying, 78
Kim, Sanho, *70*, 71
Kimba, the White Lion [*Janguru Taitei*], 88
Kindchenschema (concept), 87
King-Cat Classix, 190*n*4

378   *Index*

King-Cat Comics and Stories, 185–195, 198–199, 202
King Features Syndicate, 131, 134, 138
The King of the Golden River (book), 336
King of the Royal Mounted, 138
Kirby, Jack, 26, 57, 69, 131, 176, *177*, 254, 316, 317
"Kirby Krackle" (artistic technique), 26, 28
Kirtley, Susan, 233–234, 347
Kiss (*Marvel Comics Super Special*), 73n3
Kitchen, Denis, 322, 323
Klee, Paul, 251, 260
Kofi, 109
Kofman, Sarah, 186
Koike, Kazuo, 84
Kojima, Gōseki, 84
Kominsky-Crumb, Aline, 228
Kopin, Josh, 281–282
Korea, 32, 111
Kozloff, Joyce, 231
Krahulik, Mike, 107, 141
Krazy Kat, 5–10, *7*, 11, 14, 51, *52*, 131, 135, 219
Krug, Nora, 281
Kunka, Andrew J., 210n8
Kunzle, David, 4
Kurtzman, Harvey, 69, 316
Kushner, Robert, 231
Kyle, Richard, 68–69, 79

"Ladies First: A Century of Women's Innovations in Comics and Cartoon Art" (exhibition), 225
The Lakes International Comic Art Festival, 303
Lane, Lois, 56, 333–335, *334*
Lapacherie, Jean-Gérard, 12–13
The Last Flower: A Parable in Pictures, 67
Laydeez Do Comics, 228
Lazareff, Pierre, 315
Lear, Edward, 340
Lee, Ang, 140
Lee, Stan, 55n1, 57, 69
Leech, John, 308–310, *309*
Legends of Tomorrow (television series), 139
Lehman, Serge, 182
Lehmann-Haupt, Hellmut, 66
Lent, John A., 294
Let's Not Talk Anymore, 234, 238–241, *240*
letters columns, 56, 69, 175–176, 300, 333n5, 333
Lewen, Si, 67
Lewis, John, 352
librarians, 77, 271, 272, 327–335, 341–343
libraries, 77, 267, 271, 327–335, 341–343
  graphic novels in, 74, 300, 343–344
  manga in, 77, 343

storage issues, 272
  university, 272, 317
Lichtenstein, Roy, 315
Life (magazine), 212, 310
Life: A User's Manual [*La Vie mode d'emploi*], 113
life writing, *see* autobiography (life writing)
Lightman, Sarah, 228
Li'l Abner, 50, 131
literacy, impact of comics on, 77, 293
literary works
  intermediality and, 148–149
  references to, 335–341
  use as source material for comics adaptations, 143–163
    creativity and, 147–148
    fidelity and, 147–148, 152–157
    influence of canonical works, 152
    subjectivity and, 150–152
    visual intertextuality and, 149
  see also literature
literature
  for children, 6, 329
  co-existence with comics, 332, 333, 341
  comics as alternative form of, 2
  comics as obstacle to appreciation of, 329, 331
  comics as opposite of, 143–144, 329, 331
  comics as visual form of, 33
  initiatives by National Comics to promote, 331–333
  see also literary works
Little Nemo (*Winsor McCay: The Famous Cartoonist of the N.Y. Herald and His Moving Comics*; animated film), 42, *42*, 133–134
Little Nemo in Slumberland, 46, 129, *130*, 219–221, *220*
Little Orphan Annie, 131
"Little Orphan Annie's Eyeballs" (essay), 204
Little Sammy Sneeze, 129
Loki (television series), 140
Lone Wolf and Cub, 84
Looney Tunes (animated cartoon series), 317
Lorenz, Konrad, 87
Los Angeles Times (newspaper), *130*
Loubert, Denise, 228–229
Love, Barbara, 2
Love, Jeremy, 78, 221
Love Story Picture Library, *30*
Lovecraft, H. P., 145n4
The Loving Ballad of Lord Bateman, 65
Lucy and Sophie Say Good Bye, 8–10, *9*, 14
Luke Cage (television series), 139
Lundin, Anne, 329
Lussan, Edouard, 107

Index

Macbeth (play), 337
Macmillan, 77
MAD (magazine), 176
Madden, Matt, 148*n*9
"The Magic Card!" (advertisement), 333–335, *334*
Mahato, Mita, 257–258
Maidment, Brian, 37
Making Comics, 231, 355, 359
male readers, 295, 296–298
Malland, Julien, 107
Man, Paul de, 186–187
The Man Who Grew Younger, 144*n*3
Mandel, Lisa, 179*n*2
Mandrake the Magician (film serial), 135
manga, 32, 77, 82–99, 318, 343
    gekiga, 84, 85, 90
    seinen manga, 85
    shōjo manga (manga for teenage girls), 41, 85–86, 90, 91, 94, 302, 302*n*10
    shōnen manga (manga for teenage boys), 85, 90
Manga Punch, 90
manhua, 32
manhwa, 32
Manouach, Ilan, 282
Mansion of Evil, 67
Map of My Heart, 185*n*1, *188*, 190, 191, 192, *194*, *196*, 199, *201*
March, 352
Marion, Philippe, 16, 169, 254–255
Marriner, William, 219
Marrs, Lee, 70, 228
Marston, William Moulton, 226
Martin Luther King and the Montgomery Story, 346, 353
Marvel Cinematic Universe (MCU), 60, 132, 140
    see also Marvel Comics: shared narrative universe
Marvel Comics
    involvement in film and television adaptations, 138, 140
    management of digital archive, 277
    publishing strategy, 56, 57–59, 69, 74, 139–140, 173, 290, 301
    shared narrative universe, 57, 139, 182
    see also Marvel Cinematic Universe (MCU)
The Marvel Super Heroes (animated television series), 138
Marvel Unlimited, 110, 116, 117*n*14, 141
The Marvel Vault (book), 276–277
Marvel Zombies, 182
"Marvel zombies" (fan community), 180
Marvel's Avengers: Infinity War Prelude, 140
Marvel's Guardians of the Galaxy Prelude, 140
Mary Jane, 182
Masereel, Frans, 66, 149

"Masters of American Comics" (exhibition), 318*n*6, 318, 320, 321, 322
Matena, Dick, 148*n*8
materiality of comics, 78, 272, 273
Mathieu, Marc Antoine, 113
Maus, 74–75, 281
    academic interest in, 75
    exhibitions featuring, 320, 323
    publication history, 74, 75, 107
    sales, 75
    use in education, 1, 78, 346, 348, 352
Mazzucchelli, David, 155
McCay, Winsor, 41–42, *42*, 46, 129–131, *130*, 133–134, 219–221, *220*
McCloud, Scott, 13, 85–86, 102, 104*n*2, 108, 114, 204, 207, *208*, 322
McFadden's Row of Flats, 215
McFarlane, Brian, 152
McGregor, Don, 73
McGuire, Richard, 113–114, 187–189
McNaught (syndicate), 131
McSpade, Angelfood, 221
Méchoulan, Éric, 260–261
mediageny, 169–171, 171*n*1
Menu, Jean-Christophe, 246, 261
merchandising, 59, 117, 271
Messick, Dalia (Dale), 227
Metamorpho, 138
Metropolitan Museum of Art (The Met), 310–311, 311*n*2, 314, 319
Metz, Holly, 76
Meyer, Leonard, 27
Michaels, Marian, 226
Michaux, Henri, 251
Michigan State University Libraries, 272
Mickey Mouse, 335
microfilm, 272, 273
Mignola, Mike, 180–182
Mikkonen, Kai, 96, 195, 350
Millais, John Everett, 149
Millar, Mark, 58, 60
Millard, Joseph, 67
Miller, Frank, 58, 74, 84, 179–180
Millie the Model, 227
Mills, Emily, 355, 358, *359*
Mills, June Tarpé, 227
Mingus, Charles, 247
minicomics, 245
Miodrag, Hannah, 7, 195
Les Misérables, 156–157
Miss Fury, 227
Mr. Fantastic, 3, 176
Mitchell, W. J. T., 2, 214*n*13
Mittell, Jason, 139
Miyazaki, Hayao, 10

Index

MLJ Magazines, 56, 227
Moby Duck, 335–336
MoCCA (Museum of Comic and Cartoon Art), 321
Modern Polaxis, 113
Moebius, (Jean Giraud) 132
Moliterni, Claude, 315
Molotiu, Andrei, 208, 249, *249*
    Abstract Comics: The Anthology: 1967–2009 (book), 245–246, 249–251, *250*, 252, *253*, 260, 261
Mon Livre d'heures [Passionate Journey], 66
Monthly Halloween, 92
Moore, Alan, 63, 74, 177, 229, 299
Mopsy, 227
moral panics, 67–68, 70, 294–295, 304, 328
    see also juvenile delinquency
Moreno, Pepe, 107
Moriarty, Jerry, 76
Morrison, Grant, 181
Morton, Drew, 140
motion comics, 112–113, 126, 138, 140–141
Mouly, Françoise, 75, 77
movies, *see* films (movies)
Moya, Alvaro de, 314
Ms. Marvel, 1, 229, 301–302
Ms. Tree, 229
Muller, Jerome K., 316, *317*
multiframe layouts, 86, 195
multimodality
    comics and, 3, 125–141, 178, 195, 347–348
    education and, 347–348, 358
    films and, 132–137, 139–140
    television, 137–139
Munroe, Randall, 107, 111
Munson, Kim, 229
museum-in-a-book format, 276–277
Museum of Cartoon Art, 317
Museum of Comic and Cartoon Art (MoCCA), 321
Museum of Contemporary Art, 318, 320
Museum of Modern Art (MoMA), 310, 318–320, 321
music in comics, 245–252, 257
Musical Mose, 219
Mutt and Jeff, 48, 51, 135
My Favorite Thing Is Monsters, 14–16, *15*, 230
Myer, Peter L., 316
Myracle, Lauren, 77
Mystery Men, 50

Nabokov, Vladimir, 191
Naifeh, Ted, 182
Nakazawa, Keiji, 84, 88–90
Namor (Sub-Mariner), 138, 175

narrative agency, 114, 115*n*13, 115, 116
Nast, Thomas, 310
National Cartoonists Society (NCS), 312–314
National Comics, 331–335
    see also DC Comics
National Lampoon (magazine), 168
NAWLZ, 108
Neil the Horse, 229
Nemuki, 92
Neon Wasteland, 113
Netflix, 139
Neufeld, Josh, 78
The New Adventures of Superman (animated television series), 138
New Gods, 316
New Treasure Island [Shintakarajima], 87, *88*
New York Comic Con, 303
New York Herald (newspaper), 215, *217–218, 220*
New York Journal (newspaper), 47–48, *49*, 205, 215
New York World (newspaper), 47, 127, *128*, 205, 215, 219
New York World's Fair (1964), 314, 315
Newgarden, Mark, 8
newspaper syndicates, 127, 131, 134, 138, 219, 275
newspapers
    "Children's Corner" section, 3–4
    comics in, 206, 210, 270–272, 274–275
        comic strips, 31, 51–54, 65, 127–129, 219
        seriality and, 47, 48
    supplements to, 51, 205, 211, 215, 215*n*17
    underground, 228
Nextwave: Agents of H.A.T.E., 181–182
Nick Carter, 51
Nin, Anaïs, 2
Nobel Prize in Literature, 147*n*7
Nolan, Sir Sidney, 260
North, Ryan, 107
North, Sterling, 328, 329
Not Brand Echh, 176
Nückel, Otto, 66
nursery comics, 288
Nyberg, Amy Kiste, 328–330

The Obscure Cities [Les Cités obscures], 145
O'Donoghue, Michael, 69
Ohio State University (OSU), 272, 317
Okubo, Miné, 67, *68*
Olympia Press, 69
One! Hundred! Demons!, 73, 229, 230–231, *232*, 234
O'Neill, Dan, 70
O'Neill, Rose, 225
online comics (webcomics), 107, 111, 112, 126, 141
onomatopoeia, 83, 133

Index

Operation Ajax, 113
Opération Teddy Bear, 107
Opper, Frederick Burr, 127, 205–206, 207
Orme, Stephanie, 302–303
Ormes, Jackie, 226, 227, 318
Oseman, Alice, 86
O'Sullivan, Judith, 316
Ōtomo, Katsuhiro, 85
Oubapo, 148n9
Oulipo, 148n9
Outcault, Richard Felton, 46, 47–48, 49, 65, 127, 128, 205, 215–218, 215n17, 217–218
Overstreet Comic Book Price Guide, 275

page layout, 14, 84, 86, 153–156, 169, 195
"Pages and Progress" (exhibition), 323
Paivio, Allan, 355, 357
Pale Fire (novel), 191
Palestine, 73
The Panic, 249, 250
Panter, Gary, 76
Pantheon Books, 74, 75
Pantomime: To Be Played As It Was, Is, and Will Be, at Home, 65
Papercutz, 77
The Parade, 67
Paramount, 134–135
paratext, 13, 178, 190, 258, 335, 341
Parker, Charley, 107
Parker, Gladys, 227
Parker, Peter, 55n1
Pascal, David, 315
Passionate Journey [*Mon Livre d'heures*], 66
Patreon, 109
Patri, Giacomo, 66
Patsy Walker, 227
Pattern and Decoration (art movement), 231
Patty-Jo 'n' Ginger, 226
Paul Terry's Mighty Mouse Comics, 336–337
Peanuts, 51
Peellaert, Guy, 69
Peeters, Benoît, 145, 181
Pekar, Harvey, 75, 198
Penguin Books, 77
Penny Arcade, 107, 141
Pep Comics, 227
Perec, Georges, 113
Perfect Example, 185n1, 190, 199, 200
The Perry Bible Fellowship, 107
Persepolis, 1, 78, 229, 352
Perturbation, 248
Peter, Harry, 226
Peterson, Richard, 32
Phallaina, 111, 112

Phenix (fanzine), 315
Philbin, Ann, 318, 320
Phillips, Kimberley L., 67
"The Phonus Balonus Show of Really Heavy Stuff" (exhibition), 316
photography, 281
pictorial runes, 26, 83n4, 83
Picture This, 355, 359
Pier, John, 189
piracy, 118, 277
Pithecanthropus Erectus (music album), 249
Pixar, 318
Pixin, Weng, 230, 234, 238–241, 238, 242
Pizzino, Christopher, 1, 64, 135, 179–180
Plastic Man, 3
platform economy, 109, 117
see also hosting platforms
Platinum Age, 180
plot, 246
Poe, Edgar Allan, 145n4
The Poem of Wind and Trees [*Kaze to Ki no Uta*], 94–96, 94–96
poetry comics, 252–258
Poetry Comics from the Book of Hours, 255, 256
Pogo (comic strip), 337
Pogo Possum (comic book), 337–341, 338, 339, 341
polygraphy, 37–39, 40, 42
"Pore Lil' Mose on the 7 Ages" (comic strip instalment), 216–217, 217
Poorly Drawn Lines, 107
Pop Art, 315, 316, 318
Popeye, 131, 134
Popeye (animated cartoon series), 137
Popular Comics, 125, 131
popular culture, disposability of, 270–271
Porcellino, John, 185–195, 185n1, 188, 190n3, 194, 196, 198–199, 200–201, 202
Pore Lil' Mose, 215–218, 215n17, 216n18
pornography genre, 169
Porter, Edwin S., 133
post-comics, 157
Postema, Barbara, 258
Powell, Nate, 352
preservation of comics, 118–119, 270, 274, 275, 276, 278
see also archives
Price, Austin, 166
Priego, Ernesto, 110
"Primeira Exposição Internacional de Histórias em Quadrinhos" (exhibition), 314
The Prince and the Dressmaker, 86
Princess Knight [*Ribon no Kishi*], 41
Protanopia, 113
Proust, Marcel, 146, 149

382 *Index*

PS Magazine, 346
publishers
  approach towards librarians, 331, 341
  digital strategies, 277
  graphic novels for young people and, 77
  management of archives, 277
  narrative memory and, 276
  receptiveness to fan input, 56
  see also alternative publishers; independent
    publishers; small presses
Puck (magazine), 212, 310
Pulitzer, Joseph, 205
Pumphrey, George, 290
Punch (magazine), 127, 308–310, *309*

Qwantz, 107

Raab, Charles, 67
racial stereotypes, 204–221, 205*n*1, 215*n*17, 226
radio, 175
Radio Patrol (film serial), 135
Radway, Janice, 296
Rag-Time Cadets, 214*n*14, 214
Random House, 76
Rausch, Barbara, 227
RAW (magazine), 75, 76, *274*, 318
RAW Books & Graphics, 75–76
RAW One-Shots, 76
Raymond, Alex, 54
readers, 287–305
  adult, *see* adult readers
  consumption of other media, 168
  engagement
    affective, 83
    with comics format, 13, 351
    with extended narrative structures, 57, 69
    with intratextual metalepsis, 191
    with letters columns, 175–176
    with manga, 85, 87, 90–94, 99
    with seriality, 48–50, 55
    with variety, 46–47, 55–56
    see also agency
  ethnically diverse, 301
  expectations, 245, 252
  female, 295, 296, 301
  male, 295, 296–298
  of nineteenth-century periodicals, 37
  segmentation according to age, 85, 296
  segmentation according to gender, 85, 295–299
  young, 293–295, 301
  see also fan communities; fans
Real Fact Comics, 333*n*5
reception theory, 245
Red Barry (film serial), 135
Red Ryder (films), 137

Red Ryder (television series), 137
Red Son, 58
Reese, Ralph, 167, 168
*Reinventing Comics: How Imagination and
  Technology Are Revolutionizing an Art
  Form* (book), 108
remediation, 138
Remembrance of Things Past [*À la recherche du
  temps perdu*] (novel), 146, 149
Ren, Marietta, 111, *112*
Renée, Lily, 131
Renegade Press, 228–229
Renegade Romance, 229
Resha, Adrienne, 300
Resnais, Alain, 315
Ribon no Kishi [*Princess Knight*], 41
Rich, Adrienne, 1
Richard III (play), 337
Robb, Jenny, 271
Robbins, Trina, 227, 228, 273, 295, 320–321
  involvement in exhibitions, 229, 317, *321*,
    321, 322
  underground publications and, 228, 321
Robinson, Jerry, 316
rogue archives, 118, 277
Rohde, Mike, 354–356, *357*
romance genre, 28, 50, 178, 179, 227, 229, 295
Romero, George, 140
Ronin, 84
Rootabaga Stories (book), 6
The Rose of Versailles [*Berusaiyu no Bara*], 86,
  86*n*6, 91
Rosetti, Christina, 337
Ross, Charles, 225
Rosset, Christian, 261
Rothman, Alexander, 255–257
Round, Julia, 290
Rouse, Rebecca, 109
Rubáiyát of Omar Khayyám (book), 335
Ruggieri, Colleen, 350
Run: Book One, 141
Ruskin, John, 336

Sabin, Roger, 1, 76, 84, 283
Sabre, 73
Sabrina, 78
Sacco, Joe, 73
Saenz, Mike, 107
The Saga of the Swamp Thing, 74, 299
Saguisag, Lara, 206*n*3, 206*n*3, 210*n*9, 211–212,
  214*n*13, 215*n*17, 216*n*18, 216, 219, 221
Sailor Moon [*Bishōjo Senshi Sērā Mūn*], 84, 86,
  90–91
St. John Publications, 67, 68
Sainte-Beuve, Charles Augustin, 179

Saitō, Takao, 85, 96
Sakai, Shichima, 87
Sambo and His Funny Noises, 219
Samplerman, 282
San Diego Comic-Con, 303
San Francisco Academy of Comic Art (SFACA), 272–273, 273n5
Sandburg, Carl, 6
The Sandman, 145, 181, 229
Sasaki, Chifuyu, 77
Satrapi, Marjane, 1, 63, 78, 229, 352
Saturday Morning Breakfast Cereal, 107, *108*
scanlations, 118
scanning, 277–278
Schapiro, Miriam, 231
Schiller, Liz, 229
Schlanger, Judith, 271
Scholastic, 77
schools, 78
Schuiten, François, 113, 145, 181
Schulz, Charles M., 53, 316, 318
science-fiction genre, 84–85, 297
Scott, Randall, 272
Scott, Suzanne, 301
scrapbooks, 274–275
scratch and sniff, 171n1
scrolling, 111, 112
Secret Agent X-9 (film serial), 135
Seduction of the Innocent (book), 293–294, *294*, 346n1, 346, 348
seinen manga (youth manga), 85
Seldes, Gilbert, 5–6
self-publishing, 73, 107, 109, 245
Senate Subcommittee on Juvenile Delinquency, 68, 343, 348
Sens, 113
sequentiality, 156, 208, 251
seriality, 48–50, 51, 54–56, 73, 179, 274, 276
serialization, 46, 47, 139, 288
Seth, 267–269, *268*
Seven, John, 238
Shakespeare, William, 216, 335, 338–340
Shatter, 107
Shazam! (television series), 139
"She Draws Comics: 100 Years of America's Women Cartoonists" (exhibition), *321*
She Makes Comics (film), 229
Shelburne Museum, 197–198
Shelley, Mary, 166
Shields, Rob, 113
Shintakarajima [*New Treasure Island*], 87, *88*
Shivener, Rick, 117
shōjo manga (manga for girls), 41, 85–86, 90, 91, 94, 302, 302n10
shōnen manga (manga for boys), 85, 90

shōnen'ai, 94
Sikoryak, Robert, 282
silent films, 132–133, 135
Sim, Dave, 229
Sinervo, Kalervo, 102–103, 277
Singer, Marc, 177
The Sketchnote Handbook (book), 354–355, *357*
sketchnoting, 354–358, *357*
skeuomorphic comics, 109, 110–111, 116
Skippy, 137, 273n5
Skywald Publications, 226
slabbing, 276, 291
small presses, 73, 245
  see also alternative publishers; independent publishers; *and names of individual presses*
smartphones, 113, 116
Smith, Harrison, 66
Smolderen, Thierry, 5, 35–37, 39, 40, 41
Snake (art installation), 260
Snow White and the Seven Dwarfs (animated film), 310–311
social agency, 114, 117
social media, 109, 111, 112, 117, 141, 303
Société civile d'études et de recherches des littératures dessinées (SOCERLID), 315
A Softer World, 107
Soldier's Heart, 281, 323
soundtrack/s, 246, 247
Sousanis, Nick, 349, 360
Southern Cross: A Novel of the South Seas, 67
speech balloons, 25–26, 31, 135, 191, 251
Spider-Man, 55, 55n1, 57, 58, 59, 138, 182
Spider-Man (animated television series), 138
Spider-Man (television series), 139
Spider-Man: Bloodline, 182
Spider-Man Loves Mary Jane, 182
Spider-Man Noir, 182
Spiegelman, Art, 198
  exhibitions about, 323
  In the Shadow of No Towers, 78
  influences, 273, *274*
  involvement in exhibitions, 318, 320
  Maus, see Maus
  and *RAW*, 75
  views on
    comics, 89, 155, 204
    exhibitions, 308
    Museum of Modern Art, 319, 320
The Spirit, 131, 138, 221
Spirited Away (anime), 10
Springer, Frank, 69
Stacy, Gwen, 55n1
Star Wars, 50
Starre, Alexander, 274
Steele, Henry, 79

Index

Stein, Daniel, 277
Steinberg, Flo, 228
Steirer, Gregory, 354
stereotypes, 204, 209n6
  racial, 204–221, 205n1, 215n17, 226
Steve Canyon, 311, 312
Steve Canyon (television series), 137
Stewart, Bhob, 316
Stokes, Manning Lee, 67
Stone, Bianca, 252, 254, 255, *256*, 257, 261
Storr, Robert, 320
Stowe, Harriet Beecher, 212
Streeten, Nicola, 228, 302
Sub-Mariner (Namor), 138, 175
suffragism, 225
  see also feminism
Super Friends (animated television series), 139
Superboy, 56, 138
Supergirl (television series), 139
superhero genre, 172–176
  black characters in, 226
  divergence within, 169
  extended narratives in, 69
  female *v.* male characters in, 226–227
  and male readers, 295
  modes of reading in, 300
  rebooting within, 301
  revisionism in, 74
  transmedia perspectives, 168
  in the United States, 179, 290
Superman, 50, 56, 172, 177–178, 179, 333n5
  as brand, 58
  comic books, 48, 50, 54, 56, 57, 58, 77, 172, 333–335, 333n5, *334*
  film, television and radio adaptations, 137, 138–139, 175
  transmedia perspectives, 56
  used in campaign to promote reading by children, 331
Superman (animated films), 137
Superman (film), 139
Superman (film serial), 137
The Superman/Aquaman Hour of Adventure (animated television series), 138–139
Superman Smashes the Klan, 77
Superman's Girl Friend Lois Lane, 333–335, *334*
surrealism, 257
Sutu, 108, 111, 113
Swamp Thing, see *The Saga of the Swamp Thing*
Swann, Erwin D., 272
Swarte, Joost, 28
Sweet Time, 239
swiping (copying), 282
Sword's Edge, 70, 71
Syllabus: Notes from an Accidental Professor, 78, 231, 234, 238, 242, 355, 359

syndicates, newspaper, 127, 131, 134, 138, 219, 275
Szép, Eszter, 238

T. C. McClure Syndicate, 219
tabular reading, 13, 156, 251
Tabulo, Kym, 245, 251, 258
Tailspin Tommy (film serials), 135
Takarazuka Revue, 41
Takemiya, Keiko, 92–96, *93*, *95*, 99
Takeuchi, Naoko, 84, 86
Taking Time, Keeping Time, 257
Talbot, Bryan, 78, *292*
Talbot, Mary M., 78
Tales of Suspense, 50
Tamaki, Jillian, 179
Tamaki, Mariko, 77, 179
Tan, Shaun, 260
Taniguchi, Jirō, 96–99, *98*
Tapas, 109
Tarbox, Gwen Athene, 343–344
Tarzan, 53, 59, *70*, 71, 131
Tarzan (comic strip), 53, 131
Tarzan of the Apes (graphic novel), *70*, 71
Tate, Cath, 228
Tatsumi, Yoshihiro, 84
Tawky Tawny, 335, *336*, 341
Taylor-Ashfield, Charlotte, 301
teaching
  role of creating comics, 354–360
  use of comics, 1, 78, 349–353
Teen-Age Romance, 50
teenagers (adolescents), 77, 227, 293
  see also young people
telecomics (format), 137–138
Telecomics (television series), 138, 140
television, 295n8, 343
  adaptations of comics, 126, 137–139, 140, 169
  multimodality, 137–139
Telgemeier, Raina, 77
Tensuan, Theresa, 205
Tera e [*Toward the Terra*], 92–94, *93*
The Terrors of the Tiny Tads, 131
Terry and the Pirates, 46, 48, 131, 311–312
Terry and the Pirates (television series), 137
Tezuka, Osamu, 40–41, 82, 87–88, *88*
These Memories Won't Last, 111
Thing, the, 176
This One Summer, 179
Thor, 1, 138
Thought Bubble Festival, 303
"Three Aces" (comic book series), 48
Three Little Wolves (animated cartoon), 310
Thrillbent, 109
Thurber, James, 67
Tien, Shannon, 102–103

Index

Tiger, *289*
Tilley, Carol, 294, 330, 331, 342
Tillie the Toiler, 135
Tim Tyler's Luck (film serial), 135
Tippie, 225
To Be Continued, 112
Tobin, Paul, 78
Tokyopop, 302
Tomine, Adrian, 78
TOON Books, 77
Töpffer, Rodolphe (Simon de Nantua), 4–5, *4*, 6,
    10, 39–40, 65, 127
topoi, 51
Torchy Brown, 226, 227
Toriyama, Akira, 84
Toward the Terra [*Tera e*], 92–94, *93*
translations, 33, 84, 118, 145*n*4
transmedia perspectives, 56, 59–60, 126, 139,
    140, 168–172, 182, 277
tressage (braiding), 13–14
Trimarchi, Carlo, 112
Trollope, Anthony, 149, 153–155, 157
True Love Problems and Advice Illustrated, 279
Truffaut, François, 153*n*10
Turbointeractive, 109
turbomedia, 112, 116
Twinkle Annual, 289
Twisted Romance, 179
Twitter, 141
Tyler, Carol, 281, 323

Ubisoft, 107
The Ultimates, 169, *170*, 171
The Uncanny X-Men, 173
Uncle Remus (books), 213*n*12
Uncle Scrooge, 336
Uncle Tom's Cabin (novel), 212
underground comix, 2, 32, 69–70, 227–228,
    242, 316, 318, 321
Understanding Comics: The Invisible Art (book),
    85–86, 322
Unflattening (book), 349, 360
United Features, 131
United States, the
    anti-comics campaign, 67, 293–294
    Black Americans (African Americans), 205,
        206*n*4, 214*n*13, 221, 318
    comics archives, 272
    Comics Code Authority, *see* Comics Code
        Authority
    comics culture, 290–291
        comic shops, 71, 275–276, 290, 291,
            291*n*5, 302, 343
        superhero genre, 179, 290
    libraries, 272, 327–335, 341–343
    race issues, 211, 226

Senate Subcommittee on Juvenile
    Delinquency, 68, 343, 348
Upgrade Soul, 108
USA, the, *see* United States, the

V for Vendetta, 229
Varnedoe, Kirk, 319
Vaughn-James, Martin, 152
Verbeek, Gustave, 131
Verticalismi, 109
Vertigo (woodcut novel), 66
Vertigo Comics, 179, 182, 229
Vicki Valentine, 229
video games, 107, 171
Vidu, 113, *113*
La Vie mode d'emploi [*Life: A User's Manual*], 113
virtual reality (VR) comics, 112, 113–114
"Visions of the Floating World" (exhibition), 318
Viz, 297, 298
Viz Media, 302
Voyager Company, 107

Wagstaff, Sheena, 318
Waite, Julian, 283
Walker, Brian, 308–310, 318, 320
Walker, Mort, 272, 316–317
Walkie Entertainment, 113
Wallaby Books, 71
Waller, Leslie, 67
Walt Disney's Mickey Mouse, 335
Walt Disney's Uncle Scrooge, 336
WandaVision (television series), 140
Wang, Jen, 86
Wanzo, Rebecca, 206, 206*n*2, 221*n*20
Ward, Lynd, 66
Ware, Chris, 132, 144, 246, 273, 308
    Building Stories, 78, 110
    Jimmy Corrigan: The Smartest Kid on Earth,
        11–13, *11–13*, 14, 73, 78, 179
Warner Books, 75
Warner Bros., 59, 126
Warner Bros. Animation, 317
Watchmen, 74, 78, 299
Watchmen (motion comic), 126, 140
Watt, 157
Waugh, Coulton, 273
Wayback Machine, 118–119
webcomics (online comics), 107, 111, 112, 126,
    141
Webtoon, 109
Weekly Shōnen Jump, 89
Wein, Len, 167
Weinersmith, Zach, 107, *108*
Weirdo, 319–320
Welhe, Harry B., 311
Wells, Michele, 77

Index

"The Werewolf Hunter" (comic book series), 131
Wershler, Darren, 102–103, 277
Wertham, Fredric, 293–294, *294*, 343, 346, 346*n*1, 348
western genre, 169, 171
Whaley, Deborah, 226
What It Is, 234, 238, 355, 359
What Would Paul Klee Say?, 251
Where I'm Coming From, 226
White, Ebony, 221
White Collar: A Novel in Linocuts, 66
Whitlock, Gillian, 11
Whitney Museum of American Art, 310, 310*n*1
Whyte, Malcolm, 317–318
Wilbur Comics, 227
Wilkins, Peter, 110
Williams, J. H., 132
Willing, Jessie Gillespie, 312
Wilson, 65*n*1
Wimmen's Comix, 228
Winkler, Paul, 315
Winsor McCay: The Famous Cartoonist of the N.Y. Herald and His Moving Comics (*Little Nemo*; animated film), 42, *42*, 133–134
Woggon, Bill, 227, 229
women, role in comics culture, 225–230, 302
"Women and the Comics" (exhibition), 317
"Women in Comics: Looking Forward and Back" (exhibition), 229, 322
Wonder Woman, 139, 226
Wonder Woman (television series), 139

"Wonderworld" (newsletter), 68, 68*n*2
Woo, Benjamin, 287, 291, 292, 352
woodcut novels, 65–67, 149
wordless (poems), 252
Wordsworth, William, 337
World's Finest Comics, 57

X, 76
X-Men, 55–56, 57, 140, 173
X-Men, 55
xkcd, 107, 111

Yang, Gene Luen, 77, 78, 348, 350
yaoi, 94
Yellow Kid, the (Mickey Dugan), 46, 47–48, *49*, 127, *128*, 205, 215
Young, Dwight, 311
young adults, 77, 86
   see also adult readers; young people
Young Lust, 179
young people, 293–295, 301
   see also children; teenagers (adolescents); young adults

Z Mého Dětství [*Childhood*], 66
Zap Comix, 2, 50, 221
"Zatara" (comic book series), 48
zines (fanzines), 176, 245, 315, 346*n*1
Zippy, 179*n*2
Živadinović, Stevan, 111
Zorbaugh, Harvey, 328

Cambridge Companions To ...

AUTHORS

Edward Albee edited by Stephen J. Bottoms

Margaret Atwood edited by Coral Ann Howells (second edition)

W. H. Auden edited by Stan Smith

Jane Austen edited by Edward Copeland and Juliet McMaster (second edition)

Balzac edited by Owen Heathcote and Andrew Watts

Beckett edited by John Pilling

Bede edited by Scott DeGregorio

Aphra Behn edited by Derek Hughes and Janet Todd

Saul Bellow edited by Victoria Aarons

Walter Benjamin edited by David S. Ferris

William Blake edited by Morris Eaves

James Baldwin edited by Michele Elam

Boccaccio edited by Guyda Armstrong, Rhiannon Daniels, and Stephen J. Milner

Jorge Luis Borges edited by Edwin Williamson

Brecht edited by Peter Thomson and Glendyr Sacks (second edition)

The Brontës edited by Heather Glen

Bunyan edited by Anne Dunan-Page

Frances Burney edited by Peter Sabor

Byron edited by Drummond Bone

Albert Camus edited by Edward J. Hughes

Willa Cather edited by Marilee Lindemann

Catullus edited by Ian Du Quesnay and Tony Woodman

Cervantes edited by Anthony J. Cascardi

Chaucer edited by Piero Boitani and Jill Mann (second edition)

Chekhov edited by Vera Gottlieb and Paul Allain

Kate Chopin edited by Janet Beer

Caryl Churchill edited by Elaine Aston and Elin Diamond

Cicero edited by Catherine Steel

J. M. Coetzee edited by Jarad Zimbler

Coleridge edited by Lucy Newlyn

Coleridge edited by Tim Fulford (new edition)

Wilkie Collins edited by Jenny Bourne Taylor

Joseph Conrad edited by J. H. Stape

H. D. edited by Nephie J. Christodoulides and Polina Mackay

Dante edited by Rachel Jacoff (second edition)

Daniel Defoe edited by John Richetti

Don DeLillo edited by John N. Duvall

Charles Dickens edited by John O. Jordan

Emily Dickinson edited by Wendy Martin

John Donne edited by Achsah Guibbory

Dostoevskii edited by W. J. Leatherbarrow

Theodore Dreiser edited by Leonard Cassuto and Claire Virginia Eby

John Dryden edited by Steven N. Zwicker

W. E. B. Du Bois edited by Shamoon Zamir

George Eliot edited by George Levine and Nancy Henry (second edition)

T. S. Eliot edited by A. David Moody

Ralph Ellison edited by Ross Posnock

Ralph Waldo Emerson edited by Joel Porte and Saundra Morris

William Faulkner edited by Philip M. Weinstein

Henry Fielding edited by Claude Rawson

F. Scott Fitzgerald edited by Ruth Prigozy

F. Scott Fitzgerald edited by Michael Nowlin (second edition)

Flaubert edited by Timothy Unwin

E. M. Forster edited by David Bradshaw

Benjamin Franklin edited by Carla Mulford

Brian Friel edited by Anthony Roche

Robert Frost edited by Robert Faggen

Gabriel García Márquez edited by Philip Swanson

Elizabeth Gaskell edited by Jill L. Matus

Edward Gibbon edited by Karen O'Brien and Brian Young

Goethe edited by Lesley Sharpe

Günter Grass edited by Stuart Taberner

Thomas Hardy edited by Dale Kramer

David Hare edited by Richard Boon

Nathaniel Hawthorne edited by Richard Millington

Seamus Heaney edited by Bernard O'Donoghue

Ernest Hemingway edited by Scott Donaldson

Hildegard of Bingen edited by Jennifer Bain

Homer edited by Robert Fowler

Horace edited by Stephen Harrison

Ted Hughes edited by Terry Gifford

Ibsen edited by James McFarlane

Henry James edited by Jonathan Freedman

Samuel Johnson edited by Greg Clingham

Ben Jonson edited by Richard Harp and Stanley Stewart

James Joyce edited by Derek Attridge (second edition)

Kafka edited by Julian Preece

Kazuo Ishiguro edited by Andrew Bennett

Keats edited by Susan J. Wolfson

Rudyard Kipling edited by Howard J. Booth

Lacan edited by Jean-Michel Rabaté

D. H. Lawrence edited by Anne Fernihough

Primo Levi edited by Robert Gordon

Lucretius edited by Stuart Gillespie and Philip Hardie

Machiavelli edited by John M. Najemy

David Mamet edited by Christopher Bigsby

Thomas Mann edited by Ritchie Robertson

Christopher Marlowe edited by Patrick Cheney

Andrew Marvell edited by Derek Hirst and Steven N. Zwicker

Ian McEwan edited by Dominic Head

Herman Melville edited by Robert S. Levine

Arthur Miller edited by Christopher Bigsby (second edition)

Milton edited by Dennis Danielson (second edition)

Molière edited by David Bradby and Andrew Calder

Toni Morrison edited by Justine Tally

Alice Munro edited by David Staines

Nabokov edited by Julian W. Connolly

Eugene O'Neill edited by Michael Manheim

George Orwell edited by John Rodden

Ovid edited by Philip Hardie

Petrarch edited by Albert Russell Ascoli and Unn Falkeid

Harold Pinter edited by Peter Raby (second edition)

Sylvia Plath edited by Jo Gill

Plutarch edited by Frances B. Titchener and Alexei Zadorojnyi

Edgar Allan Poe edited by Kevin J. Hayes

Alexander Pope edited by Pat Rogers

Ezra Pound edited by Ira B. Nadel

Proust edited by Richard Bales

Pushkin edited by Andrew Kahn

Thomas Pynchon edited by Inger H. Dalsgaard, Luc Herman and Brian McHale

Rabelais edited by John O'Brien

Rilke edited by Karen Leeder and Robert Vilain

Philip Roth edited by Timothy Parrish

Salman Rushdie edited by Abdulrazak Gurnah

John Ruskin edited by Francis O'Gorman

Sappho edited by P. J. Finglass and Adrian Kelly

Seneca edited by Shadi Bartsch and Alessandro Schiesaro

Shakespeare edited by Margareta de Grazia and Stanley Wells (second edition)

George Bernard Shaw edited by Christopher Innes

Shelley edited by Timothy Morton

Mary Shelley edited by Esther Schor

Sam Shepard edited by Matthew C. Roudané

Spenser edited by Andrew Hadfield

Laurence Sterne edited by Thomas Keymer

Wallace Stevens edited by John N. Serio

Tom Stoppard edited by Katherine E. Kelly

Harriet Beecher Stowe edited by Cindy Weinstein

August Strindberg edited by Michael Robinson

Jonathan Swift edited by Christopher Fox

J. M. Synge edited by P. J. Mathews

Tacitus edited by A. J. Woodman

Henry David Thoreau edited by Joel Myerson

Thucydides edited by Polly Low

Tolstoy edited by Donna Tussing Orwin

Anthony Trollope edited by Carolyn Dever and Lisa Niles

Mark Twain edited by Forrest G. Robinson

John Updike edited by Stacey Olster

Mario Vargas Llosa edited by Efrain Kristal and John King

Virgil edited by Fiachra Mac Góráin and Charles Martindale (second edition)

Voltaire edited by Nicholas Cronk

David Foster Wallace edited by Ralph Clare

Edith Wharton edited by Millicent Bell

Walt Whitman edited by Ezra Greenspan

Oscar Wilde edited by Peter Raby

Tennessee Williams edited by Matthew C. Roudané

William Carlos Williams edited by Christopher MacGowan

August Wilson edited by Christopher Bigsby

Mary Wollstonecraft edited by Claudia L. Johnson

Virginia Woolf edited by Susan Sellers (second edition)

Wordsworth edited by Stephen Gill

Richard Wright edited by Glenda R. Carpio

W. B. Yeats edited by Marjorie Howes and John Kelly

Xenophon edited by Michael A. Flower

Zola edited by Brian Nelson

TOPICS

The Actress edited by Maggie B. Gale and John Stokes

The African American Novel edited by Maryemma Graham

The African American Slave Narrative edited by Audrey A. Fisch

African American Theatre by Harvey Young

Allegory edited by Rita Copeland and Peter Struck

American Crime Fiction edited by Catherine Ross Nickerson

American Gothic edited by Jeffrey Andrew Weinstock

American Horror edited by Stephen Shapiro and Mark Storey

American Literature and the Body by Travis M. Foster

American Literature and the Environment edited by Sarah Ensor and Susan Scott Parrish

American Literature of the 1930s edited by William Solomon

American Modernism edited by Walter Kalaidjian

American Poetry since 1945 edited by Jennifer Ashton

American Realism and Naturalism edited by Donald Pizer

American Short Story edited by Michael J. Collins and Gavin Jones

American Travel Writing edited by Alfred Bendixen and Judith Hamera

American Women Playwrights edited by Brenda Murphy

Ancient Rhetoric edited by Erik Gunderson

Arthurian Legend edited by Elizabeth Archibald and Ad Putter

Australian Literature edited by Elizabeth Webby

The Australian Novel edited by Nicholas Birns and Louis Klee

The Beats edited by Stephen Belletto

Boxing edited by Gerald Early

British Black and Asian Literature (1945–2010) edited by Deirdre Osborne

British Fiction: 1980–2018 edited by Peter Boxall

British Fiction since 1945 edited by David James

British Literature of the 1930s edited by James Smith

British Literature of the French Revolution edited by Pamela Clemit

British Romantic Poetry edited by James Chandler and Maureen N. McLane

British Romanticism edited by Stuart Curran (second edition)

British Romanticism and Religion edited by Jeffrey Barbeau

British Theatre, 1730–1830, edited by Jane Moody and Daniel O'Quinn

Canadian Literature edited by Eva-Marie Kröller (second edition)

The Canterbury Tales edited by Frank Grady

Children's Literature edited by M. O. Grenby and Andrea Immel

The Classic Russian Novel edited by Malcolm V. Jones and Robin Feuer Miller

Comics edited by Maaheen Ahmed

Contemporary Irish Poetry edited by Matthew Campbell

Creative Writing edited by David Morley and Philip Neilsen

Crime Fiction edited by Martin Priestman

Dante's 'Commedia' edited by Zygmunt G. Barański and Simon Gilson

Dracula edited by Roger Luckhurst

Early American Literature edited by Bryce Traister

Early Modern Women's Writing edited by Laura Lunger Knoppers

The Eighteenth-Century Novel edited by John Richetti

Eighteenth-Century Poetry edited by John Sitter

Eighteenth-Century Thought edited by Frans De Bruyn

Emma edited by Peter Sabor

English Dictionaries edited by Sarah Ogilvie

English Literature, 1500–1600 edited by Arthur F. Kinney

English Literature, 1650–1740 edited by Steven N. Zwicker

English Literature, 1740–1830 edited by Thomas Keymer and Jon Mee

English Literature, 1830–1914 edited by Joanne Shattock

English Melodrama edited by Carolyn Williams

English Novelists edited by Adrian Poole

English Poetry, Donne to Marvell edited by Thomas N. Corns

English Poets edited by Claude Rawson

English Renaissance Drama edited by A. R. Braunmuller and Michael Hattaway, (second edition)

English Renaissance Tragedy edited by Emma Smith and Garrett A. Sullivan Jr.

English Restoration Theatre edited by Deborah C. Payne Fisk

Environmental Humanities edited by Jeffrey Cohen and Stephanie Foote

The Epic edited by Catherine Bates

Erotic Literature edited by Bradford Mudge

The Essay edited by Kara Wittman and Evan Kindley

European Modernism edited by Pericles Lewis

European Novelists edited by Michael Bell

Fairy Tales edited by Maria Tatar

Fantasy Literature edited by Edward James and Farah Mendlesohn

Feminist Literary Theory edited by Ellen Rooney

Fiction in the Romantic Period edited by Richard Maxwell and Katie Trumpener

The Fin de Siècle edited by Gail Marshall

Frankenstein edited by Andrew Smith

The French Enlightenment edited by Daniel Brewer

French Literature edited by John D. Lyons

The French Novel: from 1800 to the Present edited by Timothy Unwin

Gay and Lesbian Writing edited by Hugh Stevens

German Romanticism edited by Nicholas Saul

Global Literature and Slavery edited by Laura T. Murphy

Gothic Fiction edited by Jerrold E. Hogle

The Graphic Novel edited by Stephen Tabachnick

The Greek and Roman Novel edited by Tim Whitmarsh

Greek and Roman Theatre edited by Marianne McDonald and J. Michael Walton

Greek Comedy edited by Martin Revermann

Greek Lyric edited by Felix Budelmann

Greek Mythology edited by Roger D. Woodard

Greek Tragedy edited by P. E. Easterling

The Harlem Renaissance edited by George Hutchinson

The History of the Book edited by Leslie Howsam

Human Rights and Literature edited by Crystal Parikh

The Irish Novel edited by John Wilson Foster

Irish Poets edited by Gerald Dawe

The Italian Novel edited by Peter Bondanella and Andrea Ciccarelli

The Italian Renaissance edited by Michael Wyatt

Jewish American Literature edited by Hana Wirth-Nesher and Michael P. Kramer

The Latin American Novel edited by Efraín Kristal

Latin American Poetry edited by Stephen Hart

Latina/o American Literature edited by John Morán González

Latin Love Elegy edited by Thea S. Thorsen

Literature and the Anthropocene edited by John Parham

Literature and Climate edited by Adeline Johns-Putra and Kelly Sultzbach

Literature and Disability edited by Clare Barker and Stuart Murray

Literature and Food edited by J. Michelle Coghlan

Literature and the Posthuman edited by Bruce Clarke and Manuela Rossini

Literature and Religion edited by Susan M. Felch

Literature and Science edited by Steven Meyer

The Literature of the American Civil War and Reconstruction edited by Kathleen Diffley and Coleman Hutchison

The Literature of the American Renaissance edited by Christopher N. Phillips

The Literature of Berlin edited by Andrew J. Webber

The Literature of the Crusades edited by Anthony Bale

The Literature of the First World War edited by Vincent Sherry

The Literature of London edited by Lawrence Manley

The Literature of Los Angeles edited by Kevin R. McNamara

The Literature of New York edited by Cyrus Patell and Bryan Waterman

The Literature of Paris edited by Anna-Louise Milne

The Literature of World War II edited by Marina MacKay

Literature on Screen edited by Deborah Cartmell and Imelda Whelehan

Lyrical Ballads edited by Sally Bushell

Medieval British Manuscripts edited by Orietta Da Rold and Elaine Treharne

Medieval English Culture edited by Andrew Galloway

Medieval English Law and Literature edited by Candace Barrington and Sebastian Sobecki

Medieval English Literature edited by Larry Scanlon

Medieval English Mysticism edited by Samuel Fanous and Vincent Gillespie

Medieval English Theatre edited by Richard Beadle and Alan J. Fletcher (second edition)

Medieval French Literature edited by Simon Gaunt and Sarah Kay

Medieval Romance edited by Roberta L. Krueger

Medieval Romance edited by Roberta L. Krueger (new edition)

Medieval Women's Writing edited by Carolyn Dinshaw and David Wallace

Modern American Culture edited by Christopher Bigsby

Modern British Women Playwrights edited by Elaine Aston and Janelle Reinelt

Modern French Culture edited by Nicholas Hewitt

Modern German Culture edited by Eva Kolinsky and Wilfried van der Will

The Modern German Novel edited by Graham Bartram

The Modern Gothic edited by Jerrold E. Hogle

Modern Irish Culture edited by Joe Cleary and Claire Connolly

Modern Italian Culture edited by Zygmunt G. Baranski and Rebecca J. West

Modern Latin American Culture edited by John King

Modern Russian Culture edited by Nicholas Rzhevsky

Modern Spanish Culture edited by David T. Gies

Modernism edited by Michael Levenson (second edition)

The Modernist Novel edited by Morag Shiach

Modernist Poetry edited by Alex Davis and Lee M. Jenkins

Modernist Women Writers edited by Maren Tova Linett

Narrative edited by David Herman

Narrative Theory edited by Matthew Garrett

Native American Literature edited by Joy Porter and Kenneth M. Roemer

Nineteen Eighty-Four edited by Nathan Waddell

Nineteenth-Century American Poetry edited by Kerry Larson

Nineteenth-Century American Women's Writing edited by Dale M. Bauer and Philip Gould

Nineteenth-Century Thought edited by Gregory Claeys

The Novel edited by Eric Bulson

Old English Literature edited by Malcolm Godden and Michael Lapidge (second edition)

Performance Studies edited by Tracy C. Davis

Piers Plowman by Andrew Cole and Andrew Galloway

The Poetry of the First World War edited by Santanu Das

Popular Fiction edited by David Glover and Scott McCracken

Postcolonial Literary Studies edited by Neil Lazarus

Postcolonial Poetry edited by Jahan Ramazani

Postcolonial Travel Writing edited by Robert Clarke

Postmodern American Fiction edited by Paula Geyh

Postmodernism edited by Steven Connor

Prose edited by Daniel Tyler

The Pre-Raphaelites edited by Elizabeth Prettejohn

Pride and Prejudice edited by Janet Todd

Queer Studies edited by Siobhan B. Somerville

Renaissance Humanism edited by Jill Kraye

Robinson Crusoe edited by John Richetti

Roman Comedy edited by Martin T. Dinter

The Roman Historians edited by Andrew Feldherr

Roman Satire edited by Kirk Freudenburg

Science Fiction edited by Edward James and Farah Mendlesohn

Scottish Literature edited by Gerald Carruthers and Liam McIlvanney

Sensation Fiction edited by Andrew Mangham

Shakespeare and Contemporary Dramatists edited by Ton Hoenselaars

Shakespeare and Popular Culture edited by Robert Shaughnessy

Shakespeare and Race edited by Ayanna Thompson

Shakespeare and Religion edited by Hannibal Hamlin

Shakespeare and War edited by David Loewenstein and Paul Stevens

Shakespeare on Film edited by Russell Jackson (second edition)

Shakespeare on Screen edited by Russell Jackson

Shakespeare on Stage edited by Stanley Wells and Sarah Stanton

Shakespearean Comedy edited by Alexander Leggatt

Shakespearean Tragedy edited by Claire McEachern (second edition)

Shakespeare's First Folio edited by Emma Smith

Shakespeare's History Plays edited by Michael Hattaway

Shakespeare's Language edited by , Lynne Magnusson with David Schalkwyk,

Shakespeare's Last Plays edited by Catherine M. S. Alexander

Shakespeare's Poetry edited by Patrick Cheney

Sherlock Holmes edited by Janice M. Allan and Christopher Pittard

The Sonnet edited by A. D. Cousins and Peter Howarth

The Spanish Novel: from 1600 to the Present edited by Harriet Turner and Adelaida López de Martínez

Textual Scholarship edited by Neil Fraistat and Julia Flanders

Theatre and Science edited by Kristen E. Shepherd-Barr

Theatre History by David Wiles and Christine Dymkowski

Transnational American Literature edited by Yogita Goyal

Travel Writing edited by Peter Hulme and Tim Youngs

Twentieth-Century American Poetry and Politics edited by Daniel Morris

Twentieth-Century British and Irish Women's Poetry edited by Jane Dowson

The Twentieth-Century English Novel edited by Robert L. Caserio

Twentieth-Century English Poetry edited by Neil Corcoran

Twentieth-Century Irish Drama edited by Shaun Richards

Twentieth-Century Literature and Politics edited by Christos Hadjiyiannis and Rachel Potter

Twentieth-Century Russian Literature edited by Marina Balina and Evgeny Dobrenko

Utopian Literature edited by Gregory Claeys

Victorian and Edwardian Theatre edited by Kerry Powell

The Victorian Novel edited by Deirdre David (second edition)

Victorian Poetry edited by Joseph Bristow

Victorian Women's Poetry edited by Linda K. Hughes

Victorian Women's Writing edited by Linda H. Peterson

War Writing edited by Kate McLoughlin

Women's Writing in Britain, 1660–1789 edited by Catherine Ingrassia

Women's Writing in the Romantic Period edited by Devoney Looser

World Literature edited by Ben Etherington and Jarad Zimbler

World Crime Fiction edited by Jesper Gulddal, Stewart King and Alistair Rolls

Writing of the English Revolution edited by N. H. Keeble

The Writings of Julius Caesar edited by Christopher Krebs and Luca Grillo